T'
b
d

⌐

SEIZE the DAY

SEIZE
THE
DAY
MIKE READ

Biteback Publishing

First published in Great Britain in 2014 by
Biteback Publishing Ltd
Westminster Tower
3 Albert Embankment
London SE1 7SP
Copyright © Mike Read 2014

ISBN 978-1-84954-767-3

10 9 8 7 6 5 4 3 2 1

A CIP catalogue record for this book is available from the British Library.

CONTENTS

Preface   vii

1.   Radio Wall of Sound   1
2.   Pass the Duchy   30
3.   On My Radio   54
4.   Top of the Pops   82
5.   On the Road Again   86
6.   Travellin' Man   118
7.   The Sun Always Shines on TV   134
8.   I Write the Songs   151
9.   Poetry in Motion   201
10. Writer in the Sun   230
11. You're History   269
12. When an Old Cricketer Leaves the Crease   289
13. Anyone for Tennis   299
14. Skiing in the Snow   317
15. Ball of Confusion   322
16. I Could Write a Book   338
17. More like the Movies   354
18. Political Man   364
19. Tomorrow Never Knows   373

Index   377

PREFACE

MY FIRST ATTEMPT at this book was lost when my laptop was stolen. Don't ask me why I didn't back it up. Did anyone ask Lawrence of Arabia that after he lost *Seven Pillars of Wisdom* when changing trains at Reading station in 1920? Of course not. He rewrote it and it almost doubled in length. For that reason I suggested the title *Eight Pillars of Wisdom*, but the publishers weren't having it. I also suggested *Read ... The Book*, but that got the 'thumbs down' from the Caesar Sisters as being too common a phrase for Amazon and Google. As Sandie Shaw once said, 'message understood'.

In many ways this isn't a conventional autobiography, if indeed it is one at all. The stories are there, the various pathways I've followed, in my *carpe vitam* moments, for better or worse, but after much thought and consulting my diaries I've made a conscious decision not to make it linear. If it were, you'd be a sitting in a cricket pavilion or standing on a tennis court every other page and listening to the radio or watching TV on the ones in between. I have no desire to get 'buzzed' by Nicholas Parsons for repetition. Neither have I overly focused on my girlfriends. They're mentioned here and there, of course, but I'm never convinced that people are particularly interested in the intimate details of somebody else's love-life. Relations between human beings have been going since the serpent suggested to Adam that he gave up gardening, so there's nothing new. (Unless of course you're very, very weird, in which case I don't want to know.) I'm still on good terms with all my girlfriends and wouldn't want their children or partners to read anything that might appear salacious. More often than not they've been to many of the cricket matches, shows, gatherings etc., but I don't feel there's a need to drag them through every opening night, flight, cruise or event in the book. They feature, of course, but appear as and when. I have many great friends, but not all of them are mentioned here if they don't appear in the selected tales. It doesn't mean that I don't love them any less or that they're not an important part of my life. It probably means their dance with me 'upon this bank and shoal of time' was brutally slashed by an unscrupulous editor. A cast of thousands, in a biography just as in a novel, is often confusing.

Also I decided not to write a book that my mother or grandmother would be embarrassed to read. As Ernest Betjeman said to his young son when he declared that he wanted to be a poet, 'Let what you write be funny, John, and be original.' I too have heeded the words of Betjeman senior, echoing down the years and now a century old. I may have failed but I have tried. I have, in the words of Horace, 'seized the day', although the literal translation of his phrase *carpe diem* is 'pluck the day', which adds another layer of meaning to one who plucks a guitar on a daily basis. I vacillated between *carpe diem* and *carpe vitam* as a title for the book. I hope it's not too haphazard or labyrinthine.

CHAPTER 1

RADIO WALL OF SOUND

I N THE FURNACE that was Surfers Paradise on Australia's Gold Coast, ten jungle-bound sacrificial lambs were introduced to each other. The only one I'd met before was John Lydon, aka Johnny Rotten of Sex Pistols fame. I was aware of the unfortunate circumstances in which Charlie Brocket had found himself and that Razor Ruddock had ritually fallen on opponents on behalf of such clubs as Millwall, Liverpool, Tottenham Hotspur and Southampton, but some of the others were a bit of an enigma. Would Jordan lord it as a blancmange-chested page three model or pine for her horses as sweet Sussex girl Katie Price? Would Alex Best be mentally and physically battle scarred after her much-publicised bust up with George Best? Would '90s pop star Peter Andre's pecs have run to fat? Would Kerry McFadden have transmogrified from Atomic Kitten to Nuclear Kitten? Would royal correspondent Jennie Bond come on like the Queen? Would athlete Diane Modahl still be smarting over her infamous and unfair drugs ban?

My diary for 6 January 2004 reveals the more mundane matters of oil delivery, the installation of a new radiator and the revelation that I needed a new boiler. These are important January-type issues.

Admittedly, no decent autobiography is complete without at least a smattering of pointless minutiae, lest it be assumed that life is one long bunfight at the OK Corral. In this case, though, it has its value, for there on the page, juxtaposed with the words 'boiler' and 'radiator', is the name Natalka Znak. To anyone finding my diary under a tree in the year 2099, it would almost certainly conjure up a potent mix of *noms de plume*, Eastern Bloc espionage and a James Bond conquest. In reality, and I use the word advisedly, Natalka was the head honcho for the TV series *I'm a Celebrity ... Get Me Out of Here!*, and I had been summoned for a second time to the TV show's HQ on the south bank of the Thames. I had all but wiped it from my mind, as I knew they must have seen hundreds of wacky showbiz folk, the bulk of whom they could eliminate to leave a suitably eclectic and disparate mix that would kill one another on sight in the name of television ratings. It smacks of showbiz cool to say that I dismissed it from my mind, but I'd read the hit list picked up from internal tabloid spies and assumed that the die was cast and the ultimate dramatis personae of Marxists, Boudiccas, pugilists and psychos had been assembled. Still the official word came that nothing had been decided and I was still on the shortest of shortlists.

Bracing myself, I knew that I was in for more grilling from the Gestapo on the ninth floor. If I was vaguely uncomfortable at this level of a high-rise block, how the hell could I fly to Australia and why was I prepared to answer questions if I had no intention of saying 'yes'? To be honest, the importance of being picked pushed my fear of flying to a temporary hidey-hole at the rear of my brain. It was that old school throwback: it was no good being the reserve. No one remembered the reserve, however good a bloke he was and however unlucky he was not to get onto the pitch. 'I was nearly there!' 'So what?' Remember poor old Jimmy Greaves and the 1966 England World Cup squad? Well, you don't have to, but it gives you the idea. Meetings and work on a promotional DVD for a potential film about pirate radio meant that I couldn't dwell on even the possibility that I might have to fly to the other side of the world, even though I hadn't flown for over ten years and had never been in a plane for longer than a nail-biting two hours. 'Radio Cool' was a gritty, humorous and hard-hitting script that didn't see the light of day. When *The Boat That Rocked* came out, other potential offshore radio films were dead in the water.

Then came the interrogation.

'What do your friends think of you?'

'Well, I guess they all have different views, but I hope that they veer towards the "he's a terrific chap … sex god … rippling muscles … loves animals … always smiling" camp.'

'Are you a leader?'

'Only if people want to be led. Sure, I'm an adventurer, wit and flag raiser but not a control freak.'

'Are you good with your hands?'

'Yes, with one of them, but only when it's holding a pen or a tennis racquet.'

'Is there anyone you don't get on with?'

'A poisonous snake, a deadly spider perhaps … nothing personal, just a hunch that we might not see eye to eye.' Always good to bring the impending enemy into the conversation.

I felt a mixture of elation and nerves when the call came about Australia. I *was* going … I was in the team … part of the mix that I guess they hoped might kick off in some way … but the spectre of the silver bird awaited and I hadn't taken to the air for over a decade! I called Paul McKenna. I wasn't convinced, but if anyone could help, he just might.

'Hypnotise me,' I pleaded. 'I'll travel as a chicken doing Elvis impersonations. Anything.'

'I don't have to hypnotise you.'

'It's the only way I'll get to the other side of the world.'

'How scared are you, out of ten?'

I couldn't say ten, although eleven was probably the right answer. 'Nine.'

He took me through various routines for an hour while we sank a cup of tea or two and asked again. 'What about now?'

It would have been rude to say nine again. 'Err … eight?'

He saw through me, of course. 'OK, you'll be fine now.'

'Really?'

'You'll have no problem.'

'How much do I owe you?'

'Nothing. I don't charge mates.'

Top man. I left feeling I was still on eleven out of ten. What the hell was I going to do? Yet the following morning I went flat calm, like the Atlantic taking on the appearance of a mill pond. I was very relaxed and cool about the trip and almost looking forward to it. My girlfriend, Eileen, dropped me at Heathrow, convinced that I'd duck out of the airport in a pile of baggage and be back in St John's Wood before her. I wasn't. I flew to Bangkok, changed planes, continued to Sydney and changed again for Brisbane. I enjoyed every minute of it. I called Paul to thank him profusely and sang his praises to whoever would listen.

On arrival, after travelling for almost twenty-five hours, Razor Ruddock and I played tennis, having booked a coach to come and have a hit with us. The coach failed to materialise. The following day I raised the matter with the hotel.

'Are you kidding?'

'No, he didn't turn up.'

'Midday, you say?'

'That's right, twelve noon.'

'Mad dogs and Englishmen,' was his literary reply.

I traded him Coward for Coward. 'But Englishmen detest a siesta…'

He shook his head and walked away as I gave him a parting shot from The Master: '…though the English are effete they're quite impervious to heat.'

Another English tennis player, young Cliff Richard, had also materialised Down Under, having come to watch the Australian Open and support Gloria Hunniford, whose daughter Caron was living there, but far from well. I discovered later that they'd arrived at the hotel to say hello, but security was so tight that they were turned away. It turned out that we all had code names and if the incorrect name was given you didn't get in. I seem to remember that we were all colours and my code name was Mr Red. Inventive stuff from the Antipodeans.

The luxury of the Versace Hotel didn't prepare us for the jungle. Razor, Peter Andre, Charlie Brocket, John Lydon and I were taught the rudiments of survival by a delightfully grizzled and gnarled bushman. He took us out into the jungle for a day to get us acquainted with things that had the power to terminate our lives prematurely. I seem to recall that it was the brown snakes and black spiders that were the culprits in the killing fields ... or was it the other way round? We learned to use a compass, had a crash course in Aboriginal tracking and were given tasks. Like making tea in the middle of the jungle.

'Come on, guys, I'm thirsty,' growled our guide, whose bare feet had so much matted hair that he resembled a hobbit. We made such a poor show of trying to light a fire that he shook his head in frustration and shooed us away. Within seconds he got a fair blaze going, erected two tripods out of sticks, bound them together and hung leaves between them that contained enough moisture for them not to burn. Amazing. Within minutes the 'kettle' was boiling.

'Well, don't just stand there, guys. I want a cup of tea, not hot water.' Away we scuttled, to return with handfuls of likely-looking foliage. He dismissed our offerings. 'Guys, guys ... those are just leaves.' He dipped into his pocket and extracted something that he tossed into the boiling water. 'You can't make it without a bloody teabag.'

We flew into camp in two choppers flying side by side (without Sondheim but with Jordan pressing her assets against the window of the neighbouring machine). A scary start, but as we yomped through dense jungle one of the crew watching from some hidey-hole was whisked away to hospital having come off second best against a snake. We victims meanwhile, had discovered a pile of ropes, pulleys and something that was a cross between a baby bouncer and slightly weird lederhosen, on a stony bluff that was clearly meant for us to leap off into the unknown and wipe out some of our number. I strapped, leapt and although not lethally damaged, found myself dangling 200 feet above the ground like a mobile circling from the ceiling of a kid's bedroom. After a minute or two of garbled instruction from somewhere in the undergrowth I plummeted down at a rate of knots that would have given Japan's elevator at Taipei 101 a decent run for its yen.

With its canopy of trees that blotted out most of the sun, the jungle had an oppressive atmosphere, which sent us scurrying to find the odd shaft of sunlight. To ward off *ennui* I made a backgammon set out of stones for Peter, Charlie and me, learned dozens of football chants from Razor and listened to Peter working on his song 'Insania'. As the cigarette smokers were allowed something like half a dozen a day, I claimed that I had a biscuit habit and, surprisingly, succeeded in being allowed two ginger nuts every twenty-four hours. I considered this a major victory. When Jordan's breast implants came up in conversation, she circumnavigated the questions by insisting that I had a look. 'Well go on, push them up or you can't see the scars.' I wasn't sure that I wanted to, but pushed anyway regardless of personal danger. I felt more like a doctor than anything else.

If there had been any cheating, then John, ever outspoken, would have exposed it. Well, there was acceptable cheating, as in Charlie concealing several miniatures of champers about his person or me stealing pencils, snapping them in half and hiding them – in my boot, wedged in my water bottle or in the braiding of Jordan's hair. I felt this was justified as the powers that be refused to let me have both pencil and paper as my luxury; I could have one or the other. They also refused to let me take a guitar. Maybe they didn't want several contestants shouting 'I'm a celebrity … get me out of here!' simultaneously.

My most exciting moment was climbing a sheer 300-foot waterfall. Kerry Katona and I had to navigate some 6 miles of jungle to arrive at our destination, but for her every step was fraught with danger.

'It's OK, come on,' I said. 'Just walk where I've walked.'

'There might be snakes.'

'That appears to be the name of the game.'

'And spiders.'

'Arachnids pretty much guaranteed, I'd say.'

'I can't go on.'

'You can always go back.'

Neither appeared to be an option.

I'm still not certain how she managed the journey, but somehow we made it to the waterfall. Perched at the top was a treasure chest, which might contain something for starving jungle folk. All bets were off as to which one of us was to hold the check rope in case the climber fell. Up I went in full kit with thousands of tons of water hammering on my protective helmet and any other part of my body that was exposed. It was a tough climb, but I took it steadily. Returning to camp empty handed was not an option. I was about 150 feet up when I slipped. Without the incessant pounding water I might have managed to re-gain a foothold, but the force of nature was too great. This was where Kerry was to come into her own, checking my fall with the rope. I felt no check as my glasses smashed against the rock to keep my knees, hands and elbows company. I took a fair battering before coming to a dangling halt thanks to a quick-thinking cameraman grabbing the rope. Bob the medic spent almost an hour reviving, checking and test-ing Kerry, who declared that all she wanted to do was to go home and suck her babies' toes. Understandable in the circumstances. As we'd apparently failed the task, commiserations were forthcoming.

'Can I still do it?' I asked.

'You seriously want to climb again?'

'Yes.'

I climbed the 300 feet, secured the chest, got back down with it and yomped the 10k back to camp. The worst of it was that, as far as I remember, there was nothing of any great consequence in the chest. A bit like life, some pessimists might say. Not so, us *carpe diem* boys.

Always inventive, I wrote a potted version of *Oliver Twist* to keep the camp amused and occupied. Charlie was the 'toff who lived in the big 'ouse wot took Oliver in'. Razor, at eighteen stone, brought a new depth and dimension to the part of Oliver, while Jordan was Nancy and Peter Andre Bullseye, Bill Sykes's dog. The latter scenario meant Jordan leading Peter around on a lead. You can text or email your captions and the most poignant will receive a slightly used 2004 Jordan calendar. John agreed to perform as Fagin, the former Sex Pistol disappearing into the bush and emerging with floral décor that made him look a little more Fagin-esque, singing 'You can go but be back soon'. The show lasted for an hour. They didn't screen any of it. Heathens.

Nor did they show the intriguing and in-depth conversation about Keats, Byron and Shelley between John and myself. The punk and the DJ discuss the Romantic Poets – fascinating TV, one might have thought. No, they wanted more salacious stuff than that. I spent a whole day writing out unusual words for a game of *Call My Bluff*, their meanings and the necessary false definitions, but when it came to it, the camp was bribed with chocolate brownies if they played a game instead where we felt each other's bottoms and guessed who they belonged to. It was intellectual stuff, you must admit. A few years later when John's group Public Image Ltd performed together for the first time in twenty years, he asked for me to do the chat, as it was going live around the world. 'Mike and me should be running this country. We know what people want.' We'd previously understood what was wanted in the jungle.

Having had my pencil confiscated early on, I used charcoal from the fire to write a daily paper called the *Jungle Drum*, featuring the

exploits of my fellow contestants. Only half a dozen issues were published, and where they are now heaven knows. The only remaining
copies were on the stolen computer, so some oik had them before
they were probably wiped and the laptop sold for fifteen quid to some
dodgy mate. With other contestants' partners, Eileen had come over
to Australia and had been reassured, on the day they started ejecting,
that I definitely wouldn't be leaving the jungle. As it happens I did. I
was never quite sure what went on behind the scenes, but who cares,
it was all a bit of fun and a chance to raise some serious money for
your charity. The media circus at the hotel were astounded when they
discovered the amount of effort I'd put into the venture, without any
of it being screened. The programme could portray you as it pleased
and to the rest of the world it looked as though I simply hadn't turned
up. As we walked over the bridge towards the waiting cameras, Eileen
gave forth with her feelings about the way I'd been edited. She didn't
know she could be heard telling the world exactly what she thought.
I've stayed in touch with a few of the jungle crew. Charlie Brocket's
outdoor wedding to the lovely Harriet in the South of France was a
delightful affair. The ceremony afforded the congregation far-reaching
views to the sea.

'Great view Charlie.'

'It is now … I chopped down a load of trees.'

'Very decent to do that just for us.'

'I thought it'd be good to open up the vista.'

'At the expense of your trees.'

'Oh they weren't my trees, they belong to the bloke who lives
over that way.'

Imagine a blithe wave of the arm there, readers.

'Well … very decent of him then.'

'Oh, he doesn't know about it yet, he's away on holiday.'

Peter Andre's wedding to Katie Price was an extraordinary affair at
Highclere Castle, but nowhere near as celebrity-laden as predicted, with

only a couple of us from *I'm a Celebrity* in attendance. As we know, it didn't work out, but Pete has two lovely kids of his own, (three including Harvey, Katie's son by Dwight Yorke) and is now happy with his new relationship.

Another jungle chum turned up unexpectedly in Frinton-on-Sea. I had been asked by a TV company making a documentary about British tennis players for my opinion on the current David Cup squad and the game in general. We shot it at Frinton Lawn Tennis Club, but each time I got into full flow, some weird old woman kept interrupting. The director and I tried to tell her as politely as possible that we were recording, but she clearly failed to grasp the situation. She came back time and time again, during which time I learned that she was married to Derek and was staying in a caravan near the beach. All interesting stuff, but not relevant to the interview. Then she got up close and peeled off her prosthetic nose and vulcanised face. It was Jennie Bond. The long fingers of the jungle have a far-reaching effect.

So how did someone with a simple, youthful passion for words and music find himself stranded in the oppressive heat of the Australian jungle with a disparate bunch of strangers, being watched twenty-four hours a day by most of Britain? I blame a man called Neil ffrench Blake. He started it.

I'm not entirely sure that I'd come across anyone quite like this Blake cove before. He drank gin out of a cardboard cup, was once apprehended by the police for running through a Berkshire village at 3 a.m. dressed only in a pair of underpants and occasionally kept goal at Reading FC's ground wearing sunglasses. That gives you some measure of the man. When I first knew him he was married to the Duke of St Albans's daughter, but later, I believe, got hitched to a girl in the Vietnamese jungle – at least judging by his Christmas card that had them entwined round each other like lianas, peering out of rather dense foliage of a southern Asian nature.

The man with two small 'f's was an enigma, a paradox, incisive, volatile, far-seeing, passionate and like myself, an adventurer, but above all, he gave me my break in radio. I hadn't been looking for a break in radio, but he gave me one anyway. *He* knew in which direction I should be going ... I didn't. Without any real experience, except that most of us spend a certain part of our lives talking, he took me on despite my obvious apprehension. The reasons he gave were threefold and bizarre: 'You're very English, mildly eccentric and a damn good opening bowler.' Sound common sense, you'll agree, and a trinity of reasons he now strenuously denies. He retrospectively claims he took me on because of my talent. I know the truth!

One may question, and not without good cause, the importance of having someone handy with a cricket ball on a radio station. In the case of 210 Thames Valley, the latest independent to go on air, it was because Neil had decided that the outfit should have a cricket team and a football team. This was a splendid arrangement, as it made it more like school and thus was a comfort zone as I ventured into an unknown and uncertain future. ffrench Blake (it feels so good to be able to start a sentence with a lower case letter) was a blend of head boy and headmaster, with the Marquis of Douro and News International's Bert Hardy the school governors. It was Rupert Murdoch's News International that had saved the station from extinction before it was even born, after the original financial backing failed to materialise and an attempt at raising £350,000 in £1 shares by public subscription had also came to naught. Murdoch's large injection of dosh inspired others to follow suit, resulting in Thames Television and EMI taking 25 per cent between them. The promotional campaign for 210 Thames Valley was spearheaded by Graham King, who'd also masterminded the re-launch of *The Sun* newspaper.

While thousands of young hopefuls may dream of being on the radio, to me, being offered a permanent job caused much consternation, as I considered myself a free spirit and shuddered at the thought of being constricted by employment. Paradoxically, at the time, any hint of security made me feel insecure and as I ventured hesitantly along the tunnel, I constantly looked over my shoulder at the reassuring light behind me. I could always turn back if I wanted to ... it wasn't too late. Of course I soon got used to this new life and subconsciously relaxed into it. It was like starting a new school – I was afraid of losing my individuality, whatever that was.

The essentially middle-of-the-road (or MOR, as that musical genre is known in the industry) station went on air on 8 March 1976, the opening ceremony and ensuing show handled by the wonderful film buff and former Radio Two presenter Paul Hollingdale. Fellow presenter Steve Wright and I enjoyed a pupil–teacher relationship with Paul, whom we cast as the slightly stern form master who'd rebuke us, but with a twinkle in his eye and a tin of polish in his hand. He was forever in the studio, announcing that his mission was to polish it 'to a high gleam'.

Local radio was still relatively young but there was an increasing number of magazines dedicated to the world of radio, including *Broadcast*, *Needletime* and *Radio Guide*, to assist in the battle against the great rival television. When I started broadcasting, the most popular TV programmes were *The Benny Hill Show*, *This Is Your Life* and *Man About the House*, but in the daytime we didn't have to worry about competition from the small screen, and breakfast television was still some years away.

The feeling of camaraderie and teamwork at 210 was engineered brilliantly by NffB, with the result that a mix of seasoned hands and new boys pulled at least vaguely in the same direction. We felt that it was *our* station and we wanted to be there as much as we could, getting involved, throwing in ideas and as far as I was concerned, learning the craft. The new boys, Steve Wright and myself, were told to listen to the old guard and follow suit. Neither Steve nor I had broadcast professionally in our lives, Steve being a Southend lad who appeared to have done a bit of everything, from working in the BBC library to appearing in the crowd, as a boy, in the film *Ferry Cross the Mersey*. Little did we dream that we'd both end up on Radio One and that he'd go on to Radio Two, as back in 1976 we were a brace of raw upstarts while the rest were top presenters and experienced professionals. Great though they were, we studiously avoided being directly influenced by them and had our own radical and off-the-wall ideas, for which we were fired by NffB at least twice a week. We swiftly became irreverent, slightly cocky and convinced that every-thing we did was outrageously humorous and that we were the first ones to do it. Despite, or perhaps because of, our attitude, we were committed, inventive and, dare one say it, a little ground-breaking. Even now Steve and I still get people approaching us who remember the *Read and Wright Show* with fondness.

In 1976 there were only a few local radio stations, which meant that major artists felt it important to promote themselves and their latest offering in various outposts of the country. Of course, Read-ing was easy to get to from Heathrow and London, which made it fairly popular with both stars and record companies. It meant that I got to interview many great names from the world of music who up until that time had merely been a bunch of letters on a record label. David Cassidy arrived straight from the airport and the legendary Fly-ing Burrito Brothers turned up in their tour bus on the off-chance of an interview. These days they wouldn't get past the receptionist and no DJ would be allowed to interview anyone 'on spec' without prior agreement from the hierarchy, but I welcomed the Burritos with open arms and was later congratulated for the impromptu interview. Knowing your music history and the characters that fell unexpect-edly into your lap was part of the game, which is why NffB beamed, 'Brilliant, you knew all about them, it was a great interview … they were happy and I'm happy.' I'd made an instant decision to change the show round to accommodate them, so I set the microphones up, got a balance, got them to play some live stuff and kept the chat fairly pacey. These days if you so much as think about changing even one track of the pre-programmed playlist you risk landing in the mire and being transported to the Slough of Despond. There was no Google to swiftly check their history either. You had to know it.

When the chart-topping singing phenomenon (his own words)

Demis Roussos came to see us, it was a hot day and Steve and I put some armchairs in the garden (oh yes, we had a garden), where, on this occasion, we intended to discuss the life, times and circumference of the Greek singer. Being a gargantuan twenty stones at the time, his great frame needed regular sustenance. 'Cake,' he boomed like an Athenian Brian Blessed. 'No cake, no interview.' The chances of any cake remaining on the premises for long with Read and Wright around were minimal, so we offered to send someone to buy the big man a slice. 'Slice? I want a cake.' A whole cake, one that would serve a family of six, with enough left over for supper. Desperate pleas over the radio led to a kind soul donating a large sponge she'd just made to the cause. He dined on it, that listener probably still dines out on it, and we got our interview.

I really enjoyed interviewing, with guests such as the Shadows, Mary Hopkin, Lena Zavaroni, Showaddywaddy, Gene Pitney, the Bay City Rollers, Alvin Stardust, Alan Freeman and Johnny Mathis all providing different challenges. Marc Bolan particularly seemed to enjoy coming to 210, often contributing live jingles to my programme, which he would write, play and perform during the show. I also did some outside broadcasts with Marc as well as roistering in local hostelries, where we'd sing Buddy Holly and Eddie Cochran songs until we were thrown out. He always talked about his love for those early rock & rollers and how much they'd influenced his songwriting and the tracks that gave him a string of number one records. Marc would always have his chauffeur sitting outside, which is something that would have irritated me no end. The thought that someone was sitting in a car at my behest, while I was inside eating and drinking wouldn't have sat as comfortably with me as it did with him. Once I asked him why he didn't drive himself, to which he replied that he thought it was too dangerous. Ironically, within a year he was to die in a road accident at twenty-nine, a sad waste of talent and the tragic end of a lovely man. I always think of him when driving across Barnes Common in west London, where the car in which he was a passenger hit a tree, fatally injuring him. It's now many years since his death but without fail there are always fresh poems, photographs and flowers regularly pinned to the tree and I often notice one or two people looking at the statue that's been erected there.

Marianne Faithfull was another early interview, arriving in the studio in a black shiny mac, short skirt and long boots. Heady stuff for a shiny, eager disc jockey. She sat opposite me and became progressively more provocative as she put her boots on the desk and displayed her knickers. Smiling away to herself, I think she was enjoying turning up the heat and being humorously flirtatious with a raw broadcaster.

Although I'd previously interviewed that legendary hit maker Cliff Richard on hospital radio in 1975, I did my first lengthy and professional interview with him a year later on Radio 210, when he was promoting his new album, *I'm Nearly Famous*. We ended up in the cover shot of a magazine, with me wearing my hair down to my shoulders and decked out in badges to promote the station, while Cliff sported a badge that plugged his record.

Former Shadows bass player Jet Harris came to do an interview and bizarrely turned up again the following morning. 'He's back,' I said to Neil. 'What shall I do?'

'Interview him again, he was bloody good yesterday.'

It transpired that Jet too had been so happy with the way things had gone that he'd checked into a local pub, determined to return the next day. By lunchtime on the second day, the general feeling was that he might be going for three days in a row, but the once-blond James Dean lookalike suddenly leapt up with 'My God, my God', and began staggering towards the pub door. Wright and I came to the instant conclusion that the interviews had been seriously debilitating and he was on the verge of collapse, but it turned out that in all the excitement he'd forgotten that he'd left his dog in his caravan in Gloucestershire without food or drink for two days. A month or two later I produced a couple of tracks with Jet at Sun Studios. Reading, not Memphis. We recorded 'Spanish Harlem' and 'Riders in the

Sky', the latter track sounding like the old Jet. I added some ghostly backing vocals and banged two blocks of wood together for the highly essential whiplash effect and the result was pretty good. Ten years earlier and we might have had a hit, but neither track was released, although 'Riders in the Sky' somehow escaped onto YouTube and has had 20,000-odd hits. Ah, if only YouTube hits counted as sales, how happy we'd all be.

As a kid, there'd been a lot of records that I'd found inspirational, but I never linked them together until later. Many of them had been produced by the legendary Joe Meek and the best ones written by a chap called Geoff Goddard. I knew only a little about Geoff, but I discovered that he lived in the catchment area of our radio station and so, not surprisingly, put a call out. At length a very shy and reluctant Geoff turned up at the station, which is when I discovered that he had actually played the organ on the global multi-million-selling single 'Telstar'. I came to know Geoff over the years, writing a couple of songs with him and hearing how, after Joe's suicide, he never really wrote again except for the odd creative excursion. He told me how one of his songs was stolen from him and went to number one. He had the squeeze put on him and even Joe, who knew that Geoff had written it, failed to support him, with the result that the courts ordered him to desist from claiming ownership. The deception not only destroyed his will to write, but also left him with severe headaches for many years. I consider myself privileged to have written and recorded two songs with Geoff, 'Flight 19' and 'Yesterday's Heroes'. Geoff died in 2000 and I feel that, as he was probably my earliest influence in wanting to write songs, I should record here the fact that he was a truly great songwriter, a gifted musician and an unusual man. He worked in the refectory at Reading University, clearing away the plates at lunchtime and generally cleaning up. He didn't have to do it, as he still made enough from his royalties, but he enjoyed the camaraderie and it gave him something to do. He was heavily into the spiritual world and confessed to me that he often left his tape machine running while he was asleep in case it picked up any alien or spirit voices. I still experience both joy and sadness when I listen to the two songs we wrote together and which feature Geoff's voice. I feel proud to have known and worked with him and I hope the future brings belated recognition. In 2013 Reading University erected the first of their Red Plaques to Geoff in a ceremony that I hosted; two of the recipients of his great songs, John Leyton and Mike Berry, performed afterwards, so perhaps that recognition is beginning to come about.

But back to Neil ffrench Blake's outfit. At the time I remember being slightly peeved at having to interview non-music people, such as the local bin men's leader during a strike, the organiser of the local cycling club, or a spokesman for the Thatcham Walkers ... we wanted to play records! However, I now confess to being retrospectively grateful for the horizon-broadening opportunity. One of the most bizarre of those interviews was with the Duke of Wellington, the interview taking place while we had a putting competition. Had it not been for my stature, non-Gallic countenance and the fact that I didn't stuff baguettes down my trousers whenever I marched on Russia, I'd have felt decidedly Napoleonic going head to head with Wellington. I would return for a further encounter at Stratfield Saye, the Wellington digs since 1815, almost 200 years after they moved in, for the BBC. I must have been damned impressive in 1976 to get that re-booking.

Being on the radio didn't mean that I stopped doing gigs with my guitar in various pubs and clubs, or that I stopped writing songs and poems. My first book of poems was stolen, presumably by mistake, when a miscreant entered the house I was sharing post-college. Unless the break-in was the work of a literary madman, I'm certain that my verses weren't his main target. I was pretty peeved, though. Still am, I suppose; no one likes losing creative stuff. If some of those gems within, like 'Autolycus' Satchel', 'Trinitrotoluene Triolet' and 'The Last Journey of the Fuscous Gnomes', ever turned up I'd probably be horrified at how ghastly they were. Luckily most of my diaries have survived, so I can vaguely see what I was up to. I recorded in my

17

diary that for compering the first International Drag-Racing Show at Crystal Palace I trousered the princely sum of £25. I continued to play cricket for Tim Rice's Heartaches, for whom I'd turned out since the team's inception in 1973. I'd known Tim since 1968, when he and Andrew Lloyd Webber had been given a breathtaking advance of £200 each, in the hope that their writing bore fruit. I remember sitting with them in the Lloyd Webbers' flat in west London as *Jesus Christ Superstar* came together, working on the PR for *Joseph and the Amazing Technicolor Dreamcoat* and singing on the demos for one of their musicals that never came to fruition, *Richard the Lionheart.* Tim even sang backing vocals on my first ever single, which you can read all about in Chapter 8. I also turned out for the 210 cricket and football teams, for which NffB kept wicket and goal respectively and always in shades. Hey, we were in showbiz … that's what you did. NffB was a hard taskmaster, once making me turn out for a match when I had chickenpox and a temperature of over 100.

Not only did I get flannelled up for cricket matches, but I also put in some hard batting and bowling practice at the Alf Gover indoor cricket school at Wandsworth. Alf, the one-time England and Surrey fast bowler, was still around then, having begun his career in the late '20s, and was on hand to give invaluable advice to anyone who wished he could bowl as Gover himself had in the '30s. His bowling action was once described as 'a little disjointed and exciting; rather as if he were exchanging insults at extreme range with the conductor of an omnibus that had the legs of him by half a mile per hour'. Be that as it may, I was happy to be gleaning any words of wisdom from the man who'd taken four wickets in four balls against Worcestershire in 1935. My best for 210 was six wickets against the local police, but at the cost of many runs and an imagined persecution that lasted for my eighteen months at the radio station. In retrospect it was an unwise thing to do, but you can't appeal against your own bowling, and one of the opposition subsequently booked me the following week for reversing all of 2 yards into a one-way street. The music press reported that I was robbed of a hat-trick against another local team, when rain stopped play after I'd taken two wickets in a row. It's quite possible that I even wrote the piece myself. Many singers and musicians were drafted into the team on occasions, including Billy Ocean, Robin Sarstedt and members of Mud, Sailor, Kenny and Cockney Rebel.

Not content with having cricket and football teams, NffB took the station into the realms of pigeon-racing! A squad of the finest flyers were donated, including a brace from the country's leading owner, Louis Massarella, and a fine specimen from the royal loft at King's Lynn, owned by Her Majesty the Queen. We certainly had to be all-rounders to work at 210; there was no shirking. A surviving press release points out that Steve Wright and I had virtually become stunt men. During one outside broadcast I had to participate in golf, cricket, basketball, judo, bowls, gymnastics, table-tennis, weightlifting and roller skating, as well as scale a sheer wall commando style and sit on the bottom of a pool in a frogman's outfit; terrific for a non-swimmer! (ffrench Blake was clearly flirting with the spirit world, as this would stand me in good stead for the jungle in the future.) Steve had to fly with the Rothmans Aerobatic Flyers! The boss also got me signed up as a member of the local drag-racing team, made Steve and me broadcast in drag (of another kind) for the Silver Jubilee and made me do a show from the back of an elephant. The animal and I clearly had an understanding, as there was not a hint of defecation. Eat your heart out, *Blue Peter*. The punishment didn't stop there: during the Reading Rock Festival, Steve and I clocked up forty-one hours of on-site broadcasts.

On one occasion, after interviewing the much-vaunted teen group Flintlock, Steve Wright and I were invited to write some sketches for the programme in which they featured, Thames TV's *You Must Be Joking!*, which later became *Pauline's Quirkes*. With the aid of our younger listeners and the TV show's producer Roger Price, who came up with the wheeze of getting us involved, we crafted live on air some material for the show, with Roger then inviting us on to take part. I don't recall watching it, but I'm sure I didn't miss much as we were a couple of amateurs alongside the talented on-air team that included the young Pauline Quirke, Linda Robson and Flintlock's Mike Holoway. If I ever get my hands on the person that suggested the script that accompanied our appearances ... it was a cringeworthy long-running gag over the misinterpretation of our names, Read and Wright. This'll give you an idea, but I'll trim it to about a hundredth of the actual length.

'No, I'm Read, that's Wright.'

'He's right.'

'You just said you were Wright.'

'I am.'

'So you see we've both been right all along.'

There was also some kissing involved, which bizarrely got past the pre-watershed censors. Not, I hasten to add, between Wright and myself.

The press proclaimed this fun excursion into writing sketches for television via radio as the first-ever TV and radio link-up of its kind, but it was in the heyday of people claiming firsts. It was the aim of Flintlock's guide and mentor, the omnipresent, blue-blazered Newton Wills, to establish them as the new Bay City Rollers. A handful of girls were always outside Thames TV to scream on demand and Newton was always whisking the boys away from interviews in the 'Flintmobile' to their 'Flint Manor' in the depths of the country. Both were figments of the fanciful but effusively charming Wills's imagination, which, as a wonderful PR man, he had by the truckload. I remember introducing one of their concerts at Reading, which was meant to be live. When the tape, five-part harmonies included, began, the group were still some 5 or 6 feet away from the microphones and their instruments! They were good lads, though, and I guess it was all part of a learning curve with a good laugh thrown in; much like life really. (Whose life I'm not exactly sure.)

When we weren't interviewing Flintlock, or Aerosmith in the cloying mud of the Reading Festival, the Read and Wright show would often broadcast from the roof or from the pavement outside the station, just because we felt like it. It was in amazement that we sat with tea and cake on the kerb and asked drivers to wave or hoot if they were listening to us. This was Neanderthal audience research at its finest and a quick fix for us, as it proved that someone was actually listening. We also had the habit of running out of the studio to listen to our own show going out on a transistor, again to prove to ourselves that we were really 'on air'. Read and Wright were decidedly odd creatures. We also had a blast inventing a series of fictional characters that we then interviewed, doing all the voices ourselves. There was Greenfingers Hothouse, the station gardener with a cod Berkshire accent, Micky Striker, the Liverpudlian footballer who only ever scored *off* the pitch, and pop singer Zoot Furnace, who only ever mimed. The bizarre thing was that listeners would often turn up to get their autographs, imagining them to be real guests.

Evidence of the swiftly changing standards on radio are borne out by the fact that there was an almighty debate as to whether Greenfingers Hothouse should be allowed to say 'dung' on the wireless. We skirted round it for a bit, using 'manure' and 'something that's good for the roses', until finally pushing out the barriers of decency and plunging headlong into the 'dung'. Laughable now of course in an age where even a certain ratio of fellatio is considered laddish and *de rigueur*. Those sweet old-fashioned things Read and Wright always referred to the radio as the wireless and were apt to come up with catchphrases and non-station jingles as well as regularly junking commercials in favour of playing more records! That is now a sacking offence. We regularly used to add our two bits' worth to existing on-air commercials, especially for some reason, the advertisement for Yellow Pages. We realised we'd done it once too often when NffB came bearing down on us like a rhinoceros with sciatica who'd just been told that his annual holiday to Bermuda had just been cancelled.

It transpired that Mr Yellow Pages himself was heading in our direction and NffB was going to make damn sure that we were in the front line to take the flak. The 'I'm going to watch you boys get a flogging' sadistic smirk soon faded from Neil's face as Mr Pages declared how many more enquiries they'd had in the area since we'd started fooling around with his commercial. We even had to record a re-enactment of us being naughty with the advertisement in question. Now as all naughty boys know, it's hellishly difficult to be mischievous when the mischief is being condoned and I suspect that we fell rather short of our usual mark.

The motley collection of DJs on 210 gradually changed as members of the original team fell away. David English departed at an early stage. An actor, cricketer, Bee Gees manager and loveable bloke, he was wont to personalise the news, as will become clear in Chapter 12. The cool and laid-back evening jock Alan Symons, a former Radio Caroline DJ, disappeared over the horizon after NffB suspected him of imbibing certain substances on air. Alan defended his inability to string a cohesive sentence together by claiming that he'd got chapped lips! A bold attempt, but just not plausible enough. Australian broadcaster John Flower handed in his notice in grand style. He began by committing the treasonable action of reading out the schedule for other radio and TV stations that he felt would be a better option than listening to his show on 210. I daresay he was technically right, but that, as every DJ knows, is a firing squad offence, or at least transportation, which was almost certainly his goal, with a big pay cheque into the bargain. John soon got into full flow as more heinous wireless crimes followed, capped with a glorious once-in-a-lifetime offer to his listeners in which he invited them to 'stick their heads up a dead bear's bum'. Whether he was implying that there were so few listeners that their heads would collectively fit into said ursine orifice, or whether indeed he knew of such a bear, fit to grace a travelling Victorian freak show, I never actually found out. Needless to say, that was the last we heard of John Flower, the bear and that unique offer to the 210 listeners. 210 was a family. Tony Fox fixed anything and everything that needed fixing, Tony 'Jogger' Holden took the listeners jogging, those that is that weren't having their heads extracted from the hind quarters of the bear, and Mike Matthews did his programme with a pipe full of something that smelled of thick black shag, with his Labrador asleep at his feet. The fastidious Paul Hollingdale, when not on air, would be busy yet again, 'polishing the studios to an even higher gleam', with a yellow duster and a can of furniture spray, while Vera the cleaning lady would interrupt any programme to vacuum the studios, whether the microphone was live or not: 'I can't hang around, I've got to get back to get Ron's lunch on.' 210 was a second home and a cosy microcosm of all that was fun, exciting and at times perplexing. That era of local radio has long gone, to be replaced by stations linked together by virtue of being owned by the same corporate, run by accountants and without a heart or soul.

NffB also handed a lifeline to TV's former golden boy Simon Dee. Since his dramatic fall from grace, the '60s small screen icon had been famously out in the cold, seemingly unable to find a way back into the business until Neil offered him a presenting job. It was small beer compared to the national glory that he'd once enjoyed, but at least it would give him a chance to prove himself. Steve and I seemed to click with him right away, as we displayed a mixture of awe at his one-time status coupled with our usual irreverence, which appeared to appeal to him. On the Friday evening before his Monday start, I gave him a lift to Reading station in my old Mini and while we sat in it for half an hour waiting for his train, he chatted about his enthusiasm for getting back into radio and how much he loved the atmosphere at what was to be his new workplace. Steve and I made him laugh, he said (presumably in a humorous way), and he talked about it being a great opportunity to show people in the industry what he was made of. When he eventually unfolded his willowy 6-foot-plus frame from my little tiny car, like a rather elegant heron, and we'd said our goodbyes, I reflected that I was going to be working with a guy who had been a seriously big name in the business, and that felt good. He was urbane, suave and utterly charming, but somewhere I guess was a well-concealed self-destruct button.

Sadly, the anticipation proved to be greater than the reality. Mr Dee breezed in on the Monday morning, seemingly ready to take Reading, Newbury, Basingstoke and their environs by storm, when an innocuous comment by NffB appeared to knock the new boy off kilter. Neil informed him that his guest on the first day was Alvin Stardust. Now Alvin is one of nature's gentlemen and a decent cove to boot, not a reticent monosyllabic interviewee, so when Simon refused point blank to interview him it threw the proverbial spanner into the works. This was a disturbing echo of the situation that had apparently led to his previous demise, that he should be the one to decide on his guests, not anyone else. In a nutshell Dee and Blake reached an impasse and a cold war began to escalate out of control, culminating in our new presenter, who was due on air within minutes, storming off and decamping to the pub across the road. NffB followed and tried to reason with him, but it proved to be useless. Before he'd even got on air the demons that seemed to invade at the moment of impact, swarmed on board like pirates of the Caribbean and he didn't get to broadcast a single word on the station. It was a bad day for all of us, as it would have given 210 a national awareness and Simon a much-needed lift back to stardom. I found Simon Dee charming, genial, friendly, intelligent and extremely sartorial – he was always elegant and immaculately turned out – but he proved to be a troubled legend and was destined to remain cast in that particular role.

More legends were to loom large and confirm my suspicions that the entertainment industry was a fascinating and exciting arena in which to work. Having acquired the publishing rights to the Buddy Holly catalogue, in September 1976 Paul McCartney organised the first Buddy Holly Week, a celebration of the great singer and songwriter that would become an annual event. A letter from the McCartney office dropped through my letterbox confirming that Buddy's group, the Crickets, would be coming over, as would his former manager and producer, Norman Petty. I was lucky to be able to interview them. The Crickets agreed to meet me at Selfridges Hotel, where they were staying, and I imagined PR men, managers and record company representatives organising dozens of interviewers and reporters, allowing a few minutes each. I couldn't have been more wrong. Buddy's main men, Sonny Curtis, Jerry Alison and Joe B. Mauldin, welcomed me like a long-lost friend, invited me to join them for lunch and chatted freely about their days with one of rock & roll's most enduring legends. I got the strange feeling that I was sitting in Buddy's seat. At the Westbury Hotel, Norman Petty and his wife Vi were equally hospitable and open over afternoon tea in their rooms, leaving me with the feeling, after spending so much time with them all, that I was as close to the Holly legend as I'd ever be. A bonus was a telephone interview they organised for me with Buddy's parents, Lawrence and Ella Holley. Over the next twenty years or so, I'd attend and become involved in many of the annual celebrations organised by Paul McCartney, including hosting a national rock & roll pop quiz, reading Buddy Holly poetry and performing live with Paul, the Crickets, Marty Wilde, Mike Berry and Joe Brown. The events were always enormous fun, but I think the musical highlight for me was performing an up-tempo version of Ricky Nelson's 'Believe What You Say' one year, with Mike Berry's Outlaws. It just felt as if it flowed completely naturally. It was a most incredible experience. Many people including Paul and Marty Wilde were very complimentary. You can't ask for much more than that! Well ... maybe a wad of cash and a '30s Lagonda in mint condition.

From the 210 days Steve Wright and I still text or chat when the mood takes us and I later worked with the station's head of news, David Addis at Classic FM. Tony Fox, the afternoon show presenter, was my agent for many years, a lovely man who sadly left us too soon. I never fail to salute when I go past his old office in the Shepherd's Bush Road.

In tandem with a radio career, I was in the studio recording new songs, inspired by having had a minor hit in the Benelux chart with 'Have You Seen Your Daughter Mrs Jones', and 'Are You Ready' having done something in the Belgian chart. Another project gobbling up the waking hours was a book with Tim Rice, his brother Jo and Paul Gambaccini: *The Guinness Book of British Hit Singles*. None of us had a clue then that it would go on to become Guinness's second-best seller of all time after *The Guinness Book of Records*, and sell millions of copies.

As well as playing cricket with Tim and working on the book, I was also able to have him as a guest on my radio show, during which he let me have world exclusive plays of songs from *Evita*; jolly decent when you consider that every TV or radio station in the world would have gone to war to have some of those numbers before anybody else. Tim also wrote me a very complimentary note about my broadcasting career, which contained the following far-sighted paragraph!

> *I honestly think that you are far and away the best on the station. Your Saturday morning show had some amazingly good records on. Why not call yourself Mic [which most people had called me up until now] not Mike? Nothing wrong with Mike (a great name!) but there already is a bloke operating with that name … you know, the 'Ugly Duckling' merchant. I reckon you could become a big name in radio so this could be important.*

Of course he was right and I should have stuck with Mic (despite being pronounced 'Mick'); it is after all short for microphone and may well have been a more suitable nomenclature for radio, but I wasn't as far-sighted as he and didn't think I would ever be broadcasting to a wider audience than the Thames Valley area.

Having always been a bit of a quiz buff, I approached NffB with the idea of presenting a quiz show with local teams competing against one another on music, general knowledge, sport, history and news. To my delight he agreed enthusiastically but informed me that I'd have to not only find the teams, but engineer and edit it, write all the questions, do the scoring, organise buzzers and bells and host it. He could have made it easy for me by providing engineering back-up, a PA and a scorer, but the responsibility of doing it all myself gave me an incredible insight into the problems of organising a weekly quiz and was to prove to be an invaluable experience. By pure chance, Yorkshire TV producer Ian Bolt heard one of the quiz pro-grammes and I got a call asking me to go to Leeds to audition for a new national pop quiz show for young people. I called back two or three times to check to see if it was really me they wanted and there hadn't been a mix-up somewhere along the line. After a trio of con-firmations I was finally convinced and was given a date to travel to the studio for my screen test.

In 1977, towards the end, although I didn't know it then, of my time at 210 a new music swept in. Through the Sex Pistols, the Clash, the Ramones and several bands on the Stiff label I became so enam-oured of it that I put together and presented Britain's first punk top twenty. There were barely enough tracks to fill twenty spaces, but bulked out by bands like Eater and the Adverts I managed to cob-ble together a chart of sorts which seemed to find favour with the younger listeners, especially the university audience. The manner in which Neil ffrench Blake fell upon me like a wolf on the fold after the fourth show told me that he'd somehow missed the first three. There was no fifth punk chart. I gathered from the histrionics that there was no room, on what was ostensibly an MOR station, for frenetic, anarchic singles that seemed to flash by at 100 mph. I had to be content with playing my beloved 'White Riot' and 'Blitzkrieg Bop' at gigs and parties.

At last I was about to undertake the journey to Yorkshire TV in Leeds for my audition, but wasn't exactly holding my breath, as I knew that several guys with previous experience were also up for the job. It seemed incredible, but I'd also been called up to the Radio Luxembourg head office in London for an interview, as they were replacing Peter Powell, who was off to Radio One. Two major auditions in one day was almost too much. It could be all or nothing, so I had to give it my best shot. Not being a fashion guru, you understand, I found it extremely difficult to decide what to wear, but in the end I decided on a nasty zip-up plastic jacket that I picked up from a cheapo shop somewhere in the vicinity of Victoria station, a crass decision that was only surpassed by foolishly going along with two suggestions from my then girlfriend Annie Evans, who decided that I was too pale and would stand a better chance if I had a suntan. I short-sightedly pointed out that October wasn't the greatest time to lie on the beach, whereupon she produced a bottle of instant tanning lotion that smelled as foul as it looked. She decreed that a liberal application should do the trick and promptly applied. Her second wise thought was that straight hair was maybe not quite as cool as curly hair, with the result that I was dispatched to Joshua Galvin in London for a mild perm. There was nothing mild about it; the slightest movement of my head and my shock of hair shifted en masse and threw me off balance. I looked like the love-child of Kevin Keegan and Leo Sayer. An orange love-child, that is, as the vile tanning lotion had finished its work and turned my face into a ripe tangerine. Two important auditions and I was already dead in the water; a skinny white body topped by a mango with ears and finished off by what resembled a joke wig.

Despite the bizarre look, I landed both jobs. I'm sure my experience at 210 worked in my favour at the audition for *Pop Quest*, as I'd been so used to hosting radio quizzes that the mechanics were second nature and I was used to putting the contestants first, and acting as a conduit, pacemaker and timekeeper. The Luxembourg audition I had to do live in front of the bosses, as I'd been too busy to make a demonstration tape, so I'm sure I got the job because it was easier for them to take the guy they knew could do it live rather than trawl through hundreds of tapes. At the time they told me they had so many people to listen to that they'd let me know the outcome within a couple of weeks. The following day they tracked me down to the dentist's chair, so they must have made up their minds pretty swiftly.

October 1977 turned out to be a major turning point in three ways: I was off to Luxembourg to broadcast to Europe; I'd landed a national TV series; and my first book, *The Guinness Book of British Hit Singles,* was published, making it a great ending to only my second year in broadcasting.

CHAPTER 2

PASS THE DUCHY

I WAS ON MY way to the Grand Duchy of Luxembourg. The station's managing director, Alan Keen, wrote to me confirming the basic salary of 53,403 Luxembourg francs, which I seem to recall was about £11,200, explaining that there would be additional payments and of course gigs back in Britain.

The other new boy, Rob Jones from Radio City, and I were thrust into the limelight overnight. Radio Luxembourg was still a big deal then, so we received a lot of media attention, even appearing on the front of *The Sun*, by which time my Shirley Temple curls had thankfully settled into a more acceptable mini Jimi Hendrix. A flurry of telex messages between Neil ffrench Blake and Alan Keen established that I would join my new station on 4 December 1977 and that Alan agreed to buy NffB 'several drinks' in, for some reason best known to themselves, Jersey. Possibly because the gin was duty free. Gin was NffB's tipple, usually out of a plastic cup. That's style ... or, more likely, polystyrene.

A theme that was to repeat itself with the run-up to the Australian adventure of 2004 began at the end of 1977. Knowing that I would have to commute to and from Luxembourg, I convinced myself that I would be able to make every journey by boat and train. Unfortunately everyone else remained unconvinced, while I continued to fool myself right up to the last minute. Rather bizarrely I even contrived to be late for the flight so that I'd *have* to go by boat, an off-the-wall notion that could only be conceived in the mind of someone who didn't like flying. Somehow I hadn't allowed myself to realise that there'd always be a 'next plane', however many I missed. I was aghast to learn that my winged chariot was still on the tarmac and that if I hurried I could still make it. I must confess that Olympic anti-hero Eric the Eel could have swum it faster with house bricks tied to his feet and a full suitcase in each hand, yet still I was thwarted in my attempt to miss the flight and found myself being welcomed on board by a smiling, or was it gloating, stewardess, as they were called then. As I staggered blindly towards the blunt end trying to find the back door I was hauled into a spare seat by a familiar face. Well, the face didn't do the hauling, but you get the gist. I couldn't say 'familiar hands' as I wouldn't have known the hands from Adam's, although on reflection Adam's probably had a film of sandy loam under his fingernails. As a dedicated non-flyer I mused that if the flight came to grief, I could actually be enjoying a one-to-one with Adam, about the Garden of Eden fruit cages and autumnal crop, within the next couple of hours. Provided, that was, that paradise didn't have a boring holding area like Heathrow or Gatwick, with those passing over banking up, due to an industrial crisis. The 'hauling' chap was actually Big Norm, a radio lover and great supporter of 210, especially Read and Wright. Norm, when not listening to the radio and passing on his well-informed and incisive thoughts, worked as an air traffic controller at Heathrow and had not only organised to be on the flight to hold my hand, but also managed to hold up the plane by devious means known only to air traffic controllers.

It proved to be not quite as bad as I'd imagined, although I avoided looking out of the window and rather pointlessly gripped the seat in front. Before long I'd be an old hand, hopping on and off planes two or three times a week, often disembarking with a goodie bag of leftover milk, sandwiches and cake, purloined for me by a stewardess. A similar theory, one imagines, as the one where folk put butter on a cat's paws to make it feel at home.

I was met at the Duchy's airport by the gravel-throated former pirate radio hero 'Baby' Bob Stewart. Not sure whether to call him 'Baby', 'Bob', or 'Baby Bob', I took one look at him and decided to navigate around all of them. He looked mean, and in his deep American tones informed me that everybody got hit by a regular dose of the local disease, the 'Luxembourg blues', and that it was bound to happen to me. Sooner rather than later, it seemed. This wasn't exactly the happy-go-lucky Luxy atmosphere that I'd imagined, as Bob ploughed on, asking if I swore. I bleated out something pathetic along the lines of 'Well maybe, if I'm extremely peeved, I might say "rats" sometimes, but on the whole I keep a fairly clean sheet, except in the excusable circumstances of traffic warden confrontation.'

'Everybody fucking swears here, sunshine, so you'd better fucking well get used to it.'

'Sure, Bob. Well, in that case, "fuck". Will that do?'

As he fell into what I ascertained to be a slightly aggressive silence, I changed the subject. A spot of pandering should do the trick. 'So when did you first bring that great, rich, deep brown voice over from the States?'

'I've never been to the States in my life, sunshine.'

The words 'so how come the American accent?' failed to materialise into actual sound, which was probably just as well. Maybe he noted my puzzled look as he took me back to his apartment, where he 'cooked' me a plate of hash browns that were still frozen in the middle when he served them up. I said nothing. Well, I might have said 'Mmm', or 'Yummy', but nothing derogatory, as I crunched on the unappetising centre of this haute cuisine and watched him train his binoculars on the middle distance. I would later discover that he was watching a girl with whom he was obsessed, but at that moment felt it prudent not to be too inquisitive.

The Villa Louvigny, which housed not only the English but also the French and German services, was situated in the middle of a charming park. Well, it held a certain appeal for the connoisseur of run-of-the-mill continental shrubs by day, but by night it had a distinctly different feel. To avoid marauding men (not always dressed as men) asking if I had a light for their Gauloise I strode through as fast as possible with an unconvincingly butch gait. I was no Eric the Eel in *this* instance, as I swerved past moderately hung exhibitionists flaunting their wedding tackle for passers-by to admire and deftly sold dummies to chaps who wanted to be my new best friend for ten minutes. I could be doing some of these blokes a disservice. Maybe they only wanted to learn about Britain's foreign policy or slide me a request for their girl back home in Wasserbilligerbrück, but somehow I doubt it. I had my finger on the pulse all right ... but only on my own pulse. I was also strongly advised not to attempt to make idle conversation with girls in the local clubs. From that, I wrongly deduced that the Luxembourgers were be a prudish nation and that a stranger may well be clapped in irons for such an outrageous offence, but it turned out to be more of a warning, as most of the girls were blokes. Yes, it was a hotbed for transsexuals and cross-dressers, a far cry from Radio 210, which was all Transit vans, transitory disc jockeys and cross bosses. The clubs played a mixture of Euro disco and the more popular face of punk, the latter regularly allowing me to pogo away the hours until I was due on air. Lest it be misconstrued and people imagine that I'm a loose-limbed one-man dance machine, I have to come clean and admit that pogoing, if that's how you spell it, is my *only* dance. From a tender age I'd had lessons in tap, tango, waltz, quickstep and countless other forms of ballroom torture, but had proved a dismal failure through a lack of ability and the total absence of any enthusiasm. Pogoing (the word still looks strange written down) was undoubtedly my forte so I'll always be grateful to whichever punk invented it, presumably one whose parents refused to buy him a pogo stick when he was a kid but he still wanted to act like his mates whose parents were pro-pogo. Anyway, this great, unnamed inventor allowed me to behave like Zebedee from *The Magic Roundabout* and still look cool ... well, cool-ish. Maybe that should be foolish.

Former Radio One DJ Stuart Henry was also part of the team. His slow delivery led many listeners to believe that he'd been flirting with his substances of choice on a nightly basis. In fact Stuart had multiple sclerosis, but bore it stoically and with great humour. Despite his problems, he and his wife Ollie were always inviting people round and on more than one occasion I had to help Stuart up off the floor. 'Excuse me, darling [don't read anything into that, that was Stuart's style], I appear to have fallen over and I can't get up again. Not a good thing for a grown man. Can you help me?' He asked for no special treatment, which is why I played the same tricks on him that I played on the other guys (well, apart from Bob as he was a bit scary.)

When I was on after Stuart, I'd sometimes find the studio empty and guess he'd shuffled off down the corridor to the loo, as his condition increased incontinence. He'd have to make sure there was a long song playing to give him enough time, and the studio door would be ajar. I would wait until I heard him coming back down the corridor and slowly turn the volume down as if the record was fading. I'd hear the shuffling increase in intensity and the muttering of unrepeatable oaths that could only be made by a true Scotsman as he attempted to hurry to the studio. Rounding the door breathlessly the realisation would dawn on him. 'You bastard,' was his usual line.

The incontinence was an unfortunate side effect of Stuart's condition, so much so that once when we were driving down one of the main shopping streets of the Grand Duchy, he suddenly swerved over and stopped.

'Are you allowed to stop here?'

'Nope, but nature calls, my friend.' He made it to the nearest shop doorway and I held his coat around him as he did what a chap in his situation had to do. After drawing many hostile looks, one passing Luxembourger looked down his nose and sneered, 'Filthy Englishman.'

Stuart was incensed. He wheeled round, still in full flow, so I had to be nimble and fleet of foot as he yelled indignantly, 'I'll have you know I'm bloody well Scottish!'

After one particularly late night, I stayed over at Stuart and Ollie's place. Following three hours' undisturbed sleep, the man with the drill that haunts hotels started up next door. He can clearly move from country to country at will. At first I thought he was inside my head. Nothing for it but to switch on AFN and listen to some music. I was awake in an instant. What was that? A French song tore through the room at 100 mph. As soon as I'd wiped the crumbs of the breakfast croissant from my lips, I was back in town waiting for the record shop to open. I had no idea what the song was called, but a combination of actions, Franglais and desperation eventually won the day and I walked out with a gleaming copy of Plastic Bertrand's 'Ça plane pour moi'. Of course I played it on my show. Of course I got told off. Of course I played it again. Of course I was reprimanded.

'We don't play foreign songs. Nobody buys them.'

'But it's got "hit" written all over it.'

'Not in Britain.'

'Follow your instincts not the rules.'

Within a month it was in the top ten.

In the late '70s, the telephone was our lifeblood. No mobiles, no faxes, no emails, no texts, just the office phone, but it wasn't always easy to make calls to record companies or to anyone in the industry. When you tried to make a call, the guys on the switchboard would either cut you off or refuse to connect you. Not only was it seriously frustrating, but you were being treated as if you were a naughty schoolboy. Just as with Plastic Bertrand, I confronted the main man early on. Well, you knew I would.

'You're making personal calls. Not allowed.'

'They're to people in the industry. I'm trying to do my job here.'

'You make private calls.'

'It's like working in divers' boots.'

He looked puzzled, and although I couldn't explain, my nose was so close to his that he got the drift. He reported me, of course. But I didn't need reporting. I needed connecting.

Mark Wesley, former pirate radio man, songwriter and good bloke, helped me to retain my sanity at 'the Great 208'. He and his wife Pierette invited me for supper countless times and helped me to settle as best I could. The programmes and popping round to Mark's were the highlights of the day. Heading back unusually late from one such evening I found that I wasn't allowed into my road. Further down was a collection of fire engines and police vehicles where all hell was breaking loose. Explaining that I lived in the road, I was eventually escorted through. The fire was obviously very close to where I was living. No it wasn't, it *was* where I was living. The apartment block was on fire and flames were leaping from my windows, which had been smashed, I presumed, by the boys in helmets. People were gasping, some were screaming and sirens were still emitting from newly arrived vehicles. Hoses were pouring hundreds of gallons of water onto my bed, furniture and probably my record collection. It transpired that the emergency services were too busy saving someone's life to answer my questions. Someone from the apartments saw my predicament and grabbed me by the arm.

'The boy on the first floor. They cannot reach him. They think he may have perished.'

'That's me,' I said.

'No, you are safe, the boy up there, he dies, I think.'

'No, listen, I *am* the boy up there, only I'm down here.' I gesticulated in what I considered to be a reasonably Gallic manner.

'It's me. Look.' I thrust my face in his.

He grabbed the nearest gendarme and presumably made him understand. A shout went up, then a cheer. It turned out that I was alive. Well, hurrah, I'll drink to that. Best news of the week.

I salvaged a few of my meagre possessions (vinyl actually scrubs up quite nicely, apart from the warped ones) but it was some while before the place dried out enough for me to resume occupation. I was still finding slivers of glass months later. Usually with my feet.

I have never been a club person, but sometimes there was little else to do and if one or two of the others were going, I'd tag along. I avoided the girls who looked like girls, as they were generally men. Those that looked like men were also questionable I was told. A hell of a learning curve. The record company guys regularly flew out and occasionally fell foul of the previous rule, including one who actually got as far as his hotel with his new friend, only to discover when they were both between the coarse European sheets that he was handling a whole greengrocer's shop. He thought he'd died and gone to Covent Garden. He was ahead of the game in getting three of his five a day. We were told by the hotel staff that he'd fled semi-naked into the night. We didn't see him for some months after that.

Don't imagine that being a Radio Luxembourg DJ in the Duchy itself meant that everyone bought you a drink, slapped you on the back and wanted to be your best friend. With some it cut no ice at all. I was with a couple of friends one evening in one of the more pleasant bars when a chap informed me that I was sitting on his stool. Now we'd been there for at least an hour and this newcomer had just breezed in. I'm a friendly fellow, to which many will attest, but I'm also no pushover.

'Sorry' – we English always start with 'sorry', it sets the tone quite nicely – 'but we've been here for an hour.' There were plenty of other seats. I indicated this with a sweep of my hand.

'Get off.'

There was something in the no-nonsense manner of this guy that told me it might be sensible to 'get off'. I got off. Most times I would feel a wimp at backing down, in fact most times I wouldn't back down, but the tone of his voice and the cold, steely look in his eye told me there was no shame in taking silver in this particular event.

My instinct proved to be correct. I was told later, in hushed tones, that he was a serious player who, with the help of the odd firearm, steam-rollered over anyone that got in his way. Good job I didn't try to reason with him then. An opening gambit of 'I say, old chap', or 'Come off it, old boy' might have created a sudden vacancy at the radio station. Call me selfish if you like, and far be it for me to deny anyone a break in radio, but in this case it was justified. I'm sorry if you were next in line.

If anything had ever kicked off, I wondered if he'd have remembered me. 'Hey, buddy, I was the chair guy. You know, the one who gave up his seat for you? My seat is your seat, you know that. Any time.' Our comradeship wasn't put to the test. Thankfully I never saw him again.

The longest-serving member of the team was Barry Alldis, an Australian who started at the station in 1956 and went on to become chief announcer. After a long spell on the BBC Light Programme and Radios 1 and 2, he returned to Radio Luxembourg in 1975. My very first show for 'Luxy,' as it was fondly known, was one that followed Barry's. We'd all listened to him under the bedclothes, presenting the Top Twenty, and here he was ... *the* Barry Alldis. I hung around while he pumped out those great catchphrases (everyone had catchphrases), 'Your DJ, BA' and 'Whether at home or on the highway, thanks for tuning my way'. Bob Stewart also had a few choice lines. My favourite was 'The clock on the wall says "that's all", it's time for me to go, there ain't no more of this here show'. I was also rather fascinated by Bob's method of giving a time-check: 'It's three little ones east of midnight.' Classic. Anyway, Barry welcomed me ... and then left me to it. No technical help, no training, no advice – straight in at the deep end. The control panel was as complex as the flight deck of a 707.

Barry was delightfully old school. I was alone in the office late one night and I heard the station output stop suddenly. Maybe it's the speaker. No, not the speaker. Transmission breakdown? No. After two corridors and two flights of stone stairs I stuck my head round the door of the studio.

'All OK, Barry?'

He was on the phone but moved his mouth away to whisper. 'Sure mate, sure. Just on a call.'

'And that thing you're waving around in your hand?'

'What?'

'That record in your hand? Is that the one that's meant to be playing?'

Down went the phone, on went the record and live went a very embarrassed DJ in apologetic mode. Now, we'd make light of it. Claim idiocy or whatever. Someone of Barry's vintage saw it as an unforgivable and unprofessional error.

The Villa Louvigny was a spooky place at night. The Nazis had captured it during the war and used it to transmit William Joyce's (Lord Haw-Haw's) propaganda speeches. The broadcasts were recorded onto shellac and then transmitted, the records playing from the inside out, i.e. you placed the needle in the centre and it moved outwards. By the time I got there, the last of them was just about to disappear. Graffiti from French prisoners of war still adorned some of the walls. You didn't want to be there alone in the dead of night.

We tended to eat sometimes with a few of the expats that lived out there, including one guy called John Bond. One night he called the station during the show and invited me to a party. 'Come on over when you've finished and bring your guitar.'

'You want me to play?'

'We all want you to play,' he announced over the noise.

I hadn't been there more than a few weeks so it seemed a good way of meeting people. Collecting my guitar from the apartment, I scooted over to the address. John met me at the door and welcomed me like a long-lost brother. Inside there was a general introductory wave of the arm around the room and a drink was brought. They'd been partying for hours and clearly couldn't wait for me to play.

Nobody mentioned the radio, but I assumed they all listened to the German service or the French service, so they wouldn't have a clue who I was. That was fine, but by now they were almost chanting for me to play. It sounded like 'Hey Mick, Hey Mick, Hey Mick', but only my old cricketing pals called me Mick and that was M-I-C. Locals, eh? Still I forgave them the pronunciation and sang a couple of songs. The disappointment was tangible. What had they expected? I didn't know. But somehow I'd let them down.

'Just play guitar solo,' shouted one enthusiast. That wasn't really my forte, but I managed to pick out a rather plodding twelve-bar blues. The dwindling audience seemed perplexed, though not as perplexed as me. Suddenly I wasn't the life and soul of the party any more and decided to go home rather than look for explanations.

'I'll give you a lift,' said the man who got me into this mess.

I was surprised after the dismal failure of the gig. Safely in the car, I had to ask, 'Was it that bad?'

'I told them you were Eric Clapton.'

'Whaaaat?'

'I thought you might get away with it.'

'Don't they know what Eric looks like?'

He shook his head. 'I thought we might impress them.'

No wonder they were disappointed. And of course they hadn't been shouting 'Hey Mick' but 'E-ric, E-ric, E-ric'. Years later, there were probably parents dotted around Luxembourg, telling their children, 'I went to a party once where Eric Clapton played. He was rubbish.'

Some DJs, like Bob Stewart, were very happy living in Luxembourg long-term, and of course, some of the guys had married local girls so felt more settled. I had no plans to stay. I had little furniture and I didn't buy a car. Rather than embracing the local lifestyle, I flew back to England every weekend to play cricket. Looking at my career statistics, which were recently sent to me, I realised it probably cost me in the region of £50 a run ... if I even got a bat. It seems that I became flannelled some seventy times for Heartaches CC, but was required to bat on only forty-nine occasions. Now either my more cavalier colleagues further up the order executed their shots with such style and panache that I wasn't needed, or Tim Rice put me so low down the order that they might as well declare rather than waste everyone's time on me traipsing to the crease. It's hard to write those words without biting the bottom lip of reality and facing up to facts, but it has to be done. The statistically cathartic part sorted, I can now turn to greater deeds. Tim put me in to bowl on no fewer than 319 occasions (319.1 actually, for the more fastidious statistician), during which I took a 'very respectable' (the Leader's words, not mine) seventy wickets. This gave me an average of 17.61, with my best figures being 6-51 against the one of our regular foes, the Blues. Admittedly 'Heartaches against the Blues,' sounds so like a Loretta Lynn song that I fleetingly wondered whether she was fielding at long-stop for the opposition. Tim's statistics also show that I took ten catches, 'stunningly panther-like', (my words of course) meaning that I took a catch around every ten matches. Before you start, that doesn't mean that I dropped dozens of them. The Heartaches annual for 2014 records that I won my cap in 1975 and was Bowler of the Year in 1980. For three seasons I took more than ten wickets (once twenty) and still hold the record (with 'Burly' Johnny Chuter) for the tenth-wicket stand. Our seventy has not been beaten since that golden summer day in 1980 when we dug in against our oldest opponents, Heaths Gents. More on this golden sporting era can be found lurking within the boundary of Chapter 12.

Any chance to jump on a plane to Blighty from Luxembourg and I took it. I jetted back for gigs when I could, as well as coming back to interview Peter Green for his new album. Much later I did Ned Sherrin's radio show, *Loose Ends*, with Peter. He fell asleep. I was also allowed to return for the premiere of *Evita* and was invited to a dinner, where I found myself sitting opposite the then Radio One controller, Derek Chinnery. I thought it unbecoming to overdo the chat. So I underdid it. As the evening broke up and we all said our goodbyes, he shook my hand and gave me an enigmatic smile. 'No doubt we'll meet again soon.' Maybe just a throwaway line. Maybe deliberately mischievous. Maybe not.

I was also flying back to record *Pop Quest* for Yorkshire TV. It was such fun to have landed a national TV series as well as doing Luxembourg. It was a forerunner of my BBC One show *Pop Quiz* in many ways, only for young people, and each show featured an interview section where I chatted to someone in the heady world of showbiz. I had John Peel on and we discussed his record collection, Brian May demonstrated his intricate guitar techniques, and pioneering TV producer Jack Good talked about the early days of his music shows on television, *Six-Five Special* and *Oh Boy!*

Flying over the green patchwork of Sussex every weekend made me realise just how much I loved England. That made me all the more determined to come home.

After nine months of living in the Grand Duchy and as the Luxembourg leaves of 1978 began to turn from greng to brong (I was becoming moderately fluent) I had a phone call from my agent, Michael Cohen. On the strength of a programme that I'd done for 7-UP that someone had heard, Radio One wanted me to come over for a chat. I knew it could be something or nothing. My initial meeting was with the station's head of music, Doreen Davies, who thankfully made me feel welcome and comfortable. I'd chipped a tooth playing cricket and was making an effort not to show the offending ivory, so I smiled very little. But Radio One was all about smiling, not guys with chipped dental displays. I must have looked, and sounded, a bit weird. Still, thirty minutes later, having appeared to have passed the first test, whatever it was, I was ushered in to see Derek Chinnery. Although I'd met him at the *Evita* launch, Derek wasn't an easy man to read. With his distinguished bearing and horn-rimmed glasses – or should that be horn-rimmed bearing and distinguished glasses? – he was the epitome of BBC hierarchy.

'We do have a vacancy.' He made it sound as though I was applying for a job at the mill. I wasn't sure what I was meant to say. He hadn't offered it to me so I couldn't presume. 'You're doing, what, five nights a week at Luxembourg?'

I nodded.

'You probably wouldn't want the programme we need filling, then, it's only one day a week.'

If you're confident that you can move up and play in a higher league, you go for it. If you're unsure and feel that you've reached your level, you stick. I knew I could do gigs to make up the money and I also knew that I would almost certainly get a shot at standing in for holiday relief. I told him that I'd like it. I certainly didn't fall to my knees with gratitude or trot out any old clichés about lifelong dreams. That wasn't my style.

I left feeling positive, but within an hour I received a call from Michael Cohen. 'Do you want the Radio One job?'

'Absolutely.'

'I've just had Derek Chinnery on the phone. He thought you were rather matter-of-fact about it and asked whether you really wanted the show.'

'Of course I do.'

'He assumed you had independent means as you had a totally different attitude to other broadcasters that he'd interviewed.'

'Really?'

'Yes. He thought you were a dilettante.'

The programme wasn't even in London. In a sort of early broadcasting devolution, some forward-thinking executive had deemed it to be a worthy thing to have a couple of national programmes a week coming from Manchester. That wasn't too bad. They put me up at the Grand and I could invite my grandmother down for the odd afternoon tea in one of the many hotels where she and my grandfather had tripped the light fantastic in the halcyon days of their youth. Actually they didn't always dance together, as is borne out by a charming photograph of Granddad Mitchell taking to the floor with a different partner: pre-dating the lyric in Elvis Presley's 'Jailhouse Rock', he was snapped in a ballroom in his black tie and tails, dancing with a wooden chair.

Tony Hale, my producer in Manchester, greeted me as I arrived for my first show. 'It's not happening.'

I knew it was all too good to be true. 'What's happened?'

'Follow me. I'll tell you in the office.'

It was bad, I knew it. Something had gone wrong. Or maybe they had mulled it over and decided that I was, after all, a dilettante.

'Lovely photograph of you in this morning's paper,' he smiled.

Did I pick up a trace of irony? 'Which paper?'

'Oh, you haven't seen it? The one with you and the very scantily clad model.'

My mind whizzed back to a recent photo session I'd done on joining the station. Most of the shots were pretty normal until a semi-naked woman appeared. 'It's OK,' said the Fleet Street photographer (we'll call him George, because that was his name), 'all the guys do shots with the girls.' I wanted to refuse, but didn't want to look like a puritanical wimp. So that was why I wasn't doing the show. Derek Chinnery had seen it, called Tony Hale and it was all over before it started. I waited for the axe to fall.

'There's a strike. Until it's resolved we can't do any shows from here.'

I smiled wanly. Well, I think it was wanly. I'd certainly expended too much energy being way off beam to have smiled more than wanly.

Bizarrely I ended up hosting *Top of the Pops* before presenting a Radio One show, but it was only a short while before I was standing in on various daytime shows, eventually landing the Monday-to-Friday mid-evening slot before John Peel at 10. I loved that programme: bringing artists in for sessions, championing new singles and new groups as well as getting heavily involved with the music. I soon discovered that Radio One wasn't simply about playing music and that some of us were cast in an ambassadorial role. One of my first forays to represent the station saw me heading off on a train to the north-east. It was a little like school. I was told to wear my BBC jacket, which rather embarrassingly had my name on it, so wear it I did along with trainers, jeans and a T-shirt. They told me it was casual and all I'd be doing was handing over the keys to a new Variety Club coach, the money having been raised by a recent Radio One football match at Roker Park. Easy. I'd joined a month or two after the charity match, so I wasn't conversant with how it all worked, but nevertheless the trip didn't appear to present much of a challenge.

Within minutes of arriving it was clear that this was more than a cursory shake-of-the-hand, nod-of-the-head, back-on-the-train operation. It was a formal luncheon. The number of local mayors almost reached double figures and between them carried more chains than Jacob Marley. The ladies were dressed as if they were to be presented at court. I half-expected to see a fashionable Chihuahua or two pop out of the odd handbag. It was patently obvious that they'd expected a Noel Edmonds or a Tony Blackburn, and I was clearly an enormous disappointment. I was the new boy that nobody knew – I hadn't actually done any Radio One shows yet. I hid my jeans under the gleaming white tablecloth as I took my place on the top table in the middle of a row of sharply creased trousers, but there was nowhere to hide my lack of celebrity. Initial embarrassment over, I'd tuck in, shut up, keep my head down and within an hour or two I'd be set free. My positivity was short lived. The speeches began. Even worse, one of them was mine. I had no idea until I heard my name. Well, that's not strictly true, the mayor in question had totally forgotten my name, if indeed he was ever informed of it.

'I'd like to call upon, er ... er ... the, er ... Radio One representative ... to, er, say a few words.'

I wasn't even a broadcaster, I was a 'representative' and had no name. I heard the introduction but initially failed to comprehend the fact that the entire room had fallen silent and were waiting for someone to say something. Cripes! It was me and they expected beguiling words of wit and wisdom. I was vaguely aware of getting to my feet and hearing myself speak. I hadn't been at the fund-raising match, didn't really know any of the other guys, hadn't done any programme, had no funny Radio One stories and had only been announced as a 'representative'. Hardly the stuff of which epoch-shattering speeches are made. I cannot recount a single word I said. I faintly recall an etymological whirligig spinning like a John Emburey off-break in my head, but whether the words came out in order I have no idea. Of the 400 or so overdressed and disappointed souls, at least one or two clapped as I fell back into my chair. For that, at least, I was grateful.

As Eddie Floyd once sang, 'Things Get Better', and he was right. Thank goodness for Eddie. Actually, come I think of it, I sang backing vocals with him for Paul Young's Q-Tips at Bristol University. There was a period where I broadcast my show from a different university each week. The idea behind those shows was that I did my radio show, followed by a live set from such artists as the Tourists, the Photos, the Lambrettas and Nine Below Zero. The Bristol night was memorable for not only sharing a mic with the man who sang 'Knock on Wood', but also the terrible news that Led Zeppelin's drummer, John Bonham, had died. The seasonal show featured Slade and was storming along at a rate of Wolverhampton (or whatever the Uni was called at the time) knots towards the inevitable Christmas finale when Noddy Holder announced a special guest that was going to sing 'Merry Xmas Everybody' with them. I'm not quite sure who I was expecting, but I wasn't expecting it to be me. Well, this would be a moment, then. Sadly not. A chord was struck, the power went and the place was in darkness. My small but heartfelt groan of disappointment was drowned by the vocal lament of hundreds of equally disappointed West Midlands students, probably scarred for life by this musical *coitus interruptus*. How could the god of music, 'Mr Apollo', of whom the Bonzo Dog Doo-Dah Band once sang, be so cruel? Would the chance ever come again? For those folk, like Dave Hill and Don Powell, only reading this book for the Slade bits, fast forward to 1991 and then again to 2013, when at last I got to join the band on stage to sing one of the country's favourite Christmas songs.

In complete contrast to the first debacle representing the country's number one station, hosting *The Year of the Child* was a pretty smooth ride. The UN had proclaimed 1979 the International Year of the Child and this show formed part of the celebrations. It was organised by Major Michael Parker, now Major Sir Michael Parker, although I can't remotely lay claim to the fact that my hosting the event helped steer a knighthood in his direction. With many military tattoos and the Silver Jubilee under his belt and Charles and Diana's wedding yet to come, he was at the helm of this great occasion, which included some 10,000 young people from around the world, in a torchlight procession down The Mall. Hundreds more, technically known as 'the Choir', were squashed into the forecourt of Buckingham Palace, flaming torches in one hand and words in the other. I was hosting the event from a specially erected platform on Sir Aston Webb's 1911 Victoria Memorial in front of Buckingham Palace, the façade of which he'd also redesigned in 1913. Do not for one moment imagine that this is mere architectural posturing. There is a point to it. Admiralty Arch was his too, incidentally. For many years I would go out with his great-niece, Alison Jenkins, and later become godfather to her delightful boys, Milo and Rawdon. The great news for architectural historians is that Aston Webb will re-appear, albeit briefly, a little later on. Anyway, on The Mall I kept the crowds entertained and abreast of the order of events, before announcing HM The Queen and HRH Prince Charles as they appeared on the balcony through the pall of smoke rising from hundreds of flaming torches. I introduced Cliff Richard, who was down to sing a few carols and whip the crowd into a seasonal frenzy. After a few songs he graciously invited me to come and join him at the microphone. I wondered how many artists, in that situation, being filmed, with footage going around the world and in the presence of the Queen and the Prince of Wales, would be happy to share the moment.

We were invited into the Palace after the event and waited for HM to arrive. Cliff whispered, 'I'll bet she brings the corgis.' Was he a seer and clairvoyant as well as the purveyor of hit songs? Clearly. In came the Welsh canine vanguard right on cue. We talked with HM about the magnitude of the event and the children losing time during the singing.

'Oh,' said Her Majesty, rather abashed, 'I'm afraid that was my fault. I was wafting the smoke away and all the children thought I was keeping time and followed me rather than the band.'

As well as Cliff, there was a liberal helping of rock royalty in my own corner of Surrey. I'd grown up in Walton-on-Thames and Weybridge so it was home territory and I bought a house there. An increasing number of rock stars and the like began to move into the area. I'd known Kenwood, John Lennon's house in Weybridge, through my early teenage years as there were often parties there before it became the home of a Beatle. The big mock-Tudor mansion had been owned by Ken Wood, the founder of the eponymous food mixer company, and his kids had parties there. With Lennon in residence it seemed ideal to try for an article for our Brooklands College rag magazine, the establishment where I'd attempted to balance studying English Literature, Art and British Constitution with guitar, girlfriends, parties and tennis. The crest on the door read *Lennon Hibernia*, which appeared friendly enough, but he had a rather tetchy Welsh chauffeur who was pretty scary and very security conscious. John very kindly gave me a large Chelsea boot which had been sitting in his garden. Very decent, I thought, although it was probably a major obstacle for anyone mowing the lawn. The 7-foot-high boot had been used as a prop in *A Hard Day's Night*, in the scene where Paul McCartney shrank, to make him look small. We hired a lorry and towed it around the town a few times before it came to rest near the old wall of death at Brooklands race track and eventually fell apart. Nobody seemed too bothered, but these days we'd have been looking at selling it to a Japanese collector for £100,000. I still have a photograph of it.

Lennon eventually sold the house to a local car dealer, Billy Atkins. When we were kids Billy could be seen on his second-hand car lot complete with camel-hair coat, flogging old motors. How he came to buy Kenwood and several other houses in St George's Hill, heaven knows, best not to ask, but he was more than generous in throwing open his doors to the regulars of the Flint Gate pub and letting the locals hang out at the house where many classic Beatle hits had been written. 'Bring your guitar,' he'd say to me, 'and go and sit in the Blue Room, you'll get some inspiration there for your songwriting.'

The room had no furniture, so I had to sit on the floor, and it was empty except for a pair of old leather sandals that had escaped the famous division of property between John and Cynthia. Maybe I tried too hard, maybe I was expecting too much, but I only wrote one complete song there. All the same, while it might not have been as good as Lennon's songs that came out of that room, I still have the demo I made of 'London Town' and it stands up pretty well. I also worked there on a song called 'Cinema Saint', which I felt was perfect for David Bowie. Of course he never heard it, but I was writing highly diverse material with very out-of-the-ordinary lyrics. No trite 'I love her, she loves me' lines from this lad. The demo is probably where it belongs, on an old cassette in a box somewhere, and I think I can say without fear of contradiction that 'London Town' was the least successful song to escape from that room.

Billy was a bit of a villain, there was no doubt of that. There was something of the underworld about him. Everybody knew him around Weybridge, where he'd commandeer a desk in somebody's office or shop, use the phone and order tea, and nobody would dare ask him to leave. He was rather Fagin-esque, sending boys to the shops on petty pilfering raids. He was probably the love-child of Fagin and Walter Mitty. He could be hellishly embarrassing. If you were in a restaurant with friends and Billy came in he'd shout 'Don't pretend that you don't know me' in a loud voice that silenced the place. The premise locally was 'Keep on the right side of him'.

The embarrassment was multiplied to the power of ten when he turned up at Radio One after my show one morning in December 1980. 'Come with me,' he insisted. He was a dab hand at 'insisting'.

Rather than make a scene, I followed him down Regent Street, asking several times what he wanted. My blood ran slightly cold. It was rumoured that he knew some, shall we say, shady characters.

'Here we are … down here.'

I cautiously walked behind him down a flight of rubbish-strewn steps. He knocked on a door, shouted his name and was admitted. Unfortunately so was I. So this was where the 'shady characters' hung out. The place froze as I walked in. Everybody stopped whatever they'd been doing and turned to statues … all staring in my direction.

'It's all right, he's with me.'

For the first time I was pleased I was.

'Drink?'

I shook my head.

The conversation was wide of anything I might have been expecting, not that I'm sure what that might have been. 'I've sold Kenwood and I want you to have the door.'

Everyone had to pass through the door to get to the house. I knew it well; the names of all four Beatles and many other interesting people were carved on it. 'Why?'

'Because you're a music history aficionado, you've spent time at the house and I know you have more respect than to flog it to make some easy money.' He was right and I was grateful, but there seemed an unnatural sense of urgency about his pressing this extraordinary gift on me. 'It's sitting in the Reardons' garage next door. Go round tomorrow morning and pick it up. Promise me now. Tomorrow morning. Don't leave it any later.'

I promised him, thanked him and scuttled back into the overworld.

I lay in bed the next morning and reflected on the strange encounter and his absolute insistence that I should collect the door first thing. 'Waste no time,' he'd said. It'd be fun to have Lennon's door.

Maybe I could make a coffee table out of it or hang it on a wall. I switched on the radio. John Lennon was dead. Shot. I barely heard the details. But if I didn't collect that door immediately I knew that I never would. Then my father happened to call round about something. I don't think he'd ever seen me cry. He did that morning but had no idea what to do, or what to say to me. Not his fault, of course, but he stood there looking very uncomfortable.

What's more, that night I had to put together and present a Radio One special programme about John Lennon. It was a tough one. Emotions were running high across the country. There were a few personal stories I was able to tell, both about Kenwood and Tittenhurst Park, John's house in Ascot, having gone to the latter the same year that the 'Imagine' video was filmed there, 1971. As well as the grand piano featured in the video, there was an upright piano at the house with a small plaque fixed to it listing five or six songs that had been written on it. I may be wrong, but I seem to remember 'Lucy in the Sky with Diamonds' and 'For the Benefit of Mr Kite' being two of them.

The coincidence, Billy's insistence, the sudden and furtive meeting and the timing have made me think about it many times. Did he know something? Was there any involvement? He was, after all, obsessed with Lennon, bought his house, and the word 'imagine' ran through his conversation like lettering through a stick of rock.

A few years later Julian Lennon and his girlfriend came down to my home in Holmbury St Mary, near Dorking. He talked quite extensively about his childhood at Kenwood, even expressing an interest in buying it if it ever came onto the market. Acting upon Jesus' suggestion to 'render to Caesar the things that are Caesar's' I gave the door to Julian. His mother, Cynthia, later told me that he'd hung it by four chains over his bed. As a footnote, Billy Atkins sold Kenwood to songwriter Bill Martin, the man responsible for such songs as 'Puppet on a String' and 'Congratulations' and Billy told this story against himself. Just about to complete on the deal, Billy turned up at Bill's office, pointed a sawn-off shotgun at him and demanded £25,000 in cash before he'd sign the contract. Billy played the tough guy, but he met his match with Bill, who took the gun from him, threw it out of the window and told him to leave … Glaswegian style! (i.e. forcibly and just possibly, although who am I to say, with some persuasive use of the forehead.) He left. Well, you would.

At the end of 1980 Radio One did a week out in Birmingham, with John Peel and me holding the fort at Broadcasting House. I was just handing over to John, when a call came through asking me to race up to Birmingham as Dave Lee Travis, who'd been doing the breakfast show for a couple of years by that time, was under the weather. It was already ten o'clock and I had nothing except the clothes I was wearing – no doubt some iconic fashion items that became dated three weeks later. Nevertheless I headed off, but only got as far as St John's Wood before my car plunged into a large unlit hole in the road where it wheezed like a newly discovered Mesolithic creature and gave up the ghost. I ran back to Broadcasting House, phoned the AA and tried to call for a car.

'Don't do that, it's ridiculously expensive,' said John. 'I'll take you up there.'

What a decent fellow. By the time we left it was past midnight and we didn't pull into Birmingham until sometime after two o'clock. That colourful wiz(z)ard Roy Wood was at the hotel when we arrived, so there were late-night drinks all round and just two hours' sleep until being prised out of bed to present the breakfast show. It was a pattern I'd get used to.

I took over the breakfast show during the first week of 1981, but it wasn't all accolades and bouquets. I was and always have been a music lover and as such have always been passionate about it, so what was more natural in my new slot than to keep playing the artists that I'd played in the evening? If music's good it's good, at any time of day. Obviously I used a modicum of common sense in tandem with what was perceived as my maverick attitude, but was pulled up about it week after week. DLT had been relatively disco orientated, but I was the guy who'd cobbled together the first punk top twenty, four years earlier, at least if I could find enough records to fill twenty places, and I was keen to incorporate new musical genres. I was strongly advised to knuckle down and play the more conventional music that people were used to at breakfast or possibly lose the gig, but I soldiered on with the groups and artists that I liked, and gradually they became more acceptable as 'daytime' music for the station.

It was a bumpy few months. By playing what was deemed to be 'night-time music' I was made to feel as though I was practising the dark arts.

CHAPTER 3

ON MY RADIO

I LOVED EVERY MINUTE of my stint on the breakfast show. Those five shows a week are enough for some, but as well as two weekly TV shows, (*Pop Quiz* and *Saturday Superstore*) and *Top of the Pops* every few weeks, I hosted the review programme *Round Table* (aka *Singled Out*) and for periods *Chart Quiz* and *Pop of the Form*. *Singled Out* threw up so many giants of music on a weekly basis there is simply no room for all the stories. One rather odd show, though, was with Pamela Stephenson and Brian Setzer from the Stray Cats. While Brian and I were deep in conversation dissecting some new release, Pamela slipped under the table and undid our trousers. How we struggled. 'Stop,' I drawled slowly, without much conviction. The ratings did an about-turn as people tuned in to the audio romp. After another edition of the show, Phil Everly told me that he was staying in Walton-on-Thames that night, a mile down the road from my house. I was having a few people round for supper and invited him to join us for a drink later. We were still eating and had a good atmosphere going when the doorbell rang. A collective sigh went up. Was this the twentieth-century equivalent of Coleridge's 'person from Porlock', come to ruin the moment? No it wasn't, it was Phil.

To say the company was awestruck would be a slight understatement. But soon everyone re-gained their composure. My Radio One colleague Paul Burnett talked Americana with him, and with Shakin' Stevens and producer Stuart Colman there as well, a few songs were sung. When the Everly Brothers played Hammersmith, Phil invited me backstage after the gig. Getting there proved trickier than I had expected. People were being turned away, denied access, and the place was crawling with security guys. Now it goes without saying that the Everlys are unique, inspirational and much revered and I could have understood such behaviour had it been 1960, but it was 1984 and Duran Duran were the outfit that needed protecting. I was eventually ushered to a small dressing room that I assumed was Phil's. I knocked, and sure enough he came to the door. 'Hey, Mike, come on in. This is my brother Don.'

Wow! One hundred per cent of the Everlys … in the same room. But there were two more guys there. One of them approached me and extended his hand. 'Hello, Mike, I'm George.' Phenomenally unassuming, but I *do* know a Beatle when I see one, or in this case two, for Ringo was also there. I re-did the maths: 100 per cent of the Everlys and 50 per cent of the Beatles. No wonder security was tight. I seem to remember Don giving George his black Gibson (possibly a J200) as a present that evening. I spent an amazing half-hour in that room and felt incredibly privileged to be invited. Apart from being musical legends, George Harrison and Phil Everly were real gentlemen who had so much more to give.

As well as the opportunity of working with the musical greats, the breakfast show brought with it a fantastic, and possibly unwarranted, clutch of national trophies down the years, with such accolades as a brace of Sonys and several Sun Awards and Smash Hits Awards being thrust into my grateful hands at various times. If I ever felt too comfortable, Doreen Davies, our head of music, was always at hand with a delightful early-morning outside broadcast at a time of year when the weather wasn't particularly clement. Oh, and the town or city almost always, for some reason way beyond my comprehension, began with the letter B.

Bromley for example. I was a milkman in Bromley. In fact I was a milkman wherever I ended up. In Barnsley the sleet drove sideways through the float as I was given my instructions by the roundsman, who I rather gathered would have preferred to have done it alone and in half the time. A tough, gnarled finger pointed and shouted a number over the prevailing wind as I, gloveless and hopelessly under-dressed, trotted with yet another two pints of gold top to yet another unwelcoming doorstep. By golly, this lactic sergeant major, with a voice like a rough-hewn Michael Parkinson, wasn't making it easy. I was also expected to make my frozen lips move at the end of every song and say something moderately intelligent. I'm not sure that I did. Was there any heart in this fourth-generation roundsman I was assisting? Any shred of humanity? Did he never stop for refreshment?

'We stop over there for tea.' He nodded towards a terraced house.

I was stunned. I almost offered him my goods and chattels and prostrated myself before him.

'I always get a cup of tea there.'

I was so overwhelmed by the moment I almost forgot my job. He hadn't. 'Well, go on then.'

I took the milk, rang the bell and was invited in. The lady of the house ushered me down the passage to the kitchen, where her husband had the kettle on. The back of an old pair of pyjamas greeted me with-out their occupant even bothering to turn round. 'Put them on the table', I was instructed by this strange northern voice, 'and sit down.'

I sat. He continued some odd conversation in an even odder dialect. I couldn't even be sure it was Yorkshire. It seemed to be a rather weird mixture, but he didn't appear to be in the mood for me to question his accent. I hoped his blend of tea would be easier to swallow. I explained that we were broadcasting and that I was about to do a link to the rest of the country from his kitchen. That'll get his attention, I thought. I was right. As I began to speak, he turned round. It was Noel Edmonds.

Another milk round, another place beginning with B. Bristol was too close for comfort to Smiley Miley country for me. Smiley Miley, for the uninitiated, was the guy who ran the Radio One Roadshow and my sometime nemesis, but let's not squander words on this rascal yet, there'll be time for that. So, as you can imagine, I had to be on my guard. My round this time took in some of the more unusual buildings and sights of the city, including Bristol Zoo. As an experienced assistant I was now allowed to deliver to some of the more important customers. The milk float could only get within a certain distance from the delivery point at the zoo, meaning that I had to carry a crate of bottles some 100 yards or so. No problem, I'm a big, strong chap. No Tarzan, but more than capable of holding my own on the crate-carrying scene. I was just contemplating imitating the old 'milko' cry that these cheerful chaps apparently executed in the days of yore, when someone beat me to it. Actually it was more a cry of desperation, as two characters hurtled out of the shrubbery and vanished at a rate of knots. It was only after they'd gone that the actual words registered. If they hadn't actually shouted 'The gorilla's escaped', it was something extremely similar. There was a thrashing sound a few yards ahead in a thicket. More cries went up from another location. My eyes, though, were fixed on the area of the thrashing. Putting two and two together I should have bolted, but I had no idea how fast a gorilla could run. I knew that a polar bear could do 40 mph if there was a raw takeaway seal at the end of the course, but gorillas, either in the mist or in the shrubbery, were an unknown in the Olympic stakes. In case the situation ever occurs again, I have since checked up on how a gorilla compares to say, Usain Bolt, and the answer is, at 20–25 mph, you can hardly get a cigarette paper between them. Mind you, you'd have to crack on a bit yourself to have even half a chance of achieving such an improbable and pointless feat. To be honest, in 1986, I stood more of a chance against Usain then a large runaway primate, as Mr and Mrs Bolt's new arrival was having his umbilical cord cut at the time and I was, if I may use a little poetical licence, loose-limbed and lithe. The milkman's guild, if there is such a thing, would have been proud of me. I stood my ground and gripped my crate as the creature came thundering through the undergrowth. OK, herbivores they may be, but if they take a shine to you, they can give a chap one hell of a 'man-hug'. This was my 'Ernie' moment, with the ape, in all likelihood from the Rwandan Virunga Mountains, cast as 'Two-Ton Ted from Teddington'. Maybe they'd write a heroic song about me as my mangled body was dragged unceremoniously away from the battlefield, still courageously clutching my crate. We've seen extraordinary images of the human-like behaviour of these great apes on YouTube, but I'd never seen one unzip itself before. Until now. This was surely taking anthropomorphism too far. Before you can say 'Excuse me but are we related?' they'll be working as librarians or as customs officials at Heathrow. This one, though, contained a human being. Noel Edmonds. He certainly got about a bit.

While we're deep in zoo territory, I was never more than a few hundred feet away from wild animals while presenting the breakfast show. My neighbour in Weybridge was Gordon Mills, manager of Tom Jones, Engelbert Humperdinck and Gilbert O'Sullivan, also locals but not the wild animals to which I refer. Gordon had a private zoo with gorillas, a puma, Siberian and Sumatran tigers and other such cuddly creatures not a stone's throw from my bedroom window at his house, Little Rhondda. If the alarm clock didn't wake me at 4.30 one of the apes did, beating out a tattoo on his chest which resembled a drum battle between Carl Palmer and Keith Moon. My prayers included his safekeeping along with my nearest and dearest, for if he were to take it upon himself to embark upon an early morning stroll and present his calling card to his nearest neighbour, Radio One would be one breakfast show presenter short. I was never certain which ape was my wake-up call, but of the tribe of primates that were my former neighbours, Memba, Winston and Janey, now all well into their forties, appear to be alive and well in various parts of the USA. Presumably still beating their chests to terrify some poor American breakfast show jock.

Continuing to deliver milk to the calcium-deficient in places beginning with B, we sailed to the Bailiwick of Jersey. Talk about coals to Newcastle. They practically invented the stuff. I also presented several non-lactic and orangutan-free breakfast shows from the Channel Islands in 1985 for the fortieth anniversary of their liberation. The islands had been occupied by Nazi Germany for much of World War Two, the only part of the British Isles to be invaded and occupied. Despite a resistance movement, the period from July 1940 to May 1945 was a dark period for this beautiful archipelago, with some 4,000 inhabitants being sentenced for breaking draconian Nazi laws. Four concentration camps were built on Alderney, and 6,000 souls were imprisoned there. It's reputed that those areas still have a strange feel about them. We captured the atmosphere in St Peter Port and St Helier as tanks, bands and hundreds of veterans of the three armed services took to the streets of Jersey and Guernsey. Old comrades hugged, reminisced or just fell silent. It was impossible to imagine their thoughts and emotions, impossible not to be respectful, humble and grateful. While in Jersey we stayed at the Pomme d'Or, where the owner relived his boyhood; he was a young lad when the German soldiers marched into his parents' hotel, informing them that their home would henceforth become the Nazi HQ. In Sark and Herm, the reflection and memories were of a more intimate nature. When I first visited the Channel Islands in 1980, there were still families and friends split due to the ongoing conflict between those that had collaborated with the enemy and those that had resisted.

I've returned regularly to the islands, even being their Mr Battle in 1987. The Battle of Flowers festival had been inaugurated back in 1902 to celebrate the coronation of Edward VII and Queen Alexandra, hence them choosing an annual king and queen, a Mr Battle and a Miss Battle. I was proud to be a part of the family, with previous Mr Battles including Stirling Moss, Sacha Distel, Roy Castle and more recently Gareth Gates, following a revival of the role after a period in abeyance. This Mr Battle gig was not a slow canter by any means.

Interviews, float inspections and a host of other duties kept me busy for several days. The inspections of the floats necessitated some dozen questions a minute. I felt like Prince Charles, and certainly borrowed a few of his time-honoured phrases. 'So how many flowers did you use?' 'Really, and how do you keep them fresh?' 'Extraordinary, and what happens to them afterwards?' 'Marvellous, and how many of you worked on it?' 'Amazing, so who's the boss?' The last question always guaranteed a degree of guffawing, at which point one could respectfully move on amid the mirth.

The Governor of Jersey came down to join me on one such excursion. What a delightful chap Bill Pillar was, or Admiral Sir William Pillar GBE KBE FIMechE to give him his full title. He was also a Knight of St John, an ancient order whose ranks I would join in 2011, and a veteran of World War Two and the Korean War. He and Ursula, Lady Pillar, rather decently invited me to Government House for tennis, supper and drinks at various times during my stay on Jersey, treating me like one of the family. I stayed in touch with one or two members of their tribe for some while with Bill and Ursula continuing to send Christmas cards. I was soon back on Jersey again, promoting and performing on Channel TV with their presenter Liam Mayclem to promote my first Betjeman album. Guitar in hand I wove my poetic way through a handful of songs and a good time was had by all. Well, I can't be certain about the viewers, but Liam and I enjoyed ourselves. This was clearly the boost he needed. He moved to the USA to host the coast-to-coast show *Tomorrow's World America*, and continues to be a major player in US TV.

Doreen Davies was always open to programme ideas. When I suggested *Three Men in a Boat* to her (see Chapter 5) she was onto it at once. She got it. She always did. Astute, inspirational, wise and never seeking the limelight. Peter Powell and I did *Ticket to Ryde* with 100 or so Radio One listeners on a round trip to the Isle of Wight. I did shows from Shire horse centres, stately homes and even a submarine. The submarine would have seriously troubled the claustrophobic. You squashed down a small tube into a longer but not much bigger one packed with sailors. If there was one thing I learned that day, it was what it feels like to be a Smartie.

During that period of the breakfast show I thought that it might be an amusing interlude to pretend I was learning the guitar. It was inspired by legendary guitarist Bert Weedon's *Play in a Day* tutorial book and my idea was to deliberately get the wrong end of the stick. It just seemed a mildly off-the-wall thing to do, to get to page thirteen and discover that Bert was wearing cufflinks and that was the reason you weren't as good as him, or after ten pages notice the guitar strap and realise that was why you'd broken so many instruments ... they were simply falling on the floor. The only problem was that after some months of that, people didn't believe I could play. At one of my group's gigs, with Monkee Davy Jones in our line-up, a girl came up to me and snorted, 'You were obviously miming. We know you can't play.' Although I'd been giving it my all for over an hour she was unconvinced, walking away with a final, dismissive 'Everybody knows you're only just learning'.

Davy sang with my group a couple of times and I saw quite a bit of him socially as he and his then wife, Anita, came to various gatherings when I was living at The Aldermoor, Holmbury St Mary. On one of these occsions he asked me if I'd edit and possibly add to a book he'd written, *They Made a Monkee Out of Me*, handing me bundles of copies of Screen Gems paperwork along with the manuscript. I read it, and assured him that he didn't need any input from me. It was well written, amusing and spoke from the heart, but tinged with a frustration that none of the guys in the band really made any money out of a group that was meant to rival the Beatles. Davy and I performed a track the Monkees had covered, 'Cuddly Toy', on *Saturday Superstore*. I played guitar as we duetted and again someone asked if I was miming while a real musician offscreen performed. Pretending to learn was a reasonable idea, but I did rather shoot myself in the foot. It was a gag that took a lot of living down and I'm still not quite sure that I have. It did wonders for Bert Weedon, though. He thanked me profusely on many occasions for introducing him to a whole new generation of fans. He told me he'd been performing for a family function at a holiday camp on the south coast, when one very young child came up, looked him up and down, walked round him and then stared up at him, asking, 'Are you really Bert Weedon?' He said he was. 'Oh,' said the girl. 'We thought Mike Read had made you up.' I'd later play a one-off gig with Bert in a band you couldn't buy or make up.

I also performed with Spanish flamenco guitarist Juan Martín, who has not only played with Miles Davis, but has been voted one of the top three guitarists in the world. Sure, I'd played a bit with him for fun on *Saturday Superstore*, but when he asked me to accompany him for a major gig at the Institute of Contemporary Arts I thought it was some kind of Spanish joke. Not so. He informed me that I was one of the best rhythm guitarists he had performed with. Reason? 'You're not the greatest lead guitarist.' I can live with that. Accompanied by a visual wall we performed 'Guernica', inspired by the Picasso paint-ing that he swore would never hang in Spain while Franco remained in power. This was no gig where you could have a laugh, smile at the crowd, pose a little and strut around with your guitar. I have to say it went down pretty well with an audience for whom I was off the radar. I doubt whether many of them had ever listened to Radio One or watched *Top of the Pops*. A delightful lady who I would swear had a virtual 'Radio Four Listener' tattoo somewhere and looked as if she'd deposited her trug by the herbaceous border for a second drawled, 'Have you and Juan been playing together for years?' More like hours, but I maintained the mystique, such as it was.

With the breakfast show came a series of one-hour specials with the likes of Phil Collins, Wham! and the Everly Brothers. These led to later specials with Queen and Paul McCartney.

For the show *Queen for an Hour*, I was warned that certain areas of discussion with Freddie Mercury were off limits. No one mentioned any specifics so I was told to tiptoe through whatever minefield I might stray into. No trained sappers at Broadcasting House to go in first to check the ground. However, all uncertainties were dispelled by Freddie, with a casual wave of the hand. 'Ask me whatever you like, Mike, anything goes.' The hour's show has, I believe, been attached to various box sets.

The Paul McCartney special, which would turn out to be a much more comprehensive affair, was spread over a couple of days in the studio with him in East Sussex. Great vegetarian food, I have to say. We ended up with eighteen hours of conversation, Paul debunking myths, and discussing his relationship with John Lennon, the early days of the Beatles and how many of the songs were written, occasionally illustrated with a burst of live guitar and vocal.

Prior to travelling down to Sussex, a BBC informer tugged my sleeve and in a covert voice reliably informed me that Paul was a Wordsworthian pantheist. OK, why not? There's no reason why a left-handed bass player shouldn't believe in the pagan concept of a life force in all of nature. It wasn't too hard to believe that he had Spinoza-type views and I reasoned that if he were indeed a Wordsworthian pantheist, he must have seen the light via the former Poet Laureate's 'Tintern Abbey'. Looking in depth at the former Beatle's left-field animism was going to be a fascinating and illuminating part of the interview. When I asked him about it, he hadn't got a bloody clue what I was talking about.

Recovering, I asked Paul about the first song he'd ever written, at which he picked up the guitar and launched into it. He'd hardly got into his stride when the excited tones of my producer, Paul Williams, became audible through a layer of supposedly soundproof glass. 'It's a first,' came the voice, 'it's a bloody first!'

Paul McC. glanced at me but, ever the professional, refused to be thrown. It became tougher to continue after the door to the studio burst open and the aforementioned producer, cigarette cemented to his lips, bellowed triumphantly, 'You've never played this before in public!'

I'd have said that there was a pretty good chance that McCartney was aware of the fact. The situation deteriorated as an overenthusiastic Williams grabbed the neck of the guitar and began to shake it, repeating his mantra of it being 'a first'.

Even a world-renowned pop star can't continue under these unforeseen circumstances. Like someone who's been electrocuted, Paul W. seemed unable to let go of the guitar and Paul McC. seemed equally unable to shake him off. Paul W.'s 'dead man's grip' made the former Beatle's strumming sound like a muted, out-of-tune ukulele. The Fab Four had been experimental, yes, but this was taking things a little too far.

Paul McC. took control of the situation. Of course he'd known Paul W. over his years at the BBC and was aware of his eccentricity. 'Paul.'

'Yes … yes?' He was still excitable but had at least let go of the guitar.

'Why don't you go back into the control room and do your job and let us do ours?'

He needed no second bidding. 'Absolutely, right, quite right, yes…' And as he'd arrived, so he departed, unabashed.

If for a moment I'd thought that Paul McC. was going to storm out diva-like at this untimely intrusion, I'd have been wrong. He took it with a grin and a chuckle, or something that was a kissing cousin to a chuckle. 'Eccentrics, don't you just love 'em?' What a nice chap. Well actually they're both nice chaps. It was a pleasurable experience making this special, which finished up as an eight-part series for Radio One. It crops up now and then on Radio Two and Six Music.

I was privileged to compere an elite lunch at the Savoy for a special presentation to Paul McCartney, attended by several luminaries including the Bee Gees and Tim Rice. At lunch I was seated next to a delightful gent in his late eighties. We chatted about songs and he asked me about Radio One. He admitted that it wasn't his station of choice but conceded that it was doing a splendid job for young songwriters, singers, musicians and composers. Eager to let him know that my musical taste and knowledge spread beyond the top forty I declared, rather grandly, that I often featured an element of light classical music as a 'bed' when I was talking.

'Oh I see ... and you have it underneath your voice?'

'That's it.' He caught on fast for a non-listener.

'Why don't you play these pieces in their entirety?'

'Well, it's a pop music station really.'

'So you put them on and then talk all over them.' I could sense the change in his tone.

'Yes,' I admitted, rather lamely I thought.

'I see, these tunes aren't on your official playlist?'

'Well ... no ... I just put them in when I feel like it.'

'And which tracks do you use?'

I use *Coronation Scot* a lot. Do you know it?'

The old boy nodded. 'And does someone make a note of this extra music so that the composers get their money from PRS?'

I think I might have winked at this point. I know I wasn't vulgar enough to nudge him. 'Well, you know, when I remember.'

'You will remember, every time.'

'I'm sorry?'

'I said, you will remember every time. Not only am I the chairman of PRS, but I also wrote *Coronation Scot*.'

If only Sir Vivien Ellis had introduced himself before kicking me into touch.

Having said that, there were times when I was comparably wicked and, what was worse, there would often be an element of premeditation. Andrew Lloyd Webber and I set up one rather elaborate wheeze at the expense of impresario Robert Stigwood. Back in the mid '60s, Stigwood had blown all his money on marketing and promoting a young singer called Simon Scott, who was cast in the mould of Cliff Richard. He had busts made of his protégé, paid for the front page of the *New Musical Express* and probably explored many other avenues in order to break the new singer. It didn't happen and it cost Stigwood dearly. Unaware as he was of the phenomenal success that was about to come his way with the Bee Gees, it must have irked him that Simon Scott didn't make it.

The single had been a small hit, but nothing to set the world alight. I actually liked the song and had recently played it, so hit upon the idea, with Andrew, of pretending that, after all those years, the single was finding popularity with a new generation. On the day that Andrew was due to collect Stigwood at Heathrow and take him to lunch and a meeting in Mayfair, the traps were set. I'd had giant posters made that had been strategically placed on the route. These were to be subtly pointed out. With the car switched on to Radio One, I organised with Mark Page, who was doing the lunchtime show that day, to play the single at a specific time. Stigwood was apparently speechless. I had it played again later. Andrew had been sent a 'new' copy of Simon Scott's bust which was prominently on display during lunch. It was, in fact, an original from the '60s. Stigwood couldn't get his head around it: Radio One playing the song, new busts, new posters and a whole new marketing strategy. Not only was he baffled, but he still owned the track and wondered, as an impresario would, who the hell was behind this new campaign when they didn't even own the product. I assume that the word 'litigation' might have been playing on his lips by the time he and Andrew hit the cheese course. What fun.

There are hundreds of tales I could tell, but too many for one book. However, I couldn't write about my time on the breakfast show without mentioning one particular song and the stories that surround it.

I am genuinely baffled that people are still fascinated by the saga thirty years on. When asked about it (three or four times a week on average) I offer the choice of truth or myth. The truth might be less interesting, but the myth clearly isn't the truth. A tough call for any media journalist or presenter. The truth is, I had no plans to ban 'Relax'. It was a good dance track that powered along. It was well produced and had firmly established Frankie Goes to Hollywood in the top ten. I've heard some rather splendid yarns that involve Anglo-Saxon words at whose meaning I can only guess and actions that would enhance the CV of a demented cage-fighter. For these outrageous tales to have even a grain of truth, there would have had to have been at least a hundred people with notebooks and a variety of recording equipment squashed into the Radio One studio. They would also have had to blag their way past Reg, our commissionaire. Not an easy task; Reg and his ilk had kept the Nazis at bay forty years earlier, so upstarts from a red-top on a mission were a pushover. No, the studio in Broadcasting House that morning, as I ploughed my way through the top twenty, contained only me, until Adrian John glided in behind me with a brace of teas from the canteen on the eighth floor. In those days the chart came out at lunchtime on Tuesdays, and we always repeated it on a Wednesday morning, but there was never time to fit all the tracks in. I had ten minutes left and four or five songs, as I remember. I was pondering what to drop, when Adrian pointed out a phallic picture and a few choice words on the back of the Frankies' record, including the claim that they'd make 'Duran Duran lick the shit off their shoes'. Hmm, hadn't spotted that. Well, maybe if I was going to drop something, I'd drop that. It'd be in tomorrow's show anyway. I don't recall saying that I was going to ban it; after all I was a BBC employee and had no power to ban anything.

In the meantime, the video had been circulated. My Radio One producer, Paul Williams, arrived home to find his two young daughters watching a couple of sections of the video over and over again, and was horrified when he saw what they depicted. At the same time, it had arrived at TV Centre and found its way to the *Saturday Superstore* office. Our editor, Chris Bellinger, told me that the programme couldn't be seen to be anywhere near it and as one of the faces of children's TV, neither could I. Directed by Bernard Rose, the video was set in an S&M-themed nightclub and featured simulated sex, urination and a few other choice scenes that of course they couldn't show on *Saturday Superstore* or *Top of the Pops*. The song had already been played on both the radio and TV, but in the light of the video it was reviewed. The BBC, I believe, also took the overt advertising campaign into account. I have no idea who took the decision to ban it, but I know who took the rap. The Frankies' manager, Paul Morley, quite rightly exploited the situation for all it was worth, with me cast as Wicked Witch of the West. Fair enough, I'd have done exactly the same in his position. The myth that it went from nowhere to number one that week is, of course, exactly that, as was the story of me smashing it violently against the studio wall or uttering a string of expletives that would have made Johnny Rotten blush.

It became *de rigueur* at any dance, disco or party, whether respectable or of ill-repute, to play 'Relax' as soon as I walked in. The expectation varied, apparently, between me wrecking the place, storming out, becoming apoplectic and breaking the record. I disappointed many an expectant throng by simply dancing – to the best of my ability, that is. There were erroneous reports that I'd punched the lead singer, Holly Johnson, and tales of heated arguments. Nonsense. I even gripped the olive branch and did the voice-over for their first album.

Twenty or so years later I was at lunch with some silver-screen luvvies at the Cannes Film Festival. As I sat at a table on the beach with a glass of something that was warming up as fast as Icarus's wing wax on his attempted escape from Crete, a smiling stranger plonked himself opposite. But he wouldn't be a stranger for long, for it turned out that we shared a page of musical history. This was none other than Bernard Rose, the miscreant who'd directed that leather-laden video. The chance meeting, a few prawns, a hint of Chablis, a soupçon of verbal jesting and the circle was complete. What made the whole thing even dafter was that only Holly Johnson was performing on the single and the group strenuously and robustly insisted that it was about inspiration. But then, as Mandy Rice-Davis might have said, 'Well, they would, wouldn't they?' Only after it had sold a couple of a million did they fess up that it wasn't actually about inspiration. I saw Holly a year or two back in Soho and we posted a selfie on Twitter. Hell, we may even have invented the term that day.

I was asked recently if 'Relax' would be banned in 2014. I had to think about it. In the '90s or first ten years or so of the 2000s, no it probably wouldn't, but I had to admit that 'yes, I rather suspect the video *would* be banned in the current climate'. To that end I checked it out on YouTube, which revealed that after more than one and a half million hits, the video is now not available to view. Maybe that will catapult it back to number one.

In May 1985, after five and a half years, my tenure of the breakfast show came to an end. There's never a specific reason, these things just evolve. New bosses are appointed, new ideas are mooted and new brooms come in, 'to sweep the dust behind the door'. The press eagerly raided their 'damning vocabulary' drawer and liberally spread words like 'axed', 'chopped' and 'sacked' across the headlines and front pages. Not strictly true, of course, as I was simply changing positions on the field of play. The main thing, as far as I was concerned, was that – for now, at least – the crazily early mornings were over.

I was certainly getting opinionated after leaving the breakfast show. The headlines were full of my immediate plans: 'Bossy Read aims to revive tired Radio Two'. I'm surprised no one pushed me up against the wall and uttered dark threats. 'They are doing everything wrong at the moment,' I opined, 'it's all bits and pieces with all sorts of odd bods working there. Teenagers don't want to hear Donald Peers.' (Donald Peers was a Welsh singer first recorded by the BBC in 1927 and, unaccountably, still enjoying regular outings on Radio Two nearly sixty years later.) 'The departure of disc jockeys like David Hamilton and Johnnie Walker have left the place in a shambles,' I ranted. I made some pretty rash statements. 'I would lay down guidelines which would guarantee Radio Two the biggest audience in the land.' This was risible stuff at the time, but the vision I had gradually happened and the unthinkable occurred. Radio Two now consistently beats Radio One in the ratings. Always listen to the crazy man … you never know, he might just be right. I was always that guy, the one with the flag, first out of the trenches with more 'gung-ho' than actual planning. Do it first and think about it afterwards.

As it turned out, I stayed at Radio One until the end of 1991. I did weekend shows, I did evening shows, I depped on daytime shows. I fronted the newly devised Sunday Roadshows, which got fantastic ratings, but when my then producer, Chris Lycett, pointed this out to a less-than-impressed controller, the reply was, 'Yes. Ironic, isn't it?' At that time I'd co-written Cliff Richard's latest hit, featured heavily on Slade's new single (their first top thirty hit for seven years), and was producing the premiere of my Oscar Wilde musical. These days, when multi-tasking is encouraged and is often financially essential, it seems strange that Radio One was suggesting that I should decide whether I wanted to be a broadcaster, a songwriter or a stage producer. I was having to choose between apples, oranges and grapefruit, but I couldn't eat them all. What nonsense. I needed my 'five a day' before it was advocated.

I'd had a couple of meetings with Capital Radio's Richard Park, as he was trying to encourage me to jump ship to his outfit, who'd got the nod that they would be given the franchise for the first national commercial radio station in the form of Capital Gold, their oldies station. Always to be relied on for a good sporting analogy, Richard affirmed, 'I'd like you to open the batting for us.' After two false starts, I signed up. It made sense … go when you feel the time is right. In doing so I avoided the infamous 'Blood on the carpet' moment when the chariot wheels of the new Radio One Controller, Matthew Bannister, scythed down several of the station's broadcasters. Only once I'd leapt across the great divide did Capital decide against going for the national franchise. Great. However, the station had a strong line-up including Tony Blackburn, Kid Jensen, Paul Burnett, Kenny Everett, David Hamilton and Dave Cash, so all was not lost.

I arrived at Capital Gold at the tail end of 1991, in time for the station's third birthday. Richard Park commented, 'It's great to welcome Mike to our all-star line-up. He has a huge following and his presence can only add to the success enjoyed by Capital Gold.' I was hired to present the drivetime show, and I also fronted up Capital Gold's Work Experience Scheme, which was designed to help schoolchildren to prepare for working life. This was becoming increasingly important both for London's young people and for prospective employers, so the idea was to provide pupils approaching their last year at school with short periods in various organisations in order for them to get a taste of the working world and what might be expected of them. Hopefully people became more switched on.

That can't be said of everyone at the station, though. On one occasion I was at an awards ceremony, sharing a table with a mix of sales, management and broadcasters. As something indescribable but creamy appeared on our plates, looking like a mass entry for the Turner Prize, the sales guy I'd been sitting next to all through lunch wiped his mouth and cheerfully asked, 'Well, Mike, what are you up to these days?'

'Me? I'm on the drivetime show every day from four o'clock.'

'Really? Which station?'

'The one that you do the sales for.'

My drivetime slot meant that I followed Kenny Everett. The studio, once Ken was done with it, was like delicatessen fall-out, but after a quick mopping-up process while Kenny said something surreal like, 'Ooh, I'm going home to count my toes,' all was presentable again. Kenny shared a passion with me for the Lettermen's version of 'The Way You Look Tonight'. Every so often he'd shoot me a sly glance, take a deep breath and whisper, 'May I borrow *it* again?' The problem was getting the single back from him. It was like tug of love with a vinyl child.

I heard the announcement that he had HIV when I was on my way to the studio, so I stopped at a florist in Oxshott and bought a small bunch of flowers. At Capital I walked into the studio with them. 'Damn! You're still alive. I wasted money on flowers.'

He teetered between the emotional and the comic. 'Thank God

for someone with a sense of humour,' he said, and gave me a hug. It seemed that no one had come into the studio as they hadn't known what to say or do. He then proceeded to lie on the floor, placing the humble bouquet on his chest. 'So this is what it feels like to be dead! I'll kill that bloody waiter when I get up there,' he said, referring to the guy who he assumed had infected him.

When the day of reckoning came for Kenny, and one assumes a second reckoning for the waiter, Richard Park asked me to put together a tribute. With only an hour's preparation, we dug out songs he'd recorded such as 'Knees', his TV theme tunes, clips of him on the pirate ship with Dave Cash, sections of his radio cartoon serial, *Captain Kremmen*, multiple sketches and characters from his TV show and some of the songs that I knew to be his favourites, including, rather inevitably, 'The Way You Look Tonight'. It could have been emotional, but like a funeral, you're too busy to grieve. That comes later.

In 1994 Capital Gold overtook Radio One in the ratings for the first time, their share going up to 7.6 per cent in London, while Radio One's went down to 5.8. Pretty decisive. The press release announced: 'Drivetime host Mike Read has increased his audience by a phenomenal 41 per cent.' At this time I was also writing a weekly showbusiness column for the *Tonight* newspaper, Mike Read's Capital Chat Show, and interviewing many American artists who I'd never met. Among the most engaging were Johnny Tillotson, who'd topped the UK chart with 'Poetry in Motion' and whose ancestors included Oliver Cromwell, and John Denver. John was a great storyteller as both songwriter and interviewee, as was Roger McGuinn, who even let me sing and play with him on the Byrds classic 'Mr Spaceman'.

Way before TalkSport, Richard Park laced the station's output in the later part of the day and the evening with football talk and football commentary. In some ways he was a visionary; in others he had his own brand of leadership that wasn't everybody's idea of man management. I know that several of the broadcasters felt intimidated by his style. One DJ went to talk about a rise and emerged delighted to still have a job. Another, who had been at Capital for almost twenty years, was frog-marched from the station without being allowed to collect anything from his desk.

I was asked to have a think about doing the breakfast show. I wasn't happy with that because Tony Blackburn was presenting it and, for my money, doing an excellent job. I was then informed that there was going to be a change round, just to mix things up a bit. Well, that happens, so I promised I'd think about it over the following week. I was still in need of some guidance when the day of the meeting arrived. 'I have been thinking about it,' I said.

'Oh, it doesn't matter, I've already made the decision.'

Well, at least that shows positive management. 'And the decision is?'

'You're fired.'

'Sorry?'

'You're fired.'

'But you've asked me to think about doing your flagship show.'

'I know, but I've changed my mind.'

'But hold on … my ratings are good.'

'Yes, not bad.'

'So this is the reward for working hard, getting good ratings and being a team player?'

Emerging from the meeting I was met by a sea of expectant faces. 'Well, are you doing breakfast?'

'No, I've been fired.'

Gales of laughter.

'No, seriously.'

More gales.

'I can't even hang around. I have to leave the building immediately.'

Stunned silence.

I drove home listening to someone I'd never heard of presenting my show. I seem to recall one or two others left the building that day as well. Even before my somewhat abrupt departure from Capital Gold I had misgivings. When I started, the station had some six or seven producers, but by the time I left it had one. My main frustration was a lack of musical input as we were fairly straitjacketed on that front.

I drove home listening to someone I'd never heard of presenting my show. I seem to recall one or two others left the building that day as well. I won't spoil the memoirs of others shown the red card by repeating their even weirder stories here, as those tales will be more credible from their own mouths, although en passant I recently heard from one senior broadcaster who was fired and not even allowed to collect his headphones from the studio. They were sent on by car the next day. In my book, not only does this bespeak a total lack of respect and decency towards a very experienced, much-admired and diligent professional, but it is bad for the image of the industry.

Even before my somewhat abrupt departure from Capital Gold I had misgivings. When I started, the station had some six or seven producers, but by the time I left it had one. My main frustration was a lack of musical input as we were fairly straitjacketed on that front.

So, with the doors at Capital Gold firmly shut behind me, where next? One place I certainly hadn't considered was Classic FM, the national commercial classical station. But the boss, Michael Bukht, aka Michael Barry, radio and TV's 'Crafty Cook', seemed to think that despite my pop background, I'd be ideal for the station. I was more convinced when he admitted that he'd already run a serious test on my profile and acceptance factor with the audience. It seems I'd emerged with a top rating.

Michael had previously set up a radio station in what was the Republic of Transkei, from where came a story that I pray was not apocryphal. Visiting one of his presenters for supper one evening, he arrived on what was a building site as the house was being renovated. It was already dark by this time and, unable to see, he stumbled into a deep, unlit hole and had to call for help. The host emerged from the house shouting, 'Who's there?'

'It's Michael Bukht,' came the reply from the bowels of the earth.

'Where are you?'

'I'm down here.'

His host looked down and allegedly exclaimed, 'There's a Bukht in my hole.'

So, I landed the gig, if indeed they called it that in the classical domain. Gounod, Berlioz and Bruch here I come. Admittedly some pronunciations went awry, but the audience were a decent and forgiving bunch. One of the highlights was the phenomenal response to the request for poetry. The two volumes that resulted from this response, which I edited, are still selling today (see Chapter 16).

My old Radio One colleague Phil Swern was brought in to produce a classical quiz. Nothing stuffy, you understand. For a start we were going to take it on the road and as a bonus the team captains were to be Barry Took and Tony Slattery. It worked beautifully, and it was fun and full of improvisation. For example, Tony would randomly start a classical limerick, I would add a second line, Barry would chuck in a third, I'd maybe sling in a fourth and Tony would dig out a stunning punchline. I was always asked how we learned our scripts! It was all off the top of our heads and wonderfully challenging.

We also ran a short series called *The Three Fivers*, a spoof, rather obviously, on the Three Tenors. Barry and I wrote the scripts, and while it might not have 'run and run' as they say, it was a delight to work with one of Britain's greatest scriptwriters. Among Barry's finest TV writing moments were *The Army Game* and *Bootsie and Snudge*, while on radio *Beyond our Ken* and *Round the Horne* were national favourites. He was also responsible for helping to bring together the Monty Python team and, rather later, hosted a regular quiz for us on *Saturday Superstore*.

One day I was dispatched to Jersey to broadcast from the 32-acre Durrell Wildlife Park, which had been set up in 1958 by the late Gerald Durrell. What they lacked in wide and high varieties, they more than compensated for with an abundance of short-toed treecreepers, blue-crowned laughing thrushes, red-cowled cardinals and lesser Antillean iguanas. We were looked after by Gerald's delightful wife

Lee, who came from the rock & roll town of Memphis, and spent the night having a couple of looseners with the Red Arrows, who were staying at the same hotel. As promised they altered course to come over the zoo the following morning and give us an official flypast.

One of the historical Classic FM outside broadcasts was from Rutland on 1 April 1997, the day it re-gained its independence from Leicestershire, having been absorbed into that county in 1974. Many doubting Thomases welded the date and their knowledge of my despicable character together and came up with … well, whatever they came up with. 'A transparent joke,' said those more inclined to humour, dismissively. Others turned on their heel with a knowing air and a demeaning shrug. I faintly remember some ancient don calling to complain that I was trivialising the gravitas of such an august radio station. I broadcast live from Oakham and the Old Uppinghamians partied like it was 1584. Even the school's founder, the Archdeacon of Leicester, Robert Johnson, might have considered selling his soul at the crossroads on hearing the glad tidings.

The ratings were excellent, as my creative producer, Tim Lihoreau, and I injected classical *joie de vivre* into the breakfast show, but alas and alack, the station was taken over and I was moved to weekends to save money. At least my show was sponsored. The big cheese from Cathedral City was clearly a wise old bird who knew just where to place his chips.

'How am I involved?'

'Oh, you don't have to do anything, we just play out a couple of ads each hour.'

'Sorry, guv'nor, not in my nature to simply push a button.'

'Well that's all we need you to do.'

I say it was more through inventiveness than belligerence, but I decided I could satisfy both the sponsors and my professional pride by drip-feeding clues to a different cathedral every week. It was absolutely right for our demographic, and despite the long faces it carried the day. Assorted incumbents danced with ecclesiastical glee when their phone rang. 'Ooh, I wondered when you'd get around to us,' was a typical response from a long line of deans and bishops, 'I have some clues prepared in case you need them.' Manchester Cathedral fooled a lot of people, as one of the clues was that it was on an island, resulting, rather obviously, in callers going for coastal guesses. But, strictly speaking, it *is* on an island, between three rivers, the Irwell, the Irk and the Medlock.

I really enjoyed the station, but it changed when GWR took it over. The quizzes were repeated ad nauseam until every listener knew the questions, the answers and the jokes, such as they were. I remain baffled that no one has yet volunteered them as their specialist subject on *Mastermind*. The new owners of Classic FM also owned the Gold network and made a bold decision to remove all the breakfast show DJs on each station and have me broadcast across them all. The icing on the cake of the deal they offered was a healthy tranche of shares in the company if I doubled the figures. It was essentially a '60s and '70s station, and despite being shackled by members of the hierarchy coming out with inane questions like 'Who is Clifford T. Ward?' or crass statements such as 'I've never heard of this track "Alone Again Or" by Love', I managed to more than double the ratings. I knew this from other stations, as we all got the same figures, and our rivals had told us how well we'd done. Still, my employers dithered around pretending they were still trying to work out the figures. Needless to say they reneged on the deal, pleading poverty, as they'd just spent £27 million adding an extra group of stations to the portfolio. Whatever happened to 'An Englishman's word is his bond'?

Well, their answer was to get an Australasian in to head things up. 'He used to work at Radio One,' we were told when the Gold presenters and staff were introduced to him.

'When was that?' I asked him.

'Oh, in back in the '80s.'

'We're only in the '90s now. What did you do there?' It wasn't so much that I had an enquiring mind, but I remember everyone that worked at the station. Here's a tip. If you're going to give your CV a little embellishment, don't make the mistake of equating Radio One with the BBC. The station has always been a small family unit.

'Oh, I was nothing, really, I didn't have a very significant role.'

'Really? Doing what?' He could only have been a presenter, producer, engineer or PA and he denied being any of those. I mentioned his name to Doreen Davies, who'd been at the station since its inception. Her response? 'Never heard of him.'

My next encounter with him was priceless. Following my show one morning, he sat and dissected it. 'The first half-hour was too '70s based.'

'But there were four '60s songs in there, that's fifty-fifty.'

'I know, but you made it sound '70s.'

I wondered how I managed that. It'd be a good trick to learn.

'The second half-hour was a fraction slow.'

'Compared to what?'

'The first half-hour.'

'You mean the one that sounded too '70s?'

'And the third half-hour was fractionally too fast.' The man was either a genius or had escaped from the set of *School for Scoundrels*. My education continued unabated. 'You played a track by the Who.'

I wasn't absolutely certain whether it was a question or a statement, so I played a straight bat. 'It's not unknown. "Pictures of Lily" fits our remit.'

'Would you say it was a rock track or a pop song?'

'That must be in the ear of the listener, surely.'

'You mean you don't know?' Before I could even clutch at a reasonable answer to such a pointless question, he started to get physical. I was poked in the arm by a finger. The finger was illustrating the speaker's point and jabbed me firmly with each syllable. 'What you have to learn is the difference between rock music and pop music.'

More jabbing. I did point out, in a gentlemanly manner of course, that if the poking continued I might just poke him on the nose. Not an unfair trade, I'd say. It goes without saying that I didn't get my shares, moved on and left him to bank what was presumably a beefy salary for some years.

There followed a spell on Jazz FM, where I was playing artists of whom I had never heard. Now I'm no slouch when it comes to your Basies, Shearings, Barbers, Brubecks and so on, but these cats on my playlist had clearly been operating undercover in heavy camouflage.

I built a beautiful and not inexpensive studio which was often depicted by the media as a 'shed' at the bottom of my garden. True, it had once been a series of sheds, but with a super architect, a herd of builders and some serious dosh, I transformed it into a stunning radio studio and record archive. As it faced acres of farmland, I was also on 'lambwatch' during the season, as many were born in deep mud and struggled to survive. In between tracks I'd send an SOS to the farmer.

In 2005 I was asked to join the re-launch of the old offshore pirate station Radio London, or Big L. This time it was to be land based, but to keep as much of a mid '6os feel as possible, the studio was at Frinton-on-Sea, spiritual home of the station from 1964 to its demise in 1967. I helped station boss Ray Anderson recruit a few other radio rascals including two former Radio One jocks, David Hamilton and Adrian John, along with an ex-Capital DJ, Randall Lee Rose. It was a great adventure with a swashbuckling crew. What more could we want? Hoist the Jolly Roger and let's set sail! I invited Cliff Richard to open the new Big L as one of his songs had opened the original station. His new single 'What Car' got us underway and to add to the fun we hired a double-decker bus to bring him to the station. The Cheeky Girls were also guests that day, treading the station's very own mono-grammed carpet and peering through the porthole-styled windows.

We rather lavishly took a Big L Roadshow up the east coast for a week, with the old Radio One vehicle and Smiley Miley. It was like old times. On one occasion Smiley guilelessly allowed himself to be blindfolded and put in a tank with some rather vicious crabs and at Clacton he was almost crushed by boa constrictors. Well, that's what the media said and they had the photographs to prove it. There was Smiley with two paramedics struggling to free him from his brace of newly acquired 8-foot scarves that appeared to have him in a grip of which Big Daddy would have been proud. We hadn't lost our touch.

A new station. Free musical choice. Roadshows. A great team of broadcasters. What could go wrong? Well, gradually, everything, but for now we were having fun and sharing a six-bedroomed house. On any evening there could be anywhere between one and six of us in residence. We all had other lives with wives and girlfriends, but actually we enjoyed each other's company and laughed a lot. There'd be sing-songs, football, tennis, TV and terrific suppers, and I have to say, I don't recall a single heated word or a falling-out. No one complained that I didn't do any cooking or washing-up, but I led the sing-a-longs and in doing so appeared to pay my dues.

Adrian John had to rise earlier than the rest of us for the breakfast show, and therefore climbed the wooden hill to Bedfordshire early, just as many an evening of merriment and mirth was getting underway. There was so much shrieking and noise one particular evening that I felt compelled to promise him that we'd be quieter in future.

'No, don't ... I love it.'

'What, the welter of noise? The cacophony of sound? Loud jokes with feeble punchlines?'

'Oh yes, it's so comforting.' I suspected irony. He demurred. 'It's *very* comforting. As it was when you were very young and you could hear the murmur of your parents' voices downstairs. It makes you feel secure.'

I agreed with him about the parent thing.

'I drift off very happily hearing your laughter and knowing that I'm in a house with a bunch of guys with good hearts. I feel spiritually uplifted.'

Big L was enormous fun ... well, if you call nearly drowning at sea in a brave attempt to re-construct the 'halcyon' days which the original guys had been desperate to leave behind fun. If you call a complete lack of marketing strategy, which the original stations had in spades, fun. If you call believing you're going to be paid and running into a brick wall fun. Actually that's where the fun stopped. But not until we'd all had a smashing time at the seaside for three years. Sadly the station was full of good intent, good heart and goodwill but the business side failed to hold a candle to the on-air atmosphere and the excellent music. A wasted opportunity.

We knew those times wouldn't last, though. Nobody will try to re-create that period of the pirate ships again. That's probably a good thing. Many got out in good time. I tried to see it through and became unstuck financially. After an attempt to put a string of independent radio stations together in the Cotswolds and beyond I realised that we simply didn't have the right team for the job. Enthusiasm, yes. Work ethic, no. I'm now very happily ensconced doing the Magic Network breakfast show on Saturday and Sunday mornings and the BBC Radio Berkshire afternoon show from Monday to Friday. One is a music-based show where I choose the playlist and the other is an interview- and speech-based show with some music. A great balance. When he heard that I'd moved into Henley, my mate John Baish from Classic FM and Jazz FM asked me if I wanted to do some programmes for BBC Berkshire. I was delighted and it gives me the opportunity to expand my broadcasting into other areas whether it's putting together and presenting a D-Day Special, a series from Country Houses, covering Hampton Court Flower Show, broadcasting from, and walking, the Thames Path or simply getting out and about broadcasting on the road. My old pal Tony Blackburn is there … mind you he's everywhere, as are a host of other seriously good national broadcasters.

CHAPTER 4

TOP OF THE POPS

HAVING GROWN UP watching *Top of the Pops*, I was now pre-senting it. What larks. Skimming through some of the first ones now, with the benefit of hindsight, I appeared a shade too eager to please at times and even a trifle bouncy in places, but I think I was doing what I imagined was expected of me. It took me some while to find myself, if indeed I ever did. Let's be blunt, there were plenty of very dodgy outfits and implausible hairstyles (I use the term loosely) through the years on *TOTP*.

Blondie appeared on one of my earlier jaunts on the show. Debbie Harry and I had a degree of parity. She was performing on the show and I was hosting it. This clearly gave me the God-given right to talk to her. Of course it did. She was wearing that short green-and-white striped affair, which, let's be honest, looked damned sexy. She walked across the studio floor. This was my moment. Closer. Now. I opened my mouth and nothing came out. According to onlookers, there may have been a barely audible squeak but little else. Pathetic. I would admit to embarrassing myself, but I don't think she was even aware of my presence … dear.

The head honchos (executive directors) that spanned my period presenting the show were the dapper, bow-tied Robin Nash, who reminded me that only cool black dudes could get away with wearing shades indoors, the occasionally irascible Michael Hurll and Paul Ciani. Michael was one of the top BBC producers, also being responsible for shows including *The Two Ronnies* and *Seaside Special* as well as founding the British Comedy Awards. I worked with him for seven years on *TOTP* from 1980 but it wasn't always easy if you crossed him in any way. Despite my office making Michael aware that I might be a tad late for one particular run-through, he was seriously angry when I arrived. Never one to toady or turn on the obsequious smile, I stood my ground. We'd let him know, after all. He let *me* know by not using me for several months. The show didn't book the presenters very far in advance, there were no block bookings for the year or anything like that, just a phone call a week or two before.

Michael also penalised me slightly on another occasion. I was in the middle of explaining the timings to one of the newer groups, when Michael barged in and overrode the conversation without so much as a by-your-leave. I wasn't having that. I attempt to be polite to everyone, and treat them well, unless they do something that warrants me behaving otherwise. So I made my feelings clear, which led to another wee period in the sin bin. Most of the time, though, Michael was fine, as was everybody else.

In the summer of 1979 I was lined up for what would have been a *TOTP* first, presenting the show and performing in one of that week's chart videos. I'd been hosting the show for less than a year when my pal Jimmy Pursey asked me to be in the video for Sham 69's new single, 'Hersham Boys', playing the fiddle. We shot it in a barn at Weylands Farm, midway between Hersham and Esher. The song had extra meaning for me, as the chorus was an adaptation of an old chant sung by supporters of Hersham Football Club, which later became Walton & Hersham, the main side that my father played for. Jimmy had taken the group's name from graffiti that was part of the slogan 'Walton & Hersham '69'. Unfortunately, there was a strike the week I was due to be presenting as well as scraping the fiddle in 'Hersham Boys', so the historical moment didn't happen and nor did that week's *Top of the Pops*.

There would always be a call sheet so you knew who'd be playing live, who was on videotape and if there were any post-recordings. We'd usually record the chart rundown between the run-through and the show itself. Here's a random, but typical call sheet, from a show I presented in 1988 with Andy Crane. Gloria Estefan, Michael Jackson, the Proclaimers, Yello and Jane Wiedlin were all on videotape, while Phil Collins, who was at number one with 'Groovy Kind of Love', Marc Almond and Spagna were live in the studio, so a light week in terms of the number of artists actually on site, but the studio crowd weren't short-changed, because there were live post-recordings from the Four Tops and Rick Astley. The omnipresent floor manager Ian McLean was there as usual to add to the fun, while running the ship at floor level, for the director and producer.

An atypical *Top of the Pops* would be one of the commemorative or seasonal variety. The 25th-anniversary show, for example, was recorded over two days and featured artists that spanned the whole period. On the Wednesday we had Peter Powell, Paul Gambaccini and me presenting, with the Swinging Blue Jeans, Engelbert Humperdinck, the Four Tops and the Tremeloes performing, and we ended with a retrospective piece about *TOTP*'s first home in Manchester. For the following day's recordings, the three of us were joined by a whole host of DJs from down the years to help with celebration: Kenny Everett, David Hamilton, Pete Murray, Alan Freeman, Jimmy Savile, David Jacobs, Simon Bates and Mark Goodier. Mud, David Essex, the Pet Shop Boys and Status Quo played in the studio, and additional on-screen guests included Robin and Maurice Gibb, Go West, Brian May and Roger Taylor, Living in a Box, Beach Boy Mike Love, the Troggs, Hot Chocolate's Errol Brown and former Bay City Rollers singer Les McKeown. On top of that many artists were featured on film, including Procol Harum, the Dave Clark Five, the Kinks, the

Animals, the Hollies, the Beatles, Slade, the Police, Adam and the
Ants, Frankie Goes to Hollywood, Duran Duran, Village People, Free,
T. Rex, Abba, the Sex Pistols, ELO … the list of fantastic artists went
on and on. No wonder the show got viewing figures of fifteen or sixteen million at times.

The banter in between songs was always left up to the DJs, but
there was usually something like ten seconds in which to back-
announce the artist you'd just seen (three seconds), introduce the
next one (three seconds again) and in the remaining four seconds,
indelibly stamp your personality on the great British public. Now
there may be some cynics with a cruel and preconceived image of
disc jockeys that might ask how we managed to spin that out so long.
I'd say that's harsh and uncalled for. It was a fantastic phenomenon
to be a part of.

Before the axe fell on what had been a much-loved British institution, the ratings had been pretty dire. That's because they hadn't kept
abreast of what was happening. OK it might never have got those
fifteen or sixteen million again, but it needn't have been allowed to
deteriorate into the corporation's sickly child. I called Peter Fincham
and asked if I could take it over on a no-ratings, no-fee basis. I knew
what I'd do with it. I'd move it to late afternoon/early evening on a
Sunday, double the length to an hour, and have a mix of songs from
the singles chart, album tracks (which would mean major heritage artists also being featured) and a sprinkling of material from old *TOTP*.
I'd give a slot to a really good new act that deserved a break, and feature a YouTube chart each week with variable genres. But no go.

It was great to be part of the programme's history for so long and
to have co-presented the very last show, in 2006. The extraordinary
thing is that BBC Four is now screening them all in order and I have
a whole new retrospective career, popping up every few weeks. I still
query some of the clothes, why I should have been dressed in a sailor
suit one week and leather trousers the next. Still, it makes for good
banter on Twitter.

CHAPTER 5

ON THE ROAD AGAIN

MY FIRST ROADSHOW week was in 1980. My debut was at South Shields, followed by Scarborough, Bridlington, Cleethorpes and Skegness. I know DLT must have been with us on one of the dates as the schoolboy in me came to the fore and the first of the infamous pranks was unleashed on him. Not for me that well-worn and overused cling-film-over-the-loo gag. That would have been childish and unworthy, disgusting and rightly frowned upon. I considered my wheeze a step up. Classier. It was the stink-bomb-under-the-loo-seat gag. Well, more than one stink bomb. Several actually. One has to make an impact or be found wanting. I subtly purloined the key to DLT's room, sneaked in with the dexterity of Raffles, lifted the loo seat and gently laid three or four of the vile vials on the porcelain. With rock-steady hands worthy of a horologist I delicately rested the seat on top of them so they didn't crack immediately. However, once subjected to the full weight of a large man with a beard they most certainly cracked. DLT's bathroom must have been like the Black Hole of Calcutta before Suraj-ud-Daulah's gang of rotters let out the remaining few survivors.

Was the subject amused, you may wonder? He was not. Far from it. In fact he was livid. One might have imagined him being in the

Black Hole himself and trying to break down the door to kill the sleeping Daulah, only it was me he was trying to kill. I really thought the door to my room was going to smash into a thousand pieces. I sensibly kept out of his way for the rest of the evening. What a lack of appreciation for a lost and underrated art form.

My 1981 roadshow week took in Morecambe, Blackpool, Southport, Rhyl and Colwyn Bay. In Southport I was reminded of another near-death experience there years earlier, when my father and godfather rather bravely pulled me out of deceptive quicksand as I sank up to my chest. My clothes were thrown away, new ones were purchased and I was chucked into a bath at a nearby hotel. Actually, that sounds uncannily like a roadshow stunt. If my father had known then that he would cross the street to avoid me in my later teenage years he might well have left me to struggle in the mud. I like to think that it was because of my attire more than my attitude. If I couldn't locate the World War One knee-length cavalry boots and milkman's cap that I preferred to sport in those days, I only had to look in the dustbin. I lost count of the times I retrieved them.

Morecambe too was memorable. It was there I had a phone call telling me that our current *Guinness Book of British Hit Singles* had hit the number one spot in the bestsellers. Of course, as soon as you're able to look at the *Times* bestseller list, your eyes drop below that dizzy height to see which serious authors are running to keep up. The news gave me a decided boost for that afternoon's game of rounders on the beach.

My 1983 holiday, sorry, roadshow week, took in Devon and Cornwall. What a treat: Torquay, Plymouth, St Austell, Falmouth and St Ives. Of course there were practical jokes galore, but let me single out St Austell for special mention. After a leisurely breakfast with my producer, Paul Williams, I sauntered back to my room to slip into something a little more Radio One, whatever that was, and to collect my guitar. But there was no guitar. The window was wide open and my pride and joy was no longer present. A footprint on the window ledge confirmed my suspicions. Half an hour later, accompanied by a concerned producer, I'm giving details of my loss to officers of the Devon and Cornwall Constabulary.

'Could you draw the guitar for me?'

I could.

'And from the side?'

Yes, even easier.

'The back?'

I had to admire their dedication to detail.

'Strings?'

'Six when it left here. I couldn't vouch for the number now.'

'Do you know anyone who might have had a grudge against you and your guitar?'

'Only the 15,000 roadshow audience, my producer, the controller of Radio One, the entire road crew, Smiley Miley and ten million people listening on the radio. Apart from that, no one.'

They were thorough to say the least, but how could I find a replacement at the eleventh hour? Paul Williams came to the rescue. 'Kid Creole and the Coconuts are in town and they've offered to lend you an acoustic.'

'How lovely. We'd better play "Stool Pigeon" a few times then.'

Now my guitar spot on the show, where I'd lead the children of St Austell, or wherever, into the musical wilderness, was normally an uphill battle, but Paul was actively encouraging me to play near the top of the show. Had he had a change of heart? Had there been a gradual realisation that my talents were worthy after all? Whatever the reason, I gave forth with my own personal battle-cry, *carpe diem*, and seized the day. With hindsight it should have been *cave ne cadas*, as I was about to be knocked off my musical pedestal. I was cantering along in full flow, making a decent fist of it, when the guitar exploded in my hands. Not only exploded and splintered, but showered me with that distinctive orange dye reserved for bank robbers. I was stunned. No, hang on, shocked and stunned. For a good two minutes the radio was filled with the cheering, howling, applauding and whooping of the multitudes assembled on the beach. What the hell had happened? I knew not. Only the appearance of Smiley Miley told me that all was not as it should be. There had been no robbery. It was an inside job. My guitar was safe. Even the members of the force making me draw the guitar from every conceivable angle were in on it. The guitar wasn't from Kid Creole, it was one specially doctored by Smiles. It contained a small amount of explosive and a very large amount of orange dye and had been detonated by him from a safe distance. Right! His future wasn't bright, but mine, for the moment, was definitely orange.

I had reverted to my normal colour and guitar when playing a duet with Justin Hayward at Falmouth and had gone with the full whites for St Ives. Wham! had just released the wonderful 'Club Tropicana' and were my guests on the last day of the week. We entertained the crowds by playing kazoos all in white shorts and shirts, which seemed like the cool outfit of the summer. I normally dreaded the final day as it signalled the end of the festivities, but Andrew Ridgeley and I decided to stay on for an extra day, not that I remember much about it. I do recall Andrew playing tennis against himself for half an hour. I didn't ask why. Maybe I was meant to be on the other side of the court. George Michael flew back from St Ives, while I drove Andrew back in my Mercedes with the roof down and 'Club Tropicana' pumping out of the radio every hour. What posers ... but what fun.

I was due to be at a twenty-first birthday party that day, so I called ahead to ask if I could bring a friend. 'Sure.' Birthday girl Penny was surprised to say the least when Andrew Ridgeley walked in with me, but her girlfriends were open mouthed. Wham! were about the hottest thing around at that time and Andrew had that heart-throb Mediterranean look that seemed to make the girls melt.

The summer of the following year, 1984, saw my group, the Rock-olas, undertaking our most extensive tour to date, performing in Hastings, Portsmouth, Southampton, Bournemouth, Plymouth,

Exeter, St Austell, Newquay and Hendra Tourist camp. Then it was off to another roadshow at Gateshead with Midge Ure, before my own roadshow week took me back to the east coast, calling in at Scarborough, Bridlington, Cleethorpes, Skegness and Great Yarmouth. In 1985 I was once more in the West Country, taking in Torquay, Plymouth, Carlyon Bay, Falmouth and Marazion. We spent one night at the Carlyon Bay Hotel, former hideaway of Edward VIII and Mrs Simpson. Mind you, they seemed to have bolt-holes everywhere. My abiding memory of that evening is sitting completely alone outside the hotel writing, as the sun hit the top of the Scots pines and the sea was flat calm. The twelve lines of 'Carlyon Bay' made it to my first book of poetry: 'But the days are growing shorter | From Black to Gribben Head.' It was one of those tranquil English evenings that I wanted to last for a week or so, but I was also acutely aware that the twilight was approaching and it would soon be over. So would the week. And the years would fly. They have. The era of Edward and Mrs Simpson seemed a world away, but they would have watched the gathering dusk there less than fifty years before that evening in 1985. Now it's 2014 and the evening I sat there is itself almost thirty years away.

My first action on any roadshow day was to tentatively draw back the curtains praying for sun. A sunny day and a blue sky put a different spin on everything. Hurricane Charley put paid to that at Exmouth in 1986: the wind howled, flags flapped crazily, the rain swept in from the sea and yet some 20,000 souls braved the elements. Those at the back were virtually enveloped in a thick, wet, mist. If Smiley wasn't in a mist he was certainly a laughing stock.

En route I'd spotted a character making gates and benches. I persuaded him to set aside these menial tasks and offered him far too much money to knock up some stocks.

'Stocks?'

'Yes, stocks.'

'You mean like ... stocks?'

'You've seized upon my meaning *instanter*.'

'You from the local council?'

Two hours later I was on my way, roof down and stocks on board. You're ahead of me. Smiley, stocks. It would be a marriage made in Devon. Of course he wasn't a willing participant, but there were enough burly blokes who rigged the roadshow to convince him otherwise. In he went and there he stayed. There was a heck of a lot of rain but I did treat him to an ice-cream. Tragically, his hand wasn't able to reach his mouth, but being a good neighbour I fed him myself. Almost as tragically, my aim was terrible that day. The ice-cream went everywhere, the remains turning a rather ghastly amalgam of tartrazine E102 and sunset yellow E110. Maybe his face was already yellow. In truth I can't remember. The rotten tomatoes may or may not have been thrown by me, but it would have been a shame to waste them.

Having taken Barry, Keith and Paul, my fellow Rock-olas, for the week, we couldn't play on that first day. Horizontal rain, a stage that resembled Victoria Falls and a ton of electronic equipment just didn't seem to be ideal soul-mates. Weymouth was also hit by the weather, but I managed to scrape up a few tarantulas and the like to keep the party going for Smiley. By Swanage it had perked up a little and by Bournemouth we were rocking. The group were in full swing and we were joined by the Real Thing, Bobby Ball and Stu Francis. I coerced some burly lifeguards to enlist Smiley to help with their drill. For demonstration purposes, they were forced to throw him in the drink. Then came the payback and ignominy of the final day at Southsea, when I was challenged to get all the answers correct to a special 'Bits and Pieces' competition or face a spell in my own stocks. They couldn't. They wouldn't. I got them all right. What? I missed one? Impossible. The last track turned out to be the dog whistle from the inner groove of *Sgt. Pepper*, which was inaudible to the human ear. Now if I'd been a Jack Russell … but then getting the other questions right may have been a little tricky.

Smiley was racing off on holiday at the end of the programme, so thank goodness I'd had the foresight to pay four bricklayers to build an 8-foot wall around his Range Rover while he was busy with the roadshow. Did I pay them? No. I told them that Smiley would pay them … to knock it down. He had no alternative. Know your enemy.

As well as the conventional, if that word applies, seaside roadshows, there were weeks away, where we all charged off to Leeds, Edinburgh, Bristol or somewhere and were sent into the market place, often literally, to impose ourselves on the inhabitants. We were also woven into the local fabric, as when my producer got me to fire the famous one o'clock gun at Edinburgh Castle. This six-day-a-week ritual had been in place since 1861, when it gave ships in the Firth of Forth an audible time signal. I was marched up through the Portcullis Gate and, at the far end of the Argyll Battery, given the relevant instructions. The idea had sounded terrific over a drink in the hotel bar the night before, for here was history. Mary, Queen of Scots had given birth to James VI here and Bonnie Prince Charlie attempted to take the castle during the Jacobite Rising, and here we were adding our minuscule contribution, by letting the rest of the country hear the one o'clock gun. The gun I fired was the 25-pound Howitzer which had been in place since 1952, although they've since replaced it. My instructor was Staff Sergeant Thomas McKay (later MBE), who went by the wonderfully scary nickname of 'Tam the Gun'. The force and the noise at close range were extraordinary. I felt as though I'd been simultaneously punched by half a dozen chaps from the 105th Regiment Royal Artillery after a night on the town. You know that feeling. The castle was built atop a 350-million-year-old volcano, so I wouldn't have considered it the ideal place to let off a jolly big gun on a daily basis.

If Radio One failed to kill you with conventional weaponry they tried to drown you. Come with me to the Plymouth of the mid '80s and let me introduce you to a man attempting to emulate Sir Francis Drake. I will refer to him only as 'Peter Powell'. An unlikely name, I know, but it will have to suffice. PP, proud possessor of a splendid-looking speedboat, brought it with him on the week away. Would we like a trip round the bay? Of course we would. With five of us on board, including Paul Williams, off we went, 'sailing on a summer breeze' and 'skipping over the ocean like a stone' without having to engage in any 'banking off of the North East winds.' Perfect, really. No, not really. Not wishing to sound like a landlubber who squeals like an especially savvy pig on its way to market when just 5 yards off-shore, I waited until the water was around my ankles before I spoke.

'That's normal, matey,' came the reply. OK, Peter was the captain. Five minutes passed before I passed further comment on the increasing depth of the water.

'Oh shit!' came the not-so-nonchalant response.

Somewhere we'd hit an underwater rock. We were about half a mile out to sea and *Pop One Up*, as the ailing craft was called, was close to popping five pairs of clogs. Baling with our shoes proved useless. With five of us on board and nothing to bale with, the weight was increasing by the minute as the sea washed around our knees. Step forward M. D. K. Read with a master plan. It occurred to me that the boat contained one lifebelt and one non-swimmer. Would it not make sense to put the two together? I donned the lifebelt, jumped overboard and tried to pull the boat towards *terra firma*. The Highwaymen had a number one back in the day about Michael rowing the boat ashore, but I don't recall anyone on our craft using the US group's tagline of 'Hallelujah'. Over the side I went, rope in hand and lifebelt around my chest. I might not be able to actually swim, but I reasoned that if the lifebelt kept me afloat, I could do something through sheer strength. Gradually, gradually the boat nosed towards the shore. After what seemed like hours (they always use that line in books, but in this case it was no exaggeration) I felt sand and rocks beneath my feet, enabling me to get some purchase at least. The boat and four crew were getting heavier and heavier and I could feel the rope cutting into me. Peter also helpfully pointed out that there was hardly an ideal place to land anyway on this section of coast, even if we made it. It was true. Jagged rocks dotted the shoreline. Then he spotted what appeared to be a tiny sliver of beach. I'm not certain my sense of direction was up to much by then. I felt like Geoff Capes pulling one of those 20-ton trucks with his teeth. This was strength-sapping stuff.

After another half-hour, and almost leaning horizontally backwards, I felt myself falling onto a sandy beach. The boat was still some yards out as I got unsteadily to my feet, thoroughly exhausted, and if I expected four grateful faces giving me a 'you plucked us from the jaws of certain death' look, I was mistaken. Their faces told a different story. They were struck dumb. With gratitude? No, they'd spotted the apparition bearing down on me like a galleon in full sail. The full-bodied female nudist swung her handbag at my head with such force that I thought for a moment that God had saved me from drowning to be concussed instead. She may have uttered something like 'pervert' or 'weirdo' but I can't be sure, as I had that feeling you get after a bottle of Great-Aunt Doris's home-made potato wine.

Others of her clan arrived at the scene. I was being berated from all sides. 'We're fed up with people like you coming to ogle.'

Fortunately for all concerned, explanation and recognition saved the day. They embraced me – not physically, of course. One of the men who had some naval experience and was a former policeman (make your own jokes here) went to help Peter with the boat while the other survivors waded ashore. The nudists were now my friends. I had become, within minutes, an honorary naturist. They gave me drinks and sandwiches. I had been accepted into their tribe. I felt like ripping my clothes off and being initiated. Well, maybe not, but I was certainly grateful to be alive-ish.

Our problems weren't over, though. The tide was coming in rapidly and we'd have to vacate the beach pretty sharpish. Peter and the ex-sailor were attempting to re-start the boat and coax it to a nearby port. Meanwhile our producer, Paul Williams, never one to panic in a crisis (yeah, right), took charge. Having discovered that the only way off the beach, unless by boat, was to scale the massive rock face via a steep and arduous set of steps, he set off in search of assistance. The stairs would be cut off at some point, so flapping his arms like a particularly inept

Bognor Birdman entrant, with omnipresent cigarette clamped firmly between his lips, he capered across the beach as if trying to launch himself, and disappeared, mumbling something about emergency services. Where he was heading nobody knew. I doubt if he did.

After what seemed a millennium, during which time the nudists had disappeared, the tide continued to menace us and *Pop One Up* drifted off towards the horizon, I came close to getting a haircut I hadn't ordered from a helicopter. It hovered and landed on the beach, and two guys in full kit leapt out and came racing over. We'd already had enough action to fill a James Bond movie, and this latest episode provided the icing on the cake. Who were they after? The answer was me.

'Which leg's broken?'

Silence. The other three members of our crew looked at me for an answer. Well, the real answer was 'Neither of them, thank you', but being a part-time student of the psychology of a Radio One producer, I soon realised this represented Paul Williams at his best. To make sure that he did his duty and behaved responsibly towards his party, he'd embellished a trifle. Why he'd selected one of my legs to be broken is beyond me. I wasn't even sure which one he'd told them had been broken. I almost asked them to pick whichever one they thought fit, or unfit. 'This one', I whispered weakly, 'hurts a little.'

I now looked like a complete bloody idiot, trying to save Paul Williams's face. The boys from RNAS Culdrose eventually dismissed me as a time-wasting buffoon. There was another twist to come, though, for their presence, albeit at the behest of a mad, fag-wielding, piano-playing Adam Faith lookalike, proved to be a boon. Just as they were about to give me a second unwanted haircut, the boat caught fire. In short order Peter Powell and the rather helpful naked policeman (an integral part of the nudist crew as I recall) were winched to safety, *Pop One Up* was towed to what might have been its final resting place and I was scooped off the beach in case Radio One was fined for littering. The following day's papers carried dramatic photographs of the near-disaster, prompting the Radio One controller, Derek Chinnery, to haul me in and accuse me of setting it up as a stunt. Crazy I may be, but I would never knowingly attempt to slaughter a handful of people for a few column inches and a blurred snap or two in tomorrow's chip paper. I assured him that no nudists had been hurt in the making of this tragedy.

For some reason best known to himself, Peter Powell dropped his shorts and bared his bottom on the penultimate day of his roadshow week, so the idea was put to me that I should beetle down the following day and 'arrest' Peter on stage. His posterior had made the national papers, including the front page of *The Sun*. Smiley had organised a uniform and helmet in my size and was convinced we could get a fun picture out of it. Always available when the word 'fun' is mentioned, I drove to Torre Abbey Meadows, Torquay and the plan was put into action. I'd turn up on stage, show him the photograph of his rear end and 'arrest' him. All harmless fun. Well, harmless until the actual police joined the party. Two constables approached me. 'We're arresting you for impersonating a member of the force.'

'Oh right, ha ha, very good.' I played along as they dragged me away. 'OK now, the media have taken the pictures and we've had a good laugh.'

They didn't appear to be doing too much laughing. I was bundled rather harshly into a police car and with sirens wailing, taken to the local nick. Lines like 'it's a fair cop' and so on didn't seem to cut much ice, so I shut up. A large sergeant, quite possibly the result of an illicit liaison between Giant Haystacks and a sturdy silverback gorilla, let me know in no uncertain terms that he wasn't messing around.

'But it's all part of the roadshow.'

'I'm not interested in who you are or what you do, you've broken the law.'

'Oh, come on, all my clothes are back at the hotel.'

'You won't be needing clothes.'

Gulp.

If he wasn't a Radio One man (he clearly wasn't) I thought that

I could maybe get away with a false name. I was taking a damn big risk. The custody record already had the reason for arrest down, 'Impersonation of a Police Officer'. I was in danger of adding to my sentence. I risked it.

'Name?'

'Peter Powell.'

'Place of birth?'

'Birmingham.'

I still have the charge sheet and Peter Powell's name beams out of it. Here are the details, Pete, in case you ever need them. The arresting officer was WPC 2497 Wignall. Your height I gave as 5 ft 9 in., occupation DJ and address c/o Broadcasting House. You were arrested at 12.42 on Torre Abbey Meadows and detained at Her Majesty's pleasure. On the 'prisoner's rights' section, I said that you didn't want a solicitor and didn't need anyone to be notified. I hope that was OK. You may be pursued for supplying false fingerprints as they remain my property. They're a weird shape.

I was led into the bowels of the station and chucked unceremoniously into a cell. After an hour in the slammer I was beginning to feel a trifle uncomfortable. I had a new neighbour, though.

'Mike Read, isn't it?'

I nodded in a custodial way.

'I was hoping to come and see you at the roadshow.'

'Not exactly the best view from here, mate.'

An hour later there was a rattle of keys. I didn't hold out any hope that they were for me. The big fella was back. 'All right, out you come.' They obviously planned to rush me to court. Instead I was shown the custody record report they'd just signed. I quote verbatim:

> *Enquiring into reasons for arrest and evidence. Determined*
> *a set-up by BBC Radio One staff. Detention authorised to*
> *continue set-up and enable evidence to be obtained by photo-*
> *graph and fingerprinting and for him to sign all autographs*

as required. Following photographs and fingerprints [notice the cunning lack of reference to my hour or two in the cooler] decided that the scam had gone on long enough. Prisoner was beginning to worry. [I can confirm that] Released from custody and even taken to his hotel, aren't we good?!

They forgot to mention that they gave me a slap-up feed in the canteen first. Did I want a pudding too before my courtesy car driven complete with flashing blue light whisked me back to the hotel? I did. From a custody suite to a custardy sweet in under two hours.

We made all the nationals the next day, including, once more, the front page of *The Sun*, which featured the arrest by WPC Marilyn Wignall and PC Keith Droudge. Both the *Daily Express* and the *Daily Mirror* deemed the prank worthy of page three, with the latter also giving us a cartoon showing me in jail moaning to a fellow inmate, 'It started as a prank, then they decided to leave me in here.' Peter's 'Super Soaraway bum' even made another appearance in some papers.

I'd have to admit it really was a fair cop, although not my first time behind bars. At college half a dozen of us caused a certain amount of mayhem having descended on the West End for our rag week. Students see rag week as an important issue. The public and the police have a different view. For some juvenile and inexplicable reason we parked our battered van outside the front entrance to the Hilton and proceeded to paint it. On being reprimanded by a couple of commissionaires we responded with the crass but reasonable student chant of 'it's a free country'. Not terribly original and straight out of the bolshie teenagers' handbook. The work of art was proceeding very nicely and the van was heading towards a new psychedelic look when an irate American yelled, 'Get that damn thing out of the way, I need to move my car.' His car was a Roller so maybe he had a bit of clout. His outburst surprised our very own Van Gogh, John Calcut, who spun round and painted a rather neat line of red emulsion across the guy's jacket.

Downing Street was our next port of call, where we painted bare footprints from the doorstep of No. 10 along the street and down Whitehall. There were no security gates then, and you could stand within a few yards of the Prime Minister's door without fear of reprisals. We were also unwittingly aided by a jostling crowd supporting the seamen's strike, which masked us. Of course we didn't get away with it. We were 'apprehended', marched across to Scotland Yard, and given buckets of water and stiff scrubbing brushes. As any painter and decorator will tell you, removing delightfully fresh gloss paint with water and a brush is impossible, but the boys in blue were well aware of that. They let us go with a warning after a back-breaking and futile hour of drudgery, after which we left Whitehall in a bigger mess than the government.

Older, wiser folk would have learned their lesson, but not adrenaline-fuelled, fun-loving kids from Walton-on-Thames and Weybridge. What possessed our student union president, Marshall Dixon, and me to sticker the four lions in Trafalgar Square with our rag week publicity leaflets and change the colour of their feet, I have no idea, but I'm sure we thought we had a damned good reason at the time. The two policemen that arrested us weren't of the same opinion and dragged us unceremoniously to the tiny lock-up a few yards east of Nelson's Column. Names, addresses and parents' telephone numbers were unwillingly mumbled, in the hope of being misheard. After half an hour contemplating our doom we were suddenly and inexplicably let go. Had the bomb dropped? Were all prisoners now free?

I felt that the decent thing to do was to come clean with my Pa, before he smouldered and exploded in his own time. I was halfway through a rather faltering explanation when it dawned on me that this was new territory for him. Despite their threat, the police hadn't informed our parents at all. Another lesson learned.

One of the best-remembered pranks that year, probably sometime in the mid '80s, took place at the Unicorn Hotel in Bristol. We'd been through the usual procedure of Derek Chinnery slowly ushering everyone towards the lifts, not unlike *One Man and His Dog*. The difference here was that the sheep didn't stay in their pens. Within fifteen minutes everyone was downstairs again. I had to be up at some unearthly hour to do the breakfast show from a boat, but nevertheless stayed the course. Not everyone was a night owl and frankly I was surprised that so many of the guys were still up at three in the morning. At last I gave in and headed for my room. There was an unreasonable fishy odour invading my space, but nothing I couldn't cope with. I hit the light switch. Not working. Could I be fagged to go downstairs to report it? Of course not. It'd be light anyway in a couple of hours. I couldn't even be bothered to go to the bathroom as I'd be up again so soon. So, clothes off, into bed … and onto the floor. Fumbling in the dark I discovered that one of the legs of the bed had been sawn off. It was going to be an uncomfortable night. Now this I would report. I groped for the telephone. It was covered in something unpleasant. I couldn't see exactly what it was in the dark, but it smelled like manure and now it was all over my hands. The bathroom after all, then.

As I opened the door, it fell in of its own accord. I later discovered that the hinges had been removed. Whoever had set up this booby-trap had real attention to detail. I flew in on top of the door and the chickens flew on top of me. At least, they sounded like chickens. I couldn't see a thing. It was impossible to take a head count, but I was obviously outnumbered. Through the beaks, feathers and flapping wings, the manured hands and kipper-impregnated nose I heard the gay, tinkling laughter of merry folk on the other side of my hotel door.

I found the handle and although temporarily 'blinded by the light' in true Springsteen fashion, I caught a 'fleeting glimpse of someone's fading shadow,' in true Bob Lind fashion. Simon Bates made it to his hotel room before he could be slaughtered by his naked assailant, but Noel Edmonds 'kept on running' in true Spencer Davis fashion. The hotel corridor went round in a square, if that's not an oxymoron. I swear I was catching him as we approached my bedroom on the second lap, but guile took over. Noel looked at my naked form, clicked my door shut and disappeared. I was aghast. I was also as God made me – well, a little taller and a little heavier, but clearly no wiser. I had no alternative but to throw myself on the mercy of the night manager. The mirrored lifts weren't flattering. I took the nude version of myself to the front desk. The manager's face told me that he could smell manure. Was this the time and place for a full-frontal bedtime story involving chickens, bed legs, kippers and late-night revellers? Probably not. I skipped the explanations and simply said, 'I appear to be locked out of my room.'

In the early summer of 1987, Gary Davies and I fronted a special series of roadshows, the Twin Towers Rock & Rolls Tour. As you'd imagine, given that we were starting in Blackpool, the rock was the edible variety, not the musical genre, measuring 10 feet long by 16 inches in diameter, weighing a quarter of a ton and needing 335 pounds of sugar. It was a far cry from George Formby's 'Little Stick of Blackpool Rock', and in fact was a world record, verified by the *The Guinness Book of Records*. To make the title of the show work, we had a brace of Rolls-Royce cars, and we would use them to drag this great, calorific lump of pink confectionery from the Blackpool Tower to the Eiffel Tower, stopping at various points along the way. Why? I really don't know. I suppose because we were raising money for the charity Insight, fund-raisers for the blind. I guess the rock played some part. The great and the good from the music world (as seen from a 1987 perspective) joined us at each roadshow. Pepsi and Shirley performed at Heaton Park, as did Marillion, while Tom Jones helped us pull a record crowd of some 30,000 at Birmingham. Sam Fox appeared at Woburn Abbey, and Steve Van Zandt and Rupert Everett, then essaying a musical career in case the greasepaint lost its allure, joined us at Dover. In Paris Kim Wilde was our guest. I seem to remember we were having dinner when the news came through that she was number one in the States with her version of 'You Keep Me Hangin' On'.

My 1987 roadshow week kicked off at Berwick-upon-Tweed, where I went for a world record. As soon as the roadshow was over at 12.30 my producer Paul Williams whisked me over the golf links to the gladiatorial arena of the tennis courts. The idea was that I'd play against 1,000 opponents. Not all at once, obviously. Anyone could appear on court as many times as they liked as long as they re-joined the queue and paid their token coin each time, which went to charity. I must have delivered my first serve sometime after midday and finished at seven in the evening, exhausted but exhilarated. I wondered what the heck I'd been thinking of when I agreed to this mad escapade, but I'd done it. So why didn't we make *The Guinness Book of Records*? We had the correct adjudication and the qualifying forms from Guinness, and everything was recorded according to the rules. Who knows? Anyway, it was time to head off to Portobello on the outskirts of Edinburgh, where we had a police escort.

This was the spawning ground for the young Sean Connery. From one-time lifeguard at the local swimming pool to international movie star: not a bad career path, unless you're a great swimmer and lousy actor. Among the massive crowd were a couple of lads with guitars who appeared at the back of the roadshow with a CD containing a couple of their demos. They seemed very normal, down-to-earth and enthusiastic. My shows were always seat-of-your-pants affairs, so I suggested they came on stage and played live. They were awesome. They sang those kinds of harmonies that you only get from siblings, or people that are on exactly the same wavelength. I was seriously impressed by their talent, songs and attitude – they wore horn-rimmed glasses and wore them with pride. This duo was worth championing. I played the demos on my radio shows, so when they got a record deal I was up for pushing their first single. I even attended a playlist meeting, but the record got knocked back by several producers, one calling it 'woolly-jumper music'. I went to two more meetings (unheard of for a DJ), whereupon they relented.

'All right, we'll put your mates on the playlist.'

'My mates? They played on my roadshow but I don't really know them.'

'Yeah, yeah. We'll stick it on the C list for you.' The C list was the bottom rung of the playlist.

'You're not doing it for me, you're doing it for a couple of talented singer-songwriters.'

'OK, we'll see what happens, shall we?'

What happened? The song went top three and Charlie and Craig Reid, the Proclaimers, had a string of hit singles and albums spanning twenty years.

Job done at Portobello, we headed north to Arbroath and then across to the west coast. 130 miles of fabulous scenery which necessitated regular stops to scribble poetry. By the time we reached Helensburgh the poem was finished.

> From the shores of far Loch Lomond,
> Over Rowardennan Forest,
> Foothills of the Drum of Clashore,
> Feed the tumbling burns that bind them.
> Coursing like the blood of demons
> From the dark of Lochard Forest,
> Forging like Buchanan smithy,
> New-born shapes of infant rivers,
> Snaking north of young Buchlyvie,
> On past Cauldhame, on past Kippen,
> Under greying summer heavens.
> Gracefully by Church of Scotland,
> Nether Gorse and Patrickson,
> The sleepy Forth creeps past the high-stacked
> Yellow hayfields of Gargunnock.

At various times during the week I'd made a point of telling a couple of Smiley's sidekicks how the water in Loch Lomond was so pure that you could drink it. I let the fact permeate. I bided my time. When we arrived at the loch I let the conversation drift naturally towards the quality of the water.

'I wouldn't like to drink that,' said my producer, right on cue.

'It won't hurt you. £20 says you won't drink a glass of it.'

'Not a chance.'

It was going according to plan. Someone had passed on my false knowledge to Smiley that the water was absolutely pure.

'Twenty quid? I'll do it.'

'You're kidding?'

'Give me a glass.'

One glass. Into the water. Out of Loch Lomond and into Smiley. 'No problem. Twenty quid please.'

I paid up, but the psychological fun I had, when he learned that it was no different from any normal lake water with its animal matter, dead fish, rotting plants and things unmentionable, was worth £20 of anybody's money. He asked serious questions of his internal plumbing for the next two or three days.

At Helensburgh we stayed by Gare Loch, but I resisted pulling the same trick twice and instead got my old pal Stuart Henry on the phone from Luxembourg, much to the delight of the crowd, as he'd done the roadshow here many years earlier. He enjoyed being there in spirit.

I saved the week's physical stunt for the final day at Ayr. After interviewing former Small Faces singer Steve Marriott, I set about Smiley. On stage we discussed his new many-wheeled roadshow vehicle. 'Many-wheeled, yes, Smiley,' I said, 'but not many-tyred.'

The crowd parted to show his truck sans tyres. Storm clouds spread over his usually sunny countenance. Something that sounded uncannily like 'You bastard' issued from his lips.

The local Air Sea Rescue had played ball. Their helicopter rose on cue, flew out to sea and dropped six tyres into the ocean. Smiley was livid. He was steaming. I'd be receiving a bill that very evening. The crowd roared their approval. At the stunt that is, not the impending invoice. He was so angry that it was a struggle to get him back on stage for the finale.

'Wait a minute, Smiles, how the heck did that happen?' I pointed. The crowd parted again. The tyres were back on the vehicle. He'd been living on anger and adrenalin for the last hour, now he was a broken man. His tyres had been safe all along, those dropped into the sea being throwaways. The Air Sea Rescue later recovered them as part of an exercise. Unfortunately, in these straitjacketed days of health and safety no one would be allowed to even entertain such an idea.

Weston-Super-Mare was always fun. The lovely Hilda (some eighty-plus years young) would turn up with cakes and presents. I'd make a point of getting her up on stage as she was a real hit with the crowd and bought records to help the groups who appeared on the road-show even though she didn't own a record player. She always got a lot of press and would call me her favourite DJ. Radio One really was a family station then, broadcasting and not narrowcasting.

In Weston we always stayed at the Atlantic Hotel, where on one occasion I organised for Smiley's room to be changed. A pretty feeble wheeze? Hold hard. I moved every single item to another room but put them all in exactly the same place they had been in his original room. Reception even swapped his key, which wouldn't work for the old room but opened the new room. A bewildered Smiley asked anyone and everyone, including reception, which room he'd been in and, being well briefed, they all played along. He began to question his sanity, something the rest of us had been doing for some while. As any decent oceanographer knows the tide scoots in pretty rapidly at Weston, so during this diversion with the rooms, we'd appropriated his car keys and moved the Range Rover onto the beach. When this was pointed out to him at an appropriate moment he broke several British sprint records in one panic-stricken burst of speed, hitherto unknown in the Miles family. It was terrific viewing from our grandstand seat in the hotel. Through the waves he ploughed as the surf broke over the top of his wheels, but there was icing on the cake for us voyeurs. He fumbled with his keys and ... they fell into 2 feet of incoming tide. We couldn't see the expression on his face as he dropped to his knees and thrashed around in desperation, but we didn't need to.

Weston is also tinged with a sad memory. At each town we were expected to be available for local press interviews and on this occasion I was asked to give an interview to a local reporter out on the seafront. It was one of her first interviews and although she professed to being a little nervous, she was actually pretty confident and very professional. We sat on the railings, did the interview and had a good laugh until some half an hour later Paul Williams appeared, shouting from the hotel doorway that it was time to eat. I asked my interviewer if she wanted to join the crew for supper where she could get a few more views on how the roadshow ran and even try to interview Paul. She said she'd love to join us, but then decided she'd better get back and write up the interview. It had been one of Jill Dando's earliest assignments and years later she admitted that she desperately wanted to come and have a laugh with us but realised that she had absolutely no money and if she'd been asked to pay for her dinner would have been acutely embarrassed.

Summer 1988 got underway at Great Yarmouth, and it was while driving from there to Skegness that I stopped at an intriguing junk shop in a small hamlet. It was crammed with everything from stuffed parrots and milking stools to hundreds of paintings and piles of old furniture. Not knowing where to start on this alluring Aladdin's cave of things that I couldn't possibly fit in the car, I made straight for an old photo album. I have no idea what made me select that item out of the thousands arrayed before me, but I opened it to find that it contained the relatives of an early girlfriend of mine, Gillie Palmer. There was her grandmother as a young girl in an Edwardian landscape, early cars, family gatherings and many other atmospheric images. They were astounded when I presented them with the long-lost photo album.

Obviously buoyed up by my find I later screeched to a halt in the middle of nowhere. My subconscious had registered something a mile or two back. I turned the car round and re-traced my journey. What the hell could it have been? Then I spotted the sign: 'Ferrets for sale'. A gift from roadshow Heaven. The following day they made their public debut. Come to think of it. I'm not sure whether there should be an 'l' in 'public' as the little chaps went down Smiley's shorts. If you think *he* struggled, you should have seen the ferrets. The crowd pleaser of the furry duet brought the roadshow attendees to their feet as it pushed down Smiley's zip and poked its head out. You couldn't have written the script.

At Bridlington Captain Sensible and I battled it out for hours one evening on the crazy golf. No hedonistic orgy of personal destruction for us. We knew how to have fun. A pair of white shorts each, a pot of tea and an old-fashioned seaside town and we were flying. Brand us pleasure-seeking sybarites if you must. I recently wrote a rather decent song with the Captain, the lyric failing, rather significantly, to make any reference to Bridlington.

At Cleethorpes Boating Lake Paddock Smiley hired a huge crane which gently and elegantly lowered my green MGB into said boating lake. After being dunked like an oversized green digestive it re-emerged with water pouring from every orifice. Fair enough; after all I'd had a hairdresser attempt to dye Smiley's hair blond the previous day and it had turned the colour of my car. I can understand a high level of peevishness dominating his vengeful thoughts. I then brought forth an Indian elephant called Bully, which Smiles was forced to ride, but I was subsequently attacked by six tarantulas. It's a wonder we had time to play any music.

On the way there I'd phoned ahead to a garden centre. I began explaining my simple needs.

'That could only be Mike Read.'

'How do you know that?'

'I can't think of anyone else who'd ask us to turn a hotel room into a beautiful garden.'

Fair point. The target this time was producer Ted Beston, who'd had the misfortune to be assigned to this roadshow week. Not being my usual producer, Ted had obviously drawn the short straw. While the garden centre got busy turning his room into an exhibit worthy of the Chelsea Flower Show, we staged a lengthy game of rounders on the beach. Nicky Campbell was with us, and if I'm not mistaken, it was his wicked swing of the bat that Smiley took on with his face. The bat won and an ambulance was called. As they wheeled him up the beach Ted called an end to the game. Knowing that we desperately needed more time for the completion of the garden, Smiley, ever the trooper, spat blood as he insisted, 'No, no you must carry on, carry on … in my name.' A little melodramatic, I felt. I mean, he wasn't exactly slipping away having copped a packet in the trenches. We stretched the game out for as long as we could. It was enough. The front pages of the local and regional papers carried photographs of a beautifully turfed room with wall-to-wall grass, flowerpots a blaze of colour, hanging baskets, ferns, small trees and a wee herbaceous border. The only discordant colour came from the bruises on Smiley's face.

With all our banging about, worms started to emerge from the turf. It was time to go. 'What do I do about all this?' asked Ted, not unreasonably.

We shrugged, made our excuses and left.

In 1989 I did the Welsh stretch, which involved fire engines, several tons of foam and a few hundredweight of greengrocery. As was often the case, I had no idea the night before what I was going to get up to the following day. David Essex was one of the guests at Porthcawl, so I raced through the local paper, tracked down a motorcycle dealership and hired a Harley-Davidson. I knew that David loved bikes, but there had to be more to it than that. I called the coastguard, who readily agreed to let me have half-a-dozen distress flares. A path was cleared through the middle of the 25,000-strong crowd, a makeshift ramp placed against the stage and right on cue, after Adrian Juste's famous announcement, 'Today, live from Porthcawl' etc., David kicked the engine into life and with me riding pillion and letting off the flares, we tore through the crowd at speed, hit the ramp and screeched to a halt on the stage. A dangerous but great start. It wouldn't get off the drawing board in these days of caution and litigation. The end was more prolonged as Smiley, much to the delight of the crowd, removed the engine from my car, delaying my departure to the next venue by several hours.

That week in Wales was equally memorable for the look of despair my producer, John Leonard, gave me as, head in hands, he whispered in a rather defeated tone, 'What … are the flock of sheep for?' What were they for? Well, obviously, for a perfectly innocent sheep-shearing demonstration. He didn't even bother asking about the enormous sheep dip that arrived and the blokes that did the shearing. The paramedics prescribed a week or two in a rest home where he could tend the marigolds, sit on a bench and mumble away to himself about what life could have been like before the invention of roadshows. Bring on the flock. Into the bath of sheep dip. Shearing demonstration. Any more sheep. No, but there's Smiley. The 20,000-strong crowd were well aware of this inevitable conclusion and, like a crowd of toga-swathed Romans at the Colosseum, were baying for blood. Who was I to deny them? I turned my thumb down Caesar style and Smiley was duly dipped and shorn.

Smiley and I regularly spent far more money than we earned setting up elaborate stunts, and I intended the 1990 week, covering East Anglia and the south east, to get off to a flying start. For my birthday earlier that year, a friend had mocked up some silly photos of me on other people's bodies. Being visual, you'll have to take my word that it was well executed. One had my head superimposed on the semi-naked body of a female mud-wrestler. Perhaps I should choose my friends more carefully, but I was retrospectively grateful. For the roadshow, I simply intended to swap my head for Smiley's. I paid someone I knew, with the wherewithal, to do just that and deliver the picture to the national newspaper that had agreed to run with it. I childishly rubbed my hands with glee. I'd turn up at Great Yarmouth and in Monday's paper would be the story I'd provided with the photograph. Easy. That story said that Smiley formerly wrestled as Gloria Smudd. Yes, that's right, 'Mud, mud, Gloria Smudd'. Of course it went wrong. The lazy oaf to whom I'd entrusted the job delivered the original, with Smiley's head loosely stuck on top of the old photograph. The tabloid (all right, it was the *Daily Star*) leapt on it of course. That morning's edition carried the story that *I* had formerly wrestled as Gloria Smudd. Damn. Never fear, a good commander always has a back-up plan and this one was the business.

I had obtained forms for joining the Army and when I arrived at the Dolphin Hotel in Great Yarmouth on the Sunday night, I revealed the plot to a willing employee. 'Army forms. Carbon paper. Autograph paper on top. When Mr Miles arrives ask him for his autograph. I'll pre-sign it and so will our producer so it looks kosher.' It worked. Some 10,000 or so, gathered on Great Yarmouth beach to watch the antics, saw an unwilling and protesting Smiley being shown the forms to prove that he had enlisted of his own free will. 'You can't make me join the Army,' he spluttered.

'No, but these gentleman can.'

A sergeant major with a face like a sheer slab of granite and two squaddies were the enforcers. To the delight of the crowd, Smiley was stripped of his own clothes and dressed in Army uniform. 'I'm not staying in this. I'll just go back to the hotel and change.'

I had to disappoint him. 'No point, Smiles, your clothes are long gone. You can have them back at the end of the week.'

The three military types turned up all week to keep him in check. There was a proud moment at Clacton when we asked him to perform with some twenty other people in uniform. His smile turned to humiliation when he learned that they were Girl Guides and he had to sing 'Ging Gang Gooley' with them. We wouldn't let him play with Aswad. Later we told him he'd be involved in a military tattoo. 'Oh yes,' he said, 'I don't mind a military tattoo – a few bugles, plenty of flags…'

'Er, no, Smiles … not that kind of military tattoo.'

The squaddies stopped him from wriggling, squirming and squeaking while the tattooist went to work on Smiley's bottom. It was terrific, crowd-pleasing stuff.

In Margate the sergeant major rather decently, at my behest, allowed Smiles to hold the regimental mascot, a small pig. We also had Bob Geldof and his band on the show to play their new single, 'The Great Song of Indifference', and I was roped in to play guitar with them. While we were playing and the crowd were swaying, Smiles was holding the pig, but the Army chaps had gone AWOL. Come the end of the roadshow and he's still holding the pig. It's OK, it was on a lead. He was now seriously looking to unload the pig on someone. No one wanted it. 'Your responsibility, Smiles,' I said, with a shrug of the shoulders. He said something that sounded like 'bastard'. In fact it probably was 'bastard'. It would make the most sense.

The next show was in Eastbourne and the run there from Margate was certainly the longest between two venues in any one week. A local constable was on hand to forbid any attempt at abandoning the small creature and 'shoving off.' This was possibly the first little piggy to ride in a Radio One Range Rover. Better than a trip to market with your mates. Smiles tried to unload the pig at various Kent and Sussex farms, but of course, as he was a thoroughly untrustworthy character that could well have smuggled it in from Calais, no one would touch it. But by the time we arrived at Eastbourne there was a definite lack of pig. I suspect Smiley just turned him loose in a field, but I prefer my apocryphal ending, making use of an ancient schoolboy joke:

> Smiley arrives at the hotel with the pig.
> 'You can't bring that in here,' says the receptionist.
> 'Why not?' asks Smiley.
> 'I was talking to the pig.'

By the time Shakin' Stevens took to the roadshow stage at the Wish Tower Slope, the Army had discharged their latest recruit.

We finished the week at Southsea, so surely Smiley had suffered enough? No, there was more to come. I went to town the next day, performing 'The Colours' with The Men They Couldn't Hang (what a song) and sending Smiley up to the old ramparts of Southsea Castle to try to find someone to interview. We went live to him and some 15,000 people looked up to the remnants of the castle.

'You won't believe this,' said the small dot 100 feet up, 'but there are some nuns coming towards me.'

I believed it. Of course I did. I'd sent them. They were paintball specialists, with their guns under their habits. I'd spent the morning organising them. Smiley's interview was about to get underway when the 'nuns' let him have it. The crowd roared, Johnny Beerling, who had come down to ensure (or at least encourage) good behaviour, groaned and it was a bedraggled, sorry-looking, multi-coloured Smiles that trudged back to the roadshow.

Heaven knows why the roadshow turned us into shrieking third-formers for one week of the year.

Apart from the roadshows, there were many one-off outside broadcasts. Early in 1988 I did some live programmes from the Ideal Home Exhibition, interviewing all and sundry and throwing in the odd impression. All was well until I had to chat to Rodney Bewes, whose 'Likely Lad' voice I'd imitated many times. As soon as the person you're attempting to take off is sitting in front of you wearing a querulous frown, mimicking becomes well-nigh impossible. My impression floundered. On a brighter note I also did the review programme *Singled Out* from there with Carol Decker and Rick Astley, and there was a celebration dinner. Prince Edward joined us, but the guest they'd seated me next to blew me away. It was Guglielmo Marconi's widow. *Her husband had invented radio.* That was how young the medium was. OK, she was his second wife, but to lie in bed and listen to the radio with the man that made it possible must have been an incredible thing. The delightful Maria Marconi was eighty-eight at the time, her husband having died fifty years earlier. She told me that she'd married him when she was twenty-four and that Benito Mussolini had been the best man at their wedding. Maria lived to the good age of ninety-four. Without her husband there wouldn't have been radio … or roadshows. Thank you, Guglielmo.

Our head of music, Doreen Davis, was always up for programme ideas, and early in 1982 I came up with one. 'What about *Three Men in a Boat*?' It was the time of the Falklands War, so they felt the country needed something cheery on the radio.

'I like it, I like it.'

There was no messing with Doreen. If she liked it, it was as good as done.

It wasn't warm in April and early May. We even had a late frost or two. The crew had been press-ganged from the mean streets of W1, having taken the King's Shilling, and were pressed into service. I was given the unenviable task of skippering the craft on its journey from Hampton Court to Oxford. The surly crew swarmed up the gangplank, without so much as a parrot or a 'yo ho ho' between them. Knaves. The onboard security was to be handled by a four-legged guard with a large tongue and a wet nose. The driver/steerer/pilot/navigator was the bearded American with the Mafioso handle, Paul Gambaccini. In the galley was another man who sported whiskers, the gourmet chef/washer-upper Noel Edmonds. As Radio One breakfast shows went it was certainly different.

Our starting point was the maze at Hampton Court. This proved to be trickier then we imagined. It's only a third of an acre, but feels like 300, and has half a mile of paths. I swear I heard the disembodied voice of Gambaccini at some point, muttering something about a topographical algorithm from behind a gnarled hornbeam, but I can't be sure. I may have cursed William of Orange, for whom it was planted, once or twice as I couldn't remember the tip that seasoned labyrinthines, as I feel they should be called, wisely imparted to us first-formers. Was it 'always turn left', 'always turn right' or 'keep the hedge on your left'? Whatever it was, it held us up. Once on board,

Noel's dog thought better of it and decamped after a few hours and our producer, Dave Tate, fell in the river. Things were going swimmingly. The turn-out at every lock was amazing.

I'm still staggered that no one got a ducking. Knowing that Noel and I were likely to have something up our sleeves, one or two crews that we met on the journey got in first and chucked the odd tomato or egg. We may be decent fellows and all that, but a chap can't turn the other cheek when tomatoes are hurled. We retaliated. We also discovered that feeble rejoinders such as 'They started it' cut little ice with the authorities. We knew we were in trouble when a Thames Water Authority launch pulled up alongside. Someone had snitched on us. Now it would be acceptable 'whistle-blowing', but then it was most definitely 'snitching'. We were ordered off the river. The dressing-down, from a man with enough stripes to attract a zebra who was looking to settle down in a leafy suburb, brought us back to our senses. At the next lock we were to disembark, the authority having already informed Radio One of its intentions to remove the three offenders from the Thames. How could I blame the man in the galley or the chap with the wheel? I was the captain and as such would have to take the punishment for my men. 'Tie me to the yard-arm,' I insisted, 'and give me the lash.' There were no takers.

We reached the lock and sure enough there were the TWA blokes. Crikey, they looked grim. Would I be 'kissing the gunner's daughter' before noon? No, I wouldn't. Smiley Miley and the Radio One team had been rascally and devious once again. It was well planned, brilliantly executed and my crew, from commodore to powder monkey, were completely fooled.

Another intriguing Radio One creation was the annual Teddy Bears' Picnic, a roadshow where up to 30,000 people turned up with their bears. Hairy bikers came in packs with well-loved bears strapped to the handlebars, some folk pushed prams full of bears and others even dressed as bears. Ursine creatures, old, new, borrowed, blue and every other colour turned up to mingle with their fellow bears and picnic, not in the woods, but in the grounds of a stately home. It was usually Peter Powell and me on bear duty with Simon Mayo, Mark Goodier and Philip Schofield making the odd appearance. The *Radio Times* featured a wonderful cartoon of Peter, Mark and me as bears. Our first teddy bear excursion was to Harewood House, which proved so popular that the traffic jams it caused made the national news.

Assorted Sootys, Poohs, Paddingtons, Yogis and even the odd ear-buttoned Steiff, with a price tag on its head, dragged their owners kicking and screaming to Longleat for another ursine gathering fronted by the furries' best friends, Peter Powell and me. Peter always brought Edward, his bear, and even Lord Bath flourished his teddy for the crowds. He told me that he normally kept a low profile and often enjoyed putting on his old clothes and just pottering around the garden and that tourists, especially those from abroad, would often shout at him to ask for directions. 'Hey, buddy, which way to the house?' 'I say ... yes, you. Could you tell us where the toilets are?' 'Hey, mate, where can we get a cup of tea?' He never told them who he was. I think it quite amused him.

At Chatsworth House the Duke and Duchess of Devonshire made us very welcome. We set up camp in the local hostelry. When I arrived, late at night and tired, the first thing I saw was peacock marmalade for sale. 'Wow, I'll have two jars of that, please.'

'On your bill, sir?'

'Absolutely. In fact, make it three.'

'You're fond of marmalade, sir?'

'Yes, but this is really unusual. What does it taste like?'

'Very much like marmalade, sir.' It could have been Jeeves speaking.

'Is it similar to normal marmalade, you know, the kind made of oranges?'

'The very same.'

'But this is made with peacock.'

He smiled wanly and let me down gently, 'A common mistake, sir. The Peacock is the name of the establishment.'

Thankfully, I was more alert the following morning for the road-show, which was another success for the bears, with even the Duchess brandishing hers. Afterwards, she kindly showed me around the huge greenhouses, gave me some cuttings to take home and instructed one of the gardeners which fruit to cut for the Duke's breakfast the following day. The youngest of the Mitford sisters and in my opinion the most attractive, she was charming and engaging, but felt she'd been hospitable enough without discussing the family history, which has been a mixture of pleasure and pain. They inherited Chatsworth after Andrew's older brother Billy had been killed during the war. Billy had married John F. Kennedy's sister Kathleen, known as 'Kick,' but she herself, widow of the heir to Chatsworth was killed in a plane crash in 1948. With Billy the heir to the leading Protestant family in England and Kathleen a daughter of the leading Roman Catholic family in the US and sister of the future President, who knows how the future may have played out had it not been for three untimely deaths.

Kick is buried at Chatsworth, JFK flying in to pay his respects not long before that fateful day in Dallas.

It wasn't all sweetness and light though. If my group the Rock-olas were on the tour, we'd often play some gigs in the evenings and agreed to do so at one major Northern resort. The evening started off pleasantly enough and our set went down well (it was the first night we featured *Born to Run*) so I was unprepared for the promotor's wife's contribution. I was chatting with one or two of the audience after coming off stage, when it seemed like my head had exploded. This woman had smashed a heavy ice bucket full of ice over my head from behind. I had no idea what had happened at that moment, but on instinct I turned around and scythed my adversary to the floor with a sweep of the leg. I was immediately surrounded by a ring of steel. Some six or seven bouncers were rubbing their knuckles and advancing. Only some very slick and fast talking by my producer John Leonard avoided serious bloodshed. Radio One did receive an apology a few days later. Another flashpoint was at a West Country resort. As soon as a few of the roadshow team repaired to a local club for a drink, a guy inter-mittently ambled up asking a few alcohol-fuelled questions such as 'who do you think you are?' and 'you're no one special.' I knew the answer to the first one and agreed with him on the second. Presum-ably between the question and the statement he'd found out. The gist was that his girlfriend was apparently making flattering comments to which he objected. Clearly she'd had a few then. My producer on the occasion was Paul Williams, who made the sensible suggestion that we leave before things got out of hand. We left, but they still got out of hand. As we walked up the side road by the club, the aggressor re-appeared, blocking my way. I tried to reason with him and Paul tried to reason with him, but he just wouldn't be reasoned with. Then he became physical. It'd been a long day, I'd tried my best to avoid vio-lence, but I wasn't going to stand there and let him start poking me. I hit him very hard, just once and he went down like a sack of potatoes. Paul could panic at times, probably in my case with justification, but back at the hotel he woke our the Radio One PR people and made a series of phone calls to the controller and anyone else that might take the sting out of what he was convinced would be a headline story for the tabloids. We never heard another word.

Which goes to show into how many historical, geographical, agri-cultural, topographical, hysterical and sometimes physical areas the roadshow could take you. You could find yourself discussing Hitler's paintings with Lord Bath, broadcasting in submarines, hiring heli-copters, purloining flocks of sheep, injecting a cow, delivering milk, blowing kazoos with Wham!, playing tennis with a thousand peo-ple, firing cannons from castle walls, getting lost in Hampton Court Maze, shooting the breeze with Prince Philip, going down a coal mine, being the fireman on a steam train or standing next to the grave of JFK's sister. And each one began by stirring us into action with that rallying jingle 'Today … live from…'

CHAPTER 6

TRAVELLIN' MAN

M Y FIRST PROFESSIONAL excursion from these shores was in 1977, when Neil ffrench Blake dispatched me from Radio 210 to Norway for reasons now obscured by time, memory and lost tapes. It was certainly with microphone and tape machine in tow to interview everyone from the captain of the ship to people who couldn't speak English. A force nine in the North Sea thinned my stock of potential interviewees, who in turn failed to thin the smorgasbord, leaving me with a mainly Norwegian contingent with whom to make conversation in Bergen. I was so taken with Bergen harbour, surrounded by hills, that I wrote a song as soon as we docked. Never recorded, the fruits of my creativity have vaporised over the years and remain of the moment. Perhaps just as well. With its enchanting wooden alleyways, the town had the feel of a time long-forgotten. My trip also took in Kristiansand and Stavanger, but I fear I returned with far less material than was expected of me. I reasoned that I might not get the next overseas gig. But lo! I was wrong. A second chance came my way when I was sent south to the Canal du Midi for a week. My girlfriend at the time, Annie, also came on the trip, as did the radio station's engineer, Chris Harris, and his boyfriend. The guys knew the partner of a world-famous parfumier who lived in Paris and as we were motoring down they suggested we met up with him for dinner at La Canelle on the banks of the Seine. *C'est si bon*, I thought, in the style of Conway Twitty's last UK hit. One look at the menu, however, and all wasn't quite as 'bon' as I'd supposed. A mere glance at the prices sent the bank balance into freefall. They assured me that it would be fine; their fabulously rich chum would be picking up the bill. Of course, their fabulously rich chum disappeared without picking up the bill and we were relieved of a major part of the week's budget, leading to an atmosphere that was less than convivial. Still, all wasn't lost: Chris's mother had made us so much food that the boot of our car was positively groaning with it. So were we when we discovered that, having spent the whole journey to Port Cassafieres snuggling up to a leaky petrol can, everything that had been formerly edible was now formally inedible. Never mind, we are English, we can 'make do and mend'. Well, Chris was actually of Slavic stock, I recall, but heck, he'd been with us long enough to be impregnated with the spirit. Sponsored by the travel agents Cox and Kings, my brief was to record the journey and package it to make it sound as appealing as the trio of sirens were to Odysseus and his crew. My job was not, as I determined, to lure would-be holidaymakers to their deaths, courtesy of the daughters of Achelous or Phorcys, depending on your mythological leaning, but to encourage them to sample the delights of the canal.

I recorded material en route, painting audio pictures of Sète, the Venice of France, and Aigues-Mortes, the latter thought to have originally been knocked up by the local builders Gaius Marius Ltd around 102 BC. Most folk of note had turned up here before us, Charlemagne, Louis IX, Philip the Bold and a host of other colourful characters. Philip the Fair belied his name by banging up a crowd of Knights Templars here, and much later a bunch of Huguenots suffered the same fate. We had dinner in this medieval walled city complete with guitar, which the others had insisted I take so that we could burst ecstatically into song when replete. The instrument was spotted by the locals.

'You play?'

'Yes.'

'*Splendide* … you sing for us then we sing for you.'

It sounded like a fair deal, although a more acceptable scenario would have been 'You sing for us and we give you a free meal'. Still, I gave forth with a few ancient classics from the Beatles, Buddy Holly and possibly a wild card from the R. Dean Taylor catalogue. Although I felt that I'd more than held my own, there was no spontaneous applause. No rapturous shouts of 'encore', or even an encouraging 'bravo', but maybe that was their way: a deep, silent respect for a wandering English minstrel. Then two of the locals produced guitars. I smiled stiffly as they put Manitas de Plata to shame without troubling to use all their fingers. These guys were on fire and there was no escape for the humbled guitarist who'd let his country down as twenty blurred digits flicked and danced their way up, down and across the fretboards. I had to sit it out, as I dropped from number one in the Aigues-Mortes chart to number fifty before you could say 'Por el camino de ronda'. These lads were good. Obviously I declined to perform at other *auberges*, for fear of a repeat performance. Maybe they could all play like this. Maybe Bert Weedon was flogging copies of *Jouez en un jour* on the shores of the Mediterranean.

Subsequently I came to work on cruise ships. I embraced cruises, fondly imagining fascinating folk hewn in the image of an Evelyn Waugh novel lounging in steamers on the sun deck and discussing the last days of the Raj. Of course they weren't as I imagined, but I still embraced. Many of us do it: two or three talks on your chosen subjects, a splash of loot and a free holiday, with pretty decent food on tap 24/7. My subjects were Common-Sense Politics, The History of the Modern Olympics and My Songwriting Career, with the odd pop quiz thrown in for good measure. When one isn't working there's plenty of sporting activity, films, theatre shows and a library, not to mention talks by the other speakers. Plus you wake up somewhere different in the morning without having made any effort. On sunny days I can bask and lounge and on squally days I can write. Cruises are terrific.

I love the Caribbean, and have returned frequently to various haunts there, often quad-biking along beaches or through rain forests. Captivated by the steel pans played throughout the region, I tried to buy one on several islands. In St Lucia, my pal Freddie, a native of the island but now domiciled in London, tipped me the wink. Collected by one of his cousins in an old jalopy, we headed for what turned out to be a shanty town area. When the car stopped, in a district in which I'd never have stopped a car, we were approached by two rather sinister-looking guys. They didn't say anything. At some 6 ft 4 in. tall and with physiques closely modelled on Mike Tyson's, they didn't have to. Their eyes and demeanour asked the questions. Freddie did the talking. 'Don't you recognise me, man? It's Rubber.'

'Rubber! Old friend of our pappy's, right?'

'Yeah.'

Things were going well until they caught sight of me in the back of the car. 'Who's he?'

'Friend of mine. He's cool, man. He's a cool guy.'

I'm not certain whether 'cool' was the best description of me at that moment, but I tried to live up to it as best I could. I affected nonchalance. I probably looked like Johnny English in a tight corner. The brace of big lads looked as if they were making up their minds about me. 'OK,' they said at length, 'no trouble.'

I wasn't looking for any. I was looking for a steel pan.

Mangy dogs and an assortment of inexplicable odours followed us through a very run-down assortment of cramped buildings until we reached what was apparently our goal. The man sitting on the step was gimlet eyed. He surveyed me in particular. Freddie saved the day. 'Hey man, you remember me ... it's Rubber.'

The man was now wide eyed with delight. 'Rubber!'

'Yeah.'

'Can you still shake it like you used to?'

Uncertain of what exactly, if anything, either or both of them were about to shake, I respectfully semi-averted my gaze. The hut's incumbent was sporting nothing but a leather thong on his manhood.

The shaking done, the conversation resumed, this time in the local patois. The request for a steel pan resulted in much shaking of the head. It looked a lost cause until Freddie started to plead in earnest. I – well, Freddie – was given a small, highly decorated pan, the sort of thing you'd find in a souvenir shop. I began to tell him that wasn't what I had in mind, when I was encouraged to say goodbye and follow my leader. Out of earshot, Freddie told me that the man didn't have any and wouldn't sell me one even if he had, because I was white. I couldn't do much about that.

As we passed an old shed, I could see shafts of sharp sunlight bouncing off dozens of steel pans. 'Freddie,' I hissed, 'look.'

'You haven't seen them. Come on quick now.'

After getting a similar reaction on three other islands, I eventually struck lucky in Tobago. After kicking an imaginary football around the Dwight Yorke Stadium, I headed to a music shop to further my quest.

'You a musician?' said the owner.

'Yes.'

'Whaddya play?'

'Guitar.'

He handed me an acoustic. 'Play.'

I did and he was impressed enough to recommend me to someone who made the elusive percussion. I'd clearly come on a bit since Aigues-Mortes. It was another slightly dodgy area, but I got in, got my steel pan and got out. I have it still, but where the beaters are, heaven knows. I can see I'm going to have to go through the rigmarole again to get replacements.

My sojourns weren't always of the lecturing variety. There were also pretty decent broadcasting trips too. I broadcast from my hotel balcony in Bermuda, surrounded by tea and breakfast, from where I could gaze down on the sea, golf course and tennis courts. A living hell, you'll agree, but I soldiered on, even forcing myself to play a few hours' tennis each day. Saints have been martyred for less.

In Bermuda I got to be a mod. My father would never let me have a scooter, so of course the injustice has burned within me ever since. I wanted the chrome, the symmetrical lights and, on the whippy aerial at the back, the obligatory squirrel's tail. In fact I'd have been happy with any tail: vole, badger, weasel ... actually I'm not certain how many of those have proper tails. Maybe because the mods had them all. Before I'm accosted by animal rights activists, let me point out that I am an animal lover myself and would only have used the tails of fauna on my imaginary Lambretta or Vespa had they expired naturally after a long and happy life (the fauna, not the scooters). With a 30 mph speed limit on the island, scooters were the order of the day. Singing a few choruses of 'We Are the Mods' from *Quadrophenia*, I made my way eagerly to the hotel's hire shop.

Only once had I driven a scooter. I was fifteen. It was a private, gated road and the friend who owned the Lambretta in question assured me that it was quite legal on a private estate. After just twenty seconds in the saddle I discovered that he was wrong and the two policemen that emerged from a side road were right. It wasn't a heinous crime, so the superintendent, who knew my Pa, gave him the nod. 'Needn't take it any further. Not serious.'

My father, it seems, had other ideas. 'No, let him go to court, it'll teach him a lesson.'

So I went, nervous, apprehensive and unsure of what to expect. Despite being in school uniform of course and putting on my best 'shining morning face', I was told off and crept away 'unwillingly to school'. Now, here I was on only my second venture on a scooter.

'I assume you're ridden one before?'

'Yes, absolutely.' Nothing but the truth, to which you will attest, but the man who I was trying to convince wasn't convinced.

'Do you need me to show you anything?'

'Everything.'

'Everything?'

'Well, you know, they vary a bit. I've only ridden in England.'

'These *are* English.'

'Are they? Oh yes, I can see that now.' After a little more blustering I was allowed a couple of practice laps around the hotel.

Within ten minutes I hit the highway. 'I'm free! Look at me! I'm a mod! I'm a mod! Let's go to Bognor and see Bluesology at the Shoreline Club!' With a head full of soul anthems I cruised 'Beautiful, Beautiful Bermuda', a classic song by local heroes the Merrymen. The sea was the deepest blue I'd ever seen. Really, it made me gasp.

I also love Jamaica. I know Noel Coward, Errol Flynn, Ian Fleming and co. beat me to it by many years, but I did sample the echoes of that post-war atmosphere by visiting their homes. Although Flynn died back in 1959, his wife Patrice, who has just died at the age of eighty-seven. I scaled the dizzy heights to Firefly, Coward's house some 6 miles east of Orcabessa on the north coast of the island. The view is so spectacular that it is no surprise that Sir Henry Morgan, one-time governor of Jamaica and sometime pirate, made this lofty viewpoint his home in the 1600s. He may have gone, but Noel remains, for he is buried here and a statue of the self-styled 'Master', seated, stares nonchalantly out to sea, cigarette dangling languidly from his hand, clearly waiting for my selfie with him.

The mid '50s house is very basic, almost Spartan, considering that this is where he entertained the Queen, the Queen Mother, Sir Winston Churchill and numerous luminaries from the acting fraternity. Firefly is intriguing because it is just how he left it. The monogrammed towels hang from the rails in a rather cramped bathroom and a wall of the unprepossessing bedroom still has books from the period on the bookshelves. Downstairs, the gramophone sits patiently by a pile of vinyl LPs, waiting for the next party of revellers to arrive. Perhaps it might include Sophia Loren, Elizabeth Taylor or Vivien Leigh; they were all here in this room at one time or another. So was Charlie Chaplin. The ghosts of the greats are all around. By a strange coincidence, the LP on top of the pile when I visited was by Olivia Breeze, the daughter of our one-time neighbours Alan and Renee Breeze, friends of my folks. Alan had been a featured vocalist on TV's *Billy Cotton Band Show*. Outside, the old swimming pool, where the likes of Laurence Olivier, Audrey Hepburn and Marlene Dietrich once frolicked, is now filled in and film stars frolic no longer.

Taking as his basis the Keats poem 'When I Have Fears that I May Cease to Be', Coward wrote a few lines that never fail to move me. If you ever make it to Firefly look out for them on one of the walls:

> *When I have fears, as Keats had fears,*
> *Of the moment I'll cease to be,*
> *I console myself with vanished years,*
> *Remembered laughter, remembered tears,*
> *And the peace of the changing sea.*
> *When I feel sad as Keats felt sad*
> *That my life is so nearly done,*
> *It gives me comfort to dwell upon*
> *Remembered friends who are dead and gone*
> *And the jokes we had and the fun.*
> *How happy they are I cannot know*
> *But happy I am who loved them so.*

Every time I read those words, the Master reaches out across the years and tweaks the tear-ducts. Now that's powerful writing.

I also visited Goldeneye, Ian Fleming's house where he wrote his James Bond novels. It occupies an idyllic spot with the garden dropping dramatically away to the sea and boasts unusual ablutionary arrangements. Each of the three bedrooms has an outside wash basin and a yard further along, a shower. OK as long as the weather holds, or maybe they just don't shower when it rains. At the bottom of each section of private garden is a fully plumbed old-style bath. One might imagine a summer's night, with Fleming, Coward and Flynn holding forth at volume from their respective tubs, Fleming's lover Lady Rothermere tut-tutting in the house that 'boys will be boys'. Many of the trees in the garden were given and planted by Fleming's guests, among the most notable being healthy specimens from Princess Margaret and Sir Anthony and Lady Eden. Ian Fleming invited the then Prime Minister for a holiday to escape the stress he was under from the Suez Crisis and the impending failure of the government's Middle East policy. I suppose planting the tree might have afforded a cathartic moment, away from the enormous pressure under which he found himself. His premiership lasted less than two years, but the tree still grows with the plaque to the Edens at its base. So now you know, the Garden of Eden is in Jamaica.

I couldn't miss out the ranch of Johnny Cash and June Carter up the hill from Rose Hall, home of the 'white witch', more of whom in a moment. Like Noel Coward's retreat from the world, the Cashes' ranch, when I saw it, was just as they left it, little knowing they wouldn't be coming back as they would both pass away in the States. There was toothpaste in the bathroom, books they were reading by the bed and Johnny's boots behind the door. The house was once owned by the family of the poet, Elizabeth Barrett Browning and was part of the Rose Hall estate.

They say the ghost of Annie Palmer still haunts the great house at Rose Hall and having spent some time there, it's not a place I'd like to stay the night. Many have tried but virtually all have failed to last the course. Legend has it that she was versed in the ways of witchcraft and voodoo by her adopted nanny on the island of Haiti. Said to be a beauty, she married plantation owner John Palmer, who she murdered. She married twice more and murdered them as well. It was also said that she took slave lovers from the plantation. Maybe we'll never know the real story, but the place is pretty spooky and the imagination can run riot. Johnny Cash wrote a song about her, 'The Ballad of Annie Palmer'.

One of the few waterfalls in the world that tumbles straight into the sea is the Dunn's River Falls. It rises (or falls, depending on which way you're heading) 180 feet in a series of terraces 600 feet long and empties into the Caribbean. Bursting with powerful cascades and dotted with micro-lagoons, it's a fascinating climb. The normal practice recommended to tourists is that they hold hands in a chain and are guided by tour guides, but where's the excitement in that? I went alone and it was exhilarating. The force of the water is so powerful you need to keep your base low and your wits sharp. You have no idea of the depth of your next step. What an obstacle course.

I had to do the tourist thing with the dolphins of course, and have the photograph of one of the creatures kissing me to prove it. But as for having an affinity with humans, forget it. I have the happy snap of our tender moment, but she never wrote. Not a postcard or a phone call. Not even a text. Dolphins, eh?

A more dramatic escapade was the 'cool runnings' afternoon. No snow of course, but they had the dogs, all rescue dogs, and the sleds were on wheels. The tricky bit was choosing the pack. The dogs knew. They sensed a good run. They all wanted some action: 'Pick me, pick me.' (I speak fluent canine.) I knew if they could they'd all have had their paws in the air.

Harnessed in twos, the dogs couldn't wait to get started. This was going to be one hell of a 'walkies' and at 40 mph I could hardly be community minded and stop to pick anything up in a plastic bag. I was given the commands that I had to use, in patois. So not only was my life in the hands of a dozen unruly curs, but I had to learn a new language in under two minutes. I had no idea how 'dogpower' would feel. They went off at a hell of a lick, with me groping at the Jamaican for 'right' and 'left'. Not easy when you're being bounced around on a buckboard and fighting to keep your balance. My team and I came through like heroes. The hounds got a thorough hosing down and gallons of water, while I made a quick getaway for a tennis match with one of the top Jamaican players. I slept well that night. Mind you, I sleep well every night.

Don't run away with the idea that I only work in countries with an average winter temperature of 75 degrees. I've done my share of the Arctic Circle and nights that last under an hour. I've sat with reindeer, watched the sun decide to rise again when we know, by rights, it should be sinking, and stood with arms outstretched Leonardo DiCaprio style at North Cape. I've stared towards that moveable feast the North Pole and gazed over the Barents Sea. Why do I feel strangely English in this Norwegian landscape that is the northernmost tip of Europe? Because North Cape was named by Steven Borough, skipper of the *Edward Bonaventure*, which came this way in the mid-1500s looking for the Northeast Passage. Those were the days, when you could scoot around the globe in ships, naming places on a whim. Many egotistically named towns, mountains and waterways after themselves, not considering for a moment that the people who lived there probably already had names for them. Then there were the nautical toadies, who named anything they saw after their monarch, in the hope of some tawdry title or an acre or two in Wiltshire. North Cape was where the *Scharnhorst* was sunk in 1943, by the British and Norwegian navies.

Closer to home, I did tours of Northern Ireland, where many refused to venture. I found everyone charming, friendly and welcoming. Of course the Troubles were rife, but people were still going about their everyday lives. Yes, there were soldiers on patrol, and no, everything wasn't ideal, but things carried on and folk wanted entertainment to give them a lift. Before my first trip crossing the border, I'd imagined it would be a blaze of light and a flurry of activity. It was no such thing. Complete darkness was the order of the day with shapes approaching from the shadows to check your identity. I would end up with a pocketful of requests for the radio, from both checkpoints. Saracen tanks were also fairly common on the streets and were often present at non-border checkpoints, where the only signal for you to stop was a small red light swung by a soldier as your car approached. You ignored or missed it at your peril. It was always slightly disconcerting to have a 76 mm gun pointing at your windscreen. In Belfast I avoided staying at the Europa Hotel, 'the most bombed hotel in the world', and usually managed to get checked in at the Everglades in Derry/Londonderry, with commanding views over the river Foyle to the far hills of Donegal.

The hospitality was so good in Northern Ireland that there were times when it was necessary to accept a spare bed. On one such occasion I woke up to an empty house. There was no clue in the place as to where I was so I wandered into the street, where my question, 'Where am I?', elicited a few odd responses and narrowing of eyes. Or if they'd had a night like I'd had, maybe their eyes were naturally narrow. It turned out that I was in Portrush, right up on the coast some 30 miles north east of my hotel. How the hell had I got there? I had no idea, and the identity of my hosts remained a mystery.

I arrived early in Belfast for one gig as it was snowing fairly heavily. An arms cache had been discovered in the city. The Army presence and sealed-off roads meant that those that were already in the club stayed there and those that had planned to come couldn't. Instead of 300 or 400 that night, there were no more than a dozen, so we sang songs, had a few drinks and made an intimate evening of it. The Falls Road area was often at the heart of the Troubles, but I was invited to someone's house there for tea, duly trotted along and was given a splendid welcome. It's well known that I'd even tiptoe gingerly through a minefield for a decent afternoon tea, with or without buttered buns.

The island of Malta is a delightful retreat, a part of the British Empire from 1814 until its independence in 1964. Always a strategic island, it fought alongside us during World War Two and was quite rightly awarded the George Cross for the bravery of its population during the siege of 1940–42. I spent some time out there with Robin Gibb when we both received International Music Awards. It was time that Robin remembered fondly and we spoke of it often. His favourite moment was away from the studios and the interviews when we spent a few hours at an outdoor café in Valletta, drinking tea and waffling about music and life. I remember him admitting that 'Telstar' was a major influence on him. 'Listen to the end of "Words",' he said.

'Can't see the similarity.' I was normally good on stuff like that.

He sang the last sixteen notes of the Bee Gees hit, then sang it again, speeded up, but without the words. He was right, it was 'Telstar'.

In May 2011 I was back in Malta to receive the country's most prestigious award. Cliff Richard and I were knighted together and given the most fantastic ceremony. We were flown out, with a group of supportive friends for a few days, and learned about the incredible thousand-year history of the Order of St John of Jerusalem, stretching back to 1070. This was the oldest knighthood in the world. On the day, some 100 Brothers and Sisters of the Order were there to watch the ceremony, while we were given our black robes emblazoned with the Maltese cross, and later our beautifully crafted silver crosses to be worn on suitable occasions. Our hands were symbolically tied with cord at one point, prayers were said and singers praised in song, until the moment arrived for the ancient sword to fall on the shoulders. What a moment.

That night, the island gave us a fantastic dinner with a few hundred people present. I did the introductions and Cliff sang for half an hour. Before dinner we decided that it would be fitting to wear our medals that night. It's been tricky since to know when to wear it. On one military occasion at the Honourable Artillery Club, I was rebuked in a friendly manner by some old soldiers who knew I had the award, for not wearing the medal. When I pointed out that they had earned theirs for defending our country and mine was simply for charity work it brought an unusual response: 'We had no option. Your effort was voluntary. Next time wear it with pride. It's an achievement.'

When you're a child, all things American seemed remote, romantic and almost like a film, so when I entered San Francisco by ship in the mid-2000s despite having had two hours sleep, I had to get up and stand on deck as we cruised under the Golden Gate Bridge. It was magical, better than flying in, as we slid past Alcatraz and Fisherman's Wharf to the city where hippies still hung out and you could buy some great CDs. On another trip around the same time, I flew into Nicaragua via Houston, to join a ship on which I was giving a couple of talks. The plan was that the agent would meet me at the airport, and drive me to the port. No agent. Two hours later there is still a distinct lack of agent and the airport is shutting down behind me. Armed only with a guitar and case I tried to make a plan, but one simply refused to formulate. There were not too many buildings, let alone hotels. My saviour, in the form of a Nicaraguan taxi driver appeared and agreed to drive me for C$50. My specialist subject has never been the Nicarguan Cordoba, but I figured it sounded about right, although he did agree, at length, to accept American dollars. After forty-five minutes he swerved into an alley and, as if on cue, a man appeared from the shadows (no jokes please, this is potentially heavy stuff). They talked furtively in some indigenous language, and whether Rama or Miskito I knew not, but I prepared to make a dash for it. I figured they may be contriving to steal the guitar and money. The passport would have been a serious problem. My life even more so. After much consultation the ominous chap (anyone who lurks in the shadows is clearly ominous) slid back into the inky blackness and my driver turned on me.

'Too far … he say where we go too far.'

'How far?'

'Too far. No go.'

'Yes, we go.'

'No go … turn back.'

Difficult to argue the case. It was his car. He turned round and drove forty-five minutes back, dumped me at the airport, which was not only closed but now appeared to be hermetically sealed and revealing no signs of life. I set off walking and some time later staggered into a rough-hewn hostelry with rooms. As I passed the bar with my cherished key in my hand, I was accosted by welsh voices.

'Come on then Mike, give us a song.'

'Get the guitar out.'

A group of welsh fishermen were well alight after a good day at sea, so out came the guitar and we sang. The day had been a long one and I hadn't even caught any exotic fish that I could dream of. I hadn't realised that I'd be sharing a room with a large family of geckos. At first I assumed it was gecko wallpaper until the wallpaper started moving.

Although I avoided dodgy taxi drivers in Acapulco, I was accosted on one occasion by a rather insistent chap who was keen for me to go with him to meet a 'nice young girl who in love with you'. While I couldn't argue with her alleged taste, I declined the invitation. No mention of afternoon tea or cake … what sort of woman was she? He trotted beside me for a good few hundred metres or it could even have been yards, upping his selling technique, until he hit what he must have presumed was his marketing zenith. Rubbing his hands on his chest he declared,

'She has lovely tomatoes.'

'What?'

'Lovely tomatoes … you know.' And again he rubbed in a circular motion.

'Look old chap, that's a seriously bad USP.'

'Eh?'

'Not good … tomatoes not a great analogy.'

'Bad?'

'Wrong fruit old son. You want to go for something bigger … like melons.'

A commercial light dawned in his Acapulcan eyes.

'Melons. I like! I try.'

And off he ran with a new plan and perhaps an eye on sponsorship, re-branding, or even a trademark. I hope the business model appreciated her new business model. I wonder how many tourists got at least two of their 'five a day' in Acapulco. Like Frank Sinatra and Elvis Presley back in the resort's heyday in the '50s I hope I contributed something to its lifestyle.

As this chapter is headed 'Travellin' Man', let me chuck in a few stats. The farthest west I've ventured is to Honolulu, where the visit to Pearl Harbor was chilling but atmospheric. Following a screening of news footage from the turning point there in the mid-Pacific in December 1941, you take a hushed walk to stand over the hull of the USS *Arizona*, which lies in just a few feet of water. This is the tomb of more than 1,000 sailors and marines, one of whom appears on your admission ticket. In many ways, it's a living ship, inhabited by the ghosts of men, and one can witness oil from the wreck still seeping to the surface well over seventy years later. The most southerly point I've visited is Cape Town. At least I think it is. The decent thing about South Africa is the lack of jet lag, even after an eleven-hour flight, as there's never more than two hours' time difference. It's worth the journey, though, just for Robben Island, or Robbenelland, if you prefer to browse this section in Afrikaans, a cluster of penguins (*pikkewyne*) and some good shops on the Waterfront (*Waterfront*). I hope those translations helped a little for those not conversant with the local language. The northern and eastern extremes of my travels have already been firmly established elsewhere as the tip of Norway and the Gold Coast of Australia respectively, while the highest point would be 10,000 feet up in the Austrian Alps and the deepest on a submarine somewhere off the south-west coast of Britain.

CHAPTER 7

THE SUN ALWAYS
SHINES ON TV

WHEN IT WAS announced that the Saturday morning TV show *Multi-Coloured Swap Shop* was coming to an end, the BBC also let it be known that the format would continue, but with a slightly different look. I was among many who were interviewed in the show's offices, with editor Chris Bellinger and his team scrutinising potential candidates to front the new programme. Post-interview, and not expecting too much in the face of stiff opposition, I was walking towards the heavily commissionaired entrance, across what was lovingly referred to as the 'horseshoe car park', when a somewhat breathless Chris caught up with me. 'This is just hypothetical, but were we to offer you the job, would you be interested?'

'Absolutely.'

'OK. No decision has been made yet and we have more people to see, but I just thought I'd clarify your position.'

'Oh yes, I understand.'

'Right then, thanks for coming for a chat.'

'No problem.'

He vaporised and I was left to ponder the brief encounter. Much the same as Radio One, I reasoned, they weren't sure whether I was that keen. I had no idea that I came over as being that laid back.

My agent, the lovely Michael Cohen sent the message that the gig was mine while I was at St Paul's Cathedral for a service to mark the BBC Diamond Jubilee. This celebration of sixty years of the BBC took place in July 1982 with Richard Baker and me being designated readers. As such, we had to follow Robert Runcie, the Archbishop of Canterbury, up the nave and peel off to our respective lecterns. I'd just come off a ship and was in the process of re-discovering my land legs, so I wasn't entirely certain whether it was the magnitude of the occasion or the briny that made me a trifle unsteady in the 'steering a straight course' department. My lectern was some 6 feet in front of the Queen, Prince Philip and several other royals. Beyond them were the serried ranks of famous BBC faces that had graced our TVs and radios for decades, some since the inception of the BBC. This was a seriously historical day, but I would have enjoyed it a heck of a lot more had I not been so thankful to reach the seat by my lectern. Delighted that my sea-legs navigated the passage through the cathedral without giving me the appearance of being in a Popeye the Sailor talent contest, I was more than relieved to relax and sit down. There was only one small problem. Everyone else, including Her Majesty, was still standing. The Monarch's eyes spoke volumes. I knew that look from my mother and needed no second bidding. I lurched to my feet, resisting the temptation to excuse myself by mouthing 'I've just come off a ship'. In a previous era I might have been put straight back on another one. The service was broadcast around the world and was an amazing and awe-inspiring occasion, especially when your voice is sending sizeable chunks of the Bible echoing around Sir Christopher Wren's cathedral and across the planet. It was an amazing coalescence and distillation of much that is quintessentially British: the Queen, St Paul's, the Archbishop of Canterbury and the BBC.

Saturday Superstore was live every Saturday morning from 9.00

until 12.15 or thereabouts and ran for five years, the main team including Sarah Greene, Keith Chegwin and John Craven. Our sports
presenter was David Icke, former Teflon-gloved Coventry City and
Hereford United goalkeeper and future Son of God. Maggie Philbin
was there for my first year and Vicky Licorish joined later. Every few
weeks I hindered Delia Smith in the food department, and assorted
pop stars, veterinary surgeons, England captains, ice-skaters, MPs,
magicians, astronauts, astronomers and gardeners trooped through
the store to promote, plug, inspire, educate and entertain – the
Reithian principle and beyond. It would take another tome to march
through the five years of fun, but highlights, for the wrong reasons,
would be along the lines of this exchange with the group Matt Bianco.
One can imagine the excitement. Their first hit single, 'Get Out of
Your Lazy Bed', their first live TV, and the second caller calls them
a 'bunch of wankers' in front of ten million viewers. Another group,
I can't remember who exactly, asked one Scots caller where he was
from. The reply, 'Fuck off', made their heads turn quizzically in my
direction. 'What did he say?'

'I think he said Falkirk.'

As Chris Bellinger put it later, 'a good try but we all heard what
he said'. Similarly, I was almost at the end of an interview with the
great Bobby Robson, who at the time was the England manager, when
the final caller, a young lad, piped up, 'My dad thinks you're a prat.'
Unflustered and gentlemanly, Bobby smiled and replied, 'That's the
way it goes in football, son.'

We had all three main party leaders on the show in the run-up to
the 1987 election, one a week for three weeks, Margaret Thatcher, Neil
Kinnock and David Steel. Near the end of the programme with Steel,
he glanced at his watch just before the final interview and asked me,
'What time does this finish? I'm meant to be at a meeting at twelve.'

I pointed out that as the party leader he called the shots. 'Tell
them to wait.'

He re-assessed and concurred.

Kinnock went down the populist route, pointing up his membership and sometime presidency of the Chuck Berry and Gene Vincent fan clubs. For the Video Vote, where we all sat in a semi-circle, he asked me if he could sit next to Paul McCartney, 'as we're both bass players', but Paul wasn't keen to be seen as a political pawn.

Thatcher's appearance is now legendary, for three reasons. First, a serving Prime Minister agreed to appear on a children's TV show, and second, she gave her approval to the Thrashing Doves' offering in the Video Vote, which simultaneously consigned their short career to the waste disposal unit and secured their place in the annals of music history. The third reason, and now the best-remembered of the PM's moments on the show, was undoubtedly the part of the phone-in where the appropriately named Alison Standfast stood her ground against the Iron Lady. The woman who dominated Reagan and Gorbachev failed to eclipse Miss Standfast. With the determination of a Paxman and the doggedness of a Jack Russell she set out her stall with a series of questions that appeared to have the PM on the ropes. Neither John Craven nor I could have asked her how she could guarantee that there would not be a nuclear war, nor hector her about having a private bunker, but Alison persisted and found her way into the history books. She now, unsurprisingly, works in the legal profession.

What a fun show it was to present, often flying by the seat of your pants, never quite sure who was going to drop in or what was going to happen. I even sang with the odd artist, whether it was performing 'Michael Row the Boat Ashore' with Bananarama or bashing out 'Only Sixteen' with Dr Hook.

I confess to being a trifle sceptical when I was asked to participate in a TV series on regression in the mid-2000s. I was convinced neither of the validity of these 'regressors' nor of the sense in doing it. However, intrigue prevailed and one of the country's leading exponents in the field, Lawrence Leyton, arrived with a camera crew. I'd already asked him the same daft questions that I expect every candidate asks him, especially what it feels like to 'go under'. He said that it was similar to driving a car over a familiar stretch of road and you don't recall doing it. You go onto auto-pilot.

His first attempt at regressing me failed. Not Lawrence's fault, but mine. He put me straight. 'Imagine you're going to sleep. At first you're 100 per cent awake then 90 per cent awake and 10 per cent asleep. Soon it's 50/50, until you're more asleep than awake. Just relax and don't think about it; if you do you'll stay "awake".' He returned for a second crack at sending me back in his time machine. We started chatting and moments later I returned to the surface. I looked quizzical.

'How long would you say we've been talking?' he asked.

I had no idea. 'Five minutes or so?'

The crew laughed merrily.

'One hour and twenty minutes.'

'You're kidding.'

'Seriously and you were in a cataleptic state. You were sitting in an uncomfortable position the whole time without moving.'

'What happened?'

I had to wait to find out until they showed it in front of an audience at the Maidstone TV studios. I was in buoyant mood. The hard work was done. Now I could sit back, listen to whatever crazy stuff I'd said and have a laugh. Wrong. Within thirty seconds of starting to watch the playback I had tears running down my face. I had no idea why. I didn't feel any emotion or any connection with the past. It came as a complete shock. They'd also sent a crew to film the area I was talking about and everything checked out. Now that was weird.

Here is what I came out with when under regression. I was George McPherson. I couldn't remember much before the age of fifteen or sixteen when we local boys used to stage sporting contests between ourselves. The games normally made use of the multitude of stones that littered the terrain in and around the West Linton area. We'd see who could lift the heaviest, who could throw the same stone the furthest, either individually or in teams, who could hit a mark from different distances, or who could hit a stone tossed in the air with a second missile. This was the way we passed our days, as well as learning skills with other more conventional weapons.

I talked of the kirk of St Andrew and the battle that had taken place. Lawrence Layton asked 'What was the name of the battle, George?' In regression I had no recollection of any of his questions nor any idea what the question meant. Of course you don't come face to face with the enemy and shout, 'I say, just for the record and in case anyone asks, what shall we call the battle? Any ideas, anyone?' It turned out that it was the Battle of Rullion Green, a part of the Covenanter Wars, fought here in the Pentland Hills. The Pentland Rising occurred between 15 and 28 November 1666. We Covenanters were led by James Wallace of Auchens, while the Royalist leader was Tam Dalyell of the Binns. The unrest was due to a long-running government campaign to force the country into episcopalianism, the church in effect being run by a governing order of bishops. As with so many conflicts, there was a small spark that triggered a raging fire. It started in St John's Town in Dalry. Troops beating an old man who had defaulted on a fine for not attending a government-approved church service were disarmed by a handful of Covenanters, supported by the locals.

Robert McClellan gathered men from Dalry and led them in a skirmish at Balmaclellan, where he enlisted more followers before heading to Dumfries and capturing a local commander, General Turner. The Covenanter Army then moved through Ayrshire, Lanarkshire and thence to Edinburgh to present their petition to Parliament.

Though we were much depleted through distance, foul weather and fear, our leader, James Wallace, held a parade and inspection of the 'rebel forces' as they called us, at Rullion Green. This is where I and several friends from my youth, although we were still young, joined their ranks. As the review was taking place, the Royalists burst through the hills and came upon us. There must have been some 3,000 of them, to just under 1,000 of us.

'What do you remember of the battle, George?'

I didn't miss a beat. 'The swearing and the smell.' An expert confirmed that. To this day people pump themselves up for a fight by swearing, punching the air with foul words. Letting the enemy know they mean business. The smell too, was spot on. It seems many people become loose of bowel and bladder on a battlefield, through nerves, serious injury or death. So what did I remember? I didn't recall a brothers-in-arms feeling. Not the fight for glory. Not the cause or a patriotic swell. I remembered the swearing and the smell.

'What weapons did you use, George, a sword and shield?'

Nothing so neat and organised on the weaponry front. 'A long knife and a short knife.' We failed to win the day and we lost over fifty men, while they came out of it very lightly. Not content with victory, the Royalists tortured many of the survivors and treated us with calculating cruelty. Fifteen men, including Neilson of Corsock, were hanged, drawn and quartered. Several of the boys, even younger than us, were tortured first, being kicked repeatedly by heavy Army boots.

I had no idea of my physicality, size or colouring. I liked to think that I was Big George McPherson, wielding my blades in the thick of the battle, yelling, 'To me, lads, to me.' I may, however, have been Wee Georgie McPherson, wetting myself and scuttling for the shrubbery at the first sniff of the enemy.

'You clearly survived the battle, George.'

'Yes, but no one stood around waiting to be hanged. We dispersed and were pursued. I suppose some were luckier than others. The plan was to rout us all in the end, so someone suggested appropriating a boat and heading for Holland.' I had no more information to give Lawrence, my regressor. It all went dark. He said in a gentle voice, 'I don't think you made that boat, George.'

The local historian whom the programme director consulted said that much of my story aligned with the actual history and that I should visit the area. I keep meaning to. Each November I promise myself that this will be the year. I'll walk the battleground and see if anything feels familiar.

A less daunting show was *Through the Keyhole*. I managed to appear as the keyholder on several occasions. There were probably two reasons for this: first, the programme was directed by Ian Bolt, who'd given me my first national TV series with *Pop Quest*; second, I moved house a couple of times. They seemed to like my houses because I didn't go to great lengths to neutralise them or import books and objects to create an impression. There were also enough oddities about the place without going near the giveaways of the record collection, the jukeboxes or the tennis bags.

For some reason I had acquired an army of frogs. These amphibians arrived mainly by default. There was never any intent to hoard, collect, impound or colonise these slimy but loveable creatures, yet they infiltrated my home disguised as Christmas presents, birthday presents and dinner party gifts. Some just seemed to materialise. I swear there was some reproductory thing going on. I'm reliably informed by the anuran experts in my social circle that they get into a position known as 'amplexus'. Whatever this position may be, and I'm told it's pretty normal biological stuff, I can honestly say that I never encountered any amphibious shenanigans while patrolling the corridors. When Loyd Grossman arrived to probe into my personal possessions he seized upon the frogs with the creative hunger of Aristophanes looking for a new comedy. There were frogs reclining in soap dishes, frogs playing the guitar, frogs honking saxophones, frogs on lilypads, waste paper baskets in the shape of frogs, frog mirrors, frog vases … the list seemed endless and a tad embarrassing.

'The person that lives here is clearly a toadophile,' he drawled, creating a brilliant new word in the process. He may have suggested 'looking in the croakroom', but I can't swear to it. I had been cruelly exposed and resolved to thin the ranks of these creatures as soon as was humanly possible. If Loyd returned today the only evidence of frogs he'd find would be a copy of the comedy by the aforementioned wit of ancient Athens.

The *Keyhole* camera crew, as with most crews, arrive before the presenter to set up. With frogs reduced in number and having moved house I pondered my fate as I prepared for my second appearance. Would Loyd savage me for having an *Alice in Wonderland* room, with Alice wallpaper, paintings, books and ornaments? If so, I'd get in first. It's not a well-known fact that in another life Loyd Grossman masqueraded as Jet Bronx, the frontman of low-charting punk outfit Jet Bronx and the Forbidden. I was one of the few that possessed a copy of their forgotten gem, 'Ain't Doin' Nothin''. I opened the jukebox and inserted the vinyl, to the amusement of the crew. I gave them a guitar each and as the Grossmanmobile slid to a halt on the drive, I started the record at full ear-splitting volume and the camera guys and I launched into a frenzied and badly synchronised mime of that shining example of lyrical perfection. It must have stirred long-buried yearnings, for not many years later Loyd re-formed the band. I like to think I played some small part in the renaissance of an outfit whose career peaked at number forty-nine back in 1977.

That wasn't the only record I possessed that had been released by a *Through the Keyhole* presenter. I also owned a mint copy of an amusing David Frost single which I deftly dropped into the 'on air' conversation with him during the programme. He was visibly shocked. It was as if Richard Nixon had just revealed to him that he had in fact been canonised for leading a virtuous and blameless life. The single was 'The Cricket Bag', a parody of the old classic 'Deck of Cards', only in David's version it was his cricket bag and its contents that served him as his Bible and his prayer book. I was even able to quote a line or two in the stunned silence that followed. I'm not sure which lines, but quite possibly 'When I look at the four bails I think of the Gadarene swine, or at least four of them … And when I look at the eleven men in a team I think of the Ten Commandments, plus one.' It was hot stuff, and I could swear that the man who had crossed swords with everyone from Nixon to the Shah of Iran and John Lennon to Muhammad Ali was temporarily lost for words. Forget traditional weaponry, there is nothing more powerful than an embarrassing recording that the artist has imagined is long forgotten.

No one was ever lost for words on *Give Us a Clue*. You weren't allowed to use any. It was always a fun TV show in which to take part, with first Michael Aspel and then Michael Parkinson at the helm and Lionel Blair and Una Stubbs as the captains. Liza Goddard later replaced Una Stubbs, but all this is mere scene-setting for the grimmer truths to come, the dark side of *Give Us a Clue*. David Clark was the producer and he was the man who indicated that major and incredibly vital factor: which chair was yours. Picture the scene. It's your first day. You don't know the rules. Well, you do, but you realise pretty quickly that there are more elements to this than simply playing the parlour game. The most damning thing that ever happens in a familial game of charades at home is someone squeaking, 'You're not supposed to speak!' In the murky subterranean world of the TV version, things are markedly different. As the new boy you are expected to know your place. It's no good making a desperate lunge for the chair next to Lionel's; that coveted place belongs to a senior, a Bernie Winters or a Kenneth Williams, with a sense of superiority and the ability to tip you not only off the seat but off the programme. In fact it's best not to look as though you might be thinking about it … even as a joke. Forget being a quick-witted guesser or a brilliant actor, to sit at the left hand of Lionel was the ultimate accolade. It was the pinnacle. You get the idea. As the new bug you held onto your end seat at the edge of the fray, while the big boys 'did their thing'. You got to act out one title, but rarely, if ever, did you get a second crack at demonstrating your thespian skills.

Then there was the guessing. This wasn't as straightforward as you'd imagine. There were unwritten rules. Body language and audible admonishments let you know that you'd either guessed too soon, and nobody likes a clever dick, or you didn't get it at all, which was a slight on the acting skills of those at the senior end of the line. A correct guess between the 90th and 100th seconds of the allotted two minutes was acceptable. With Bernie Winters that wasn't always easy. His clues for almost every title consisted of clutching various parts of his anatomy, pulling a few faces and using as much physical innu-endo as possible. How one was meant to guess obscure titles from an even more obscure charade, heaven knows.

After a year or two, you've paid your dues and are moved up the line. You are now one chair nearer to Lionel. This is a measure of how your career is progressing. Some have been known to fall off the end, without ever realising their hopes and dreams of making it to chair three. This move puts you in a solid position to challenge for that final seat; that place coveted by many but achieved by few.

With almost inexpressible joy that day eventually arrived for me. Somewhere between the pound note ceasing to be legal tender and archaeologists discovering the Globe Theatre, I made the grade. I watched with trepidation as David Clark's digit wavered a little, before, compass-like, it pointed at the object of my desire. This was it. Nerves of steel were needed now. I was 'next to Lionel', meaning that great things were expected. Even Gyles Brandreth was one seat below me, and poor Roy Barraclough was clinging on to the end chair as if it were a lifebelt adrift in the Caspian Sea. If a Union Jack had been handy, I'd have stuck one in the chair, informed Her Majesty the Queen and asked Sherpa Tensing to take a quick snap.

Again there is much to remember. Single cut-away shots of you are now no longer solo efforts to be admired by the sofa-dwelling viewers. Lionel has *carte blanche* to lean in and share the shot with you, and lean he will. This is part of the price you pay for this pro-motion to the giddy heights. However, and I cannot emphasise this too strongly, while Lionel may lean into your shot, you may *not* lean into any single shot of Lionel's. The distant sound of the firing squad taking out some former miscreant is a salutary reminder of this. But hey, every TV series is different. *Carpe varietatem.*

I returned to Northern Ireland for a TV show where they sent various folk to different 'retreats' to see how we'd cope away from the helter-skelter ride of showbusiness. I was given a very basic room, ate frugally and drank water, while the crew stayed at a hotel and made merry at a pub or restaurant every night. I wrote poetry, played my guitar, and was encouraged to think, contemplate and pray. I had to keep a video diary and was counselled at the end of each day by Father Patrick.

'Has God spoken to you today, Michael?'

'He might have done.'

'In what way?'

'He might have done it without me knowing.'

'I think you'd have known.'

'Maybe it was subliminal.'

'Possibly, possibly.'

I made a note to be more positive the following evening.

Chairing a forum between young Protestants and young Roman Catholics was an eye opener, as was my trip to Rathlin Island, 6 miles north of the Antrim coast. There are longer sea journeys, but when I tell you that on this one virtually everyone was seasick, including the ship's cat, you get the drift of what a riptide can do to the balance. The riptide in Rathlin Sound is notorious and I hit a bad day, with the boat pitching, dipping, rolling and tossing, which sounds like an old blues song. Hang on, let me grab the guitar. Rathlin is an amazing place with views to the Mull of Kintyre (I would have grabbed the guitar again, but somebody's already beaten me to that one) and Bruce's Cave.

One of the earliest stories that I ingested at school that seemed to have a modicum of interest about it was that of Robert the Bruce and the spider. At that age it's possible that the greater interest lay in the spider, and its ceaseless attempts to spin a web, than in the deposed Scottish king. Now, here I was ... in the very cave in which he squirrelled himself away back in 1306, after a pasting by the English at Perth. No one can of course be certain about the spider, but in the legend it embodied the moral that was hammered home to us wee ones: 'If at first you don't succeed, try, try, try again.' And here, whether under the influence of arachnid or by his own resolve, Bruce vowed to regain his kingdom, which he did after a home win at Bannockburn.

I've been interviewed in some unusual places, but being in bed was one of the most comfortable. I was a guest on Emma Freud's TV show, *Pillow Talk*, where presenter and guest shared a double bed for the duration of the interview. It may have been comfortable, but it was no easy ride. The topics were: Mike Read versus Robert Maxwell; a poem I'd written about Jeffrey Archer; being late for the Radio One breakfast show; and not being married.

My Archer poem was a parody of Rupert Brooke's 'The Old Vicarage, Grantchester', using the theme that both Brooke and Archer, some seventy-five years apart, had viewed that little corner of the world as a haven, as their sanctuary. The programme alleged that I was being supportive of Jeffrey Archer when I was actually being observational. I didn't expect my opinion on anything interesting or half-intelligent to be taken seriously. Radio One DJs didn't venture into this territory.

The MR v. Maxwell saga referred to a girl who sold an erroneous story about me to the press which had been published by the *Sunday People*. I sent a writ on a motorbike to Maxwell's HQ in Oxford and then had vast sums of money extracted from me as I fought the case. I was intrigued when my QC smilingly informed me that even though the newspaper story was untrue, I might still lose. Not what I'd imagined. The paper tried to prove that they were justified in running the story as it depicted 'my lifestyle'. When asked what that meant, the reply was something along the lines of 'He goes out with girls'. That particular aspect of human behaviour has been going on for hundreds of thousands of years, so I didn't really consider it a justification for printing porkies. The press even camped outside the rooms of a girl I'd known at Oxford, disrupting her theology finals. After running up a massive bill, Maxwell's team capitulated and coughed up. Expecting a missable two-line apology under the haemorrhoids ad at the base of page thirty-nine, I was surprised to receive a prominent half-page apology in which the *Sunday People* threw their lexical and metaphorical arms around my neck. Oh, and they gave me a large cheque.

I became embroiled in many *This Is Your Life* escapades, invariably being brought in to ensnare some poor, unsuspecting cove. I was meant to be the interviewer for Bob Geldof, who began to look doubtful at the lack of recording equipment in the scheduled theatre. Midge Ure and I discussed Bob's possible reaction. The expletives, we thought, were a given, but there was an outside chance that an element of physicality might just creep into the proceedings at some point. As it happened he was fine. Several of us waited to be part of a Mickie Most radio programme at Broadcasting House, only it was TV and the big red book for a man who was quite shy despite his success as one of the country's top record producers. We did Bert Weedon's *This Is Your Life* at Thames TV. One of the regular aspects of the programme was the subject having to recognise a voice, usually from there distant past, but for Bert they wanted to play it differently. The scenario went something along the lines of, 'do you recognise this guitarist?' whereupon I hit a string of dischords and bum notes. I seem to recall that it baffled him initially before realising it could only be me. For the hit on Alvin Stardust, my job was to take him to lunch, to keep him out of the way during the set-up. I guess things overran as we must have ploughed through many courses.

'More pudding Alvin?'

'You're not serious?'

'Absolutely, I'm going to.'

'You're kidding, you've had a starter, a main course, another starter and two puddings.'

'I'm still a bit peckish.'

'I'll leave you to it then.'

'No … no … stay and watch me … no hang on … coffee? You must have a coffee. Great for the digestion.'

And so it went. I could see him appraising me; assessing my mental state. I took a hell of a lot of calories on board, but the ruse worked. Eamonn Andrews was still presenting the show when the subject was my broadcasting pal from Radio Luxembourg, Stuart Henry. Eamonn and I sat in a giant, hollow cake with a couple of other folk from his life. We sat on a bench in total darkness with Eamonn sweating profusely as he was prone to do. I think we all did, squashed into a cupboard sized gateau. Like Bob Geldof, there was some concern about Stuart's possible reaction and accompanying expletives. Again, the subject behaved impeccably and the audience gave him a standing ovation at the end of the show. Stuart though wasn't one to suffer fools, so when one guest bent down over his wheelchair and shouted, 'Well Stuart, how are you?' in a slow, patronising voice, he looked up sharply and replied, 'My body's not very well, but my mind's working perfectly thank you.'

For ten years I hosted the *TSB Rockschool* TV programme, started by my now long-time friend Andy Trotman, which encouraged musical groups and artists from schools and colleges around the country to enter a competition where they'd be judged by some pretty formidable artists.

It was very successful, but I imagine the programme I hosted on 5 May 1990 had the biggest audience I've ever performed to, with a worldwide 100 million tuning in for the Tribute Concert to John Lennon. I was delighted to be asked by Yoko Ono to present the show with Christopher Reeve, him representing the USA and me the UK. Ten years after Lennon's death, an eclectic mix of world-renowned names came together to celebrate the life of the cynical, short-sighted art student who became a global icon, both with the Beatles and in his own right.

I thought that Yoko might be demanding, challenging and difficult, but not a bit of it: she was charming, helpful and caring, even knocking on my hotel door to make sure that I was happy with everything. I was. Who wouldn't be? The line-up was like a who's who of music and included Lou Reed, The Moody Blues, Roberta Flack, Terence Trent d'Arby, Wet Wet Wet, Herbie Hancock, Al Green, Sarah Vaughan, Joe Cocker, Foreigner's Lou Gramm, Deacon Blue, Cyndi Lauper and the Liverpool Philharmonic Orchestra. The incredibly talented Dave Edmunds was the musical director, leading a top band.

Lou Reed, I remember, knocked out fair old versions of 'Mother' and 'Jealous Guy'.

The venue was the Pier Head, where a 45,000-strong crowd gathered, flanked on one side by the River Mersey and on the other by the Liver, Cunard and Port of Liverpool Buildings. It doesn't get much more Liverpool than that. Yoko told everyone that 'John was committed in his life and music to spreading peace and harmony in the world in his generation and generations yet unborn'.

Yoko got a leading US designer, Michael Hoban, to make around a dozen top-quality leather jackets for the occasion, with 'Lennon' hand sewn, also in leather, on the back and a bird symbolising peace over the lettering. I was really made up to be given one of these items, as apart from its rarity value and the great memory it evoked, Michael's other clients included Elvis Presley, Elton John, Diana Ross, Paul McCartney, Sammy Davis Jnr, the Rolling Stones and Tina Turner! Not bad for a guy who'd been the leader of a teenage street gang in the '50s. I still have the jacket, but I've never found an appropriate event at which to wear it.

In 1992, alongside Kim Wilde, I launched the Panasonic Rock School (the *TSB Rockschool*'s successor), the national schools rock and pop contest, at London's Rock Island Diner with the previous year's runners-up, Project X. We had the 'X' then, and the judges as well as the national contest, so you could say it was a blueprint for *The X Factor*. Bizarrely, the press seemed to question whether encouraging young bands was the right thing to do in the light of several major artists having died of Aids. Citing Liberace, Freddie Mercury, Alan Murphy from Level 42 and Billy Lyall, an early member of the Bay City Rollers, they mentioned what a great job the Terrence Higgins Trust was doing and suggested pamphlets to read. Surely the implication wasn't that music was to blame? Kim and I were press-ganged into busking in Piccadilly to publicise the event and encourage hundreds of young bands and singers to enter. Rather obviously I played guitar. Rather less obviously Kim played saxophone.

Although I've attended a few Royal Variety Performances, I've never performed in one. However, Keith Chegwin and I were the opening act for the Children's Royal Variety Show one year, doing Mick Jagger and David Bowie's version of 'Dancing in the Street' with matching all-white guitars. There were two or three attempts at starting the show, as the electrics failed more than once, plunging Keith, me, the audience and Princess Margaret into darkness. Chatting with her after the show, she was fairly gracious about the protracted start.

I love steam trains, so was delighted in 1994 to be asked to host a Steam weekend for Channel Four, live from the Bluebell Railway in Sussex. It would have been tough enough had we recorded it and the weather had been clement, but it hammered down all weekend, was completely live and jam packed with people. It was almost impossible to see the director signalling to me. Joe Brown did the 'cooking the breakfast on the shovel in the cab of the engine' trick that he'd done in his pre-rock & roll days as a fireman for British railways and his daughter Sam played on the platform with her band. With a delightful blend of a ton of water and live electrical equipment, how the hell there wasn't mass electrocution I don't know. David Shepherd exhibited his wonderfully atmospheric railway paintings and a rather spiffing steam weekend was had by all. There have fortunately been other TV shows I've done from railway engines, including one from the footplate of Sir Nigel Gresley and another from an engine they named *Saturday Superstore*. Having an engine bearing the name of a TV show you present is almost as good as having one with your own name on.

CHAPTER 8

I WRITE THE SONGS

WORDS AND MELODIES have always been a powerful and all-consuming passion. I have a pretty high percentage recall over where I first heard songs, my emotions on hearing them and how they affected me. In my infancy, a song was a song. Music appreciation was a blank canvas: there was no cool involved, nor any peer pressure, artist bias, hype or expectations. I understood at a very tender age (actually all ages are pretty tender one way and another) that it was the perfect marriage of words and music that made a great song. A sizzling tune with trite words rendered it quite useless to me, as did a strong lyric with journeyman crochets and quavers that even a small baboon could have written. Perhaps I was a strange child. On those golden summer pre-school days I'd trail my mother around the vegetable garden, prior to pea-shelling and cherry-picking duties, and catch strains of her singing 'Me and Jane in a Plane', 'Mairzy Doats' or 'Papa Piccolino'. How could I possibly imagine that in the year 2000 I'd be discussing the origins of 'Mairzy Doats' with the song's 87-year-old writer, Milton Drake, and talking about his brother Ervin's bestselling 'I Believe'? It was wonderful to hear first-hand how these songs had come about.

My paternal grandmother was not too shabby on the piano when she put her mind to it, while my maternal grandmother, Grandma Mitchell, had a pretty good singing voice. Her repertoire comprised songs from not only her youth, but my great-grandmother's. Snatches of 'Lily of Laguna' and 'I Wouldn't Leave My Little Wooden Hut for You' wove themselves around the household amid her tribe of barking dogs, whistling kettles, washing machines and a cleaning lady who made me squeal with delight by kicking her shoes up to the ceiling. Kids love stuff like that, simply because it's not what adults normally do. I had no idea where these places like Laguna were, except that they sounded too exotic to be anywhere local. My grandmother was no one-trick pony in terms of her set list, as was shown by the more raucous 'Kelly from the Isle of Man', with 'If You Were the Only Girl in the World' being her showstopper.

My maternal grandparents always had piles of sheet music lying around, in case anyone fancied bashing something out on the piano. This was where, well before reaching double figures, I discovered a treasure trove of Stephen Foster songs such as 'Some Folks', 'The Old Folks at Home' and 'Oh! Susannah'. At home we too had a much-used upright, as well as a totally unused baby grand. The radio was always on and, bizarrely, we did have an early jukebox. My two favourites were 'Mutual Admiration Society' and 'Music, Music, Music'. We were sadly lacking in the sheet music department, but one of the few pieces we did have was 'On the Gin Gin Ginny Shore'. With retrospective wisdom, I ascertained that it was a Walter Donaldson song extolling the aquatic virtues of Virginia, but at what can only be described as a forgivable age, I thought it was about Virginia Water, which was not too far from us in Surrey. Not a cataclysmic mistake, I'm sure you'll agree, but I compounded my error by singing the words to the tune of 'Davy Crockett', thereby brilliantly discovering songwriting and plagiarism simultaneously. Let's be honest, it saves time.

Let's bring in my maternal grandfather at this point, for he too had a not insignificant part to play. He opened my ears to what is, somewhat scornfully, referred to as 'light classical music'. He was naughty. When my grandmother's attention was diverted, his guilty pleasures included reading comics, eating crisp sandwiches, dressing up to amuse me and listening to radio detective serials. I had no idea then what the stories were about (I know now, for I have dozens of them on CD) but it was the theme tunes that captivated me. The theme to the radio serial *Paul Temple* was a real winner and evoked the atmosphere of steam trains long before I knew the tune was called *Coronation Scot*, or that one day I'd sit next to the composer at lunch. Sadly I never met my favourite light classical composer, Eric Coates, the man responsible for such classics as *By the Sleepy Lagoon* (the *Desert Island Discs* theme), *The Dam Busters March* and my all-time favourite, *The Knightsbridge March*, but at least he has a trio of blue plaques.

Now songwriting at an early age is one thing: you hit a few notes on the piano, tell the singer to get on with it and wait for the royalties to pour in. Simple. Performing, however, I found a little trickier. The first time I attempted to entertain my family I exposed my inability to hold a note. As my sterner critics eagerly pointed out, the weak point in my armoury appeared to be breathing. Not that I couldn't suck it in and pump it out as well as the next chap. I have a fine pair of bellows. It was the control that was beyond my grasp. My debut, a soul-stirring classic from the other side of the water called 'Roll the Cotton Down', failed to set the crowd alight. Many cried tears of mirth, but I had no aspiration to be a comedy turn. I was the romantic, angst-ridden, misunderstood songwriter and performer, and the small but unappreciative family audience needed to realise that.

My cotton-rolling period gave way to the more English 'Out of Town', a song suggested by my tap-dancing teacher, Auntie Joan. Dancing lessons were held in a spacious wooden-floored room in our house, with Auntie Barbara on the upright, plus ever-present cigarette and a glass of something medicinal. I was one of Auntie Joan's 'tinies'. Joan and Barbara weren't my real aunts, but they were in fact Julie Andrews's aunt and mother respectively, Joan Morris and Barbara Andrews. For a while I was rather proud to be thought of as 'tone deaf', following Auntie Barbara's frustrating declaration one afternoon. I could overcome this. I had passion, enthusiasm and youth on my side and they must count for something. In fact as late as 1998, and not having performed it since the age of six, I was able to bring both a smile and tears to Auntie Joan's face when I sang 'Out of Town' to her word for word in her nursing home, not long before she died. Auntie Barbara would continue to be supportive in my attempts at writing songs and performing. She was both encouraging and influential and I remain indebted.

As a lad I clearly had an open mind musically. Not for me the juvenile devotion to Pinky and Perky covers, in an almost undetectable range, nor the blinkered fascination for bland ditties accompanying children's stories. As well as the areas already covered, my appreciation also included cowboy themes like 'Riders of the Range', 'Davy Crockett' and 'Home, Home on the Range', in tandem with Celtic classics and hymns. In among the obvious and much-loved standards such as 'Jerusalem' and 'I Vow to Thee, My Country' were such aisle-rocking nuggets as 'Glad That I Live Am I', 'Non nobis domine', 'For All the Saints' and the moving (spiritually, topographically and geographically) 'Hills of the North, Rejoice'. I still enjoy delving into *Hymns Ancient & Modern*, once even spending a happy quarter of an hour absorbed in its pages while visiting Charlie Brocket and waiting for him to emerge from the shower (I know, I know, I only take five minutes too). Freshly scrubbed, the strapping former Army officer glanced at the gargantuan volume of hymns and exclaimed in a surprised voice, 'Crikey, I've got that book too.' I gently explained that it *was* his and that I wasn't in the habit of toting the world's heaviest copy of *Hymns Ancient & Modern* around the country with me in case chums were showering when I arrived.

Before I move on from early musical influences, and while we're in the Army camp so to speak, my father's repertoire also had a profound effect on me. It featured novelty numbers from the uniformed men at the front, like 'Ginger You're Barmy', from a PC LP also containing 'Kiss Me Goodnight Sgt Major', 'They Were Only Playing Leapfrog' and a song I imagined was called 'Aura chickerau, chickeracka roona', which I learned to sing (and still can when called upon) if not to spell. Heaven knows what it means. There was also a smattering of hymnal material. My father was also a keen whistler. He was good, if inclined to embellish a little rather than cracking on with the melody. If I had to select a couple of high points in his repertoire, I'd have to plump for the theme from *Moulin Rouge* and 'Oh Mein Papa'. Although a boy chorister, I rather suspect his whistling talent came from being pretty adept on the harmonica. A lifelong golfer, even in his more mature years when one guesses his handicap had slipped from a career high of six back into double figures, he habitually attempted to smuggle a mouth organ into his bag of clubs for golfing holidays. My mother of course would always rigorously check the bag for instruments and remove any she found. Another would be substituted. She thought it ridiculous and demeaning to whip up a tune on a mouth organ at the nineteenth hole, after a round of golf. Mind you, she didn't think much of the golf either. I don't recall her thoughts when he created a nine-hole putting green in the garden, complete with realistic mini-bunkers, but I loved it, although the grass tennis court was also a heck of a pull as well, despite not being particularly even.

Beyond the putting green and the tennis court were the Sherwells. They were American. I'd never seen Americans before and my first thought, as I glimpsed them through a screen of fir trees, was that they looked much like us. They turned out to be 'OK', as their two sons, Robert and Michael, taught me to say, and again, the family furthered my musical education. As well as giving me masterclasses in lengthy songs from the New World, with a minimum of twenty-nine verses, they were a conduit to important aspects of life that, until then, had no place in mine. They had streamlined bicycles that you couldn't get in England, they ate waffles with maple syrup, their family had a Dodge automobile and they read American comics. While my compatriots, and I, were reading the *Beano*, *Dandy* and *Eagle*, I was also learning to speak the US vernacular through the antics of Sad Sack, Huey, Dewey and Louie, Nancy and Casper the Friendly Ghost. The back pages were crammed with attractive offers, but there were bewildering boxes to fill in, including one that said 'My mom agrees', and another requesting your zone and zip code number. I had neither. We argued over which Dennis the Menace was the real McCoy. US Dennis was freckly with blond hair while the UK Dennis, of course, had black spiky hair and not a freckle in sight. The Sherwells also had a pretty American nanny whose voice wafted over from their orchard as she sang the first version I'd ever heard of 'Don't Let the Stars Get in Your Eyes'. Her version remains the most abiding for me.

Yet another style of music that cast its spell on me was that of the Sea Scouts band. They held their annual fete in our garden, which led to my not very secret ambition to be a Sea Scout. The fact that I couldn't swim was of no matter to me. Their music, which I could hear a mile away, heralded the opening of the fete and I loved it. There were exciting stalls like Pick a Straw and Bowl for a Pig, but I was always seconded to Ye rather tame Olde Wishing Well, which didn't do much except yield small amounts of wet money ... presumably to pay for Ye next year's Olde Wishing Well. The fact that it was neither old nor a well didn't stop the good folk of Walton-on-Thames exchanging their loose change for a wish. Years later, I discovered that Madame Notlaw, the fete's rather scary gypsy fortune-teller, wasn't genuine either. Neither the deep, masculine voice nor the fact that her name was 'Walton' spelled backwards stopped me from believing. It taught me about the cycle of life more than the Book of Ecclesiastes ever did.

The Sea Scouts fete was the first time I heard rock & roll. Heaven knows what the group was called and heaven knows what the rest of their repertoire was, but the song I remember was 'Party Doll'. Call me naive if you wish, but I was raw, inexperienced and short-trousered and knew nothing of this devil's music. I was more into the songs of adventure, derring-do and wholesome love of one's country that we sang at school, in the vein of 'The Ash Grove', 'Sweet Polly Oliver', 'The Minstrel Boy' and 'Westering Home'. However, 'Party Doll' was my induction into rock & roll, although I had no idea it went under that name or indeed why a bunch of older boys were singing about a doll. A wet subject, I thought. I had much to learn.

I'd appeared in plays, some with music and some without, while still in single figures, playing Lysander in *A Midsummer Night's Dream*, in which I wielded a wooden sword against Demetrius. A better golfer than carpenter, my father nevertheless made me the silver-painted weapon for the on-stage scrap. To Pa, a chip was not so much a piece of wood, more a shot with which to get out of a bunker and onto the green. I was apprehensive about appearing in front of an audience. My mother caught me in the bathroom with my head in a basinful of cold water. She observed for a minute before demanding an explanation. I admitted to being nervous and was trying to catch a cold so that I wouldn't have to perform.

I navigated Shakespeare's lines; the sword got broken but not my spirit. I graduated to local shows, junior variety concert parties and the like, more often than not with Mater producing. I even convinced her to let me perform some music with a few friends after I'd learned my first handful of chords.

'Do you know enough songs?'

'Yes, yes. Please ... we'll rehearse.'

'I should think so. You'll still be acting in a few sketches in the first half.'

I was fourteen and incensed, as fourteen-year-olds are. 'I can't do that.'

'What do you mean, you can't do that?'

In my mind I was already a rock star. 'It'll spoil my image.'

Cue my mother's shrieking and the wrath and frustration of the misunderstood teenager taking himself just a tad too seriously. It didn't deter me from acting, though, as I played juvenile roles in adult productions of plays such as *I Capture the Castle* and *Dear Octopus*. I fondly imagined that I might land a child's role on *The Adventures of Robin Hood* as Nettlefold Studios where the series was made was in my hometown of Walton-on-Thames. As kids we'd find rolls of discarded film in the adjacent woods around Ashley Park and sometimes would stumble across a scene being shot. One of my parents' friends, Gilbert, was an art director at Nettlefold and for the Robin Hood series. Through him, my mother was able to take me on set on a couple of occasions. Ostensibly for my sake, but I rather think as much for hers, for I feel she had no small crush on the handsome Richard Greene. To have had a small part as a child of Sherwood Forest would have been the ultimate, but as history relates, Robin stayed loyal to Maid Marion and my mother went back home to see whether my father's golf clubs had returned home. Robin and Friar Tuck did at least sign my autograph book, Alexander Gauge writing, 'lots of luck from Friar Tuck'. Almost until the time I would lurch into Radio One I was appearing in one play or another.

I could point an accusing finger at many songs and singers who pushed and jostled me along hitherto unknown and unexplored musical thoroughfares, but I feel at least some of the blame should fall on the shoulders of Ian Gibb. Later to become a top sports and boxing correspondent, at school he was the one with the *New Musical Express* folded discreetly under the desk in Paddy Skues's maths lessons. Until then I had no idea that there was a paper devoted entirely to pop music. Of course there was Radio Luxembourg, the BBC's *Saturday Club* and *Easy Beat* and the TV shows *Juke Box Jury* and *Thank Your Lucky Stars*, but within these few pages I could learn more about the singers and the songs. If this was a drug, I'd swallowed it.

Woking was an eye-opener. Not only the education side of things, but the learning of master's names, their nicknames, their foibles, their bêtes noires, the way they wrapped their gowns around themselves, and prefects who seemed to be at least 7 feet tall, with gold tassles dangling extravagantly from their pale blue caps. One prefect approached me on my first day and protectively told me that if I was ever in trouble to go and seek him out. Fights were, on the whole, left to police themselves; ice slides of some 40 feet in length attended by a never-ending queue of boys weren't cordoned off in case somebody slipped over. The prefects kept a weather eye out from the upper quad onto the lower areas, inhabited by the hoi polloi, but rarely intervened.

The school had an excellent sporting and educational strike rate as well as fiercely contested inter-house competitions. I was in Drake House, as I had been in my previous school, and continued to volunteer for everything 'for the good of the House'. Football, cricket, tennis, boxing, cross-country, chess, basketball … I was there. I've been dogged by cross-country dreams all my life, but heaven knows why, always a different course, but always much faster than in real life. I revisited the old buildings some years ago and was regaled with tales of ghostly happenings and extraordinary temperature changes. I can believe that.

Several Old Wokingians became eminent musicians, including the leader of school group The Hustlers, Mick Green, who went on to enormous success with Foreigner. He was my guest on *Saturday Superstore* one week, and just before we went live, I whispered, 'Rigby Hardaker sends his love.' Mick's face was a picture. Our deputy headmaster and head of Latin, while resembling a miniature Mekon from *Dan Dare*, wallowed in the delightfully Dickensian name of Rigby Hardaker.

As in sport, humility was also the name of the game in academia. I only discovered years later, on buying some books I wanted, that they'd been written, as had many others, by our history master L. C. B. (Godfrey) Seaman. Our biology master and leader of the school treks, Kenneth Fudge, had the appearance of a being from a much earlier period and would amuse us by watching a piece of chalk like a hawk, to see if it moved. We watched too, thinking that it just might. It never did. I have even chatted with him on Facebook once or twice over the last year or two, but didn't dare mention the chalk. Still the schoolboy at heart. Anyway, the love affair with music was definitely on ... and it looked like lasting.

Sensing my exuberance and desperation to be involved somehow, my grandfather bought me a guitar. It was a small acoustic, not a flashy electric like the real stars played, but it was a start and my attempts to convert it into something more spectacular by drawing on it failed dismally. I morphed into a piece of human blotting paper, absorbing anything I could and avidly learning rudimentary chords from anyone who could be bothered to show me. Unlike other kids with guitars, I had no desire to be a lead guitarist, as long as I was able to play enough chords to write songs. Then there was the all-important aspect of forming a group. Forget the standard of musicianship, if you had an instrument you were in. If someone you knew had a van, they were the manager. Business acumen? Forget it, a van was the way forward. Of course within a short space of time, the stragglers lost ground and were ejected either pleasantly or unpleasantly, as the group took one step nearer to becoming the next Beatles or Stones. Most of the time was spent thinking about a name. Getting the right name was surely the first step to success. At odd times I and whoever was around would play as the Layabouts, the Rivals and, for one gig, the Riverbeats.

My earliest song was an instrumental which my mother dubbed 'Sheer Hell'. What was it like? There's a clue in her title. More melodic attempts followed, with such classic lines as 'All the lights on the hills break my heart, all the stars in the sky play a part'. I can't honestly say what part the stars played and to be perfectly frank I'd never had my heart broken, but it seemed the right road to travel. Another early lyric was the deeply profound, or was it tediously basic, 'It's me and, you know, it will always be'. At least it threw up a degree of self-awareness. The title of another song was 'Ever Decreasing Circles', which just possibly summed up its direction.

Our earliest attempts at being a group were rough hewn but filled with schoolboy enthusiasm. We were rehearsing upstairs one day when the buzzer on our dumb waiter started going berserk. It was my mother. I stuck my head down the lift-shaft only to receive orders to present myself downstairs. I was used to receiving orders. I became a dab hand at giving the dumb waiter just the right amount of tug to let it free fall and knowing just when to grab it, inches before a crockery disaster. I climbed over and crawled into most places as a kid, including roofs and cellars, but the dumb waiter would have been madness and I was probably too big. We had an elaborate bell system as well, which meant I could be summoned from anywhere in the house. My mother did a lot of summoning. I assumed, on this occasion, that the bass was throbbing through floors, walls and ceilings as it was wont to do. Preparing my usual answer, 'It doesn't sound as good if we play quietly', I was surprised to see that she was with two men and introduced one of them as Mr Gomelsky. He was bearded, his colleague clean shaven. They'd heard the music from the open windows and were looking for somewhere to start a club for groups to play in. Did I know of anywhere? I knew nothing of buildings, property or suitable spaces, so probably looked rather vacant. Anyway I was keen to get back to rehearsals and left my mother chatting to them over a drink. I should have stayed a little longer. A year or two later and I'd have been more inquisitive: 'Music club, eh? Do you need a group? Maybe we should keep in touch.'

'Who were they?' I asked later.

It transpired that the sidekick was called Hamish and the other was a Giorgio Gomelsky. The mater said that he seemed to be the one in charge. Of course I knew the name. Giorgio was the former manager of the Rolling Stones and was then looking after the Yardbirds. He was heavily involved in the Richmond music scene and had helped put together the early R&B festivals at Richmond that would morph into the Windsor and then the Reading Festival. Missed out there.

One local group were head and shoulders above the rest and that was the Echolettes, who were resident at the youth club, but in reality far, far better than that. Slightly older than us, they featured Rod Roach on lead guitar, who by rights should have been up there with the greats. Rod's technique, style and execution were so ahead of the times that one wasn't sure whether to be inspired or give up. The Echolettes made it to TV's *Ready, Steady, Win*, an offshoot competition from *Ready, Steady, Go!*, and featured on the ensuing LP and later CD with their song 'Our Love Feels New'. A later line-up, still featuring Rod, recording in De Lane Lea Studios, encouraged me to turn up at the session with one or two of my songs, as Dave Siddle, the engineer/producer, might well like them. They followed me on 'Thoughts of You', but we hadn't rehearsed it and it didn't come over as I'd heard it in my head and I wasn't confident enough to relax and take my time over it.

'It'd make a great B-side,' said Siddle, whose work would eventually encompass musicians from Deep Purple and Jimi Hendrix to Herman's Hermits and the Goons. I was thrilled. At around the same time I played some songs to Screen Gems and received a similar response. I reasoned that it was a start. Surely it was but a short step from writing B-sides to writing A-sides. When older and wiser, I learned that this was a time-honoured way of someone saying they weren't keen on a song. A critic might say that my first real songs revealed a very diverse approach or, if one were a little harsher, that I was thrashing around looking for a direction.

Another up-and-coming Walton/Weybridge outfit was Unit 39, fronted by our local doctor's son, David Ballantyne, who majored on soul and blues and was bloody good at it for a white boy in his mid-teens. Within months he signed a deal with EMI, who released a few singles, including 'I Can't Express It' and 'Love around the World', the latter becoming a huge pirate radio hit. We'd later team up before he went on to play with Geno Washington and wind up as a classical DJ in the States. Another one who should have made it. He looked great and had a stunning soul voice. His sister Celia later became Julian Lloyd Webber's first wife.

At college, I ran the music club, such as it was, wrote a comic opera called *City Sounds* that leaned heavily on John Gay and Charles Dickens, and was art editor of the rag mag. I also wrote songs about Dickens ('What the Dickens' emerging on a 2013 compilation), a friend's psychedelic roadshow and Gilbert and Sullivan's *Iolanthe*, and attempted to emulate Bob Dylan's 'stream of consciousness' songs. Bob had certainly drawled something very similar long before me … and had executed it with more commitment. Even so, I like to think that lines such as 'getting caught in the spider's web of uniformity' have a certain ring even today, even if I didn't know what I was talking about. Many of the songs I put down in that period have disappeared, but just as many remain as a musical diary including 'Nicola', 'Charley Brewster's DJ Show', 'Pictures on my Wall' and 'If She's a Day', all appearing on a '90s album for which I actually got good reviews for my singing. Viva retrospection I say. I shamelessly quote: 'Well-crafted ballads with Read's folksy delivery reminiscent at times of Donovan, Mick Jagger and Bob Dylan.' The reviewer also noted that the eclectic mix included 'Edward E. James Rainbow', 'an infectious upbeat homage to poet Edward James, the godson of Edward VII, whose sizeable inheritance enabled him to become a patron of the arts'. Despite the diversity of subjects, another reviewer, who'd clearly led a sheltered life, wrote, 'For what are essentially bedroom recordings, Mike Read's early work is surprisingly strong.' Where was that reviewer at the time?

The Welsh Jesuit poet Gerard Manley Hopkins was also a big influence on my writing, or at least I like to think he was. It was more the internal rhyming and sprung rhythm that inspired me rather than the copious dollops of alliteration or the darker side of his subject matter.

It was while having tea at the house of a great-aunt and -uncle that I scribbled down the germ of an idea that was to become my first published song, 'Evening Paper'. I know it sounds like a cliché but it was genuinely written on an envelope. When writers come out with this old chestnut in interviews, they tend to be pooh-poohed by the sceptic that's questioning them. I'm no pooh-pooher. I believe them, because I wrote on that envelope.

With the song complete, and not wishing to do things by halves, I strode purposefully along Savile Row, knocked at the door of No. 17 and marched boldly in. This was the home of one of the biggest transatlantic publishers, Carlin Music. After the striding, knocking and marching came the wavering. These guys published song for Elvis, Cliff and hundreds of stars. Maybe this new song and a couple of others I'd recorded for good measure weren't that good. But amazingly I was ushered upstairs to the office of Dave Most, the brother of record producer Mickie Most. Before listening to my songs, he played me a couple of new releases, due out the following month. This was it. I was part of the inner circle. Hearing tracks before they hit the shops or even the airwaves! Maybe more out of encouragement than conviction, Dave listened to my songs and muttered something that sounded like 'suitable for Herman's Hermits' – or maybe it was 'not suitable for Herman's Hermits'. It was now surely a short step to writing for Cream or John Mayall's Bluesbreakers. Then surely the American market would open up. I was convinced I could knock up something pretty reasonable for the Byrds, or maybe the Lovin' Spoonful. I got a contract, but in the eyes of contractual law, I rather embarrassingly still needed my father to sign for the dream to become a reality, as I was under age, which turned out to be a lot harder than actually getting the publishing deal. He made me wait for a whole week before he consented, imagining that I might be signing away any meagre goods or chattels that I possessed. I never heard another word about 'Evening Paper', the song that may or may not have been suitable for Herman. The cutting-edge lyric involved a guy who bizarrely places a newspaper small ad offering 'happiness for hire'. In retrospect, a rather arrogant action, but not an earth-shattering song.

One summer holiday, I was on the receiving end of a phone call from a friend, imploring me to jump on a train immediately and only alight when I saw the sign Bognor Regis. Always up for an adventure and not getting too many straight answers to my questions, I submitted to his entreaty. OK, it wasn't exactly a blues-guitar-playing hobo riding a freight train to Milwaukee, but it was the way we English folk did it. 'Single to Bognor, if I may? Thank you so much.' The Shoreline Club and its sister establishment within the same building, the Caribbean Hotel, was a world first – a hotel run by teenagers for teenagers. What could possibly go right? Musically, everything. The story of the birth, life and death of the club lurks in my revealing tome *The South Coast Beat Scene of the 1960s*, but here let's just note a handful of the acts that performed there and opened up even more musical avenues (and a few cul-de-sacs): David Bowie, Bluesology (with Long John Baldry and Elton John on keyboards), the Equals, Geno Washington, Jimmy James, the Artwoods, Pink Floyd, Arthur Alexander, the Who, John Mayall, Arthur Brown, the Herd … the list is by no means endless, but you get the vibe, I'm sure. The place had a cast of characters that you couldn't have invented, with the all-nighters full of mods popping pills not for kicks but simply to keep awake. It was a different and more decent era, but I'm sure the older guys with a little more *savoir faire* took advantage of the situation in any way they could. Down the years I have remained friendly with some of the folk that I met all those years ago, especially Percy Nowell, Hugh Wilson and Blair Montague-Drake. We still talk with enthusiasm and love for those distant days, keep the characters alive in our conversation, both the good and the bad, extol the virtues of the camaraderie if not the food, and I rather suspect would love to take a time machine back to those heady days when the world was at our feet. The Shoreline was a unique place, where you could chat, hang out or even play a bit of guitar with some seriously interesting guys. The media, of course, had a field day, assuming it was a den of iniquity. It wasn't, at least not for me, but I was pretty naive. I had several letters from both my mother and my maternal grandmother insisting that I leave the place at once. They must have been kidding. I was discovering new music, new people, a new way of life, playing guitar each night and going to the beach every day. I could handle that.

The man behind the Shoreline and the Caribbean Hotel was the incredible and inspirational Eric St John Foti, a man who has truly lived life to the full and whose middle names should have been *carpe diem*. He is still in full flow well into his eighties, with projects, flying lessons and an inexhaustible supply of ideas and energy. He offered me a few pounds a week, which for holiday money was fine, as all the food (such as it was) was free, as were the music, the incredible camaraderie and the experience. I'd have paid him for all that. Circa 2004 my pal Eddie Grant, who played at the Shoreline with his group the Equals was so delighted to know that Eric was alive and well and living in Norfolk that he insisted we caught a train up there to see him. A great reunion. Eric was and still is a driving force that brought people together and got things done. I still go to Eric's various anniverseries, which seem unlikely to end.

Every teenager working at the place had to participate in the menial and day-to-day jobs necessary to keep the place going, but at night I was put on stage with my twelve-string guitar to play between the groups. In principle it sounds like a hot ticket. In reality the floor emptied when the heaving, sweating crowd rushed to get a drink, the sound of the Who, the Action or the Untamed still ringing in their ears, as I tottered on in my Cuban-heel boots and corduroy jacket to play a handful of Donovan- and Dylan-style songs to the few remaining souls who simply weren't in a fit state to make it as far as the Coke bar. My job, it seemed, was to leave again as soon as the crowd returned for the second half. The manager of the Untamed, Ken Chaplin, promised me an audition with top record producer Shel Talmy, who'd worked his magic on the Who and the Kinks as well as Chaplin's band, but despite sitting in the reception of Regent Sound in Denmark Street in my painted jeans and clutching my twelve-string Hoyer for the whole of an afternoon, the legend never emerged from the studio and I eventually went home. There was talk of joining the Untamed, but A-levels rather obviously won out. I was also pushed in the direction of another manager who was making a name for himself, Ken Pitt. I remember playing for him in his office in Curzon Street, but despite making promising noises, nothing came of it. Looking back, I should have pushed a little more, been more assertive and projected some attitude, but I was probably too polite.

The Shoreline was an education. It was where I grew up musically. Until then I'd bought fairly mainstream pop records. I loved them then and still do, but at Bognor I discovered other music that hadn't been on the radar. One of my jobs was to buy new records for the club, which meant heading off to the local record shop, Tansley and Cooke, once a week with a fistful of dollars to spend. The music world opened up. I bought tracks on Sue, Tamla Motown, Bluebeat, Stax and many other labels, returning with the likes of Billy Preston, Don Covay, Prince Buster, Otis Redding, the Temptations, Justin Hines and the Skatalites. The club scene was so different to the radio. I even went out on a limb and bought Frank Zappa's early Mothers of Invention single 'It Can't Happen Here'. It was weird, you couldn't dance to it and the milkman would have had a hell of a job whistling it, but it broadened my horizons.

I wrote a few songs at the Shoreline, including the Beach-Boy-esque 'Shoreline Surfin'' and the pop-orientated 'Find Her', in collaboration with Dave Hooper, much-respected singer with top south coast outfit Dave and the Diamonds. I was also challenged to write a song by a couple of holidaying Cadet Corps lads from Lancashire about Colne, their home town. I haven't played it since, but I can still remember sizeable chunks of it:

Latchkeys are fumbling | In the distance rumbling
Sounds of the rail | Aurora to the West
Silhouettes against the night sky

Seems to infest | The assembled rubble nearby
Separate echoes now of Colne.

The TV show *Whole Scene Going*, came to the Shoreline to film at that time and I borrowed a blue polka-dot tab-collar shirt from one of the cadets to wear for my scene. They filmed me playing my twelve-string Hoyer and singing 'Where Have All the Flowers Gone'. I desperately wanted to play one of my own songs, or at least something with a hint of credibility, but for them it was gentle guy plus twelve-string guitar equals folk song. Oh well.

Some summer holidays or odd gap months in the school or college holidays, I'd attempt to earn some cash as most kids do. One of my most exhilarating weeks in a school holiday was spent at the old Cheeseborough Pond cosmetics factory in Victoria Road, Acton which had stood on the site since 1923, although the Cheeseborough chaps didn't take over the Pond people until 1956. The remit was to spend the morning collecting every faulty bottle in the factory and in the afternoon smash them to pieces against a wall in the yard. Had I been an avant garde painter, I could have sold that wall five times over. A schoolboy's dream. I also used to escape to Lancashire and spend some time with my maternal grandparents. On one occasion I saw an advertisement in the *Manchester Evening News* for a group wanting a rhythm guitarist/vocalist. The Impact were based in Stockport, the other side of Manchester, but who cared about distance? If I needed to take four buses I would. I auditioned at the house of their leader, Graham, with their outgoing rhythm guitarist present, and yes, I had the gig if I wanted it. Indeed I did. We had a kind of uniform; I seem to recall matching shirts at least. The most prestigious venue we played was the Oasis, a very cool Manchester club where all the top groups from the Beatles down had appeared. The highlight of the Oasis night for me was playing The Temptations' 'Since I Lost My Baby', which I'd bought in Bognor, the day after hearing the Action do it live on stage at the Shoreline Club.

One night the Impact didn't collect me for a gig. There were no mobiles then, so I stood in the street for an hour waiting for a van that never arrived. I received a call later saying the van had broken down. I was disappointed, but these things happen. Well, they do, but not twice. I didn't realise that I was on the way out. Now I'd be on it like a flash. I'd sense something wasn't right. Their old guitarist had decided that he had made a mistake in leaving and wanted to return to the fold. It was a no-win situation for me; they were mates and had history. The third time the van 'broke down', I actually did that trip involving four buses and made the gig. They clearly weren't expecting me to turn up, but again, in my naivety, I failed to pick up on the half-whispered comments and merrily joined them on stage. I played with them one more time and only then did they have the courage to tell me, on dropping me off, that they were going to revert to the original line-up. I was devastated. Didn't I fit in? Wasn't I good enough? Did I look too different? Did I not have the right geographical credentials as a lad from Surrey? I didn't know. Years later there would have been a shrug of the shoulders and I'd have moved on. My grandmother was livid and telephoned the new-old guitarist's mother. Not one to hold back, she had a real go at her about her son's attitude, how they'd let me down and why this was not the correct way to treat someone who'd been so dedicated. Looking back, I'm not sure that I put enough into it. I was possibly enjoying the kudos without paying attention to the musicianship. But it certainly knocked my confidence at a time when it needed boosting.

Probably the first half-decent records I made were with Amber, a name I liked from reading Kathleen Winsor's *Forever Amber* at school. Having drafted a trio of very good musicians that I vaguely knew from the Bognor Regis area, Martin Bury, Dave Gibb and Alan Smith, we recorded three songs at RG Jones studio in Morden, near Wimbledon, 'Time and Tide', 'Yellow and Red' and 'Shirley'. They still sound as if we meant it, especially 'Yellow and Red'. In 1999 it appeared on the compilation album *The Story of Oak Records*, alongside songs by groups such as the Mike Stuart Span, the Game, the Thyrds and the Bo Street Runners. The sleeve notes rather embarrassingly record, '"Yellow and Red" is chiefly notable for Read's excellent guitar work … any resemblance to "Astronomy Domine" is entirely intentional…' I played it entirely with an art deco perfume bottle. As one does. The vinyl album *From There to Uncertainty* was released on the Tenth Planet label at about the same time, and contained many of my very early songs including those recorded as Mic Read and Just Plain Smith as well as Amber.

Trying to push the group meant spending some time in London away from the tennis courts and parties of Surrey. Dave Gibb's girl-friend allowed us to stay in her bedsitter in Notting Hill. As kids we thought little of there being five people in one room. Dave and his girlfriend had the bed, obviously, and we had the floor, awkwardly. Did we notice the discomfort, the cold, the aroma of socks, and the lack of food? Of course not, we were young. It didn't matter. Food did arrive, but in an unusual manner. When the communal phone in the hall rang it was never for any of us Amber lads, it was always for Angie in flat three. We'd knock on the door and let the occupant know that she was wanted on the phone. The odd thing is that Angie was never in. We heard this mantra several times a day from a voice that we presumed belonged to her flat-mate. One night we gave voice to our thoughts.

'How come the calls are all for Angie and not her flat-mate?'

'You're right. She's the more popular of the two, but she's never there.'

'What's the other one called?'

Gallic shrugs all round.

'Anyone seen her?'

Several heads shook in unison.

'Why doesn't the other one get calls?'

'Even weirder, why doesn't the flat-mate ever take a message?'

Days later I fleetingly bumped into one of them on the stairs and mentioned our bemusement *en passant*. Clearly in a rush, she shouted over her shoulder, 'If you answer the phone again, could you just ask them to call back later?' And she was gone. Which one it was, I was still unclear.

It was after the fleeting meeting over the bannister that the bags of food were discovered hanging from the handle of our door. We ate and asked no questions. Pre-occupied with life, we failed to link the food with the countless phone calls. I then encountered the same woman in more relaxed mood.

'Is the food OK?' she asked.

'Oh, it's from you. We wondered where it was coming from.'

'Well, you're answering the phone, aren't you?'

'When it rings, yes.' Always the ready wit.

'It's payment for answering the phone.'

I had to ask. 'We're slightly perplexed as to why all the phone calls are for your flat-mate, who's never there, and never for you, who's always there.'

She smiled as an ancient guru looking upon an unworldly inno-cent would smile. Or at least how I imagined an ancient guru would smile in the circumstances. 'I don't share with anybody, Angie's my professional name.'

I still didn't get it. 'So if you're working you're too busy to come to the phone?'

She thought I'd got it.

I hadn't. 'So what do you do?'

'Well, I'm with a client. I can't very well answer the phone, can I?'

My naivety marched on unabated. 'Couldn't you just leave the meeting for a minute?'

'My "meetings" are in bed, luvvie … you know … with men.'

I got it. It took me a while, but I got it. When I passed the infor-mation on, we wondered whether we should take any more phone calls or any more food.

The Mad Bongo Player of Powis Terrace was another character

associated with the house. He would arrive at any time of day or night, come in, drink tea, tap his bongos and disappear off into the cauldron of Notting Hill. We never knew his name, his purpose or anything about him. We knew even less about the transvestite that tripped down the stairs in size twelve slingbacks and make-up that looked as though he'd fallen into a basket of overripe fruit. These folk simply didn't exist in Weybridge.

Fed up with the cramped conditions, I often slept in the basement of a West Indian café called the Surfari Tent. Nights there, though, were often disturbed by the local steel band deciding on an impromptu session in the wee hours of the morning. Complain? Not me, I'm easy going and laid back, especially if the musicians were four or five mean-looking dudes from the Caribbean. 'Rehearse away, boys,' I'd say, 'Sleep is nothing to a seasoned muso like me.' It was safer operating from the stockbroker belt.

I said I owed a debt of gratitude to Barbara Andrews and I do. As well as the encouragement when I was a 'tiny', she now let me and the group live in her house, and rehearse in the ballroom. She even gave us much-needed singing lessons! Also it was her art deco perfume bottle that I used to achieve the 'Syd Barrett–Pink Floyd psychedelic guitar sound' on 'Yellow and Red', strangely raved about by record reviewers on assorted CD sleeves (see above). A very keen potential manager called Joe Nemeth appeared at the Old Meuse (for that was the name of the Andrews' house) one afternoon, offering us the moon. Instead he took us to the local shop and urged us fill our baskets with food. We needed little urging. This guy was hot stuff. Back at the house he outlined his plans; pacing, expounding and postulating, he gave a speech to put Churchill to shame. Now a real player knows exactly when to quit. You've built up to your peak, hammered home the salient points and captivated your audience. At that point you depart like morning mist, leaving everyone open mouthed and bewitched. Joe Nemeth timed it to perfection. He turned on his heel, opened the door and walked straight into the larder. He emerged with his face the colour of a beetroot, found the right door and departed, with our explosive laughter ringing in his ears. We never heard from him again.

Barbara was also indirectly responsible for my first single being released, 'February's Child'. I'm not giving any state secrets away when I reveal that my mother, Barbara and their friend Molly Edge liked a glass or two and when the mood took them (which it did quite often) they had a wee dram. From one of these sessions, which occasionally got a tad maudlin, the idea of introducing Molly's daughter to Beryl's son emerged. I have to say at this point that my mother wasn't Beryl Reid *the* comedienne, she was Beryl Read, *a* comedienne, and coincidentally happened to be a passenger in a car with the other one when they had a minor road accident. My father wasn't Les Reed the songwriter, but was the Les Read who played golf with Les Reed the songwriter. And of course, I was never in *EastEnders* claiming 'Pat'll be livid', nor presenting *Runaround* and shouting such meaningful lines as 'Wallop!' Mike Reid and I did, however, appear together in one episode of *Through the Keyhole*, as some wag, possibly Ian Bolt, thought it would be jolly humorous to have Mike Read/Mike Reid as the answers to both parts of the show. Anyway, Barbara introduced me to Valerie Edge and we became boyfriend and girlfriend, although part of the deal appeared to involve Barbara playing teenage love songs to us on her piano in the ballroom and getting deliciously weepy while we sat there with suitably reflective expressions. From this was to come my first single release.

Local musicians tend to gravitate towards each other and drift in and out of various groups like butterflies trying to find their favourite buddleia bush. At one point we drafted in Ric Parnell from the nearby village of Claygate, reasoning that as his father was one of the country's top drummers and bandleaders then Rick should be able to at least hold a pair of Premier E sticks. Hold them? Led Zeppelin's 'Communications Breakdown' with its unusual nine-beat intro, straight in, no messing. He played on one or two of my demos, including a powerful re-working of 'What the Dickens', where he and Virgin Sleep guitarist Keith Purnell really let rip. Keith also played with the seasoned rocker and highly respected singer Jackie Lynton, who popped his nose into one session and ended up kicking some life into a rather lacklustre song of mine we were recording, 'January, February, March'. Even attempting to rhyme 'March' with 'much' was lyrical madness. Ric Parnell was rising faster than the rest of us, moving on to Rod Roach's new band, Horse, and playing on their debut (and only) album, and then touring the States with Engelbert Humperdinck at the insistence of Parnell senior.

It was during the recording of the Horse album at Olympic Studios that I met Mick Jagger. We walked in together one day. 'Hello, Mick,' I said.

'Hello,' said Mick.

You could tell we clicked. I haven't seen him since.

On Ric Parnell's return to the UK, he immediately gave me his immaculately tailored midnight blue DJ, which had been made for him. He hated it. I loved it. He joined Atomic Rooster and acquired a much more appropriate snakeskin suit and snakeskin boots, which he wore until they fell apart and took on a life of their own in the corner of his bedroom. I swear I heard that suit hissing. I shared two flats with Ric. When there was no work on he'd stay in bed all day. That's just passable in itself as a part of a rock & roll lifestyle, but his culinary habits were the stuff of legend. Under his bed lived a white Mother's Pride loaf, a jar of peanut butter, a knife and a rolled-up pair of socks that existed in a world devoid of launderettes and washing powder. Following yet another slice of dry bread coated with crunchy peanut butter, the fastidious Parnell would gently place the knife, thick with spread, on the rolled-up socks to avoid getting it dirty on the floor. I swear each sandwich contained more sock fluff than peanut butter. I also swear that it was this natural rock & roll behaviour pattern that led to him becoming the drummer in Spinal Tap. He was a shoe-in. God made the rock & roll lifestyle especially for Parnell.

The key to success in those days was to release a single. You couldn't simply cut your own records back in the day. Now, anybody can do it. You set up the technology in your bedroom, record it, mix it, upload it, make a cheap video, stick it on YouTube and even cut CDs where necessary, print your own labels and your own liner notes and design the cover, all from the room that you were once sent to for being naughty. But then, to feel the thrill of holding a piece of vinyl in your hand meant that someone other than yourself, in the all-powerful record industry, believed in your talent as a performer or a writer. It was proof to friends and family that there was a chance you'd make it. I had several songs at the time that might have been considered commercial (which seemed to be the all-important byword), including a song about a Florence Nightingale-type character, 'Lady of the Lamp, I Won't Look Back', which included references to 'double-breasted businessmen' and a former Uppingham scholar who lost his life in World War One, and 'Pictures on My Wall'. The latter song, as with a few of my demos, had the delightful addition of my friend Tricia Walker on her family's great Canadian harmonium, with lyrics extolling the virtues of pictures scattered around at home. The lyric took in Chatsworth Hall, Sybil Thorndike, Katmandu and the cartoon character Toby Twirl! Heady stuff. As it turned out, the first single release that I could wave in front of my parents was 'February's Child', a song inspired by Valerie. Valerie's mother, Molly, caught us kissing in the music room (nothing really serious, but enough to put a mother's nose out of joint) and banned me from the house. Limited to riding past on my bike and waving I simply had to vent my spleen in a song. Not surprisingly, the spleen-venting was done in a very Home Counties way, via a twee little ditty featuring harpsichord and flute. Sure, it might have been released on a small classical label, whose previous single had been 'Esmeralda Fufluns', a children's song about a dragon, but at least there would be a piece of vinyl and that was what mattered. Our group, Just Plain Smith, comprised two friends from

Uppingham School, Bill Heath and Chris Hatt, and their school-mate Jake, Colin Standring from Surrey University, who'd been in the Jimmy Brown Sound and Horse, and Dick, like Bill a budding law student. Chris literally dreamed up the name, while Bill coined the song's media strapline, 'On a scene of its own'. Quite.

Our backing vocalist on this exploratory disc was Tim Rice, credited on the label as playing the 'mitsago'. At the time, and occasionally since, people have stolen stealthily up to me and whispered in a covert voice that they had no idea that people still played the mitsago, in a classic case of emperor's new clothes. The erroneous assumption that it was maybe related to an ancient instrument such as the sackbut or the hautboy was heavily wide of the mark, as, with the scintillating humour of youth that only youth considers to be scintillatingly humorous, I simply reversed Tim to get 'mit' and added 'sago' instead of Rice. For his sins, and the thrill of musical camaraderie, Tim joined the band at the odd gig and, as top record producer Norrie Paramor's former right-hand man, was closer to the hub of the business than we were. For some obscure reason he became unavailable the following year, after *Jesus Christ Superstar* shot to number one in the USA. There's gratitude. Where was the publicist who could have given us such possible newspaper headlines as 'Just Plain Smith backing vocalist tops US chart'? To date T. M. B. Rice is the only Just Plain Smith backing vocalist to have been knighted. A version of the group appears sporadically to this day, but even Tim's global glory hasn't added much to their fee or their set list over the years.

Mention must be made of the Hatt–Heath B-side, 'Don't Open Your Mind', on which we really let rip and stopped trying to be commercial. Gentle and pretty it wasn't, but it should probably have been the A-side, being described over twenty years later in Record Collector as 'a dynamic piece of freakbeat akin to "Arthur Green" by John's Children'. 'February's Child' was described as a 'beautifully crafted slice of late '60s pop in a similar mould to the Kinks'. In the '90s the single was listed at number twenty-seven in the *Record Collector* chart. No mean feat two decades on. It's now listed as a having a value of around £150 a copy. It didn't cost that to make the record!

Orlake, the pressing plant, was way out at the end of the tube line in Upminster, but there was no way I was waiting for our copies of the record to arrive by post and I hurtled up there on the appointed day. I got there early and had to wait some three hours. Would I like to come back later? No I wouldn't, thank you. I'd like to wait. You can't trust the music industry: go for a cup of tea and the factory closes and that's it. Eventually, they gave me a box containing the first six copies. I hardly noticed the long trip home as I examined each one over and over again; first the A-sides then the B-sides, then the letters scratched onto the section where the groove runs out, then the grooves themselves and then I started again on the A-sides. We got a few reviews; I think it was the *Melody Maker* who declared that we were like Skip Bifferty. We were thrilled as they were a serious musical force, but it turned out that the only likeness they were referring to was that both groups were living in a house in the country. Having the same real estate values as a genuinely talented and respected group was surely no bad thing.

In another interview I was holding forth with such earth-shattering comments as 'A deadline can work wonders and we play much better under pressure'. The only pressure I remember is that Jake's family lived in the Bahamas and he got to the studio half an hour late. The producer was also quoted in an interview, inspiring all and sundry with his *aperçu* that 'the harpsichord is an essential gimmick and without it the song will never get off the ground', which was good to know. Another of his quoted classics, this time regarding the microphones was, 'It all depends on strategic positioning. It's this that will make or break you.' Nothing to do with our songs, haircuts or youthful good looks then? How very disappointing. One interview ended with a flash of visionary brilliance from 'Just Plain Mic', as they insisted on calling me: 'Even if the record doesn't make the chart, I don't think we've wasted our time.' The jury is still out.

The record actually got some airplay: Emperor Rosko spun it a couple of times and Bill Heath's incessant and terrier-like campaigning bagged us a spot on *Radio One Club*. I hoofed up to Leicester, although I was still bearing the final scars from a horrific car crash a few weeks earlier. The axle sheared on my friend Roger Tallack's Triumph Herald and as the car somersaulted I apparently went through the gap where the windscreen had been and ended up unconscious with battery acid pouring over me. How we survived goodness only knows. There was petrol everywhere. If either of us had been smoking (luckily neither of us smoked) we'd have been engulfed in a ball of flame. I remember briefly coming to in the ambulance and muttering 'We can get some press out of this for the single'. A trouper through and through. Having done my PR I passed out again, coming round in A&E. I was naked except for a piece of elastic around my waist and a few tatters hanging down Robinson Crusoe style. Not realising that the battery acid had eaten my underpants I entered the realms of somnolent apologia: 'Oh no, my mother always told me to wear clean underwear in case I had an accident.' I couldn't see a thing for the first three days in hospital as the petrol had burned my eyes and soaked into the dozens of lacerations on my face and head. Apart from the severe pain I had no idea what state I was in. I was still semi-conscious during first visiting hours when I heard my mother say to my father, 'My God, I hope they don't let him look in a mirror.' I wasn't sure how my new Quasimodo look would fit into the image of a young pop group. Maybe I could go solo. Maybe I'd have to. My mother at that point, not yet aware of my total lack of sight, didn't know that they could have held up every mirror in the place and I wouldn't have known.

After my honourable discharge some three weeks later and a few more weeks convalescing in the sun, I bore my remaining scars with youthful embarrassment as I appeared on *Radio One Club*, alongside Jeff Lynne's underrated Idle Race and Bobby Vee. According to the music press, there was much talk of servicemen from

Walton-on-Thames taking a copy of 'February's Child' with them to the Far East, where it was copied and pressed illegally, reaching number ten in the Malaysian chart. You can't beat a good rumour.

I did a one-off gig around this time, forming a trio with two other young hopefuls to play at the Dorchester Hotel. The occasion was the second wedding of property magnate Sefton Myers, who'd recently formed a management company with showbiz agent David Land. The guests included Sefton's daughter Judie, later to find fame as Judie Tzuke. The three lads who took to the stage to entertain (I use the word loosely) were also looking for appreciation of their musical abilities and as such were still on the very shaky first rung. I played guitar and sang, my fellow vocalist just sang and our third member pounded the piano. My confederates were keen to make an impression, as they'd not long been signed to Sefton and David's management company, New Ventures. I was on board too, not as an artist, but as the young lad attempting to do their PR from their office in Mayfair, at 1 Charles Street. I had no experience of course, but the singer of our trio had rather recklessly recommended me in what must have been an unguarded moment. Had you wanted to interview Tim and Andrew and be the first to spot their global potential, you only had to call me on 01-629 **** and you would have been on a winner, or rather two winners. Too late now.

I have no idea what we served up that night. I don't remember any rehearsals. I don't remember any soundcheck. I'm not even sure that I remember any applause. We certainly weren't approached by anyone else in the room eager to book a rather odd trio. It was a case of three men in a boat without a paddle ... actually, no, make that without the boat.

'Tim and Andrew' were Rice and Lloyd Webber respectively. Their big project at the time, post-*Joseph* and pre-*Jesus Christ Superstar*, was a musical based on Richard the Lionheart, with the rather lengthy working title of *Come Back, Richard, Your Country Needs You*. They wrote some of it on a barge on the Thames and recorded the songs at

Chappell's in Bond Street, where I added my dulcet and not unharmonious backing vocals to some of the tracks. The two I can recall were 'Come Back Richard' and 'Roll On over the Atlantic'. Now if only it had been *Superstar*.

Many artists and musicians lived locally, but I was always more interested in the songwriters. I'd heard a whisper that Barry Mason had bought George Harrison's old house, Kinfauns in Claremont Park, Esher. I knew where it was as we'd played several times for Claremont School dances. The invitations (black tie or military uniform) were always worded by the headmistress as being from 'Miss Doran & the Claremont Seniors', which I thought was a cracking name for a doo-wop band. Miss Doran would utter cries of anguish at the volume of our amplifiers, in sympathy for 'Queen Victoria's ceiling', but we were sure that the Old Queen was past caring about the coved cornices, decorative roses and plaster icing over our heads. Barry had co-written many classic hits, including 'The Last Waltz', 'Delilah', and 'Everybody Knows' for the Dave Clark Five. I had it all worked out. I'd cycle down, knock on the door and offer to play him a few songs; he'd like them and my songwriting career would take off. Well, I did the cycling and the knocking, but expected little else. I hadn't counted on being invited in, being given a cup of tea and having my rough demoes played. That's when they stop sounding as good as you'd imagined. Barry listened, offered to record them in better quality if I brought my guitar round the following week and was genuinely encouraging. I cycled home on a wee bit of a high.

He was as good as his word and remained encouraging at odd times over the next few years to a hungry, eager songwriter with nothing to offer in return. He was convinced I'd make it. In the early '80s, when we were booking guests for *Pop Quiz*, then pulling in ten million viewers every Saturday evening, I suggested Barry. He was wonderfully emotional. 'I remember when you came and knocked on my door with your songs and now I'm on your TV show.' Yes, there were a few tears. Why not? Even in 2013 I had him as a guest on my

BBC radio show and we walked together for the best part of a day, broadcasting along the Thames. Our industry is a wonderful family.

Common sense might dictate that, following a modicum of media exposure (as it wasn't called then), we might have stuck with the same name for our follow-up single, admittedly two years later. Or, if we were going to change our name, we might have gone in an entirely different direction. In fact we did neither of those things, rather indecisively changing it to Just Plain Jones. We may well have discussed Just Plain Brown for a third release. This way of doing things could have taken some little time. By the time we got to our millionth Russian release as Just Plain Zvorykin the Earth would have been a cold, virtually lifeless desert inhabited by baby amoebae asking silly questions like 'Who *were* the Beatles?'

My old Walton pal Dave Ballantyne became a member of Just Plain Jones, with Bill Heath and myself hanging on in there as well. I'm not sure who else played on the track, 'Crazy, Crazy', but the publicity shot was simply of Dave, me and bass player Barney Tomes. We got even less publicity on that song. As I said, local bands are fluid, organic and sometimes socially difficult animals. Who comes? Who goes? Who plays what? Who falls out with who? In the end, those who are dedicated and mean to see it through come hell and high water do so, and those for whom it was a short but fun ride drift back to their more sensible jobs. Ballantyne and I slid rather effortlessly into a situation with the experienced Dave Mindel from Noel Gay publishing, putting together a non-performing group initially called Saturday. The idea was that the three of us individually wrote enough songs for an album and we'd record it at Sarm Studios in London. I'm struggling to recall all my songs, but 'If She's a Day' and 'Love Is Over' were two of them, while Dave B. came up some pretty diverse stuff, one being a clever anti-Johnny Cash parody called '12 Bore Blues'. Another had no title, so Mindel, imagining Ballantyne to be a Lothario, said, 'Oh just call it after any bird you know.' So Dave called it 'Chaffinch'.

From this diverse and unreleased album (no surprises there) came the single 'If (Would It Turn Out Wrong)', with Saturday becoming Esprit de Corps. Tony Blackburn made the track his record of the week on Radio One. What foresight and good taste he had … oh, and still has of course – there may be future singles. With Junior Campbell pulling out of that week's *Top of the Pops*, the vacancy was quickly filled by … yes, TB's record of the week. This was it! The third single and we were there. Well, not quite. Mindel and Ballantyne along with musicians Barney Tomes and Bill Pitt performed, while I sat disconsolate in the dressing room. I wasn't a member of the Musicians' Union. It hadn't even crossed my mind. It did then. It crossed, criss-crossed and double-crossed. This was the big moment, the one that would lead to a string of hits and tours of Britain and the States, and I was missing it. If I'm completely honest there was also an unspoken undercurrent of hostility, as happens in groups. With the impatience and intolerance of guitar-toting youth come the differences of opinion over song policy and musical direction. As it turned out, there was no UK tour, no US tour and no hit. The *Top of the Pops* performance hadn't cut it. Maybe it wasn't that, maybe the masses had been deterred from buying it because, being on the Jam label, there was a large pot of jam on the record sleeve, or maybe they knew somehow that it would in the distant future appear on the *Rubble* compilation series and they could buy it then. I consoled myself with imagining that my presence would have made a difference. Rubbish, of course, but it was a much-needed temporary boost as I bemoaned the loss of my only chance to be on *Top of the Pops*, or so it seemed at the time.

As I had since college, I continued to perform live at as many venues as would book me. OK, the pubs and tennis clubs of Surrey may not have been the Roundhouse or the Marquee, but they paid for tins of beans and sausages and Vesta curries. To be fair, there was the odd London gig, including one at the Pocock Arms in the Caledonian Road and another at a pub in Shepherd's Bush that was subsequently pulled down. As far as I could see, there was no connection. Sometimes the gigs were solo, sometimes as a duo. My most frequent partner was Big Stan (Colin Standring), although I did many with ex-Gracious frontman Sandy Davis or Dave Ballantyne and the occasional one with Rod Roach. In 1973 I got my first cover, when Henry Hadaway's Satril label released Jon Lukas singing a song I'd written the year before, 'Summer Sun'. Not a hit, but what a thrill. My version was quite gentle, and he gave it a bit more oomph.

My next recordings came via Sandy's home studio and somehow found their way into the hands of David Bryce, who worked closely with Cliff Richard. David played them to Cliff's manager, Peter Gormley, who invited me to the organisation's office at Harley House. The walls were lined with gold discs by Cliff, the Shadows, Olivia Newton-John, the New Seekers and John Rowles; these guys had really shifted some records. Surely I was motoring now. Peter informed me that he probably had a deal for me with EMI after playing the demos to Roy Featherstone, one of their top executives. Peter put me with Tony Cole, who'd written great songs for both Cliff and the New Seekers, but I found him rather scary. Older, wiser, bearded, more talented, at least that's what he implied, and, I gathered, not overly happy about being given a new boy to work with. I found him so intimidating that I didn't really give my best in the studio, despite being given Cliff's musicians to back me. The confidence has a habit of slipping away when the producer and engineer switch the intercom off and talk between themselves. You interpret every shake of the head and grimace as being a negative and imagine (with good reason) they're despairing of having to dig deep into your well of meagre talent to salvage something half-decent. Of course if you're a great singer, you rise above it with the arrogance of youth. But it was becoming clear that I was a better writer than a singer.

The three songs that emerged from the session at RG Jones studio were 'Have You Seen Your Daughter Mrs Jones', 'Beatles Lullaby' and 'Girls Were Made to Be Loved'. Sadly 'Captain Noah's Floating

SEIZE THE DAY

Zoo', a song I felt had a lot of potential, didn't make the cut, so I only have a rather thin-sounding demo of it, recorded on cassette on a boat at Maidenhead an hour after I wrote it. Although I remained part of the extended family at Peter Gormley's office, the deal with EMI fell through for various reasons, thankfully nothing to do with the performance or the songs. 'Mrs Jones' came out as a single on the Rainbow label in 1975, complete with a talkie bit which has made me (and others) wince ever since. Bad image too. We came up with the name Micky Manchester and they put me in a rather ghastly striped jacket. Not destined for the chart then? I still find the B-side, 'Chamberlain Said', quite listenable. It was a musical representation of Prime Minister Neville Chamberlain's return to Heston Aerodrome after his 1938 meeting with Hitler in Munich and his subsequent assurance to the people of Britain. I wrote of a yet unchanged Britain, with blacksmiths and district nurses still content pottering about in herbaceous borders and playing cricket! It was backed primarily by bass and mandolin. A little heavier and it would have been prog rock, a little lighter and it would have been a poem. For some obscure reason 'Mrs Jones' escaped for a second time in 1975, this time on the Satril label. Were no lessons learned from the first release? 'Chamberlain Said' popped up again as the B-side of 'Are You Ready', a raucous little number that took about ten minutes to write, if 'write' is not too elevated a word for it. The UK clearly wasn't ready for this 7-inch chunk of fun, recorded in Sandy Davis's studio with more than a dozen fairly well-lubricated mates on sound effects and backing vocals, all vying to get their individual voices heard over the cacophony of sound. It was wisely released in Belgium on the Biac label. I suppose I could pretend it went to number one, as I doubt whether you'd find a Belgian that would argue the point, but it didn't. It didn't get to number anything. No taste. That was my first and last Belgian release. The single was re-released on Satril after I joined Radio Luxembourg. The cover shot for the sleeve was taken outside the old Roxy in London in a vague

184

and ill-conceived idea to make me look punkish. I didn't, I looked like Nick Drake with a mild perm. The B-side this time was 'London Town', the song I'd written in the Blue Room in John Lennon's old house, Kenwood.

When I joined Radio One late in 1978, the station was about to change its wavelength from 247 metres to 275 and 285, and to that end, a single was being recorded as part of the awareness drive. My very first job at Radio One was to be part of the group of station DJs that were adding their voices to a song co-written by Peter Powell and Showaddywaddy, who provided the backing and the better-sounding vocals. 'New Wave Band' by Jock Swon & the Meters (you couldn't make it up ... although somebody must have done) was released in November on the BEEB label to a wave of apathy. I don't remember it being played on the station, but maybe it was. Showaddywaddy were probably press-ganged into it, but it was fun to be a part of, and it was a little piece of history. It was the only 'New Wave Band,' that was emphatically not New Wave.

By the time the next single came out I had been at Radio One for six months and was presenting the evening programme before John Peel came on air. I had a batch of new songs that I'd played to friends and thought a couple of them quite commercial, but they all went for one I hadn't considered, 'High Rise'. The song was inspired by the block of flats in Walton in which Sham 69's Jimmy Pursey lived. He was on the eighth, and top, storey. Keith West of 'Excerpt from a Teenage Opera' and 'Tomorrow' fame had once lived in another of the flats and Martin Briley from Mandrake Paddle Steamer and Greenslade had lived in yet another. The block was on the site of the old Nettlefold Studios, one of the UK's pioneering film studios, where they shot the *Adventures of Robin Hood* TV series with Richard Greene. It was also where I fell 60 feet out of a tree, when the area was heavily wooded, miraculously grabbing the last branch before I would have hit the ground at a speed from which it would have been tricky to get up. Backed by the Stadium Dogs, I went back to RG

Jones to record 'High Rise' under the name of the Trainspotters, and it was picked up by Arista, who released it as a single in May 1979. Produced by Colin Giffin, who as it happens had been at Woking Grammar School a few years before me, the single was incredibly well received and even got Radio One airplay, until the powers that be thought it a bit close to home and it was quietly dropped. Though not before I'd made personalised jingles from the backing track for many of the DJs. Even though they all used them, it was mine that seemed to catch on and find a life of its own. I was in Leeds doing a show from the university when I first heard someone singing it in the street. I was actually shocked. They sang the whole thing, unwieldy as it was. This was no snappy two-second soundbite; it was a gruelling marathon that almost rivalled Wagner's Ring cycle: 'Mike Read, Mike Read, 275 and 285, Mike Read, Mike Read, National Radio One.'

I have no idea why that jingle should have caught on and ended up being sung around the world by UK travellers. The postcards, letters and, later, faxes poured in with vivid, dramatic and often embarrassing descriptions of where the jingle had been performed: at the North Pole, at the South Pole, on the top of Snowdon, in a submarine, at Buckingham Palace, at the world's southernmost radio station, swimming with dolphins, on the back of an elephant, on top of the Berlin Wall, with the Red Arrows and thousands more. Extraordinary. Not only was the jingle well travelled globally, but it also travelled through time and is still sung (and even tweeted) to me with amazing regularity to this day.

The Trainspotters' follow-up single at the tail end of 1979 was virtually written on the day of the recording. I'd been doing a Radio One gig in Barnstaple the night before and only realised that I only had one song when the Stadium Dogs van overtook me on the M4 en route to RG Jones. I drove off the motorway, sat in the car with the guitar for thirty minutes, wrote 'Unfaithful' and arrived at the studio with a few minutes to spare. The focus of the session rather slipped away, as I had two delightful assistant producers who turned up add their input to that of producer Colin Giffin, namely Ian Page from Secret Affair and Jimmy Pursey. It was fun, we laughed, we threw crazy ideas around and everyone chipped in, but there seemed to be little cohesion. I still have no idea how to categorise that single. It appears to have a light ska feel with punk overtones but no devotee of either of those genres would have given it a home. In hindsight, the B-side, 'Hiring the Hall', was much tougher, more direct and should have been the A-side. Arista, bless them, even went for a third single, but why on earth I changed the group name to the Ghosts rather than sticking with the Trainspotters brand I have no idea, apart from the fact that we were entering a new decade. Pete Waterman had been very taken with 'High Rise', and came in to work with me on this third single, 'My Town', which probably leaned a little towards the Jam. It seemed pretty commercial to us, and really should have been the Trainspotters' third single from a completist point of view. Close again, but still no cigar.

Later in 1980 I veered off in an odd direction, when the Hot Rock label released a fun single I'd recorded full of Elvis Presley song titles, 'Big as Memphis', which came out under the wickedly witty name of the Memphis Tenor Cs. The following year saw yet another single release, yet another direction and yet another failure to trouble the accountants. 'Teardrops Fall like Rain' had been the B-side of the Crickets' 'My Little Girl', both good songs from the early '60s, but really having no relevance in 1981. The only bonus was the writer, Jerry Allison, telling me that he loved our version of it. He may or may not have actually liked it, but he was Buddy Holly's drummer, that's what he said and it was good enough for me!

Matchbox, who'd had already taken five songs into the top thirty in a two-year span, covered one of my songs in 1981. I'd already demoed '24 Hours' but hadn't really thought about placing it, when their producer, Pete Collins, asked if I had a song as they were one short for the new album, *Flying Colours*. What is now the polo bar at the Langham Hilton was an old BBC recording studio, and that's where Matchbox put the track down. It turned out well enough to be included on the album, was also a single in Germany and has notched up a few thousand hits on YouTube.

By 1982 I'd put the Rock-olas together, named after the jukebox of course, with the aforementioned Keith West, Barry Gibson and Paul Foss. We performed on the Radio One Roadshows, gigged occasionally, appeared at Oxford and Cambridge balls and even supported the Beach Boys at Alexandra Palace. No, I have to be honest we topped the bill. Seriously. Well, to be even more honest, they wanted to get away early and asked if we minded them going on first. 'As long as we can say we topped the bill and the Beach Boys supported us.' Bruce Johnston and Mike Love said that was fine by them. We were thrilled, forgetting the reality that we'd actually have to follow one of the world's most successful groups. We had Tony Rivers in the band with us that night, whose Beach Boy harmonies are as good as the real thing, so when the group left the stage after their encore and the crowd were shouting for *Sloop John B.*, we decided to open with it. I can't remember whose mad idea it was but we launched into it unrehearsed and unplanned, only to see Bruce and Mike peering back onto the stage with incredulous looks on their faces. How we had the audacity I don't know. It was like topping the bill over the Beatles and opening with 'She Loves You'. The Rock-olas also played a lot of tennis and released three singles. At one point when Pete Waterman and I were looking for our second single, quite late one night I had a sudden thought. I called Pete: '"Let's Dance", the old Chris Montez number.' Pete's reply was short and to the point. 'Print the silvers!' Despite appearances on *Saturday Superstore* (even though I fronted it, it wasn't a shoe-in) and *Crackerjack*, there were no silver discs. There weren't even bronze discs. The third single under the Rock-olas banner was what I considered a fair re-working of Tommy Roe's 'Dizzy', which as far as I recall included Ric Parnell's brother as part of the session crew. At around the same time, and I'm not sure

whose idea it was, Paul Burnett and Dave Lee Travis, who were with
me at Radio One, Radio Luxembourg's Tony Prince and I released a
novelty version of the old Four Lads song 'Standing on the Corner',
with most of the music industry appearing in the video. A bit of fun
but, not surprisingly, no chart position.

In 1984 I was back in RG Jones with Stuart Colman at the helm.
A necessarily hard taskmaster in the studio, Stuart was responsible
for Shakin' Stevens's string of '80s hits and Cliff Richard's version of
'Livin' Doll' with the Young Ones. We put down four tracks with
Cliff's backing vocal team, led by the hugely talented Tony Rivers, and
'Tell Me I'm Wrong' was released in the spring. Rather than coming
up with yet another weird and wonderful name, some bright spark
suggested that I used my own. Nick Wilson, one of our producers
on *Saturday Superstore*, directed the video, which we shot in a car
scrapyard near Wembley and which featured fork lift trucks, old car
parts and fenders (guitar meets car). Written by John David, who'd
penned classics for Cliff, Status Quo and Alvin Stardust, the song
almost made it, storming (my own word) into the chart at eighty-
something, and sitting above Duran Duran and Michael Jackson.
OK, they were probably on the way down after a blistering run in
the higher echelons and I doubt whether it affected Michael's career
one jot, but it was a 'moment'. Actually that's all it was. The following week it had disappeared from the listings. Hey ho, there was
always the follow-up, 'Promised Land'. Admittedly, a much-covered
song, but it wasn't simply a case of saying, 'let's do the Chuck Berry
number again,' as dozens of artists had before us. In the studio we'd
fallen to talking about the romance of American place names and
how they worked so well in songs. New York, San Francisco, Chicago, New Orleans … there was a great ring to them, while British
names like Basingstoke, Hounslow, East Grinstead and Bognor Regis
somehow just fell short of the mark. Never one to shirk my own
challenge, I beetled off to the local garage, bought a road atlas and
re-wrote Chuck's 'Promised Land' with English place names. I needed

a good long road that would give me as many options as Route 66, and went for the 284-mile A30, running from London to Land's End. I figured that I could make places sound moderately attractive by qualifying them, as in 'Memphis, Tennessee' or 'Houston, Texas', and so used 'Basingstoke, Hampshire'. I also pepped up the town's romantic image by having it 'bathed in the morning sun'. Unlikely, I know, but I needed the rhyme. I even attempted to make Hounslow and Staines sound thrilling. I was on firmer ground by the time I'd sang my way to the West Country and more American-sounding places like Indian Queens and Launceston.

The potential catchment area for sales was enormous. Surely folk would want a record with the name of their town or village writ large, with the bonus that it was a picture disc, bearing the features of Bert Weedon. On top of that, the song was promoted through another Nick Wilson video, featuring my old MG TF, the red-bereted Captain Sensible, the oldest surviving garage in Surrey and a Cajun knees-up at a local pub. What more can a chap do to please the record buyers? Or maybe we were just pleasing ourselves. We probably didn't please MCA Records as there was no third single.

Back on the comedy road, the Legacy label released 'Hello Ronnie, Hello Gorbi', a spoof of Alan Sherman's 'Hello Muddah, Hello Faddah', for Comic Relief, which consisted of a two-way between Ronald Reagan and Mikhail Gorbachev. Paul Burnett was Ronnie and I was Gorbi, but it was too much of a last-minute idea to pick up plays or make a dent in the listings. Let's not dismiss, though, some of the convoluted rhymes such as 'I met Maggie at Brize Norton, | She wants a long chat, I want a short 'un.' Eat your heart out, Oscar Hammerstein II.

One of the singles I released was a version of John D. Loudermilk's 'Language of Love'. A good writer is John, with songs such as 'Angela Jones', 'Ebony Eyes', 'Indian Reservation', 'Sittin' in the Balcony' and dozens of others, giving him a phenomenal catalogue. When he came to play the Country Music Show at Wembley, I met him through my old friend Trisha Walker, who'd moved to Nashville years earlier. He asked me to stop by his hotel and pick a little (see how effortlessly and naturally I've slipped into the American phrasing) so I stopped and I picked ... well, strummed. I must have slipped through the chord sequences with enough dash and elan to impress him, as he asked me to join him and his wife on stage to perform 'Language of Love' at Wembley. My new buddy and I played and sang, while his wife performed the song in Indian sign language. Somewhere there is a photograph of us on stage with me dressed in a decidedly un-country pullover and John sat on a canvas stool looking for all the world like he was casting for speckled trout. It turned out that he liked my version of the song; it's always good to get the 'thumbs up' for a cover from the guy that wrote it.

All went quiet for a few years on the recording front, but then in 1987 I got involved in a charity single. It had been conceived by *The Sun* in the wake of the Zeebrugge cross-Channel ferry disaster, with their journalist Garry Bushell securing Stock, Aitken and Waterman for the project. I'd had to cope with the news live on *Saturday Superstore* over a three-hour period, a situation that I was expected to deal with back then. Children's TV wouldn't be anywhere near a story like that now; it would be in the hands of rolling news. One-hundred and ninety-three passengers and crew had been lost when the *Herald of Free Enterprise* went down and *The Sun*, having promoted cheap tickets for what turned out to be a fateful day, spearheaded the fund-raising campaign.

Over a three-day period in March, a cavalry charge of artists invaded the PWL Studios in Borough, south-east London, to record a new version of Paul McCartney's song 'Let It Be'. Paul sang the basic track, with contributions from the likes of Kate Bush, Boy George, Kim Wilde, Nik Kershaw, Mark Knopfler, Gary Moore and Edwin Starr. I was in the choir of backing vocalists alongside such luminaries as Rick Astley, The Drifters, Suzi Quatro, Frankie Goes to Hollywood, Bonnie Tyler, Go West, the Alarm and Errol Brown.

The song went to number one in the UK, Norway and Switzerland and made the top ten in several other countries. I even presented an outside broadcast for Radio One, from a ship in the English Channel, with surviving crew members from the *Herald of Free Enterprise* going back to sea for the first time since the disaster.

Anyone who owns a horse will tell you that their feed and vets' bills far outweigh any scraps of money they might pick up in a selling plate at Towcester. I'd been a co-owner in a quartet of the four-legged fiends that sapped my bank balance for a while. From the mid '80s, Lambourn trainer Charlie Nelson selected our animals at the Doncaster Sales and brought them to peak condition. John Reid, who rode almost two thousand winners, steered our most successful horse, Sir Rufus to several victories, although every nag we had ate more than it won, as you'd expect. That earlier investment was now about to pay dividends. Not on the racetrack, but in the chart. Cast your mind back to Valerie Edge, who inspired my first single, 'February's Child'. In 1991 she and her then husband, Peter, invited me and Alison Jenkins, my girlfriend at the time, to a lunch party, which included Simon and Rosie May. Over lunch Valerie brought up my racing period and the moderate success of the final nag, Sir Rufus (some three or four wins as I recall), was discussed. Simon expressed complete surprise at my not inconsiderable knowledge of the more basic points of the Sport of Kings and probed deeper than one normally would over the gooseberry fool. I guessed that he might be hankering after squandering a few of the BBC postal orders he received for writing the *EastEnders* theme, or indeed many others, on a horse. Not so. He'd been asked to look at writing the theme for a new TV series that focused on the loves and lives of a racing community. Would I like to write it with him? Yes please. I thought the song, 'More to Life', might suit Cliff Richard, so I approached him with the idea. He liked the sound of it, loved the demo and a few months later we were back at RG Jones laying the track down, rounding the session off with rather smashing Indian cuisine and a few glasses (oh, all right, bottles) of wine in Wimbledon Village. Cliff performed it on *Top of the Pops*, wearing a shirt that rather cleverly resembled jockey's silks. We were over the first, as they say in jump race parlance, and possibly on our way to being first past the post. The run-in, though, wasn't the simple task we had imagined. There were other runners jostling us as we headed towards the top twenty. Cliff's usual team at EMI (the owners) would have dealt with it via their promotion team (the trainers), but because it was a TV theme, it was put with a different part of the company which just assumed that because it was Cliff (the jockey), and his last single, 'Saviour's Day', had been a number one, there was no work to be done. In tandem with that simplistic and assumptive approach, EMI had a major company gathering somewhere outside London the week that the song cruised effortlessly to number twenty-three, meaning that no one was around and at a crucial time, the single was left to its own devices. Despite that, we got news through that the sales had doubled and that a top ten place looked inevitable. However, as Martin Luther King said, in far more important circumstances, 'change does not roll in on the wheels of inevitability'. In fact the wheels rolled the other way and the record slipped a little. However, whenever I feel a wee bit disappointed about a chart position, I project myself back to my schooldays and the unthinkable prospect of somebody like Cliff Richard performing my songs and charting them. If anyone had suggested that to me at the time, I'd have bitten their hand off. 'More to Life' has turned up on a couple of Cliff's albums, including the re-released *Small Corners*.

Trainer was sold to many other countries, but failed to last beyond a couple of series. Directed by Gerry Glaister, it was filmed in the village of Compton, near Newbury, and featured Mark Greenstreet, Susannah York and David McCallum and was transmitted on a Sunday night. The second series was relegated to a midweek slot as they laboured to spice up the plots. One of these brought in singer Kym Mazelle as the 'love interest' for a couple of episodes, for which they also needed a song. Simon and I wrote 'Woman of the World' for Kym, a number which gave the woman the role normally associated with the man. Lovely girl, great voice, infectious laugh and by her own admission, seriously well endowed. We all wondered how, in the episode where she and Mark Greenstreet 'got to grips with each other', he managed to avoid any flicker of emotion as Kym loomed over him on the bed, displaying her more than ample assets. Again we recorded at RG Jones and mention must be made of the timeless, youthful and omnipresent Gerry Kitchingham, one of the great engineers. After the passing of old RG himself, Gerry *was* the studio. Kym arrived, Kym went. Where, no one knew – the ladies'? the shops? McDonald's? – but surely she'd be back soon. No, we discovered that she'd gone to New York. We waited. Allegedly she left a taxi with the meter running at Heathrow while she did a quick round trip to the big apple. Now that's rock & roll, and one heck of a bill for EMI. We were dealt another blow as EMI were set to release her from her contract just about the time that they put out the single. Maybe it was the excessive taxi fares.

Leaving *Trainer* on a high note, Simon and I did finally get into the winner's enclosure to pick up the Television and Radio Industries Club Theme of the Year award, a TRIC as they're known. During our speech Simon delighted the industry gathered at the Grosvenor House Hotel by thanking director Gerry Glaister for providing him with his three children. Was there no end to Gerry's talents? Of course Simon had meant that through working a lot with Gerry he'd been able to support his tribe and educate them. I had a lovely note from the chairman of the BBC, Marmaduke Hussey: 'On behalf of the BBC I would like to congratulate you on the *Trainer* signature tune winning TV Theme Music of the Year at yesterday's TRIC Awards ceremony. This is immensely well deserved and a tonic to us all at the BBC.' What a kind thought. However, having given the BBC a tonic, it was at this time that I was wooed to Capital Radio by Richard Park, as the word was that the station was going to be awarded the national commercial licence and he wanted me to 'open the batting'.

Late in 1991, I approached Frankie Howerd's manager, Tessa Le
Bars, with an idea for a cover of Right Said Fred's 'I'm Too Sexy'.
I could see him delivering it in his own inimitable way. We had a
meeting at his London house in Edwardes Square, so he could see
how the project would work. It was getting dark by five o'clock as
we put the final nuts and bolts together and in the gathering twilight
Frankie shouted to Dennis, his partner and manager, 'Switch the
light on, it's so gloomy in here.' Dennis turned on an old standard
lamp which illuminated Frankie but no one else. Imagining himself
on stage, he said, 'Oh, I'll do at least an hour now.'

We recorded the song at Red Bus studios in Lisson Grove and
during a lull I popped down to Church Street market to buy something for lunch. On the way back I spotted a bargain. Five pairs of
gaily coloured boxer shorts for £5. Unbeatable value. Frankie couldn't
believe his eyes. 'What are they?' I explained the brief history of boxer
shorts and he was captivated. In fact he was so enamoured that I
had to go and buy another five pairs for him. At least I was part of
his education. Rather splendidly, Right Said Fred let us have the
original backing track and Frankie got the feel for the song and the
doctored lyrics I'd written. I suggested he throw in the odd catch-
phrase. You know the kind of stuff, 'Nay, nay and thrice nay', 'Titter
ye not' and the like.

'No,' he said, 'you write it where you want it, and I'll say it in
those places.' I told him I felt slightly fraudulent writing his personal lines. 'Oh no,' he said, 'that's the way I like to work.' I still felt
fraudulent. Sadly Frankie died not long after the recording, so we
weren't able to give him that last hit. Hitter ye not. We used a top
British Frank Sinatra tribute act to sing the B-side, 'I Did It Howerd's
Way'. I suspect the title might well have been more amusing than
the song.

The following year I got a call from George Martin, asking me
to perform on a new album. We had worked together before on a
musical I had written based on the poems of John Betjeman, which

you can read all about in the next chapter. Anneka Rice had been asked on her TV show, *Challenge Anneka*, to put together an instant album to raise money for Tommy's, a new maternal and foetal research charity based at St Thomas' hospital in London. She called George and George called a few likely folk. Essentially a children's album, it contained songs and poems, sung and read by a variety of artists, including Joanna Lumley, Phillip Schofield, Maureen Lipman, Pam Ayres, Nanette Newman and Emma Forbes. We recorded the album at Air London studios at Oxford Circus and George asked if I fancied doing 'My Old Man's A Dustman', with Right Said Fred backing me. Of course. What a hoot. Move over, Lonnie Donegan. The album has recently appeared on iTunes, so the Fred boys and I are skiffling all over again and the charity is deservedly having a second bite of the cherry. After the recording was done I had a delightful thank-you letter from George Martin:

> Wasn't it a wonderful, crazy weekend ... I'd like to thank you especially for a super performance ... I'm so glad you did 'Dustman', it really was super,
> Love George

The same year, I was asked to write and record two children's albums for Avon (yes, the door-to-door cosmetics company), *A World of Colour* and *On the Move*. I can't for the life of me recall whether the titles were the briefs they gave me or my idea. Not that it really matters; they were fun to create and turned out extremely well, with George Martin's right-hand man, Rod Edwards, and me laying down both albums in a very short space of time in a studio in Shepherd's Bush. The songs on *A World of Colour* had titles such as 'I'm a Frog', 'Rainbow', 'Balloons', and 'Paintbox', while those on *On the Move* included 'Toby the Toboggan', 'Chummy the Funny Car' and 'Postman's Bike'. They were only meant to be for young people to have fun while they were learning, but *Record Collector* magazine later commented:

'Postman's Bike' has a distinctively psychedelic feel about it.
Had it been recorded back in 1967 at RG Jones, or at Graham
Clark's studio, it would undoubtedly have been a pop-psych
classic. For now though, it's lost among the bubble baths and
smudge-free lipstick in a discontinued Avon catalogue, await-
ing its rediscovery at psychedelia's centenary celebrations in
2067, when a mere twenty years either way won't make any
difference to anyone but the purists.

That's kind of comforting to know.

Also in 1992 I had an idea for a song based on *Baywatch*. I wrote
it, demoed it and approached Timmy Mallett, with the idea of him
being the skinny guy on the beach who beats all the muscly guys to
the girls, or something along those lines. The idea moved on and we
ended up recording the old classic, 'Hot, Hot, Hot', which involved
shooting a video in a Majorca-type resort and re-naming him. I jug-
gled with naming him Costa del something, but decided on Del Costa.
My girlfriend Alison and Dawn Andrews, Gary Barlow's future wife,
were the dancers and the result of the shoot was terrific, but it made
a hole in my pocket that wasn't compensated for by any great chart
position or sales graph. The single pottered up the charts and was
looking moderately healthy, but it staggered to a standstill outside
the top seventy-five and refused to budge. What happened to that
fan base from his number one, 'Itsy Bitsy Teeny Weeny Yellow Polka
Dot Bikini'? Timmy needn't worry about his chart career, he's actually a seriously good painter. History will re-assess him, relegating
'Mallett's Mallet' and promoting Mallett's palette.

'Hot, Hot, Hot' came out on Silhouette, the label I formed to
circumnavigate the problem of always having to do deals with different labels. Great idea, but a financial drain when the buck stops
with you. With independence comes responsibility.

The year 1992 was a great one for playing with highly unusual
groups. One you'll find in Chapter 14, but this one was a rock & roll

hierarchy gig. Well, apart from me. My old buddy Bert Weedon was King Rat that year and as we'd been sparring partners since I started in radio he asked me to bring my guitar to the annual ball. On the evening, someone kindly took it from me and put it backstage. 'I'll give you the nod,' said Bert.

'Nod for what? What are we playing?'

'Oh, a twelve-bar maybe.'

Good enough for me. After something nameless and custard had followed the other massed ranks of culinary delights in a southerly direction, I received the nod. Replete and somewhat heavier than an hour earlier, I excused myself and winched the body from the table. Backstage it was dark. Very dark. I fumbled around among a mass of what I assumed were stagehands until I found my guitar. I staggered out onto the stage to meet Bert for our impromptu duet and was outraged to discover there were interlopers trying to get in on the act: George Harrison, Bruce Welch, Brian May, Lonnie Donegan, Joe Brown and Chas McDevitt. The gig extended to one elongated song, but what a wonderful five minutes. I hoped we might stay together and tour the country. An album or two maybe and then a series of US gigs? It turned out that they had their own bands. Well, they passed up a great opportunity. I still have the photograph, though. As Frank Sinatra once said, 'They can't take that away from me.'

As I left Radio One to join Capital Gold, I found myself represented on two chart albums simultaneously, Slade's *Wall of Hits* and David Essex's *His Greatest Hits*. It had been suggested at Radio One that I should make my mind up whether I wanted to be a songwriter or a broadcaster, but I'd shown it was perfectly possible to do both. Surely it's a major plus if you live, breathe, play and write music as opposed to just doing the voice. Now, as even the most cursory glance at the Radio Six Music schedule confirms, they pull in rock stars to present programmes.

On re-visiting this period of my life, I'm frankly staggered that I had time for TV, radio, books, croquet, poetry and tennis. Being a great tennis lover and avid player, when I was asked to front a tennis single in the spring of 1993, for release in time for Wimbledon, I pondered for perhaps a tenth of a second and agreed. They needed a fun band name for the doo-wop-flavoured song, so I came up with the not terribly inventive Don Wimble and the Aces. In the video for 'Game, Set and Match', featuring former British number one Annabel Croft and Des Lynam on backing vocals, I played a match at David Lloyd, Raynes Park with that rising star of the court, Cliff Richard. Plenty of posing, lots of tennis, great fun … but no hit. I'd masqueraded under many names so being Don Wimble for a fleeting moment was no real hardship. Aficionados of the game point to this video as the inspiration for our future greats Tim Henman, Greg Rusedski and Andy Murray. 'Training, talent, stamina and mental strength are only a small part of it,' they say. 'The avant-garde armoury of shots displayed by Don Wimble and Cliff Richard were groundbreaking.' At least, that's how it plays out in my dreams.

That same year I wrote a couple of songs with a guy that I consider to have been one of the great and innovative songwriters of the '60s, Geoff Goddard. 'Johnny Remember Me', 'Wild Wind', 'Son This Is She', 'Just like Eddie' and 'Tribute to Buddy Holly' were just a few of the seriously influential songs that poured from his pen. He was a shy, modest man who had studied at the Royal Academy of Music, but along with the legendary producer Joe Meek, he challenged the chart domination of the major record companies and won a decisive victory. We routined and later recorded 'Flight 19' and 'Yesterday's Heroes' at Reading University, where he worked. As well as writing the songs together, Geoff and I corresponded as we honed them: 'I have written in riffs and basic ideas for arrangement [for 'Flight 19'] which I hope you may like' and 'Please find enclosed two copies of "Yesterday's Heroes", which I have developed from our song "Do You Remember Me" … the vocal range is one and a half octaves, the same as "Johnny Remember Me".' We planned to write some more songs. While Geoff was waiting for the muse to strike, he wrote, 'Not having felt very creative lately. I have no new ideas at the moment but should inspiration return I'll send a tape if that's OK.' Sadly Geoff died in 2000, but I was delighted to be invited to a red plaque unveiling at Reading University and a commemorative evening for him in 2013, along with two great singers who worked with Geoff, John Leyton and Mike Berry. John Leyton was keen to record the songs and even talked of me writing a musical around them, but it didn't happen.

I pick up the guitar most days and write a song a week on average, the good ones I demo, the others I keep working on and sometimes there's a bonus. A few weeks back a Matchbox singles collection landed on the mat and there was *24 Hours*. I also had the good fortune recently to be asked by Nigel Elderton at Peer-Southern Music to write English lyrics to an international hit made popular by Yves Montand. Written by Francis Lemarque, *A Paris* was full of so many notes that it was mathematical as well as lyrical, but enormous fun to work on.

CHAPTER 9

POETRY IN MOTION

I'VE ALWAYS LIKED poetry, both reading it and writing it. As a child I often, in my mind, put words to what I thought were sympathetic tunes. Somewhere around the age of ten I discovered a book of handwritten poems by my mother. I had no idea that she'd written poetry, but it was atmospheric stuff and unlike my less than fair hand, at least it was decipherable. It wasn't quite the immaculate copperplate effected by my maternal grandmother, with her bank of Swan pens, but it trounced mine by a country mile.

When I started to set John Betjeman's poetry to music, there was no plan. No rumbling strategy that had been brewing like an approaching storm. No Archimedes moment. I had a book of Betjeman's poems and had been rolling 'A Subaltern's Love-Song', also known as 'Joan Hunter Dunn', around in my head. A tune appeared and I liked it. It seemed natural and had a flow to it. A day later it was complete and I seamlessly moved on to another Betjeman poem, 'Harrow-on-the-Hill', closely followed by 'The Fete Champetre' and 'Newest Bath Guide'. I was on a mission without knowing why I was doing it or where I was heading, at a time when I was up to my ears in TV, radio and personal appearances with hardly a spare moment.

Within a short space of time I had half a dozen songs with my music and Betjeman's words but had no idea what to do with them. Step forward Charisma Records CEO Tony Stratton-Smith. Ever ready to promote Englishness and quirkiness through his label, Strat loved the whole idea and was up for putting out a six-track CD/LP. Thank goodness for inspirational characters like him in the industry. There are too few now, if any. When asked about a producer I decided to aim for the top and called George Martin. Our initial meeting was marvellous: we got on well and George visualised it immediately. He did some initial orchestrations and arrangements and we began putting down tracks at Air London, with George producing alongside Rod Edwards. After we'd done most of the tracks it became obvious that I wasn't going to stop writing and that a full-length album was in the offing. George had to head off abroad to produce an album for Kenny Rogers and left Rod in charge of production. It worked very well. I kept writing, Rod and I kept producing, and we frequently hired the Rolling Stones' mobile studio, which we parked in my drive at home. Afternoon tea, a little croquet, another song: it was an equable way of making an album.

On top of all that I was pitching songs from the album to various singers. Justin Hayward, who had once heard Betjeman reading at his local youth club, recorded 'Tregardock', Steve Harley sang 'Harrow-on-the-Hill', Annie Haslam did 'Hunter Trials' and Captain Sensible recorded 'Parliament Hill Fields'. All those were done at my home, The Aldermoor, in Holmbury St Mary. I had to collect the Captain from Crawley railway station as he'd come by train from Sussex, where he pursued his love of rabbits, Jimi Hendrix and cricket. It was rush hour and I was a little late, but unconcerned, he was sitting in his trademark white shorts, shirt and red beret on the ground, with the crowds pouring round him, eating curry from an assortment of tin foil dishes spread around him. The rest of the album, mixing, production and vocals, was done at Mickie Most's RAK studios in St John's Wood. Mike Nocito (on the brink of finding fame with Johnny Hates

Jazz) engineered, while Mickie popped in now and again to make a salient point or sagacious observation. He was also the chap that went for the fish and chips! I think he'd really done it all. With dozens of classic hit singles and albums over the previous twenty years or more, he'd got the badge, the T-shirt, the mug and the hundreds of gold discs. He was now happy to take the lunch order, get on his motor-bike and whizz off for half an hour, or watch Chelsea play at home.

I ended up singing two of the songs by default, backed vocally by Cantabile, as no ideal artist sprang to mind. Cantabile (now the Lon-don quartet) had been on both *Saturday Superstore* and Radio One many times, so I was acutely aware of their harmonies and humour. One of the songs in which they sang backing vocals, 'A Subaltern's Love Song', was parodied with appalling scansion by *Tatler*, which imagined me changing Betjeman's words to squeeze in lines like 'super-hot-shot powerplay'. I suppose I was fair game.

Ralph Allwood, Precentor and Director of Music at Eton College, was enthusiastic about the Eton College Chapel choir recording 'May Day Song for North Oxford', but practicalities meant recording it at the school, which proved an onerous task in many ways. Setting the microphones for the right balance was an intricate and elaborate pro-cess and by the time that had been executed it was lunchtime. The organist had obviously enjoyed a cracking lunch and had a wee bit of a post-prandial struggle getting to grips with the mighty instrument. That was solvable with time and a strong coffee, but the Heathrow flight path was slightly beyond my control. There seemed to be a plane every five minutes or so. Even if we couldn't hear it, the sound man's semi-permanent wince gave away the problem. This is what sound men do, they wince. A passing bluebottle 100 yards distant ... wince. A lorry reversing 2 miles away in Slough ... wince. The Queen turning the sound up on the TV across the road for the 2.30 at Newmarket ... wince. I'm not convinced these coves are that sensitive. I believe it's a power game. 'You may be the producer, mate, but *I'll* tell you when you can record. I hold all the cards.' With fortitude, determination, strength of mind and sheer luck, we got the track 'in the can' as we music biz types say and it was a corker. Earlier in the decade we might have had David Cameron and Boris Johnson in the ranks of the choir on that track. A few years later the Princes William and Harry might have been giving forth on it.

With Ian McNabb from the Icicle Works, Alvin Stardust, Simon Bowman and Cantabile also on the album, the only unknown act was an outfit called the Students of Architecture. These guys had previously gone under the names England and the Rose and they were seriously talented. We recorded their track at Abbey Road and went through the usual routine when anybody records in what was the Beatles' studio: 'Do you think Lennon stood here? He must have done ... Oh yes, this is definitely where Ringo's drums were ... Can you feel the magic?' and so on. I thought there might be an outside chance that Paul McCartney would sing 'Archibald', the poem about Betjeman's much-loved bear. I had a conversation about it with Paul outside RAK Studios and he made one or two suggestions that might help the structure. It sounded promising, but Alan Crowder at Paul's office came back to say, 'Regretfully he can't get involved in this project due to the enormous amount of things he has going on himself, but wishes you every success with the musical.' Pity.

CBS looked to be the main contenders for the album. We discussed the marketing, the sleeve design, the overall strategy and the possible first release. The most likely candidate for a single was David Essex singing 'Myfanwy'. This track almost didn't make the album. Rod Edwards was convinced that we already had enough songs and really didn't need another one and he was probably right, but you can't stop a chap when he's on a roll. I pleaded the case for a song I'd just finished writing over breakfast at the kitchen table. I have to say, it wasn't looking good until he heard it. He reasoned that if he was convinced by my live version on one guitar, then it was worth considering. Chris Rea had originally recorded it and even performed it at the Royal Albert Hall, but the Magnet Records boss, Michael

Levy, not yet elevated to the peerage, refused to let him release someone else's song.

We felt that it was a possible hit single, but were adrift until Dave
Dee suggested David Essex. He was on the money. David was absolutely perfect for it. His version of 'Myfanwy' was given the thumbs-up
by CBS and we looked set fair. Set fair, that is, until one of their pro-
motion guys heard it. His comments went something along the lines
of 'You're joking, aren't you? It's a bloody waltz with an orchestra, how
the hell can I get Radio One to play that?' They thought again, and
that effectively ended the potential single and album deal with CBS.
Luckily Arista, headed up by Peter Jamieson, picked up the single and
ran with it. The launch was at Kettners in Romilly Street, opened in
1867 and a favourite haunt over the years of Oscar Wilde, Edward
VII, Lillie Langtry and Agatha Christie. Bing Crosby once sang from
a balcony to keep hundreds of cheering fans happy. The invitation
was 'To have morning tea with Mike Read and David Essex.' We were
joined by Arista Records boss Peter Jamieson, Betjeman's publisher,
John Murray, and some of the artists on the album, including Justin
Hayward, Captain Sensible, Steve Harley and Annie Haslam.
Justin kindly dropped me a note saying, 'Lovely to see you this morning, the mix of "Tregardock" sounds great. The best of luck with the
whole project.' We all have doubts, but sometimes a few well-chosen
and sincere words keep us flying the flag.

I put together the story-board for a video and persuaded the good
master of Magdalen College, Oxford to let us shoot around the building and grounds. Not only was it Betjeman's *alma mater*, but we were
also able to use his rooms for a tea party scene and those of visiting
dons as David Essex/Betjeman's study. Mr Strutt, the head porter,
gave his staff instructions to co-operate fully, including ideal, and
sometimes very precise, camera positions, one anticipating a shot
'from New Building's Staircase 3, Room 7 bathroom'! David was the
consummate professional, insisting on discussing the shoot at length,
working at the correct dynamics between him and Rachel Roberts, the

wonderful young actress who portrayed the role of Myfanwy Piper, and even cutting his hair to give it that '20s look. He commented at the time, 'I've always had a soft spot for Betjeman. I liked the poem and I thought the music that Mike had written for it was terrific.' The lovely Gordon Elsbury from *Top of the Pops* directed the video, which we completed in just one day and which included some wonderful shots of the Oxford skyline and the town. Now, unfortunately, I can't find a copy of it. I keep hoping it's going to turn up on YouTube.

Radio One actually seemed happy to play the song. It was promoted for Arista by my old pal and first publisher, Dave Most, and slowly began to climb the chart. Week by week another ten places and another, until we were convinced by the sales pattern that it was going to be a top ten hit. When it hit number fifty-six, it was sandwiched between Percy Sledge and Ben E. King on one side and Tina Turner and Smokey Robinson on the other. I was happy to dwell in that holy place.

We found an unlikely ally when Princess Alexandra helped the single to chart with the copy she bought in Durham. The press reported that she was on an official visit to the city when she spotted a Virgin record shop, had the barriers removed where the police had cordoned off the road and proceeded ask the bewildered manager for a song she'd heard on the radio at five o'clock that morning called 'Myfanwy'. She told him that she'd been so taken with it that she 'simply had to buy a copy'. The embarrassed manager explained that he'd just sold the last copy, but, good businessman that he was, he called Virgin MD Andy Warrell in London and before the princess arrived back home at Richmond Park, a copy had been delivered by motorcycle messenger. Even Tim Rice sang the song's praises in *Punch*: 'The tune is bewitchingly simple and marvellously arranged.' He was very gracious in his comments: 'The real eye-opener is the music. Mike Read, the composer, is a totally unknown quantity, but those who might have dismissed him as a mere jock or children's TV host will have to think again.' Two things stopped it from carving its way through the forty. First, the folk that compile the chart would often 'down-weight' a single if they thought that sales weren't evenly spread. The thought was that someone could be deliberately buying copies to give the track a false chart position. This of course was nonsense. If a group were from Manchester, where the core of their fan base was, it was likely that there would be more sales in that area. They noticed what they considered an unnatural peak in Wales for 'Myfanwy' and downweighted it. Well, who'd have thought it – a song titled with an archetypal Welsh girls' name popular in Wales? But we could still bounce back as we'd been offered *Sunday Night at the London Palladium*, the last of the series. That'd catapult the song into the upper stratosphere, surely? Ah, but life isn't that easy, and this is where we encountered our second stumbling block. David's manager, Mel Bush, would only let his boy do it if he topped the bill. Dave Most protested that although David was indeed a major star, Diana Ross was on the same show and took precedence due to her longevity and level of success. Pleas, entreaties and whatever else fell on deaf ears. Either David topped the bill or he didn't do it. He didn't do it and the single stalled at number forty-one. We would have made the forty had it not been for Zodiac Mindwarp's 'Prime Mover' appearing out of nowhere and sneaking into the position above us. Frustratingly, 'Myfanwy' stayed at number forty-one for two or three weeks. Was there any consolation in being higher than the new releases from Go West, the Fall, UB40 and the Housemartins? Not really. It's a terrific testimony to the track, though, that it still spent over two months on the chart and was very popular in Australia. The weird and frustrating postscript is that when *Sunday Night at the London Palladium* began its next series, David sang 'Myfanwy', but it was too late, even though the single leapt back into chart on just that one play. Seemingly still popular, it's now notched up well over 100,000 hits on YouTube and was selected by Tim Rice as one of his Desert Island Discs, alongside the Everly Brothers, Elvis Presley, the Rolling Stones and 'Once in royal David's city'. Not bad company.

What did Myfanwy Piper, the subject of the poem, think about the song? I was invited for lunch a couple of times to the Pipers' house at Fawley Bottom, near Henley-on-Thames. Her husband John Piper, one of the great British artists of the twentieth century and not too well by that time, was nevertheless very welcoming, even showing me dozens of his of paintings that he had stashed away, presumably as yet unseen. The ladies from Myfanwy's era seemed to retain their acuity and perception. Over lunch she encouraged me to talk about my songwriting and writing in general, while she listened and gave little away. Was she interested in the written word or not? I wouldn't have known. It was only when we went into the kitchen to make tea that I noticed a well-worn poster on the wall, crudely stuck up with ancient and yellowing Sellotape. The poster proclaimed her to have been a librettist for Benjamin Britten. That generation sure knew how to deal an ace without moving their hands. She was quite kind when talking to the press: 'I wasn't mad about previous musical treatments of his poems. I'd rather they were left as they are. But I know many people get pleasure from them so I'm glad. And I'm sure he would have liked it.'

Of course I had wanted Lady Betjeman to approve and, as invited, drove down for lunch in my old MGA to the home of her daughter Candida Lycett-Green in Calne, Wiltshire. I headed off from Radio One in torrential rain and made slow progress on the M4, getting completely drenched as the car had no hood. Normally if it came on to rain, I'd pull over and shelter until it stopped. But I knew Penelope Betjeman was a stickler for punctuality so I simply carried on, got there some ten minutes after the appointed time and appeared on the doorstep looking like the proverbial drowned rat. Ignoring my condition, she informed me in no uncertain terms that I was late and stomped off into the house, leaving me dripping and having to find my own way to the table. The Betjemans' daughter, Candida, and assorted grandchildren were there and things soon eased. I think they'd all had a telling-off about something. I gradually dried off, ate a hearty lunch and played the demos. They seemed to get a seal of approval. One of the demos was of 'Hunter Trials', and Penelope told me that John had gone along to a gymkhana in which their son, Paul, was riding and was inspired to write the poem. As she pointed out, they weren't hunter trials at all and he completely misused and deliberately muddled the equine terms used in the poem.

Prior to the release of 'Myfanwy', the *Mail on Sunday* was keen to do a piece about my collaborating with the late Poet Laureate and asked Lady Betjeman if she minded doing a photograph. It transpired that she didn't mind, so off we trooped to her fairly remote house at Cusop in the Black Mountains. There was deep snow that day, so the newspaper hired a 4x4 to get to the property. It was a long hike and we struggled through some pretty deep drifts to get there. She opened the door, looked at the photographer and pointed to the camera. 'I don't know what you think you're going to do with that thing,' she said and did her stomping off thing. The photographer and journalist were crestfallen, but I was used to the stomping and reassured them. We were all dreaming of a hot meal after the long and arduous journey. We got bread and jam. It did come with tea, though, from an enormous enamel pot that would have served all the Women's Institute meetings in a 10-mile radius. The photographer was seriously concerned that he wasn't going to get his picture and on top of that, he was keen to shoot outside. He skirted round it a little, knowing that the temperature was below freezing and Penelope Betjeman was well into her seventies. She became impatient with his equivocating and let him have both barrels. She may not have actually pinned him against the wall, but she did so verbally. He was informed, in no uncertain terms, that she'd been up since seven, had saddled her horse, and ridden out some 14 miles in heavy snow and 14 miles back. She wasn't to be trifled with. The photographer ceased trifling and we trooped outside, sat on a log pile and did a few bracing snaps. In a full-page spread in the *Mail on Sunday* Penelope rather decently commented, 'I think it all sounds marvellous, marvellous. It should be very good.

Great fun.' Exactly. The paper was equally generous in calling me 'an authority on Betjeman's life' (hardly, compared to many of the folk in the Betjeman Society who keep the flame alive) and talking up the variety of genres: 'Latin through rock & roll to Irish Folk.' The large photo of us sitting on the snowy pile of logs was wackily captioned, 'Ode Couple ... Read and Lady Betjeman'.

Penelope and I corresponded over the next few months, she sending me little notes and copies of odd poems that John had written, including one about the King Alfred tea rooms at Wantage, which she ran at one time. The last communication I received was just before she set off for her beloved Himalayas (or Him-*ar*-lee-ers as she pronounced them). Her father had been Commander-in-Chief in India, hence her love of the region. She sent a note asking me to join her and Osbert Lancaster for lunch on her return. She never returned, and so we lost another great character from a disappearing generation. At the twenty-fifth AGM of the Betjeman Society I was surprised and intrigued by a comment in the speech of Betjeman's biographer Bevis Hillier. He made mention of the fact that Lady Betjeman had been 'rather in love with me'. Life is full of surprises.

Another formidable lady with whom I had to deal in connection with John Betjeman was Lady Elizabeth Cavendish, sister of the Duke of Devonshire and a very close friend of JB's. I was initially introduced to her at a meeting with Betjeman's literary executors, which also included Henry Anglesey, who was the godson of George V, and the architectural historian Mark Girouard. The four of us sat around discussing the possible release of an album and even a stage musical. They gave no quarter; it felt like a courtroom and I came away feeling that their response was going to be negative. While I thought Henry Anglesey encouraging and charming, Mark Girouard appeared inflexible and defensive of Betjeman's works. I was certain that one shouldn't attempt to canonise a man who was essentially a poet of the people, but who was I to know? All three literary executors had been personal friends and were acting in the manner they considered in the best interests of the estate. They needed clarity on my intended musical and to that end I was invited to Elizabeth Cavendish's house to explain my intentions. We drank a glass of wine or two and chatted amiably, although my eyes kept being drawn to Betjeman's battered old bear, Archibald Ormsby-Gore, who was scrutinising me from his perch on the window sill. Either I didn't explain myself too well, Lady Cavendish failed to grasp my intentions or Archie was distracting us, but she asked me to come back again the following week.

This time she had a friend with her who was introduced to me simply as Peter. Asked to explain how one goes about writing a musical, I proceeded with great aplomb. Apart from juvenile attempts and the heavily plagiaristic comic opera at college, in truth this was my first real crack at a real stage musical. Being a polite and well-brought-up chap, I didn't simply direct my explanation of how to write a musical to Elizabeth, but also to her friend Peter. I even read the opening pages of the script, which began with Betjeman going through customs at the Pearly Gates. 'Anything to declare?' asked St Peter. I used an actual line of Betjeman's as the response, which he'd spoken during his last interview. On being asked if he had any regrets, he responded that he hadn't had enough sex. A great line, I thought, so I used it as his reply to St Peter … and, crassly, read it out loud to Elizabeth, not thinking about the close friendship between herself and Betjeman. I still squirm when I think of it… After talking about the art of writing a musical play for an hour I sat back, feeling that I'd acquitted myself rather well. Not smug, but satisfied. Not for long, though. Elizabeth Cavendish turned to her friend and asked demurely, 'Was it like that, Peter, when you wrote *Amadeus*?' I'd spent an hour telling one of our greatest playwrights, Peter Schaffer, how to write. I had the grace to blush.

The executors were not keen on the proposed title for the musical, *Teddy Bear to the Nation*. Elizabeth Cavendish wrote to me, 'It is only fair to you to say that in no way will the Literary Executors of John Betjeman allow the suggested title, so by the time we meet can you have thought of a different and more suitable one. This is *not* something we will be persuaded about.' Eventually, but only after much deliberation on the part of the executors, I had an agreement. This was good news. The downside was that the musical looked like a 'no go' area. I wonder why? The album would eventually be released on various small labels, but has seemed to have found a comfortable home with Angel Air. In the view of everybody involved, it still hasn't realised its full potential.

Meetings with Betjeman's publisher, John (Jock) Murray, were always fascinating as the Murray family, from 1768 on, had published such luminaries as Jane Austen, Sir Arthur Conan Doyle, Charles Darwin and Lord Byron. Sherry and cheese biscuits were always on the agenda and of course another glimpse of Byron's shirt, which was on display. Signed to John Murray (each generation bore the same name), Byron had an instant bestseller when *Childe Harold's Pilgrimage* was published. In true pop star fashion, he announced, 'I awoke one morning and found myself famous.' We discussed Andrew Lloyd Webber's interest in staging my intended musical at his Sydmonton Festival, but even with Andrew's enthusiasm it didn't happen, for some reason now lost in a hundred historic conversations. The tabloids made much of a completely untrue story (nothing new there) that Andrew had been secretly teaching me how to become a 'superstar composer'. Risible. I can just imagine him peering at me over a glass of 1997 Romanée-Conti in his kitchen and shyly asking, 'I say, would you like to become a superstar composer?' The headline was 'Mike's Phantom Aide'. The press appeared to be moving me from Lord Reith to Lord Wraith.

In another genre, I was asked to play guitar on a song that the Duke of Kent's daughter, Lady Helen Taylor, was recording, called 'Single Girl', which led to us being erroneously linked by some of the gossip columns. Lady Olga Maitland's column majored on it at one point. With a marginally folksy feel in the style of Marianne Faithfull as I recall, it was recorded at a studio in Great Marlborough Street, a yard or two from the one-time London abode of Percy Bysshe Shelley. In the end there were questions asked about the release of a single by a member of the royal family and the producer did the decent thing and handed over the tapes. Something must have escaped, though, somewhere along the line, as in 2000 it emerged as one of Ibiza's 'hottest tracks of the season', according to *The Times*. The track was much changed from the original (essential, I'd say) but the newspaper admitted, 'Lady Helen's clipped tones are quite audible on the new version, which is the work of producers, Royal I.'

I did put a musical on stage in 1988, but it wasn't Betjeman related. I had also been working on a Rupert Brooke musical, over whose title I was still dithering. The papers got wind of it and one of them fired a not unexpected opening salvo. 'Read fancies himself as a poet, although his literary output has thus far been confined to *The Guinness Book of British Hit Singles*, a work not known for its lyrical and aesthetic qualities.' I considered drawing their attention to my two poetry books, *The Aldermoor Poems* and *Elizabethan Dragonflies*, and the various poems in the Poets England series, but why bother?

My neighbours in Holmbury St Mary, Richard and Linda Jackson, who ran Hurtwood House School, offered their wonderful theatre space for a week, so with Hugh Wooldridge directing, we were away. Having assembled a fine cast from the school, headed by imported actor Michael Dore, we were rolling. Well, sort of. The school wasn't draconian, but it did not achieve its fantastic results by standing any nonsense or rule-breaking. It was 'one strike and you're out'. So on a couple of occasions we found a cast member no longer a member of the cast ... or the school. I must point out that expulsion by the headmaster isn't the norm in musical theatre. With regard to the audience, we operated on a 'pay what you like at the end of the show' basis and despite that got a sackful of money, which I dumped on the desk of the very grateful and completely surprised PHAB centre in the village. After the final show we had a farewell bash, where I got ceremoniously thrown in the swimming pool fully clothed. Indecent behaviour, you'll agree. I had been particularly attached to that green pullover with its country motif. The following morning it would have been a tight fit on an Mbuti pygmy, or indeed any pygmy.

Within a year, producer extraordinaire Bill Kenwright picked up the show and decided to stage it at the Thorndike Theatre in Leatherhead, although he wasn't especially keen on the title we'd used at Hurtwood, *The Most Beautiful Man in England*. It's a hell of a thing to live up to if you're playing the lead, out there each night, gingerly treading the boards dreading some wag shouting, 'I've seen more beautiful men in gurning contests.' I was on the phone to Bill from the end of a platform at Kings Cross station when we finally agreed on calling the show *Young Apollo*, thus creating a vague link, in case it should ever come up in some obscure quiz, between Queen Boadicea (or Boudicca as they now call her), allegedly buried under one of the platforms, Harry Potter and Rupert Brooke. Hugh Wooldridge directed again and organised a superb set that drew applause in its own right.

Alex Hanson played Brooke, and stayed with me at The Aldermoor for some of the run. Over a glass of something with a fancy label one evening, he suddenly looked quizzical. 'Wasn't Brooke blond? I'm very dark, won't that look odd?'

I smiled. That slow, knowing smile that I fancied would look good on the silver screen. It probably just looked ridiculous, but I smiled it nevertheless. 'You're dark at the moment, but it won't last.'

Realisation dawned. 'Oh no,' I believe were the actual words that came from his mouth. I nodded slowly. Again very filmic, I thought. Within two days he was blond, his head shining like the Eddystone lighthouse on a foggy night, and full of disbelief that he'd been well and truly bleached.

Now when I was doing amateur dramatics, the prompt stood to the side of the stage and if you forgot your lines, you'd sidle as unobtrusively as possible towards them, hoping they'd spot your dilemma and whisper the words audibly enough for you to pick up. It was a covert operation. Not so with the Alex Hansons of this world. On the dress run, with full audience, when he dried, he screamed 'LINE!' like an elephant protecting her young from a pride of lions. I jumped. I'm sure several in the front row were thrown into the second row with the force of it. It was all over in a flash and the musical moved on. No whispering, no edging towards the side, Alex took it full on. 'Crikey,' I thought at the time. 'Bravo,' I thought afterwards. Another incident wasn't quite so well received. We're still with the dress run and a full house, but Clive, our musical director, was desperate not to miss England v. Poland and took it upon himself to listen to the match on headphones, while playing keyboards and directing the music. No one would know, so where's the harm? There was no harm at all … until Gary Lineker found the net after twenty-four minutes. During a quiet and particularly moving moment in an early scene, Clive's voice (and we all shout louder with headphones on) rang around the auditorium, 'England have scored!' I don't recall any of the cast or the audience yelling back 'Oh, jolly good' or anything similar. Maybe some in the back rows went away thinking it was a particularly avant-garde moment in the show and I was the new theatrical Messiah. Actually there were messianic writers already present in the shape of Tim Rice and Andrew Lloyd Webber, who both turned up to give their support. Andrew even brought a bunch of flowers. Bill Kenwright's plan to move it to the Mermaid never materialised, even though I was convinced by his tears during one performance. 'That's it,' I thought, 'he's visibly moved … the West End (well close enough for me) beckons.' I later learned that Bill is always emotional at his musicals. The West End actually wouldn't beckon until the new millennium, and without *Young Apollo*. While I laid down most of the demo tracks for the musical, the duet 'Too Young for Love' was beautifully demoed by Michael Ball and the young actress who had played Myfanwy in the David Essex video, Rachel Roberts.

Speaking of Myfanwy, we debated which of the Betjeman songs would be a suitable follow-up for the autumn on 1987. I was keen on

Captain Sensible's 'Parliament Hill Fields', or Justin Hayward's 'Tregardock', but in the end we decided to go for David Grant's 'Conversion', with the Eton College Choir on the B-side. We used Mickie's RAK label for this release, but David's manager thought it was rather a distraction as he was pushing him in other areas so it wasn't really promoted heavily and consequently failed to chart. In 1989 the two Alvin Stardust tracks, 'Christmas' and 'Executive', were released on the Honeybee label, but we were thwarted by a total lack of distribution. Undaunted we pressed on, thwarts and all. Despite several TV appearances, a lot of hard work by the lovely Alvin and a jolly seasonal video shot at my house and the church at Holmbury St Mary, and involving a terrific new scheme of colouring in each frame by hand to achieve a truly unique effect, it failed to trouble the scorers. The only bonus was having a fully decorated Christmas tree in my drawing room in September. In our defence, it did make the top ten of several Christmas listings. 'Myfanwy' re-emerged on my Silhouette label in 1990 and was also on the *Poetry in Motion* album, which came out in the same year. I decided to release the album on my own label as everyone felt that it had legs, but no one had had the opportunity to buy it. In 1991, 'Myfanwy' escaped for a fifth time on David Essex's *The Christmas EP*, along with 'A Winter's Tale', and, for a sixth time, on the *His Greatest Hits* album, which climbed to number one and spent thirteen weeks in the chart.

In the end there was no Betjeman musical as such, but I re-wrote it as a vehicle for a charity evening, with interlinking dialogue for a JB-style character. It got its first airing as *Poetry in Motion* in the spring of 1992 at the Richmond Theatre, in aid of the Royal Marsden Hospital. Jeremy Irons and John Wells undertook the narration, while the impressive list of artists included Donovan, David Grant, Tim Rice, Peter Sarstedt, Carl Wayne, Cantabile and Alvin Stardust. Christopher G. Sandford directed proceedings, with the Wren Orchestra lending their weight to it, Rod Edwards supervising the music and Tony Rivers leading the backing vocal team. It sold out and was well received by the audience and the press.

I staged *Poetry in Motion* a second time in 1998, at the Criterion Theatre in the West End for the Children with Leukaemia Trust, run by the tireless Karen Sugarman, now of Shooting Star Chase Hospices. This time, Tim Rice, his daughter Eva, Cliff Richard, Leo Sayer, Tony Hadley, Colin Blunstone, Carl Wayne and Dean Sullivan took part, with the wonderful Bernard Cribbins taking the role of Betjeman. We raised more than £10,000 on the night, so bless all those who give their time again and again for good causes.

We released another track from the *Poetry in Motion* album as a single in 1992, Donovan's 'Newest Bath Guide'. We hit upon the novel idea of shooting the video in Bath, utilising the weir, the architecture and the Roman baths with Don looking suitably moody. Driving from the hotel very early in the morning, I noticed a rather pungent smell in the car. 'What's that, Don, have we just passed an Indian restaurant? It smells like somebody's day-old takeaway.'

'Very perceptive,' said the minstrel. 'It's the remains of *my* Indian takeaway from last night. I thought I'd have it for breakfast.'

I pulled into a garage, deposited the 'Remains of the Takeaway' (as another Old Wokingian, Kazuo Ishiguro, almost wrote) in the litter bin and re-started the car. We drove to our destination in silence. Not a good start to the day. But, ever the professional, an Indian-free Don rose to the occasion. Having breakfasted on something far more appropriate, we got a spiffing and historically weighty video in the can. Don sang the song live on *Pebble Mill*, but maybe the single was too whimsical, folksy and literary to take on Gabrielle, Queen, UB40 and Shaggy for a chart placing.

In between all this musical activity, radio, TV and social stuff, there were gigs. What fun to get up and play live music. Well, fun for us, if not the audience. I discovered a shot from one such event, in Hampstead, lurking on the front page of the *Hampstead & Highgate Express*, fondly known as the *Ham & High*. This isn't unusual in itself, but it remains the only photograph of me with a full beard, which in tandem with a suntan and long locks made me look, as Alison, my girlfriend at the time, commented, 'like a terrorist'. *The Sun* reported that I looked 'like a cross between Dustin Hoffman in the film *Papillon* and George Best on a bad night'. A little harsh.

In 1991, just before I moved from Radio One to Capital, my musical on Oscar Wilde was staged for the first time. It was billed as a world premiere, which although technically true, sounds a trifle pretentious. But who cares? It *was* a world premiere, so let's run with it. My friend Martin Miller (of the Miller's Antiques Guides) and his then wife Judith, today one of the experts on *Antiques Roadshow*, owned the beautiful Chilston Park in Kent. At night the house was lit entirely by candles: very romantic – or very sinister, depending on your mood. Either way, it offered the ideal setting for a musical play, so together we hatched a plan and it came to fruition. A cast, a couple of weeks, a hundred and something people a night, black tie, champagne and canapés before and dinner afterwards, the cast joining the audience as they were all staying at the house. Oscar would surely have approved.

His grandson certainly did. A year or two earlier, after writing the first draught, I'd sent it to Merlin Holland, who approved of it to such an extent that he became involved. He felt that it was the most balanced piece he'd seen on the subject. We also became good friends, and I even helped save his son Lucien's life.

I was round for dinner and drinks one evening at their house in Wandsworth and after a few hours of bonhomie felt I should be beetling off. 'Have a tea or something before you go,' insisted Merlin. I refused, then relented. 'Well, if I do I should really pop to the loo while you put the kettle on.' At the top of the stairs I smelled smoke. It was coming through the gap at the bottom of the door to his son Lucien's bedroom. I yelled to Merlin, who came pounding wild eyed up the stairs. We opened the door and billows of dense fumes poured out. Keeping a clear head, Merlin dashed to the bathroom, wet a flannel, put it over his face and dragged an unwilling Lucien from the room. Within twenty minutes electric blue flashes were rebounding off the walls and two fire engines stood at the gates. It seemed Lucien had nodded off and a bedside lamp had fallen onto the pillow. The smouldering had continued for some while, until the whole room was filled with smoke. A very lucky escape. I was pleased I had agreed to that cup of tea.

Before every performance, Merlin did a superb preamble about his grandfather, setting the scene and bringing a sense of history to the occasion. He made allusion to the fact that had Oscar lived to find success again, he would have written about the tragic part of his life. 'This is the tragedy that Oscar lived, but didn't live to write about it. Mike Read has written it.' What a lovely testimony. Merlin was clearly so good in his role that one lady, sitting next to him at dinner, assumed he was an actor and asked him how he got the part. 'You'd better ask my mother,' came the quick riposte, which went over the lady's head.

'Why, was she in the acting profession too?'

'No, I *am* Oscar's grandson.'

'Oh, go on … you can stop acting now.'

The talented Don Gallagher played Oscar, and Alvin Stardust surprised everyone (I knew he would) with a powerful performance as the Marquess of Queensberry. After one show, a guy sidled up to me, told me he'd enjoyed it and then declared himself to be a 'serious' clairvoyant. As opposed to a jokey one that's just teasing you, I supposed. Anyway, he first told me in no uncertain terms that I had a very strong spirit guide called Emily. I stared. 'She's a very old member of your family.' There were no Emilys in my family that I knew of, but the sage insisted. 'Ask your grandmother.' I did, the following day, and waited for the gales of derisive laughter. No laughter. 'Oh gosh, that's a long time ago. That would be my great-aunt Emily. She was a devout spiritualist and used to take me to meetings when I was a little girl.' Well, I wasn't expecting that. I now think of my disapproving ancestor looking over my shoulder and silently chiding me when I wander off piste. Is she helping me write this? It's a thought. Maybe Great-Great-Great-Aunt Emily could knock out a few thousand words of this book each night when I'm in bed. Meanwhile the clairvoyant had more to offer. 'This musical will one day be known across the world,' he announced with a smile. 'It will be talked about globally.' Did his smile betray the fact that he also knew *why* it would attract such attention?

Oscar got some very encouraging reviews, one magazine commenting that after 'You Always Want the One Who Doesn't Really Want You', there wasn't a dry eye in the house. Must have been the champagne. It has a tendency to make some folk maudlin. Attendees were also mentioned. 'Mr Cliff Richard enjoyed the show and stayed for dinner, as did Mr Tim Rice. Mr Rice believed there were at least three hit songs in the show.' What taste, what perception! The article also gave honourable mention to 'His Excellency Dasho Lhendhrup Dorje, who had come all the way from the small, exotic Buddhist kingdom of Bhutan in the Himalayas.' That's one heck of a bus ride.

One night I got chatting to a guy called Mike Eilers, who liked the show so much he offered to put up some money if it was produced again. Top man. Thanks largely to his generosity the show appeared at the Old Fire Station, Oxford the following year. Cliff also helped out towards the production costs, as well as lending me his main man who looks after him on tour, Roger Bruce. Well grounded in musicals, Roger had worked on *Time* in the West End among other stage shows. He even took the cast's shirts home to wash. You couldn't have asked for more. Well, maybe if the collars and cuffs had been starched…! At Oxford, the one-time-blond Rupert Brooke, Alex Hanson, was now dark enough again to take on the lead role.

Again it got some great reviews. Baz Bamigboye in the *Daily Mail* said, 'Having heard the score, I think Mr Read can safely give up his day job.' I loved Baz for that and instantly forgave him any previous reporting on my love life. I loved *The Stage* too, for writing, 'The whole piece may be described as the thinking man's musical. Scholarly libretto … the music is mature … he [Read] is clearly no Wilde popularist but a scholar too.' The theatre publishers Samuel French added, 'The libretto is extremely literate with some amusing use of language and a general air of sophistication.'

Oscar's next outing (insert your own third-form jokes here) was at the King's Head Theatre in Islington, with Nigel Williams in the title role, and was again well received, by and large. Nigel was a brilliant Oscar, despite *The Times*' review: 'His Wilde with his toothy grin and arresting yet vacuous eyes, looks suspiciously like Tony Blackburn in a cravat.' Unfair to Nigel, Oscar and Tony, I'd say. I didn't escape, of course. 'If you like several tablespoons of sugar on your tragedies this show might make you happy.' I was happy with 'sugar'. Thank heavens it wasn't 'saccharine'. *The Guardian* couldn't resist the inevitable radio link either despite it not being remotely relevant to the piece: 'Listen up mates! Deep beneath that bouffant hairdo that is DJ Mike Read a creative literary talent is fighting to get out.' Bouffant? The *Daily Express* claimed in a full page, 'Mike Read would rather have guaranteed press than a fair press.' Is there a choice? Nick Curtis of the *Evening Standard* was the only one to completely tear it to shreds, dredging the hacks' dictionary for useful words such as 'gauche', 'bathos', 'stereotypes', 'trivial', 'doggerel' and a few other choice barbs to help me sleep at night. Was this the same *Evening Standard* that had recently written, 'Mike Read is a man of untapped intellect'? Other reviewers who were adjacent later told me that Nick had quite liked the piece, but that any hint of admiration wasn't likely to appear in print. We've since had a laugh about it. Well, I bought him a drink and he laughed all over again. The critics are, after all, only a handful of people trying to make a name for themselves. The real critics are the public and I continue to hear great comments from paying customers who were baffled as whether the reviewers had watched the same show.

It was the fourth outing that brought disaster. I'd had so much positive feedback from *Oscar* that it was mooted, by several enthusiastic mooters, that I should re-stage it as a commemorative piece for the 150th anniversary of Wilde's birth in 2004. It certainly proved memorable. In casting around for a theatre, I was told that the Shaw in Euston Road was intending to re-open. It had stood dark for some while and on inspection proved to be more suitable for conferences than performances, but they promised that they'd wave a magic wand. The spend on re-marketing and re-launching was said to be in excess of £250,000, and *Oscar* was the very first show. I was told that very little could go wrong. In retrospect a hell of a lot went wrong. All right, everything went wrong.

In 2004 the banks were still encouraging entrepreneurs to borrow wads of cash to fund, well, almost anything. They kept throwing it at me, so I kept taking it, while the whisperers were telling me that this show was so good that it was going to be the making of my script-writing career. But I broke several rules.

- *Rule one:* never fund your own show. A wise man, let's call him Tim Rice, once told me that you don't have to win twice. If a show you've written is successful, you don't need to be the producer as well. He was right of course, but when the hare is running, as they say in greyhound racing, there's no stopping the race. There were times when I should have called a halt to the whole thing.

- *Rule two:* never try to wear a multiplicity of hats. I was writer, director, producer and the frontman for the media. This was a bad idea. In fact several bad ideas.

- *Rule three:* don't open in London. Let the critics discover it in the wilds.

Despite this, we had a great cast, terrific musicians and a script that had already worked three times, so all was looking good – until, that is, we came to the theatre itself. The Shaw had no website, nor was it in any telephone listings. Those people who did, against all odds, manage to get the number never had their calls answered and the phone rang off the hook all the time we were rehearsing. There was no re-launch money and we had zero co-operation. Furthermore, the theatre was in such a terrible state backstage that we had to clean it from top to bottom before we could even get in. By now money was leaking through my pocket, I was juggling directing with producing and doing publicity and became general gopher. My team were exemplary, but they had the burden of Sisyphus.

When the media wolves later descended on the fold, they triumphantly declared that the musical closed after one night. Good headline stuff, but a myth: we'd had a week of runs before the press night and audiences were healthy. The cast had a well-deserved day off before the proper opening night, which is when the demons set in. On the opening night itself, our sound man told me that the beautiful and perfect balance had been destroyed by forces unknown. Some head microphones had also been seriously tampered with and others were missing.

My questioning began as calmly as I could muster. The repeated answer to my enquiry as to who had been in the theatre the previous day was 'No one'. I was paying for the damn place, so that should have been the correct answer. I knew it wasn't. I'm an easy-going guy, but my face got increasingly closer to the head honcho, who wasn't unaware of my physical presence either. After five minutes of protestation I eventually pushed the truth out of him. Unbelievably, they'd allowed a twenty-piece Brazilian jazz-rock outfit in behind our backs and wrecked our sound. On top of that, this amateurish theatre only had one, hired-in, machine for processing tickets, meaning that every ticket holder, including celebrities and, crucially, journalists, had to wait for ages in a long, long queue that straggled down the street. Once again, the delightful Merlin Holland had agreed to say a few words before the performance on behalf of his grandfather, but someone from the adjacent hotel made such a long and tedious speech that there was no time for him. The sound on stage and in the auditorium was atrocious and with some of the head microphones not working properly, many of the cast were understandably thrown, despite their professionalism. I spent much of the performance walking the street.

I pulled the show. I had to. The press destroyed it. The TV crews, newspapers and magazines who'd been invisible when I needed the publicity suddenly manifested themselves and showed an unbelievably keen interest in the show. Funny how everybody loves a failure. One of the lines reflected that 'they adore a persecution, but abhor an absolution'. Oscar would have enjoyed a fine example of life imitating art.

I didn't shirk the attack. It came from all fronts, with everyone jumping gleefully on the bandwagon. I was happy to justify anything except my stupidity, as Oscar might have said, but didn't. As well as answering the press, I agreed to be interviewed on several TV shows, including one where a journalist attacked the rhyming couplets. 'Good enough for Shakespeare,' I retorted, which brought a gasp of horror that I dared compare myself to the Bard. I wasn't, I was merely pointing out that many of the greatest and most durable plays in the English language employed rhyming couplets from time to time. Then I had the audacity to liken some of the script to Gilbert and Sullivan. I wasn't saying that I was as good as G&S, but was simply alluding to an accepted style for which I was now being criticised.

Remember the clairvoyant who announced that one day the musical would be known globally? He was right. I had calls of sympathy from Australia, the United States, South America, South Africa, Spain and all points east and west. The global cuttings laid flat reached floor to ceiling several times over. Bad news travels fast, but smirking, self-satisfied, lead-him-to-the-scaffold news travels at Mach 2 with an upgrade. I got the upgrade. I'd been hoping for the Lew Grade.

Wouldn't you think that after that I'd leave it alone? I'd capitulate, surrender to the barbarians at the gate and desert the Oscar who'd served me so ill? Nope. Against all odds, there were still believers who knew the piece would work. Peter Kosta, who had worked tirelessly on the production at the Shaw, pushed for the show to do a week off Broadway. His determination paid off, and with him and musical director Michael Reed on board we flew to New York for another crack at it. The York Theatre and the cast were terrific, but it proved tricky to get producers there in what was an icy, snowy March with some biting winds whipping off the Hudson River. I fondly imagined that staging it in the States for a week would mean no UK media attention, but I really don't learn. They were onto it in a nanosecond, but this time round not quite all the coverage was negative. *The Independent* called me the Stephen Sondheim *du jour*, and reckoned that *Oscar* was 'monstrously underrated'.

At least it proved there was life after the Shaw Theatre. Unlike Genesis's Lamb, *Oscar* wouldn't lie down on Broadway or anywhere else and continues to periodically twitch and kick. The continued interest means that it will re-appear, sometime, somewhere, probably with the strapline 'The musical that dare not speak its name'.

A coincidental culinary *ménage à quatre* occurred during the time we did *Oscar* in the Big Apple when Tim Rice called me, only to find that we were walking down adjacent streets of the city. Another call revealed that our choreographer friend Anthony Van Laast was also in town, checking on the city's production of *Mamma Mia*. With Michael Reed, who'd worked extensively with all three of us, making the fourth corner, we had a rather jolly evening being excessively and deliberately Englishmen in New York. Luckily it was a night off, unlike the night the legendary guitarist Les Paul played just around the corner. It coincided with a major rehearsal and my bitterest regret while there was not getting to see and hear him.

In the late summer of 1991 I'd had a call from Slade, who were in the studio putting down a new track that they thought just might put them back in the top twenty (where they rightfully belonged). They felt that the song, 'Radio Wall of Sound', needed a punchy American-style DJ delivery to give it some pace, but it wasn't really working with any of them doing it, so they asked if I'd pop up to the studio in north London. No problem. They already had a few phrases, I scribbled a few more and after a few playbacks of the track, I was able to push some hard-hitting US-style lines into the gaps. The more I heard Jim Lea's song, the more I thought it was going to be a monster. It had a great tempo and a seriously catchy chorus, and was a terrific idea overall. The band graciously asked me to appear in the video, which was great fun, with me recording the studio scenes at Broadcasting House. It's not easy to lip-synch at speed when you've forgotten what the hell you babbled about at the original recording session. The video was brilliantly shot and, like the single, laden with atmosphere. I didn't see how this could fail to put them back in the chart. Their last top twenty hit had been in 1984 with 'All Join Hands'. 'Radio Wall of Sound' did climb to number twenty-one, their highest position for seven years, but I honestly felt that it was going all the way. It remains a radio favourite and re-emerges periodically on greatest-hits albums. Dave Hill later approached me with a view to writing a musical as a vehicle for Slade's hits, much like *We Will Rock You* and *Mamma Mia*, and I worked on an angle for a possible script for a while, but nothing has come to fruition. Dave and I still discuss it from time to time, so who knows? Dave and Don Powell are still out there on the road, playing Slade's great catalogue of hits and enjoying every minute of it.

During 1992, Peter Powell, encouraged Apollo Leisure to look seriously at two Dickens-based musicals for which I'd written all the songs, *A Christmas Carol* and *Great Expectations*. Rather decently, they saw the value in them and we began auditioning for a run at Theatr Clwyd at the end of the year. After spending a heck of a lot of time in the recording studio and finely honing the numbers, I went up for the opening night of *A Christmas Carol*, or rather, the opening matinee. I was staggered at one point to hear the audience singing along to one of the songs. How could this be? The songs were new. Had I unwittingly plagiarised some classic? To my relief, I discovered I hadn't. The theatre had rather cleverly sent out four of the songs on a cassette to various local schools, so they could learn the story, hear the music and be encouraged to read Dickens. By the time they came to the show, they were almost word perfect. Smart marketing. Chris Corcoran took the role of Scrooge and expertly played the part to include humour, fear, contrition and pathos. Not all went smoothly for our talented if sometimes volatile director, Christopher G. Sandford, as one of the cast, in a fit of pique over something, sneaked back one night and cut up every single wig with a large pair of scissors. Cue the understudy. I discovered only recently from a member of the cast that another of the team was putting several noses out of joint to such an extent that a few tins of cold custard were wilfully poured into his boots just before he was due on stage. He apparently squelched his way through the whole scene, with the viscous yellow liquid slopping onto the stage and making a rather decent slide for the rest of the cast.

A Christmas Carol later re-appeared for a healthy run at the Theatre Royal, Nottingham with the great Anton Rodgers playing Scrooge. It nearly didn't happen, though. With a hectic schedule at Capital Radio and busy writing new material and film scripts, I hadn't had time to get to rehearsals and work through the songs as I would normally have done. When I heard the rough demos that the cast had laid down I went ballistic. Several melodies had been changed by the arranger, with the blessing of our director, who then had the gall to insist on a royalty. I'm sorry, but you can't simply change someone else's songs just like that, and then claim part ownership. I was livid. There were long and angry phone calls, but I made damned sure that I got my way. It's like defending and fighting for your children.

At the end of 1993, *Great Expectations* also made its debut at Theatr Clwyd. Prior to the opening, and with the musical having been cast, we took all the performers into a studio by Wembley Stadium to record all the songs. They arrived not having heard a single note, so we had to rehearse, routine and record from scratch. It was chaotic and frenetic, but we got everything down. Of course, later, when everyone had bedded in and knew the numbers intimately, they wanted to go back in and do them again, but it was not to be. The album was released in that form. Having forked out a not insubstantial amount of loot for the scenery, Apollo Leisure then decided that the show should go on tour. Great news, except for the fact that this scenery wouldn't fit the venues. So new scenery was built and more costs incurred. But it was very good, I have to say, even if not quite to the standard of Frank Lloyd Wright. In fact *Great Expectations* toured twice. On the first tour Darren Day played Pip, with Nyree Dawn Porter and Brian Glover portraying Miss Havisham and Magwitch. *Hello!* magazine gave us a wonderful double page spread. Nyree said, 'I consider it an honour.'

For the second tour, Darren and Nyree were back, and Brian was replaced by Colin Baker, making an effortless transition from Dr Who to Magwitch. Colin graciously wrote to me after the run: 'I would just like to thank you, both for providing such a splendid show for me to lurk and menace in and for turning up to see it from time to time so that we felt that someone out there cared.' On the last point, certainly, Colin was right. You don't bring a child into the world, nurture it, educate it and then ignore it. Nor should one with a musical. As in life, show a keen interest and keep touching the tiller imperceptibly. Don't let the boat hit the bank before you try to correct your course.

For the national tours we re-recorded four of the songs, 'Great Expectations', 'The Loneliest Night in the World', 'Estella' and 'Heart of Stone', for release. 'The Loneliest Night in the World' emerged on the 1998 compilation *Musicals of the Night*, alongside songs from *Miss Saigon*, *West Side Story*, *Phantom of the Opera* and *My Fair Lady*. The tracks were laid down at Abbey Road with a full orchestra and my great pal Michael Reed as musical supervisor and arranger, which he also had been for the tours. We always refer to each other as 'Your Majesty'. I should probably explain. I heard that every time the switchboard operator at Buckingham Palace connected the Queen with the Queen Mother, because they had the same Christian name, his official line had to be, 'Your Majesty, Her Majesty, Your Majesty.' As Michael and I had the same name I started using the line on our phone calls and it stuck, eventually being shortened to 'Your Majesty'. It certainly makes people look up when the mobile goes in a public place and you answer in respectful and regal tones, 'Your Majesty.'

The *Mail on Sunday* magazine proclaimed that it could 'see no reason why he [Read] can't take the West End by storm'. By storm? Even by bus would have been good. The paper's theatre critic, Baz Bamigboye, seemed confident that it would be staged in London: 'Mr Read has become a one-man music industry, with productions of his various shows touring the country. Now there are plans for his *Great Expectations* to hit the West End later this year.'

One night I was driving back home from Nottingham, after watching the show. There had been dense fog the whole way and I had had to concentrate intensely. I was only a few miles from home, then in deepest Sussex, when my thoughts began to run a second or two ahead of themselves. I knew what I was going to think a brief moment before I thought it. It's a tough symptom to describe, but that's the best I can muster. You might counteract with the rational response, 'Well, you've just thought it – the "premonition" is the actual thought, so the repeat is simply an echo.' It wasn't that, though, and it scared the hell out of me. I've tried to rationalise whatever happened to me many times, even putting the blame on eating a whole bag of liquorice allsorts during the journey. I've since have been assured by experts that it wasn't the liquorice. I know they say that the brain always runs slightly ahead of itself, but this was a very different and scary feeling. I pulled over several times before making it back to the farm. Alison had come round for supper and was rather bewildered at my state. It certainly shook me up. I can only assume that my level of concentration had been such, peering into thick fog for some hours, that it affected my thought process in some way. Maybe the brain slowed down to the speed of consciousness and thus had a problem dealing with the surroundings and conditions.

CHAPTER 10

WRITER IN THE SUN

B Y THE MID '90s I was on the Classic FM breakfast show, where one of the regular features was the Morning March. In fact the station trumpeted, 'The Pope is Catholic, Judith Chalmers has a passport, and just after 7.30 a.m. on Classic FM you can hear a good, rousing march.'

The Morning March had become one of the favourite features of the breakfast show, attracting an audience of devotees that included celebrities, journalists and even the odd MP. I thought it odd that no composer had ever written a tune called 'The Morning March', but maybe pre-prandial marching wasn't too popular. Jogging or walking alone is socially acceptable. Marching alone, with or without uniform, is considered weird and makes the watcher feel marginally uncomfortable. I had some workings for a march that I was going to use in the *Young Apollo* musical, so I suggested to the station that I might finish it and call it 'The Morning March'. They loved the idea, which led to HM Band of the Royal Marines, who'd played live at Classic FM, recording it. I journeyed to Portsmouth for the occasion, under the beckoning baton of Lieutenant Colonel Richard Waterer and the watchful eye of the arranger, Mike MacDermott. What a thrill it was to be later invited into Richard Waterer's box at the Royal Albert Hall to hear the Massed Bands of Her Majesty's Royal Marines play 'The Morning March' to a very responsive audience, for the Mountbatten Festival of Music 1998. Being on the same bill as Rossini, Delibes and Bach wasn't rock & roll, but I liked it.

It was an equally big thrill when the piece was included on Classic FM's successful *Morning March* CD, alongside works by Elgar, Prokofiev, Verdi, Strauss, Dvořák and Sibelius. A bonus came when it was also featured on a *Radio Times* classical CD and I found myself joining the ranks of Tchaikovsky, Rachmaninov, Rimsky-Korsakov and Bruch. It was definitely my 'Roll over Beethoven and tell Tchaikovsky the news' moment.

Let it not be said that I merely mingled and rubbed shoulders with the ghosts of the revered creatives of old; I also had the current crop in my sights. An old friend from Weybridge, Bob Grace, by then one of the country's leading publishers, suggested a writing session with Albert Hammond. It'd take a few pages to list all the great songs that Albert has written, although my favourite is '99 Miles from LA', and he did have a couple of classic hits of his own with 'Free Electric Band' and 'It Never Rains in Southern California', so I was delighted to have the opportunity to write with him. I arrived at his London flat in Holland Park, probably looking a little too eager and clutching my guitar case. I was tuned and ready to go – let's start writing those hits, Albert. But I sensed a lack of urgency from my co-writer as he flicked on the TV.

'Do you like football?'

'Absolutely.'

'Great. There's a match I want to watch.'

Ah well, that'll be a hitless hour and three quarters, then. We might have knocked off our first album in that time. My hopes rose again as the final whistle blew, but there was a further question. 'I'm really hungry, aren't you?'

I could be, I suppose. Off we trotted to Julie's Wine Bar, normally a favourite, but tonight a mild frustration. By something past midnight we were back outside Albert's place. Super chap, great supper, decent match, no songs. 'Well, goodnight.' I managed a weak smile, slightly embarrassed by the unused guitar that I had toted around all evening like an expectant child.

'Coffee, tea?'

Why not? Tea finished and the clock gathering pace towards sunrise, there was a third question. 'Got any ideas, then?' I think I beat the dawn home, but at least we'd written a song. 'The Power of Life' is parked on a shelf, and may not be the greatest song ever written, but it still stands up pretty well.

Some writers like to work together and kick ideas around while others work independently of each other, returning with their latest contribution as and when. The song I wrote with Andrew Lloyd Webber in the summer of 1997 was one of the latter. I was having lunch at Sydmonton to discuss something or other and after we'd watched Venus Williams doing amazing things with yellow balls at Wimbledon, Andrew mentioned a couple of songs he had that needed lyrics. If he sent me his rough instrumental could I have a go at some words? I could indeed. Nothing turned up for a couple of weeks so I assumed he'd forgotten. I was pottering around a local mill that had once been the home of the composer John Ireland, when, by interesting coincidence, Andrew called to say one of the tracks was in the post. With Peter Ainsworth, then an MP, I'd been suggesting turning the mill into a South Downs musical museum, for the likes of Ireland, Havergal Brian, Hubert Parry, William Blake and Edward Elgar. The excuse that was given for not being able to do it was that the surrounding area was landfill and therefore the ground (and the mill) could be unsafe, apart from any noxious gases that might emanate from the area. That, however, didn't affect the tune from ALW. I pounced on a good title almost immediately, 'No Smoke without Fire'. The lyric took shape, but I really needed to play with the tune and add a middle eight. I knew Andrew well enough to ask him if I could move his melody around where necessary and he readily and graciously agreed. I was definitely pleased with the result and did a pretty good demo, much in the style of UB40. Andrew loved it too, which was good news, and decided to have it performed at the next Sydmonton Festival, along with his workshop for *Whistle Down The Wind*. It went down very well and Andrew was confident that our song was going to be a huge hit. Any congratulations from those present that came my way were tempered by experience. Andrew was so busy that today's great idea might well slip down the chart of priority within a week or two, plunge even further after a month and then slide under the radar and off into the ether. I didn't want to be right, but I was.

Fast forward to the launch of Tim Rice's autobiography. After the event, Andrew and I headed back to his London house to watch an England match. It won't have escaped the more astute among you that there is a theme here, with songwriters inviting me round to watch football. The screen was so large that at times I felt that I was playing in midfield, especially after a glass or two from Andrew's cellar. After the game we listened to some Bollywood music of which he had become enamoured, before he treated me to some tunes on the piano from his forthcoming musical *The Beautiful Game*. Andrew is a great writer of melodies, no doubt about that.

A month or two later I had calls from a couple of friends, delighted that the song I had written with Andrew was in his new musical. Was it? No one told me. Someone played it to me. That was it, all right, with different and to my mind inferior lyrics (no offence to the hugely talented Ben Elton, whose name was on the credit) but the same re-structured melody. I mentioned it to Tim, who wasn't unduly surprised, and I wondered if Andrew would bring it up. He never has. I've seen him on many occasions since then, but not a squeak. My publisher suggested suing him. I laughed. Not that 'hollow, mocking laugh' used by crime writers to create an atmosphere, just a normal laugh with no hidden agenda. I wasn't going to go down that road, for several reasons: I've known Andrew for ever, he wouldn't have done it deliberately, it would cause a rift in an old friendship, it was only one song in a musical that wasn't one of his blockbusters, and frankly I didn't mind. The original 'No Smoke without Fire' still sounds good. When Andrew stages *Pyrotechny, The Musical*, the song will come into its own.

Like me, Andrew is a big Bobby Vee aficionado, Bobby having performed at various of his functions in the '90s, but the press jumped the gun rather by announcing that I planned a musical about the early '60s US heart-throb. They announced that Bobby would play himself in the show, but in reality it had got no further than drawing-board stage, with him and me kicking round a few ideas. The idea was for Bobby to have been the pivotal narrator with a young singer portraying him from the day he stepped in for Buddy Holly and through the '60s. Back when I bought his records, I never imagined I'd get to meet him, let alone to be able to call him a friend and that he would call me whenever he was in the UK. A lovely man, with a lovely family, though sadly he's not in the best of health now.

I'd also been a fan of Ricky Nelson's records. He sang in a range that was achievable by chaps such as myself, and had dozens of hits and a great image. He'd also been a child star on his parents' long-running TV and radio series across the States, *Ozzie and Harriet*. Tragically, he died in a plane crash on New Year's Eve 1985 when only in his mid-forties. The news came through on the car radio while driving back from a party with Janet Ellis, whom I went out with a few times. I was so shocked that I cried. She was probably shocked that I did. Later I began work on an idea for a stage musical on Ricky, using the title *Teenage Idol*. By 1995 *The Buddy Holly Story* was in its seventh year as a stage musical and had grossed an incredible £100 million worldwide, so there was clearly a market for shows like this. While the Bobby Vee one hadn't worked out, perhaps this one would. While I was working on it, Andrew Lloyd Webber, also a Ricky Nelson fan, said that he'd like to stage it at Sydmonton. Again, we had a lot of press coverage up front, including a double-page spread in the *Daily*

Express, where I gave my reasons for choosing this subject: 'The story has it all ... fame, success, glamour and tragedy. It's a gripping subject. In America, by the end of the '50s, not only young people adored him but their parents did as well.' It seemed reasonable. He was a pop star at seventeen and sold millions of records.

I took a gamble on the unknown Richard Sharp, then just twenty, in the lead role and Tony Rivers and his boys as the backing vocalists, also singing radio jingles. We rehearsed in Chelsea with director Nicola Treherne and got up to speed before heading off to Andrew's for the show. It was a busy weekend for me as the Sunday morning service at the local church (as part of the Sydmonton Festival) featured the choir performing my setting of Rupert Brooke's war sonnets. *Ricky Nelson – Teenage Idol* was well received by an audience that included Charlie and Martin Sheen, George Martin and Don Black. I'm sure it was daunting for Richard, who'd never acted before in his life, but he pulled it off and the piece was a success. As I've never been certain what to do with it after Sydmonton, that remains its only performance.

One musical play that didn't even make it to the stage was my adaptation of Alan Sillitoe's classic *Saturday Night and Sunday Morning*. I used music from the period and met with Alan, who liked the adaptation and gave me permission to go ahead. That was good news. More good news was that Bill Kenwright called, wanting to stage it. But back comes that old phrase, 'life is what happens to you while you're busy making other plans', and somehow it slipped away, despite me renewing the rights to stage it for several years. I did write a title song, with Chris Eaton, but despite being a strong song, that too remains on the shelf, hopefully waiting for its moment to shine. I'm convinced that 'shelf' will give way one day under the not inconsiderable strain.

I mentioned the Rupert Brooke sonnets as in 1996 there was action on the Rupert Brooke front. Imagining I'd need music for the film, I had set Brooke's five war sonnets to music. I'd written a film script and there was a heck of a lot of interest from production companies, with letters flying backwards and forwards and meetings galore.

Pleased with the result after a few months, I'd asked Ralph to work on the arrangements, which turned out splendidly. From there we played my demos to the head of music at King's College, Cambridge, Stephen Cleobury, who agreed that the King's College Choir could record them. I organised the recordings to be filmed, fondly imagining the choir to be dressed accordingly, looking angelic and with candles guttering to throw wild and fanciful shapes across the fan vaulting of King's College Chapel. I hadn't reckoned on casual dress – rock T-shirts, jeans and trainers – but we filmed everything anyway, including Stephen ticking off one lad whose shirt was hanging out. The cameras were still rolling as he reluctantly and sullenly made his way outside, only to re-appear with it tucked in in a token manner. Henry VI had first instigated a choir here in the mid-1400s a few years after what was initially known as Our College Royal of Nicholas opened its doors to scholars, and here we were more than 500 years later with microphones suspended at every angle. What would Henry (incidentally our youngest-ever king, at nine months) have made of that? Stephen Cleobury made me realise how lucky I was to be having my songs recorded here when he reminded me how much of the music sung in the chapel was by greats that had long departed such as Mozart, Bach, Tallis and Taverner. The Eton College Choir later performed the Brooke settings from the chapel for a BBC World Service programme, in which I was one of the readers of the secular and non-secular narrative linking the pieces.

In the mid '90s, Simon May had been commissioned to write the music for a new comedy film, *Caught in the Act*, and he asked me to come up with some ideas for a title track. I needed no second bidding and soon knocked up a demo that included a basic melody for Simon as a starting point. It failed to start, although listening to it years later, it's pretty damn good. As happens with films, the idea for a title was sidelined and instead there would be an opening operatic dream sequence. Fine, getting onside with a soupçon of W. S. Gilbert wouldn't be a problem. What was a problem, though, was this. They wanted the lyrics in Italian. 'Sorry,' said Simon, 'but that's what they want. I'll have to find an Italian lyricist.'

'I can do it.'

'I didn't know you could speak Italian.'

'You give me the tune and I'll give you a great Italian lyric.'

'If you're sure.'

I was sure. I didn't actually say that I spoke the language, simply that I was capable of writing the words. The nearest I got to speaking it was ordering a Four Seasons at Pizza Hut. Undeterred, I lashed out £6.99 on a Collins Italian dictionary and a few quid on a teach-yourself publication, *Beginners' Italian*. I made a list of all the words that might come in useful, familiarised myself with the way tenses were constructed and knuckled down to it. I decided that 'Ci vedi-amo' ('We'll Meet') might be a good title and that as the opening sequence was an over-the-top spoof that I could easily get away with a cheesy, over-the-top lyric. Bizarrely it flowed quite well, with lines like '*Nella luce della luna*' ('In the moonlight') and '*E in tutti il mondo | Tutte le stelle scintilleranno* ('And all over the world | All the stars will shine'). It was heady stuff, you must agree. Had I been born in Venice in 1823 I might have paddled the operatic gondola big-time. As it was, the opening sequence was shot in Wimbledon, with my moving lyric, '*Non vedo niente solo te*' ('I won't see anything but you'), ringing out across SW19. It sounded jolly clever in Italian. In English it would have sounded ghastly. Before submitting my lyric, I'd run the whole thing past an Italian acquaintance who pointed out certain errors that might lead to his country declaring war on me. The film won the Jury Award of Excellence at the Laguna Festival in the USA. Probably because of an all-star cast that included Lesley Phillips, Nadia Sawalha and Sarah Crowe, rather than my Italian lyric.

In 2000, I re-visited a musical show I'd previously put together featuring music and news through the centuries, *Journey through Music*, to raise funds for a new clock in Pulborough village close to where I was living. We bounded like eager musical puppies through the centuries, playing a variety of instruments usual and unusual, and extolling the virtues of folk, blues, jazz, skiffle, pop and the like. It's only clock & roll but we love it.

Another show I regularly compered and often sang at was *Songs from the Shows*, organised by the aforementioned Michael ('Your Majesty') Reed and staged in his rolling acres in the shadow of his historic mansion Prince Hill House. I was normally consigned to some fun song from the West End, but I once got to read a serious piece, in the form of Rupert Brooke's 'The Soldier'. In World War One uniform I strode purposefully out to centre stage. Move over, Sir Larry. But I was baffled at the audience's response to my incredibly moving declamation of Brooke's classic poem. They were laughing. I mean really laughing. Many couldn't contain themselves. Tears of mirth fell from their eyes, as did the scales from mine, eventually. Other things nearly fell as well. In my rush to change, I'd forgotten to do up the buttons on my trousers and a piece of shirt was sticking through the large gap. The seriousness of the poem made it all the more hilarious for the crowd. I even had my own room at Prince Hill House as a host of folk stayed on the show weekends. After one spectacularly late night, I stirred at some unearthly hour as the grey fingers of dawn were afoot. (Mixed metaphor intended.) Was that a figure squatting at the end of my bed? It was. Were they naked? They appeared to be. I might not have been fully *compos mentis* but it was definitely female. And ... oh no ... going to the toilet.

'Stop ... don't do it ... not here.'

'But answer came there none.'

She squatted, soaked the carpet and was gone. Like a relief in the night.

For one of the shows (with trousers securely fastened) Michael and I wrote a millennium hymn, '2,000 Years', which was performed brilliantly by the local choir, and also another Italian song emerged. I used the same trick – *non c'è problema*. I was becoming an old hand now. This time I checked my past participles and adjectival agreements with a waitress in an Italian restaurant in Devizes, as you do. The song, 'È stato amore' (delicious with a glass of Perrier-Jouet), along with 'Ci vediamo' (on or off the bone), could become the foundation for my first Italian album. No, wait! There's a third I'd completely forgotten about. When we had the group Amber on the go, way back when, Dave, our drummer, and Martin, our bass player, had this wheeze that it might be easy to get a recording deal in Italy. Not only did they have a contact there, but Martin's father was a director of KLM Airlines, which enabled them to procure a couple of very cheap flights. They said that songs with English lyrics were perfectly acceptable, but it might be the icing on the cake if we had one in Italian. I don't remember forgoing food to buy an Italian dictionary back then, and there was no internet, so I have no idea how I managed it. Their destination was Milan, so I wrote a song with a title that might impress, which when translated meant 'People of Milan, we love you'. I didn't know the inhabitants of the city, nor was I cognizant of their behaviour, but suddenly I felt close to them. I'm not even sure of the spelling now, but it phonetically it was something like 'Milanese noi amore, Milanese noi amore, noi piacca on y giorno, tutta cosa da qui et buono' and so on. Heaven knows what it meant after we got past the title, but with a little brushing up, a following wind and the English-Italian dictionary it could be the third track on my ever-growing Italian CD. Of course we didn't get a deal from the Milan record company, who obviously saw through my rather thin and weedy plan, but the guys did come back with a case full of free airport sugar and condiments, so it wasn't a complete waste of time.

In the mid to late '90s I began to write the songs that would become the second Betjeman album. There was no real plan or sense of purpose, they simply started emerging and were written on a beaten-up guitar, lying around at Alison's flat, that wouldn't even tune up properly. It's odd that I used a severely impaired instrument when I had plenty of good ones, but that's how it goes sometimes. It's not the guitar, it's what's inside your head that's important, and indeed whether you can extract it to satisfaction. I was introduced to producer Jon Sweet, who got what I was doing straight away, so it seemed natural for him to work with me on the album. Most of the demos were done in his studio at Yeovil and there was a feeling that something really creative was happening. There was a vibe, as they say in more cosmic moments.

Again, as we were working we talked about who could sing certain tracks, but as with the first album I'd only approach an artist if I felt that the song was absolutely right for them. The power and pace of 'Narcissus' seemed ideal for Marc Almond and to my delight he delivered a really dramatic and highly polished performance. Colin Blunstone bravely took on two songs, 'In Memory' and 'Peggy', and was sensitive and unique as always, while the late Paul Young, of Sad Café and Mike and the Mechanics fame, was equally superb on 'Greenaway'. Leo Sayer rushed into the studio having hardly had time to listen to his song properly, but pulled out the stops to sing in a very different style for him, amid trumpets and Spanish guitars. Richard Sharp (who you'll recall from *Ricky Nelson – Teenage Idol*), still relatively unknown, really delivered on the Byrds-esque 'Pershore Station'.

The melody for Cliff's song, 'November Night', I wrote at Jon Sweet's house on the morning of the funeral of the Princess of Wales. I woke while it was still dark and felt this compulsion to get up and write. By the time Jon emerged I'd completed it. I played it to him and he agreed that it was right up Cliff's street. He was an ideal judge, having written 'Ocean Deep', one of Cliff's most enduring songs. Cliff got into the spirit of it and we shot a moody-ish video for it at a church at Bakewell in Derbyshire followed by a slap-up tea with what we were told were Bakewell puddings, not Bakewell tarts. It was worth going, for that knowledge alone.

The album also included another version of 'Myfanwy', this time sung by Gene Pitney, and again we did a video for it. It was meant to be set on the Cherwell at Oxford, but due to Gene's commitments, we had to make it on the Granta at Grantchester. Thanks to my friend Robin Callan I was able to use the Orchard Tea Garden, bag a punt and shoot on that section of the river. Here was the guy who'd had hits with 'Twenty-Four Hours from Tulsa' and 'Something's Gotten Hold of My Heart' singing in the garden where Philby, Burgess and Maclean had plotted over tea, where Virginia Woolf, Henry James, Lytton Strachey and Rupert Brooke discussed literature and where Wittgenstein and Russell wrestled with the problems of the day. Another moment to add to the tableau of the Orchard's rich history.

Gene had recorded the vocal in the States, calling me up every twenty minutes so that he could get his head around Betjeman words that belonged to a time long gone. Much of the lyric would have baffled many Englishmen, let alone a boy from Connecticut. I explained more lines with every call. What a professional: not for him just singing them, he needed to understand them. At last he felt that he'd cottoned on to '20s Oxford-speak. 'Hey Mike, I got one. I worked it out. You ready?

I was indeed, ready.

'The line "Tom and his 101 at nine".'

'Yes?'

'It's a cricket score, right?'

I had to disappoint him. I felt bad. He'd been so sure of it. I guess I could have pretended, but that's not my way. 'Sorry, Gene, it's not.'

'I was so certain. What the heck is it then?'

'Well, the Tom in the poem is Great Tom in St Aldate's in Oxford, which is the main entrance to Christ Church. The bell is rung 101 times for the 100 original scholars at the college, plus one, which was added in 1663. It's rung at five past nine every night, corresponding with what was nine o'clock in old Oxford time.'

'You sure it's not a cricket score?'

Another wonderful singer taken far too soon.

One of the most atmospheric tracks on the album turned out to be 'Youth and Age'. We pitched the demo very high as I felt that's where it should be, so my thoughts strayed to counter-tenors and one of the finest at the time in my book, Andreas Scholl. The young German singer had recorded a stunning version of the old ballad 'Barbara Allen', which I'd been playing a lot on the Classic FM breakfast show. I then decided that a classically trained singer might make it too rigid, but how many pop singers had a voice in that range? I didn't exactly smite my head with the palm of my hand Homer Simpson style and shout 'D'oh!', but suddenly I knew exactly who I wanted. I'd always loved Yes and the unique voice of their singer, Jon Anderson. I was given an address in the States for Jon and duly, with little hope to be honest, sent him a demo of the track. A week or two later a note from Jon snaked out of my fax machine (what sweet old-fashioned things they seem now) saying that he loved the song and would record it next time he was in England. That time came round and he arrived at the studio, full of apologies that he wouldn't be able to sing it as the key was too high, but if I lowered it he'd come back next week and do it. I wasn't going to let him go. He might not come back. I thought with the speed of a good guy in a radio serial trussed up by the villain with little chance of escape. 'It would help…' I began, not exactly sure where I was going. 'It would help … if … you … er … that is, it'd help me … if … er, you could possibly … just go through the vocal in the current key so that I can see how much I need to lower it.' Genius. We ran through it once, the key was perfect and Jon sounded fantastic. He surely couldn't have doubted himself.

Jon Sweet thought we should get his vocal down quickly in case there was some sort of problem we didn't know about. The purity of his tone gave us goose-bumps. I heard what was needed. 'We must get him to do a trademark three-part harmony in the B section.'

'No, we'll put that on later.'

'It won't sound the same. Jon harmonising with himself will have a magic we won't be able to get.'

'Best not to ask him, it might be pushing him too far.'

I was about to ask anyway and pressed the talkback button to speak to him, but he got in first. 'Mike, I think it'd sound good if I did a three-part harmony in the B section.'

Another result, especially as 'Survival' by Yes, with Jon on vocals of course, is my all-time favourite song.

I was very surprised that Don McLean agreed to sing one of the songs on the album. His own songs were of such a high standard that he rarely recorded other people's numbers, but he was up for it and I was delighted. We had to fit in with his UK tour schedule which meant taking the Stones Mobile to Liverpool. Don's agent, Malcolm Feld, did warn me that Don was very much his own man and we might or might not get a recording from him that day. The latter began to look very much more likely. He didn't appear to be leaving his hotel. Apparently he was watching TV.

'What do we do?'

'You could call him,' said Malcolm, with some hesitation.

I tried to interpret the hesitation part. Then I called Don. 'Hi Don, How's it going?'

'Hi Mike, yeah, good, just hanging out looking at some TV.'

Had he forgotten? Had he changed his mind? Maybe he just wasn't in the mood.

'Nothing much on in the afternoon, Don.'

It wasn't a lie: even fifteen years back, there wasn't the choice there is now.

'No kidding? What kinda stuff do they show?'

'Oh, children's shows, cartoons for the very young and probably a chunk of horseracing from some distant course like Kelso.'

'That doesn't sound too good. What else is happening?'

'Well, we've got the Rolling Stones Mobile here, we could always record that song you wanted to do, "Farewell". Better than being influenced by sub-standard TV.'

'Too right. I'm on my way.'

Don treated the song as if it were his own. He made it appear effortless. And to think we nearly lost him to the 3.30 maiden handicap at Kelso. It doesn't bear thinking about.

The remaining song, 'Distant View', I ended up singing by default, as we couldn't find a singer that really fitted it. I think I got away with it.

This second album faced an early and enormous hurdle, unwittingly brought about by the second Betjeman charity evening, in aid of the Children with Leukaemia Trust (see Chapter 9). I'd already had one or two very pleasant meetings with Betjeman's agent, Desmond Elliott, over tea at Fortnum and Mason at which I kept him abreast of the album's progress. We would discuss his early connection with Tim Rice and Andrew Lloyd Webber and their first attempt at a musical with *The Likes of Us*, nibble on a few splendid gateaux, and get outside several pots of Earl Grey. OK so far, but the invitations to the charity evening went out while I was away at a tennis centre for a few days and by a complete oversight Desmond failed to receive his. When I returned from pounding tennis balls for a few hours a day I was too busy with the show to check that everybody had received their invitations. We'd got the great news that some twenty radio stations would be featuring the album and that many of those had even made it album of the week. Everyone involved felt that this was going to be a major success. Then the sky fell in. Desmond Elliott had stopped the album he'd been so keen on a week or two earlier dead in its tracks. My baffled and bemused solicitor was contacted and the project slithered to a halt. Toys were not only thrown out of the pram, they were thrown in my direction. At first he refused to take my calls, despite an apology for the oversight with regard to his invitation. When I did speak to him, he was sharp and bad tempered, insisting that I should stop calling him Desmond and refer to him in the future as 'Mr Elliott'.

I wanted the album out, but I sure as hell wasn't going to grovel. If a man can't accept an honest apology in good faith he's not much of a man in my book. His unreasonable and intransigent stance made the release of the album impossible at that time, despite a year's hard

work, creativity, time, money and an opportunity for John Betjeman's wonderful poems to reach younger generations. By the time
the album was released, much later, the momentum had been lost. I
feel I should balance my opinion by stating that he was very highly
thought of in the industry but we can't all see eye to eye.

From poetic rock I lurched headily again into clergy rock as my
musical settings of Rupert Brooke's war sonnets were featured along
with Elgar, Parry and Betjeman during an Armistice evening at the
church of St Andrew and St Mary in Grantchester. Never commer-
cially released, they've certainly had live airings from four or five choirs.

In 2002 I worked with five really talented Russian girls, two of
whom were gifted classical pianists. They were here doing some shows
and recorded three of my songs, 'City to City', 'Moscow Nights' and
'The House of Usher'. Great tracks but as they weren't in the UK per-
manently it was tricky to know what to do with both the songs and
the girls. I recorded them under the name of Russia, with the 'R'
turned backwards. I guess I must have misguidedly thought that it
looked vaguely Russian. It did to me, but probably not to Russians.
They performed at both of Cliff Richard's Christmas shows that year,
the Tennis Foundation dinner at Hampton Court and the big bash
with tennis and music at the Indoor Arena at Birmingham.

Early in 2004, while still languishing in Australia following *I'm
a Celebrity* and enjoying summer barbecues at Peter Andre's family home, I thought it might be an idea to record something with a
jungle feel. I didn't recall anything similar from previous series and
wondered why no one had thought of it. Now when you're watching
I'm a Celebrity from the relative safety of your sofa, it's not uncom-
mon for the sound to be muted and an apology to slide along the
bottom of the screen. 'Smut,' you might think, 'scandal.' There is
clearly a dark, unfathomable reason why this deeply personal conversation is not fit for transmission. Not so, say I. It's usually because
the happy campers have launched into a campfire sing-song and no
one wants to pay for the right to broadcast the music. Simple as that.

It was during these quiet moments that Razor Ruddock would trawl the Gilbert O'Sullivan songbook and treat us to his gruff but passable bass rendition of something like 'Alone Again'. This was a man who'd accidentally floored the odd referee and broken the occasional leg... Who was I to argue with his impeccable taste? One of Razor's ambitions was to be on *Top of the Pops*, and Charlie Brocket concurred, with something along the lines of 'I say, what a spiffing idea.' How could I deny my two new acquaintances?

The idea didn't exactly come to me in the Versace Hotel bathtub, but I seem to remember that I was within feet of it, which almost makes it a 'Eureka' moment. Hank Mizell's 'Jungle Rock!' I could re-write the lyric to include a bunch of indigenous Australian animals and do a deal with a record label. I was sure they'd bite (a record company, that is, not the animals). I called Woolworths (and no, it wasn't our fault they went under) and they went for it, with the promise of a follow-up. I found a studio, got the track down and the song was ready for release by the time we touched down in Blighty, with our version of 'The Lion Sleeps Tonight' as a second track and the *I'm a Celebrity* theme as a third. Top value! When we first performed it on *This Morning*, Peter Andre was part of the gang, but his label also planned a release so he had to put all his marketing and PR into that.

We got plenty of TV, including a morning show that Terry Wogan was presenting and *Top of the Pops*, and a bucketload of radio plays. Our studio performance for *This Morning* was brilliantly edited into a video for the single, complete with odd creatures ... yes, and animals from the jungle. I took to the road doing signing sessions, being joined at some by Charlie. We were delighted when it made the top thirty and I was able to inform Charlie that he was now the second most successful peer of the realm in the history of the singles chart, sandwiched between (Lord) David Dundas and Spinal Tap's Nigel Tufnel, Christopher Guest (Baron Haden-Guest). The single loitered on the listings for a heady five weeks, before sliding off to the great archive in the ether.

We performed at various charity events, including the Chase Children's Hospice, CLIC Sergeant Cancer Charity and the Cliff Richard Tennis Foundation. We also performed at the Roy Castle Foundation Dinner in London, where, much to the delight of Razor, Cliff joined us on stage for the performance, while former jungle boy Uri Geller swelled our ranks for yet another charity gig. Of course Uri played spoons, promising to bend them at the end of the song and also to break one of my guitar strings simply by staring at it. On cue, the spoons bent and the string broke.

For the follow-up we recorded our version of Mungo Jerry's 'In the Summertime'. No new lyrics needed here, apart from amending the line, 'Have a drink, have a drive' and changing 'We're not dirty people' to 'We are jungle people'. OK, it may not be Byron or Keats, but it worked. We had a riot making the video at Brighton (see YouTube to gauge levels of riotousness) and the CD slipped into the chart at number seventy-two. It slipped out again the following week. At least it charted, gave us a second hit, pushed the Jungle Boys' number of weeks on chart up to six and gave the song its first appearance on the chart since 1970. It also appeared briefly in the ringtone top twenty. Listen, all charts count, trust me. There was no third single. Jungle Boy mania, if it ever existed outside our own minds, was over. The screams subsided and lovers of good music were blissfully unaware of the group's passing.

In the spring of 2004 I appeared in a short run of the stage musical *American Patrol*, alongside John Altman as Glenn Miller, but of course wrote none of the music. Later that year I found myself directing, rather than writing, a stage musical. I'd been asked by Mike Bennett, one-time member of the Fall and a damned fine actor, if I'd take the wheel of his satirical musical play, *White Wedding*, a look back at the '80s. It was certainly different and received many plaudits, *Blues & Soul* magazine calling it 'a comic triumph!' Thank goodness it was *meant* to be funny. I wasn't absolutely sure that I understood it, despite getting good reviews, including plaudits from, of all periodicals, *Lloyd's*

List: 'More power to the elbow of such companies when they allow full rein to the skills of directors like the prolific Mike Read.' 'Mr Newsagent,' I said, marching into my local shop, 'add *Lloyd's List* to my regular order as well as the *Beano*. It's a ripping good read.'

In 2003 I teamed up with my pal Trevor Payne, the singer/director behind the phenomenally successful show *That'll Be the Day*, to put together a musical on Cliff Richard. It would feature a wagonload of hits woven together by a fictional story. In this case the storyline was based around the eve of Cliff's eightieth birthday, as he and his butler, (Bruce) Welch, plan the festivities and go through a list of songs for possible inclusion in the celebrations. As Cliff muses over various highlights of his long career, the story goes back in time to include scenes from *Summer Holiday*, *Oh Boy!*, Eurovision, *Blind Date*, *Sunday Night at the London Palladium*, Wimbledon and more. The action, apart from the retrospective scenes, took place at Cliff's residence, the Keith Richards Health Farm.

We featured four Cliffs with me playing Lord Cliff, initially in a platinum wig, until the heat forced the producers to march me to the hairdressers to have dozens of streaks put into my own hair. We did a lot of TV, radio and press, but even more rehearsing, under the eagle eye of Trevor Payne and the pitch-perfect ear of our musical director, Steve Etherington. The dancing was the worst. I've never been a natural dancer. I've not even been an unnatural dancer. It took weeks of gruelling, cruel and agonising dance routines until I could get away with it.

I'd had plenty of amateur dramatic experience as a kid with audiences that were not too discerning as they comprised friends, relatives, schoolmates, local burghers and those enforced by a three-line whip or press gang. We'd generally be playing to about sixty-seven people and a few rows of empty chairs. We'll find our way back to Cliff the Musical in a moment. Even while at Radio One and Classic FM, I was still treading the odd board. I once played Pharaoh in a production of *Joseph* at Dauntsey's School in Wiltshire, dressed in giant blue suede shoes, an unfeasibly large fake quiff, a drape jacket and other extraordinary garb. Despite being in this insane outfit I was still working while not on stage. During rehearsals I dodged off to interview legendary rock & roll songwriters Doc Pomus and Mort Shuman down the line. With Potiphar and co. bashing out a song over and over again, the quietest spot I could find was in the middle of the cricket square. Trying to conduct a sensible interview with a 2-foot plastic quiff dangling in front of you and 2-foot-long clown shoes making you look incredibly foolish was pretty tricky. The weird thing was that Pharaoh was based on Elvis and here was I as Pharaoh, talking to two guys who'd written countless classics for the King. Cliff also recorded some of their songs and my next stage appearance would be *Cliff the Musical* playing to theatres that could hold 1,000 or 1,500, and those that turned up would have forked out serious money.

We did our press/dress opening night at Blackpool Opera House. Now that place was cavernous and could seat almost 3,000 happy holidaymakers. The history of the place was daunting. This stage had been graced by the likes of George Formby, Arthur Askey, Morecambe & Wise and the Beatles. As I stood in the wings trying to give an impression of a relaxed thespian, for this was only the dress run and surely just a handful would turn up, Colin, one of the show's producers sidled up and whispered, 'About a thousand in already.' Thanks, Colin. Five minutes later he was back. 'Well over a thousand now.' Stop it, Colin. He's clearly on a roll. 'Quite a few famous faces in.' Colin, this may get physical. He can't keep away now. 'Shane Richie and his family are in.' At that moment, the stage manager announced 'Curtain up in five minutes' and bloodshed was narrowly avoided.

I was nervous but there were no hitches and I got away with it. We moved on to play a week at the Liverpool Empire. More history. More to live up to. More stars from yesteryear who've trodden these boards: not surprisingly George Formby and the Beatles again, but also Frank Sinatra, Judy Garland, Laurel & Hardy and even Roy Rogers & Trigger. I knew I wasn't yet on top of the part – if only a small amount of their confidence lurked in the drapes, footlights and dressing room I'd be fine. Maybe it did. After two or three performances I settled into the role and began to feel comfortable. I reasoned that most people had come, not to be critical, but for a fun night out. I also realised that sometimes even the costumes were getting a laugh, so I let the part breathe. There was no rush to deliver the lines if they were chortling at my blue velvet Eurovision suit with the white ruffled shirt. I started adding lines. All my radio work was ad-libbed and that's what the audience were used to, so why not? I let them laugh at the suit for a few seconds and then came out with a random one-liner. 'I think you'll find it's called fashion', 'We even have one in your size, sir' or 'What's funny ... is it the wrong colour?' Not side-splitting stuff I grant you, but right for the occasion.

We marched around the country, taking in places like the cavernous Sunderland Empire, Manchester Opera House and the Derby Playhouse. We could have kept touring the show year in, year out, but the producers, and I guess the cast to an extent, were wooed by the prospect of a West End run. The Prince of Wales was due for refurbishment, but there was a three-month period free prior to that. The deal was done and initial ticket sales were excellent. Then two things happened. The congestion charge was announced, with the prophets of doom predicting that it would herald the death of the West End, and there was an escalating terrorist situation with the media reporting expected attacks on London. The capital was so empty at times that you could have roller-skated down Piccadilly. Well, you could if you had roller skates. I remember signing programmes after the show and ladies saying things like 'My husband was so worried about me coming to London with all the bomb threats'. Those two factors seriously affected our ticket sales and the producers panicked. We had the option of going to another London theatre at the end of the run, but they decided against it. As people got used to the congestion charge and the threat of terrorism diminished, sales picked up again, but it was too late to find another theatre and the Prince of Wales closed for refurbishment.

In the provinces we got good press. In London we got mixed reviews. The piece, however, was written and tailored to suit the audiences, not the critics. The *Evening Standard* devoted the whole of page three to the show, saying that it was OK if you were the sort of person who liked a cup of hot chocolate and a biscuit before you retired early. It was meant to be a barbed comment but actually hit the nail on the head. We were catering for a specific audience. If it had been sharp and edgy and had made the public feel uncomfortable, we would have been aiming at the wrong demographic. In fact we had it right. The *Daily Mirror* let its hair down, the banner headline proclaiming, 'Effervescent, irresistible and sure to be a success. Sod it, this is FUN.' The *Daily Express* was also jolly decent: 'The show is a total hoot. The music sounds great, the girls are gorgeous and a superb band doubles for the Shadows … it's Cliff-tastic.' Quite.

The writers of a show normally get paid their percentage at the end of the week, but I was asked if I minded getting it in one lump at the end. Actually that quite suited me. I was getting paid as an actor, so that would be a lovely bonus at the end of the run. I didn't get it. On several occasions I sat in the office of one of the producers, who was spending a fortune on other things, and politely asked for my money. I heard a heck of a lot of lame excuses, but learned a sharp lesson. Take the money when they need you, because you stand less chance of getting it when they don't. I've always called it the 'pied piper' syndrome, you know, where the mayor of Hamelin promises the piper 1,000 guilders to rid the town of rats. After the job's done, the mayor has no more use for the piper and tries to fob him off with a derisory fifty guilders. You know the rest of the story, but I had nothing to bargain with, nor power to wield. In the end I let it go as it's a small industry, but I haven't forgotten. Every now and again, producers and backers show an interest in getting the Cliff musical back on the road, so who knows.

Just about here I had another bad car smash. I was en route to see a friend for lunch, when a Polish lorry driver nodded off at the wheel.

The M3 was pretty busy, with those on the inside and middle lanes doing 70 mph and those on the outside lane a tad more. I could see the great truck veering towards me, but with continuous traffic on my right I had nowhere to go. He smacked me amidships and spun me in front of him. I found myself travelling sideways at high speed, wrestling with the wheel. If I hadn't been in a Porsche with a low centre of gravity my vehicle would have rolled. No question of that. All four tyres actually wore right through crossways. I kept thinking 'He must have seen me,' but he was so high up and possibly not even awake, so I don't think he did. I had a damn good close-up of his grill for a few hundred feet … and then he came again, crushing the passenger side and inching towards my side. Eventually the madness stopped. The M3 ground to a halt. Amazingly, I stepped out of my car completely unscathed. A fellow motorist ran up and said, 'You drove your way out of certain death.' Instinct, I guess. I was bloody determined not to die. I was standing on the grass verge when the police arrived. The sergeant's first words were, 'You were bloody unlucky in the jungle.'

'Luckier here, though.' I'm glad it was that way round.

That evening I was giving a talk at the English Speaking Union. I'm sure many speakers' opening gambit involves something along the lines of 'I'm delighted to be here' and 'It's good to see you all.' Never had the lines been more apposite.

My girlfriend Eileen Johnston and I had been spending Christmas 2004 with my friends Ros and Paul in Sussex with the usual bouts of banter, Monopoly, tennis and a few other seasonal pursuits. I knew them well enough to have rapped their wedding speech in a near-the-knuckle style wearing an inappropriate wig and to have been unceremoniously dragged feet first from their house and dumped in the drive when they considered I'd overstayed my welcome. Anyway our festivities hit the buffers on Boxing Day when the images of the Indian Ocean tsunami first flashed up on the TV screen. They had friends out there and had not long returned themselves – there but for the grace of God etc. There was talk from the news reporters that these wounds and memories would take a long time to heal, if ever, and they spoke of the grief of those who'd lost relatives and friends. The following day it dawned on me that a song I'd written, 'Grief Never Grows Old', echoed the emotions and pain I'd subsequently heard from people interviewed on the television. I wondered whether it might be put to some use with regard to this situation and the subsequent devastation that was unfolding before us by the hour.

The Disasters Emergency Committee welcomed the idea of releasing the song. I did point out that it might well raise an irrelevant amount compared to the tens of millions pledged by countries like the United States. They countered with the fact that the record, especially if I had major names on board, would create profile and awareness, so it wasn't necessarily about the money. It was also mentioned that pledges didn't always materialise, as new needs and events often overtook and superseded the previous crisis. Their third point was that within a month the media would have left and the focus would have shifted elsewhere. The news crews would only stay for a finite period, but a suitably apposite song would hopefully keep the needs of the stricken communities in people's minds.

I headed to a café on the seafront at Worthing, armed with my mobile, pen, notepad and a hell of a lot of determination. I wanted real singers. Singers that were instantly recognised. Cliff Richard had just gone to his house in Barbados, having completed a tour and overstretched his voice. Only a week earlier he told me that he was looking forward to relaxing and not singing a note for some while. Because of that I was slightly reluctant to ask him to participate. Five minutes and one positive phone call later I had my first singer. No hesitation. He was happy to do his bit for those less fortunate. What a trooper. Fortified by his response, another tea and more toast, I ploughed on. Robin Gibb, the most generous of souls when it came to helping others, also committed *instanter*. Then his brother Barry came on board. Within a couple of days I had a pretty unbeatable list of singers, including Boy George, Russell Watson and Jon Anderson, with

253

members of America, the Beach Boys and Celine Cherry from the Honeyz agreeing to do the backing vocals. Brian Wilson then agreed to join the line-up. Things were moving. Sky News had me on talking about the project and even played my demo.

The following day I was on a mission for top musicians who were on a par with our vocalists. I called Bill Wyman. His immediate response was, 'When do you want me?' He'd seen the piece on Sky and knew exactly why I was calling. Rick Wakeman, the only keyboard player with four arms and four hands, agreed, even though he normally steered clear of charity records, and producer Steve Levine, who'd also been heavily on the case, brought in Gary Moore on lead guitar. Kenney Jones agreed to provide any percussion that was needed. There was no getting away from it, they were a quartet you couldn't buy. Just before we started recording I had a call from Steve Winwood asking if he could contribute. Are you joking? Yes please! What a lovely gesture. Steve Levine's studio in south-west London was buzzing as singers and musicians milled around and did interviews with various TV crews while waiting to record. Calmly and with technical precision, Steve oversaw recording artists like Cliff, Boy George, Barry Gibb, Jon Anderson and the backing vocals from assorted members of The Beach Boys and America live from different parts of the United States, sometimes conversing with them via Skype.

The Sky news piece had caused a bit of a stir in Sri Lanka, which led to the most fantastic group of young female singers from that country, Soul Sounds, and their musical director, Soundarie David, contacting me to ask if they could participate. All the vocal parts were spoken for, but I asked them if they'd like to record their own version which we could use as a bonus track on the CD. Thankfully they agreed and recorded a very different but equally moving version.

The National Children's Orchestra of Great Britain were also keen to be involved and although I wasn't quite sure how they'd fit in, I instinctively felt that it would be right to include them in the project. Again, I suggested that they might like to record an orchestral stand-alone version. I was delighted that their musical director, Roger Clarkson, was keen on the idea, but wondered how to go about finding a suitable studio. 'Aim high,' I thought, so I talked Abbey Road into letting me have the studio for nothing. They couldn't have been more helpful. Only by actually watching the video would anyone know that it was a children's orchestra. It could have been the RPO or the LSO. They were fabulous.

I called the boss of Universal, who was holidaying in Barbados, persuaded him to release the record and then set about purloining tsunami footage for a video. I made my presence felt at Sky, ITV and the BBC until I had several hours of visuals. Working through the images with Robert Garafalo at Classic Pictures, Shepperton Studios, I found much harrowing material that was far too disturbing for a video so I had to be judicious and cautious. We intercut and dissolved the footage with the artists, as tastefully as possible, weaving our way through the appropriate and inappropriate news items, some of which hadn't even made it to the TV screens. For the front cover I had no hesitation in selecting a photograph taken two weeks after the disaster of a man clinging to the remains of a coconut tree in the middle of the ocean. He later revealed that one by one his family and friends had weakened and slid away into the water. Against all odds he survived and against all odds he was rescued, a tiny dot in a vast ocean.

Just as we were beginning our press campaign, Sharon Osbourne announced that she was organising something similar. Names like Eric Clapton and Elton John were bandied about. I spoke with Sharon on the phone and agreed that anything that helped or raised awareness could only be positive, but proposed that she might hold their release back for a week or two, which she graciously consented to do. The press suggested that maybe people should wait for that CD, as the song that they intended to release was a version of Clapton's 'Tears in Heaven'. A great song, there's no denying. There's no question that it diluted our sales, especially as the other single never happened. No recording, no Elton, no Eric, no release.

I gave the artists on our record the collective name of One World Project. Heaven knows why, as I've never been too keen on the word 'project' when applied to music. It sounds a little pretentious. Even so, the media were talking of it being a possible number one. It was just about the time of the thousandth UK number one, so we were in with an outside chance of making history as well as raising the profile of the cause. In the end, that accolade went to Elvis Presley, although Woolworths had our single at number one above Elvis on their in-store chart. Robin Gibb and I did a signing session at HMV and the buzz was good. I even found myself back at TV Centre presenting *Top of the Pops*, alongside groups including McFly, introducing the section of the show that featured the video for 'Grief Never Grows Old'. It had been a while since I'd done it, but it felt very natural although unexpected.

On 5 February 2005, the single went straight to number one in the Independent Singles Chart and straight in at number four in the National Singles Chart. A great result – we may not have made the thousandth number one, but who could deny Elvis that position (with a re-release of one of his finest hits, 'It's Now or Never')? Within an hour of the chart being announced, I had calls of 'condolence' from the press. 'Wasn't it a pity that it failed to get to number one ... You must be distraught ... Do you I feel deflated?' No I bloody well didn't. I was delighted on every level. We'd made a great record, the Disasters Emergency Committee were happy, it was helping to raise awareness and we were sitting up at the top of the chart with Elvis Presley. I projected myself back yet again to being a kid and never daring to imagine that I'd learn to play the guitar, let alone write songs or make a record. Being in the chart was unthinkable. Being in the chart with Elvis was as likely as a day trip around Venus.

Jon Christos later recorded a version for an album. He played it to his mother but she felt it was too sad, so it was rejected. It has been used at many funerals down the years, so I hope that it may have brought a little comfort to those who were left behind. A couple of years ago Geno Washington put down a great blues version of the song, with Clive Carroll on guitar and Paul Jones on harmonica. Geno is without question one of our greatest soul and blues singers, but he knew the way that he'd recorded it wasn't exactly how I'd envisaged it. Crazy and hilarious he may be, but he's a consummate professional and insisted on doing it again. 'How do you want me to sing it?' he asked.

'Listen,' I said, 'imagine it's 1927, you've sold your soul to the devil at the crossroads, your wife's left you and you've got outside of a couple of bottles of hooch.'

He became animated. 'I gotcha, I gotcha, yeah, I know where you're coming from.' He dissolved into his trademark manic laugh and then nailed the track in one. Wow.

I've been moved by many people affected by the disaster who've said that they felt 'Grief Never Grows Old' was so appropriate. Some 170,000 lost their lives and more than 130,000 are still missing, the tsunami and preceding earthquake having brought devastation to ten countries. I spoke to one couple who'd been drinking coffee in a hotel lounge one moment and the next became creatures in a vast aquarium. They subsequently lost each other for several days. Apart from the guy who I featured on the front of the CD and DVD, possibly the most extraordinary tale to emerge was that of an eight-year-old girl who was swept away, only to turn up seven years later.

In 2006 a Japanese label released a limited-edition CD featuring twenty-four songs from my catalogue, including several singles and some unreleased material. They sold all 1,000 copies pretty swiftly. 'Big in Japan', eh? That's what they all say. I was small in Japan, but at least I was there. The Angel Air label picked the album up for the UK and also re-issued my two Betjeman albums as *Mike Read & Sir John Betjeman: The Sound of Poetry*. After the Japanese tsunami in March 2011, images uploaded onto YouTube were accompanied by 'Grief Never Grows Old'.

It wasn't all work, by the way. There were a couple of trips to

Venice with Eileen, for friends' birthdays and the like. It certainly lived up to my expectations, with its singing gondoliers, maze of waterways and incredible architecture. The highlight of one visit was an extravagant masked ball, which could have taken place centuries earlier. What an atmosphere. We also dashed up to the island of Bute to take in the Highland games at Rothesay, my first Highland games. I learned that it's not how far you toss the caber, but how straight it lies having gone over once. The nearer the twelve o'clock position the better. (Make up your own jokes here.)

In 2003, I had a call asking me if I'd be interested in writing the book for a musical based around the music of the Village People. It's never wise to say yes to anything and everything, but I'd always liked the theatricality of the group and their songs and duly scooted off to Paris for a *tête-à-tête* with their producer and co-writer, Henri Belolo. We got on well. I threw a few ideas at him, he threw a few back at me and after a rather robust *déjeuner*, I Eurostarred myself back to London bursting with creativity. I was going to enjoy this. 'In the Navy' became a major dance number featuring the waltz, tango and cha-cha, while 'YMCA' was sung classically as well as in the style that we know and love and to which we do misspelled hand movements. Of course 'Go West', 'San Francisco' and 'Macho Man' were in the mix, as was a humorously staged version of 'Sex over the Phone'. The storyline worked really well, but I needed a song about the New York police that reflected 'YMCA'. I had the audacity to write one. I used one of Elgar's marches, *Pomp and Circumstance No. 4*, which he'd first performed 100 years earlier, back in 1907.

I assumed the melody must have had a lyrical setting at some point, although I'd never been aware of one. Calling the song 'NYPD', I used the word 'liberty' to great effect, only to discover a year or two later that A. P. Herbert had written words to the tune during World War Two, calling it 'The Liberty Song'. How weird is that? I wasn't sure how Henri would respond on my next visit to Paris. He'd written all the Village People hits and more. There was a good chance he'd dismiss an interloper out of hand, but he didn't; he surprised me by embracing the song and agreeing that it'd be good for the musical.

On one occasion, probably when things started to look seriously good, Henri took me, his son and his son's girlfriend out to dinner. We discussed the project at length and Henri became so animated, in the Gallic style, at one point that he got to his feet and, gesticulating in my direction, shouted, 'Mike, you must fuck us ... you must fuck us...' The other diners, intrigued by whatever Parisian perversion was on offer in this *ménage à quatre*, stopped their conversations and swivelled their heads, only to be bitterly disappointed by Henri's son's swift rejoinder, 'Dad, the pronunciation is "focus".'

The project floundered after the production companies we approached felt that the Village People hadn't had enough hits to make the show viable. Just because the Queen, Abba and Madness musicals were full of hits didn't mean that this one wouldn't work. It was theatrical and colourful, it featured some great songs, and the audience would have dressed as members of the group.

I was recently approached by a UK producer who loved the script, the whole presentation, and wanted to tour it. He offered Henri £500,000, but he turned it down. Crazy in my opinion. No point in having a shelf full of dreams.

There was another single in 2006 when 'England My England' was released to coincide with the FIFA World Cup. W. E. Henley had written the magnificently stirring words in 1892 and I'd added the music over 110 years later. It had been at Jeremy Beadle's insistence that it came out, after he attended one of the *Dead Poets* shows (see below). He thought it was a wonderfully patriotic marriage of words and music and deserved to be heard. I grafted on some anthemic Elgarian chants and a soupçon of the old Elgar/Parry classic for good measure and the press picked up on the song. They also picked up on the other fifty-three artists and writers who'd had a similar idea for a football anthem. Elliott Frisby handled the lead, with him, Steve Etherington and me doing the backing vocals. I'm sure the rather nifty video that we made, which included some classic footage from old Wembley matches, helped ease the song into the all-time top twenty football songs as featured on Sky TV. Let me tell you, it's good to be in any chart! The *Daily Mail* quoted odds of 100/1 on it reaching number one, making it a far more inviting bet than the Cumbria Tourist Board's single, 'Baarmy Sheep' at 50/1 or Leicester City FC's 'Swinging For England' at 33/1. The *Daily Star* printed the lyrics to 'England My England' with the comment 'What the FA want us to sing'. A little premature perhaps, but it was to point up the English-ness, as the other half of the story was Germany asking the Kaiser Chiefs to record an anthem for their team. We were deemed to have a better chance of topping the chart, though, than Showaddywaddy at a grossly unfair 125/1.

I'd met Elliott on a ship in the Caribbean in the early 2000s. He was performing and I was giving talks. Elliott's voice was exceptional and after chatting one evening on deck we wrote a couple of songs. Now you can't just write songs with anyone, it doesn't work like that, but with us it did. There were many cruises and we wrote a new song most evenings. They seemed to come very naturally, they were unusu-ally varied and there was hardly any friction. In fact there was usually a wagonload of humour in the mix.

I guess we have about forty or so pretty strong songs that so far haven't seen the light of day, although a new female singer has recorded 'Just a Little Bit Crazy'. The idea for the song came from a story I'd remembered about Nelson's youth. In his mid-teens while serving as a midshipman, he had an encounter with a polar bear at Spitzbergen and was lucky to escape with his life. The ship's captain described him as being, 'just a little bit crazy'. The song isn't about Nelson, but about a fictitious relationship; ideas, however, can come from anywhere. Two of our collaborations were released on a charity single for the Shooting Star Children's Hospice, now Shooting Star Chase. Elliott and I had been discussing Christmas singles over a pot of tea and came to the conclusion that every title and angle had been covered, but on a journey to Hull later that day I had time to reflect on the fact that Christmas cards had somehow become less important than they were when I was a lad. Then there was the excitement of the cards dropping through the letterbox, the anticipation, the opening, the revelation (who was it from?) the reading of the message and the decision where to put each one. All part of a festive ritual that was fast disappearing. For many, the thrill of the Christmas card has ceased to exist. Cards have been largely eclipsed by presents and group emails, Skype or texts. I mused on the fact that Christmas Eve was no longer represented by sleigh bells ringing, but by mobiles pinging. So why not send a song, I thought. Forget robins, snow scenes, and shepherds with their flocks … let a song be the Christmas card. I worked on it all the way to the banks of the Humber, stopping periodically to update Elliott … or 'Slacker', as I perversely call him, because he works so hard. Within a few days we had the song finished and demoed. I couldn't help feeling that part of the verse was reminiscent of something. I was sure it was one of Wizzard's songs, so I emailed the demo to Roy Wood, who'd written them all. It did indeed turn out to be similar to 'Angel Fingers'. He was delighted to be credited as co-writer, confessing that I'd rounded the verse off in a way that he hadn't managed to back in the '70s. What a gracious man, and one of our great British songwriters in my opinion.

Karen Sugarman, who headed up Shooting Star, was delighted for us to release the song for the children's hospice, so I started to think of ideas for a video. In the end, Andy Park, known to all as Mr Christmas, came to the rescue with an offer that we couldn't refuse. His house looks like Christmas Day all the year round; decorations and cards are displayed for 365 days and his larder groans with foodstuffs that would be the envy of Billy Bunter *and* Mr Toad. Elliott and I were joined by Mr Christmas, in a starring role of course, Dave Hill from Slade, my fellow DJ David Hamilton and Scott Ottoway, who is now drumming with the Searchers. We tipped our hats to the charity by calling ourselves the Shooting Stars and the single picked up a fair amount of airplay as well as notching up almost 20,000 hits on YouTube. The Slacker and I wrote a second seasonal song as a bonus track for the CD, 'Christmas Day'. We agreed that we didn't need a third, but we wrote one anyway. Unlike Henry I with his surfeit of lampreys, we overindulged and survived. Our festive song count is now five and rising. We struggle to determine our favourite.

I also worked on stage with Elliott between 2006 and 2008 on *The Dead Poets' Society*, a piece on which I'd collaborated with many great wordsmiths, including Byron, Kipling, Shakespeare, Auden, Masefield and Wordsworth. It's terrific working with these legends: no arguments, no contrary moments, no hissy fits. I used two narrators (me and an available actor) with Elliott singing and playing guitar and Steve Etherington on keyboards. I staged it at the Gatehouse Theatre, Highgate, the Frinton Library Festival and Home House, London.

I once asked Neil Sedaka which of his songs were his favourites. 'Oh Mike,' he beamed, 'they're *all* my little babies. I send them out into the world and they send me money home.' I thought of that recently when the contract came through from Cherry Red for the inclusion of 'What the Dickens', a song I wrote between O-levels and A-levels, which was being released on the compilation album *Love, Poetry & Revolution*. Far out, man, peace and love, power to the people and let's light another joss-stick. Coolly juxtaposed with the likes of the Spencer Davis Group, the Crazy World of Arthur Brown, the Alan Bown!, John's Children and Fat Mattress, I'm joined on drums by future Atomic Rooster and Spinal Tap drummer Ric Parnell with Virgin Sleep's Keith Purnell on lead guitar. A song I'd started work on at school is still sending me money home. Not as much as Neil Sedaka's send him, of course, but the same principle applies.

I was thrilled to write a song with my old friend Robin Gibb near the end of his life and I'm very moved that it's appearing on a posthumous album later this year. I never discussed Robin's illness with him. It wasn't what he wanted to talk about. He wanted to make plans, discuss the future and pretend that everything was fine. He was still planning tours of places like Australia for goodness sake, but what a positive mental approach. I understood that. He also liked to imagine that Maurice, his twin, hadn't actually died but was living on some vague island somewhere overseas. That was how he dealt with it, and as John Lennon said, 'Whatever gets you through the night, it's all right, it's all right.' We talked about and watched documentaries on the US Civil War, discussed English history and politics, swapped books and sometimes sang classic songs. He dragged me off one afternoon to look at a disused aerodrome that had last been used to land planes bringing soldiers back from World War Two and wandered round in wonderment gazing at rusting fuel pipes and worn markings. We had the same sense of what was a great song, a good song or simply an average song. Robin was adamant that one should never aim to write a number two, always a number one. It worked for the Bee Gees. In not wanting his illness to become public, his team often had to come up with some wild tales to disguise the truth, but Robin battled on relentlessly whenever he could. I directed the video for a re-working of 'I've Gotta Get a Message to You', which he had recorded for the Official Poppy Appeal 2011 with a trio of serving Army soldiers known simply as the Soldiers. The day of the shoot, Robin made a herculean effort to get out of his sick bed, dress and give 100 per cent for me, the Soldiers, the camera crew and the press.

If his positive approach appeared to wane, I sometimes gave him a gentle kick up the backside. We were due to talk to Peter Andre about the song we'd written that he was going to record but Robin's wife Dwina said he was very tired and probably wouldn't make the trip. I decided he might need a little incentive, so I wandered into the garden, stood underneath his bedroom window and shouted, 'Gibb, get your backside down here now, the bus is leaving.' There was no bus of course, we were going in his Range Rover, but there's nothing wrong with a hint of weak humour if you're ailing. The terminology wasn't along my usual eloquent lines, but I felt it might hit the mark for that reason. He was downstairs within ten minutes.

'I didn't sleep much last night, there was a fly in my room,' he said.

'Why didn't you swat it?'

'I shouted at it.'

Brilliant. 'Get dressed and we'll head off.'

'I'm still tired, let me have another hour's sleep and then we'll go.'

'Half an hour.'

'Forty minutes.'

'OK, forty minutes.'

Within ten minutes he was back down, dressed in a roll neck and jacket and ready to go.

'That was a quick forty minutes.'

'The fly was back.'

All the way there and back Robin was in fine form; we sang, the surreal humour flew, we discussed the world in general and I'm sure that was far better medicine than lying in bed, being crowded from all sides by unbidden and unwanted thoughts. When we went back to record the demo with Peter, Robin was very impressed with his voice. I think Peter's range and interpretation surprised him. Peter in turn was, I think, a little apprehensive at having to record in front of Robin. I was pleased to be able to introduce them and that mutual admiration and respect was the result. Peter came to Robin's funeral to pay his respects and later we erected a blue plaque on the gatehouse of Robin and Dwina's home, The Prebendel, in a small ceremony with Tim Rice and me offering a few words.

When the news from the clinic started to look pretty grim, I began to write a little song, which was my personal way of saying what I wanted to say. It was really a letter to Robin. Songs are how we do it. Taking Robin's way of dealing with bereavement, I wrote 'This Is Not Goodbye'. There was one verse that hit my tear ducts every time and I couldn't get past it, which was about his favourite dog, Ollie, waiting patiently for his return and the empty chair outside the studio where he'd sit in the sun. Sunny days seemed to cheer him. I was still concerned about being able to sing those lines when I demoed it at

British Isles behind, Fair Isle in front.

In the words of the Stephen Foster song, the 'Old Folks at Home'.

Not sure about my batting stance, but my mother's wicket-keeping is exemplary.

Aged fifteen: my first electric guitar and my first-ever appearance in front of an audience.

A moody quartet comprised of Peebles, Powell, Peel and I in the Radio One studios at Broadcasting House.

At the start of 500-mile walk assisted by The Proclaimers and Dennis the Menace. Another normal day, then.

The Rock-Olas – myself, Paul Foss, Barry Gibson and Keith West – on tour with the Radio One Roadshow.

A cuppa with Macca.

All together now:
'We're all going on a
summer holiday…'

The moment before mine
and Richard Branson's
prank misfires and a friend's
wedding cake crashes to the
ground. We are reminded
of it annually.

Chris Farlowe, Cliff Richard, Sue Barker and I at the Abbey Road studios.

The *Guinness Book* boys
– me, Tim Rice and Paul
Gambaccini – with Kate
Bush. It was humorously
captioned: 'Three men with
Kate Bush in their eyes.'

'All the nice girls love a sailor': in the Mediterranean
with Olivia Newton-John and Gloria Hunniford.

Hanging out with the Brisbane boys,
Robin Gibb and Peter Andre.

The launch of the first Betjeman album at Kettner's with rascals such as Captain Sensible, Annie Haslam, David Essex, Steve Harley and Arista boss Peter Jamieson.

Alvin Stardust, Cliff Richard, Andrew Lloyd Webber and I share a bottle of something highly carbonated at the launch of the *Pop Quiz* board game.

A Guinness World Record: two dozen broadcasters and none of them talking.

Our party at the House of Commons for the number ones of the '70s. One point for every one you can name.

It's all very well, but she held my hand for a full twenty minutes.

Prince Philip about to land me one at Buckingham Palace, although as a royalist with concern for my knighthood I offer no resistance.

Peter Fleming, Cliff and myself all behaving like the gentlemen we are. But what the heck is Michael Chang looking at?

Lady Betjeman making me work for my tea.

With Margaret Thatcher in 2002.

Our skiing gang in Lech, Austria.

Tennis giants. Well, three of them: Bahrami, Leconte and Nastăse to you.

The Radio One team are victorious at Old Trafford as Bobby Charlton and I lift the coveted trophy. Between us we have 106 England caps. He has 106 of them.

In traditional cricket shorts for Heartaches CC, much to the displeasure of skipper Tim Rice lurking loftily in the back row.

It's an unfair
cop, guv.

As Tina Turner. She was very impressed.

Union Mike.

Elliott's studio, but I got through it. A few days before he went into the clinic for the final time, Robin had asked me to film him in the garden. He instructed me how to use the machine and I attempted a few atmospheric sequences while he posed in his frock coat and trademark blue glasses and looked moody. I used that final footage, in slow motion, to go with 'This Is Not Goodbye' when we put it on YouTube.

The night he died I'd only been in bed for half an hour when I had the call. There would be a taxi at the door sometime after midnight to take me to London. Dwina was happy for me to do the interviews as she felt that I would be able delicately to handle questions on personal issues, the Bee Gees' career, Robin's career and his enormous capacity for charitable causes, including the Bomber Command Memorial, of which more below. It was a harrowing two days of interviews with hardly any sleep, so sometimes it verged on the emotional. One interviewer asked me, 'All this media coverage. What do you think Robin would say if he could see it?'

I said, 'He'd say, "I'm bloody annoyed because I want to be down there, living my life and writing songs."'

Robin was fiercely loyal to people that he felt had been supportive and even wrote and recorded a moving song about one of the early champions of both the Bee Gees' songs and his own solo material, Alan Freeman. He went to visit Alan at Brinsworth House, a nursing home for people in the entertainment industry, and secretly wrote a very large cheque for the charity that runs it.

Robin could also be sharp and on the offensive if he felt he hadn't been treated correctly. When the edition of *Who Wants to Be a Millionaire* on which he and I appeared wasn't transmitted on the day we'd been told it would, he was on the phone demanding the tapes back, insisting that they were biked down that minute. He calmed down when it was re-scheduled, although we didn't do too well. During the run-through in the afternoon, which is played as if for real, we notched up £250,000, but cometh the hour, where were the men? We couldn't answer that. We did get to £20,000, but then we blew it and didn't make as much for Shooting Star Chase as we'd hoped. We weren't sure whether to stick at £20,000, I seem to recall, although I could be wrong, but I do remember trying to catch the eye of the tireless Karen Sugarman for a 'thumbs up' or a 'thumbs down'. I couldn't work out why I didn't know who'd won that year's FA Cup Final. Nor could a bewildered John Inverdale, who thought he might be called up on 'phone a friend' for something a little more challenging than saying 'Chelsea'. It was only later that I realised I'd been in Jamaica at the time.

In 2012 I was drafted onto the Lords and Commons Entertainment Committee, working with Macmillan Cancer Support to raise money for cancer care. This long-running institution meets every month in preparation for an annual show each March in which the participants are all MPs or peers. For the 2013 event, I wrote and directed a show titled *100 Years of Prime Ministers and Prime Music*, with Margaret Jay, Jeremy Hunt, Danny Alexander and me narrating. I became chairman of the committee that spring and put together and directed the 2014 show, *Best of British*, celebrating our music, poetry, art, literature, architecture and sport. The narrators included Michael Fabricant, who decided to do his own thing, which rather threw the timing and created a slightly anarchic and unwelcome twist to the evening. I feel rather privileged at being the only person that's not a member of the Lords or Commons to perform. You may surmise, and you'd be correct, that putting words into the mouths of politicians isn't that easy, nor is asking them to learn new material so that the shows have some degree of variation from year to year. Yet somehow, after weeks of writing and hundreds of phone calls, emails and texts, it comes together. Shows always do, but it's often a close-run thing. My maxim has always been to wait at the spot where the rollercoaster will inevitably come to a stop and then deal with the situation, rather than taking the white-knuckle ride, screaming and shouting en route while fellow passengers' minds are otherwise engaged. I'm in and out of Parliament so often that that the gatekeepers have suggested that I should have my own peg in the Lords cloakroom now! As one of the policemen of the door put it, 'Are you sure you're not a Lord? You're in here more than they are.' Measure me for my ermine.

In May 2013 I undertook my first solo gig for a long time, appearing at Paul Clerehugh's prestigious Crooked Billet, near Henley-on-Thames, and performing several of my own songs in the set, including 'Grief Never Grows Old', 'In Flanders Fields' (from *Dead Poets' Society*) and 'Myfanwy'. Fortified by an enthusiastic response I played an entire two-hour show of my songs and poetry as the final night of the Wantage Literary Festival.

Uncertain of being able to hold a sell-out crowd with material they might well not know, I landed on stage with a certain amount of trepidation. It worked so well that is was decreed one of the most popular events of the festival. A dangerous pronouncement. A year later there was a UK tour … two nights at the Crooked Billet (with Elliott Frisby) playing all my own songs and a return to the Wantage Festival as well an appearance at the Fawley Festival. At Fawley I played and sang with Chas McDevitt and Sam Brown in Chas's skiffle group, the personnel for 'Freight Train' having changed a tad since he performed it to a US TV audience of forty million back in the summer of 1957 on *The Ed Sullivan Show*.

There was a further flurry of activity at the end of 2013, with Santa (Alan Williams from the Rubettes) and his Christmas Crackers recording 'Christmas Day', another festive offering I'd written with Elliott. Another track that escaped over Christmas 2013 is a single written by my first radio boss, Neil ffrench Blake, coupled with a rocky version of 'Good King Wenceslas'. Neil is far from well but facing what future is left with fortitude. It was fun working with him again.

In 2014 I went back into the studio to record a new album, with John Mitchell, the lead singer with It Bites, producing. As I'd written music to the words of various World War One poets and with the hundredth anniversary looming I thought I might put together an album along those lines. I already had collaborations with Rupert

Brooke, John McCrae, Alan Seeger and Siegfried Sassoon, but found myself veering away from World War One specifically and bringing in other conflicts as well, including World War Two and the American Civil War. Alan Seeger was the uncle of Pete Seeger, the pioneering folk singer, civil rights campaigner and champion of international disarmament, and one of the first US soldiers to be killed in World War One. Only after presenting an obituary on the BBC for Pete Seeger, who died in January 2014, did I think that maybe I should have sent him a copy of my setting of his uncle's poetry. Not for any commercial reason, except that it would have been a good thing to do. It's always too late, isn't it?

CHAPTER 11

YOU'RE HISTORY

M Y FIRST ENCOUNTER with history was being taught to play chess by a friend of my parents, John Liulf Swinton. John was some twenty years older than my mother, but enjoyed a similar intellect, and he taught me to play before I even started school. Where's the history in that? The answer is in the stories that came out while he was trying to instruct me on the King's Gambit or the Bishop's Opening, for John's father was Major General Sir Ernest Dunlop Swinton KBE, CB, DSO, RE, credited with inventing the tank and appointed official war correspondent on the Western Front by Lord Kitchener.

Being the son of such a man must have been a hell of a thing to live up to. That's possibly why I remember John as a somewhat nervy man whose wife rather dominated him. Ellen Schroeder Swinton certainly scared the life out of me when I was young. Later, for reasons best known to herself, she became our cook, but I found her food quite unpalatable, the main reason being her long, greasy hairs that got entangled in the contents. She'd frequently, and rightly, scold me for folding over the bread on a jam sandwich when I should have been cutting it, but I'm sure she had a good heart as she often gave me her loose change. Even as a kid always on the lookout for some extra sweet money I was loath to take her coins, though, as they were always dirty and stuck together with something unsavoury of, I suspected, human origin. I always gave the money a seriously good clean. Indeed, even as I write this a historic queasiness washes over me. I always thought she was Swedish or Norwegian. It turns out she was Danish. The actress Tilda Swinton is related somehow – I believe Ernest was her great-uncle, which makes her John's niece, but that doesn't really affect the action here.

Putting history on hold for a moment, unless you count the history of cooks, let me wander briefly onto the subject of cooks. Our first was Cookie Dawson, who had a rather bland brown dog and still wrote to Father Christmas. I chanced to see her list of festive wants one year and it was headed by something called a 'dunlopillo,' which seriously made me question whether I'd go on writing to Santa when I got to an age where a dunlopillo was the one thing that would make me shriek with joy on Christmas morning. Cookie Durr was tall and quite austere, while Ann Brice, a Geordie through and through, was jolly decent and sent me birthday cards and the like. Somehow she never had the 'Cookie' tag attached to her like the others. Her son Leslie, who was to die tragically young in a road accident, gave me my first vinyl records. Whether it was stuff he'd grown out of and suddenly found uncool or whether it was simply a philanthropic moment I couldn't say, but I was certainly grateful and it started me on a long and winding road.

In any child's life there is a queue of adults asking you the tricky question 'What do you want to be when you grow up?' My answer, even at a tender age, was that I had no intention of growing up. I'd seen the film *Peter Pan* and knew categorically that such a thing was possible. On the off-chance that I was wrong I usually went for veterinary surgeon or archaeologist. Once I'd ascertained that a vet dealt with sick animals and not frisky types that were full of life, I came down firmly on the side of archaeology. Uncle Jack Haslam (Uncle Zak when I was younger as I had some trouble with my 'J's) had other ideas. He was a larger-than-life, dominant character who felt that my future was in the chemical industry of the north. I didn't quite see it that way, but was reluctantly wheeled around massive and forbidding factories that neither excited nor inspired. Bleaching, dyeing and other unnamed aspects of it had, I suspect, been founded the previous century to work in tandem with the great Lancashire cotton industry. It was not talked about that much, but there was an underlying sadness, in the only son of Jack and his wife Dorothy having been killed in a car accident. More than that I was never told, nor did I seek further information. Their house was called Brooklands as Jack had raced there in his younger days, and by coincidence I would attend Brooklands College years later. I must have been seen as the lad designated to step into the role they'd assumed their son would take, with a view to one day becoming lord and master. My dreams and aspirations, though, lay elsewhere and not in the dark satanic mills of Lancashire, where affluence and effluence had become acceptable bedfellows.

I guess I was about eight years old when I went on my first archaeological dig. Not an official dig, you understand, but Ken Lewis, the father of two friends of mine, Brian and Jeremy, invited me to join them on their part-time forays into the past. I warmed to it immediately and was soon identifying arrowheads, scrapers, borers, sickle blades and other prehistoric tools. Spotting knapped flints, the bulb of percussion and those little fissures incurred by the shock of knapping became second nature. If I'm walking over likely terrain, I still look to the ground, where others may look to the sky. As other children gathered flowers, conkers, acorns or tadpoles, I'd arrive home with pockets full of stones. My mother was supportive, my father bemused.

I haunted Weybridge Museum when I could, listening to the stories of the curator, Dorothy Grenside, herself, I suspect, a great age. I discovered later that this lovely old lady had been a champion swimmer, a tennis player, an eminent watercolour artist and poet, and one of the pioneering women motorists. I only knew her as someone who fired my enthusiasm for exploring the past. I was able to track down and buy a copy of her 1917 book of poems, *Open Eyes*. Museums now have a designer air about them; then they had nothing more than rows and rows of display cases with the name of the piece and the donor handwritten in ink on a small, yellowing card. Having had a deep fascination with history from an early age, the lure of a museum was great.

A favourite spot for us flint hunters was somewhere we called 'Flint Hill'. That wasn't its proper name, if indeed it had one, but it was close to the deep railway cutting between Walton-on-Thames and Weybridge and the excavations a century earlier must have churned up thousands of Neolithic implements, many of which ended up in our box room jostling with the model railway for shelf space. I found looking for flints exacting, rewarding and highly compelling. Complete arrowheads were something of a rarity as their fragile tips tended to snap easily, but the more solid tools were usually complete and slipped comfortably into your hand. Great workmanship, and it was extraordinary to wonder who had held it in 4000 or even 9000 BC, only to be discovered in an age that those toolmakers could never have imagined. Our findings were fashioned before the discovery and use of copper, bronze and iron, and on the site of what to them would have been a terrifying vast iron road haunted by monsters with red eyes that pierced the night, shrieking and belching steam.

When I left home I donated thousands of Palaeolithic and Neolithic flints, Roman pottery, ammonites, crystals and a whole range of historic goodies to the Weybridge Museum. I kept one tin trunk full, but on a clear-out one day my father tipped the contents out into the garden. 'Well it's where they came from,' was the reply to my indignant pose. I made sure that I was well out of reach before chipping in with, 'Huh, if it had been a trunk full of golf balls you wouldn't have thrown them away.' My mother, more of a garden habituee than my father, encountered New Stone Age craftsmanship for years to come, almost breaking her ankle on the bigger items and snapping many of the more delicate pieces.

At Brooklands College, alongside my classes in English literature and British Constitution and art, I started to go out with Vivien Berry, with whose sister I was studying. Vivien lived at Laleham, some 7 or 8 miles from Walton-on-Thames, but I was happy to miss the last bus back to Walton for a few extra minutes with her. Those 'extra minutes', though, were often taken over by Major Berry with a few tales of life in the military. I knew any canoodling had come to an end when he marched in with the opening gambit, 'Have I ever told you about this particular skirmish in Burma…?' The pipe would be filled, tapped on the hearth, lit and the tales would begin. In youth it drew a sigh of exasperation; as an adult the response would be, 'Hey look, we can kiss goodnight anytime, but these Burma tales are gripping.' It's good that our paths still cross and Vivien and I are able to catch up and flatter each other that the years haven't altered us too much! At least we recognise each other so it must be vaguely true.

While I was at Brooklands College I got involved in a major archaeological find after a series of aerial photographs that had been taken of the River Wey just by the 'wall of death', a steeply banked section of the old Brooklands motor racing circuit, revealed the grass growing in a different direction. This was intriguing. It seemed in all probability that the meadow we'd all sat on and walked on had once been a reasonably substantial building. Very slowly, once the dig began, the outline of a sizeable structure emerged, but it was, of necessity, an extremely pedestrian process. The eventual consensus was that we had located the lost manor of Hundulsham, once the domain of Bishop Odo, William the Conqueror's half-brother. Research revealed that it had passed through many hands over the centuries but the family that held it the longest were the Wodehams. In 1290 they had 2 acres at the rent of one rose per annum. Very romantic. By 1324 they held 80 acres at a rent of 6 shillings, the area later expanding to almost 100 acres.

All was well until the late fifteenth century, when the descendants of Sir Bartholomew Reed, former Lord Mayor of London, seized Hundulsham from the Wodehams, who later would contest the ownership.

When challenged over the legality of his claim, William Reed denied that there had ever been a manor there. The Reeds were very powerful, with many connections, so whether he demolished the manor to prove a point or whether nobody dared question his word and it fell into disrepair, we'll never know. There is no further reference to the building or to any future families living there, so it seemed that we were the first to re-discover the lost manor of Hundulsham. One of the areas that I worked on was a room where a tiled hearth had gone from vertical to horizontal, so maybe the Reeds did destroy the property. I had some of the tiles at home for many years. I'm not sure where they went, but I can make a shrewd guess. Maybe a future historian will discover them cheek by jowl with the Neolithic tools and be totally baffled. The demolition of Hundulsham would hardly have mattered to the Reeds, for they had other houses, including Otelands (later Oatlands), which they gave to Henry VIII in a part-exchange deal, and plenty of land.

How marvellous it would be to stroll down the meadow today and look for any artefacts that still remain. Marvellous but impossible. The site is now home to a delightfully attractive sewage plant, easily visible from the train as it leaves Weybridge station heading southwest. Underneath it somewhere is a rose that was handed over for a year's rent. How indiscriminate progress is. I haven't checked to see if I am a descendant of the power-hungry, avaricious, bullying Reeds of Weybridge. Surely not?

The great British inventor Barnes Wallis had his office at Vickers Armstrong, later BAC, on the Brooklands site and came to the college to give us the odd lecture. He was inspirational, engaging and still so full of excitement for the future. He would show us, by demand of course, unseen footage of the testing of his revolutionary (pun intended) bouncing bombs at Reculver in 1943. One of his sons was our chemistry teacher at Woking.

Even in the years at Radio One and TV Centre, my enthusiasm for the past didn't dim and on more than one occasion I managed to sneak something historical into the shows. On *Saturday Superstore* in the mid '80s, I did several outside broadcasts from a major dig at York, complete with hard hat and trowel, for the York Archaeological Trust alongside historian Richard Kemp. The site of Anglo-Saxon York had apparently been a puzzle for many years, but now it had been located on the area previously occupied by the Redfearn Glassworks at Fishergate. The extensive dig also produced finds from a nearby twelfth-century former Gilbertine priory, which assisted with study into the cemetery population, health, diet, appearance and life expectancy. The Gilbertines were unique in that they were the only totally English religious order, having been founded in the 1130s by Gilbert of Sempringham (later St Gilbert), a parish priest from Lincolnshire. They disappeared with the Dissolution of the Monasteries, so it was fascinating to re-discover elements of their existence. We dug, uncovered, washed, examined and filed. I was also delighted to launch the trust's Archaeological Scholarship. I was enrolled onto its committee of stewards and received various papers for discussion, but alas geography and travelling time meant me falling by the wayside after a while. That summer they did find part of a Roman helmet in pretty good condition with an embossed rosette. An exciting dig. I still have my certificate confirming that I am not only a fully fledged Viking but also a comrade in arms of Erik Bloodaxe and 'entitled to conquer, plunder or trade in any lands encountered'. Take me on and you're also dealing with my pal Mr Bloodaxe.

On a broadcasting trip to Jamaica a year or two back with Adventures in Radio we were informed of an old site that had just been uncovered when some dense undergrowth had been cleared. The remains were of old Colonial buildings, with even older Spanish architecture underneath, the homes of those long gone. I was invited into what had been a crypt. The question as to what had happened to the occupants was answered as we stumbled across a handful of old graves. These were the last resting places of English settlers. All was still, hot and humid with not a breath of wind, as someone muttered,

'There must be ghosts in a place like this.' The supervisor overheard and turned on us with a loud mocking laugh, barking, 'There are no such things as ghosts.' At that very moment we heard a mighty crack and looked up to see a massive section of a huge tree break away and crash towards us from a great height. Weighing, we guessed afterwards, somewhere in the region of half a ton, it missed one or two of us by no more than a couple of feet. There was absolute silence. Everyone was shocked. Our organiser, Tim Jibson, went as white as a sheet and was shakier than an amusing jelly in the shape of Shakin' Stevens. No such things as ghosts?

I also enjoy sporting history and a long-term part-time project is the ultimate book of the history of the FA Cup Final, with a write-up of every final, photographs of every winning side and a whole load of facts to boot. It'll be full of useful and fascinating stuff: for instance jazz musician Humphrey Lyttelton's uncles both played for the Old Etonians in the 1876 final, and the 1878 final between Wanderers and Royal Engineers was refereed by a Bastard. A forerunner of many, you may think. Perhaps, but he was the only genuine Bastard, Mr S. R. Bastard in point of fact.

I also wrote a screenplay about the 1873 FA Cup Final between the Old Etonians and Blackburn Olympic. I was originally cast as consultant to Julian Fellowes, but he proved to be too busy so I landed the role and was delighted with the result. Taking in football history, social history and relationships on and off the field, it examines the eve of the professional era and the first time that the FA Cup went north. The Old Etonians, Old Harrovians, Old Carthusians, Oxford University and Royal Engineers had had it all their own way until the working-class teams from the north brought in training, diets and … money! The game would never be the same again.

My interest in history led me to becoming increasingly involved with the Heritage Foundation and the blue plaques they erected. Initially commemorating comedians, they soon progressed to plaques for all areas of the entertainment industry. For several years, I was the vice-president and Robin Gibb the president. We shared a love of history and with the foundation's chairman, David Graham, were involved with erecting plaques for such luminaries as Sir Norman Wisdom, Sir John Mills, Peter Cook, Keith Moon, Kenneth Williams, Joe Meek and Jerome Kern.

The Kern plaque, unveiled by Robin and *Les Misérables* lyricist Herbert Kretzmer, had a special meaning for me. A few years earlier I'd watched the Kern biopic, *Till the Clouds Roll By*, and had become strangely obsessed by one particular scene. This depicted Jerome and his manager cycling through an English village. One of them gets a puncture and the manager goes to find help, leaving Kern by this quaint rose-covered cottage, featuring the delightfully un-English address (on the US-style mailbox!) of something like 1093 Main Street. Intriguing how England was perceived by Hollywood film moguls. He wandered in through the open door, sat down at the very conveniently placed piano and played until a young lady appeared, questioning his presence. In a nutshell he thought she was the maid, when in fact she was the daughter of the house, and they subsequently fell in love. Why I became dead set on finding out in which village these events played out in real life I have no idea. It plagued me for weeks. I googled, I researched, I drew a blank. Three months later I was having dinner with some friends on a steam train in Kent. I asked whether they still lived by Walton Bridge. They did.

'Do you know that, on the very spot where your house is, both Turner and Canaletto, at different times obviously, painted the old bridge?' I asked them.

'We did, but do you know the two pubs across the river?'

'Yes I do, The Swan and the Anglers.'

'What do you know about the Swan?'

'More than you imagine. I often played in the garden when I was a kid and I did my very first paid gig, singing and playing guitar, for a friend's eighteenth birthday in the main room, of which a photograph still exists.'

'Ah, but what you probably don't know is that the room in which you played your first paid gig was the room in which the American songwriter Jerome Kern was playing the piano when he met his wife-to-be.'

I was utterly speechless. They had no idea of my quest and were equally speechless when I told them the story. It transpired that Kern had married Eva Leale, the landlord's daughter, at St Mary's Church, Walton-on-Thames, sixty years before I was confirmed at the same altar. Who can possibly say what made me so obsessed and that there would be a double link between us? I was so delighted to be able to organise a blue plaque for the man who wrote such classics as 'Old Man River', 'Smoke Gets in Your Eyes', 'The Way You Look Tonight' and 'I've Told Every Little Star'.

Among the regular guests at the Heritage Foundation's post-plaque lunches were a number of Bomber Command veterans. They were clearly disappointed that their efforts, and more importantly those of the 55,500 Allied aircrew who perished keeping our country free from oppressors, had never been recognised. From the first-voiced thoughts at Foundation functions that something be done about the injustice, we initially raised small sums for a memorial that, like Topsy, 'just growed'. As the wheels turned, the *Daily Telegraph* and later the *Daily Express* championed the cause and more people became involved, including Jim Dooley, formerly of the hit group The Dooleys, with Robin Gibb adding his profile and passion to the project as well as his time and energy. Architect Liam O'Connor was brought in and benefactors stepped up in the shape of Lord Ashcroft, John Caudwell and Richard Desmond. The scheme now had legs and began to take shape. Liam was responsible for the design of the memorial which he wanted to be in keeping with nearby monuments designed by his architectural hero, Aston Webb. Philip Jackson was responsible for the sculpture that provides the memorial's focus, depicting a Bomber Command crew home from a mission. There was to be no triumph or jingoism in the seven 9-foot-high figures. They display fatigue and exhaustion, with eyes to the sky, praying that their pals make it home too.

The Ministry of Defence came in for some criticism for not assisting with funds, especially after many veterans exposed themselves financially by putting up their own money. Other veterans missed out on applying for tickets for the unveiling, but very movingly, many people returned theirs so that the airmen could attend in order to pay tribute to their mates. HM the Queen, flanked by many members of the royal family, unveiled the sculpture in Green Park on 28 June 2012, with an Avro Lancaster dropping red poppy petals over the park. Vanessa Brady and I sat in the sunshine, feeling very patriotic and knowing that justice had been done for the boys of Bomber Command. Robin would have been so proud, but at least his name is, quite rightly, carved on the monument.

I met Vanessa at one of Robin and Dwina's garden parties. I say met, we were actually pushed together by Dot Most the wife of my first publisher, Dave Most. We began a gradual relationship that increased with time. It was only after a few weeks that she revealed that we'd almost met back in the mid '80s. It seems that we were both at a function and our eyes met as she walked across the room. As she was with a group of friends I didn't really have the bottle (or the glass) to go and talk to her. So being a useless bloke, I sent someone else to ask on my behalf. Wrong. Back came the answer, in the negative. By the time she decided to make another trip across the room, I'd gone … as they say in the song, 'Who know where, who knows when.' But we did meet again years later.

Three years ago I discovered that if I'd asked her myself she'd have agreed quite willingly to a glass of something from the Champagne region, with the implication that she would have been happy for the conversation to blossom as the *prunus* in May, from that point. I was swift to point out that I hadn't arrogantly dispatched a Pony Express rider to do my dirty work, it was simply shyness. You know the score. Striding purposefully towards a table hidden round a corner and containing half a dozen girls to talk to just one of them, demands nerves of steel and several acres of confidence. Then there is the question of approach. The comedic? The smouldering? The domineering? It's a tough call. That's why I sent in the troops. Well ... man at arms. After the passing of half an hour VB claims she noticed I'd gone, as she rounded the corner on her way to the ladies room. I claim she couldn't restrain herself and just had to see whether I was still there. Maybe the truth lies somewhere between the two. Being a *carpe diem* kind of chap I should have seized the moment and also heeded Horace's quantifying follow-up, *Quam minimum credula postero*, and not put my trust in tomorrow. This tomorrow was a long time coming and it was just after Robin and I had been on stage singing *Massachusetts*.

Robin and I were always keen to pursue plaques that were more historical than necessarily showbusiness. Sadly my old pal passed away in 2012, but I feel he's very much a part of the British Plaque Trust, a registered charity that we set up in 2013. In October of that year, with my fellow trustees, Vanessa Brady, Ian Freeman and Major Ian Mattison, we erected a blue plaque at Wembley Stadium to commemorate the 150th anniversary of the Football Association. Relatives of the Founding Fathers of football, who drew up the rules back in 1863, were flown in from the USA and New Zealand to join those closer to home. The former West Ham United and England player Sir Trevor Brooking made a speech and unveiled the plaque, assisted by one of the youngest descendants present. The FA historian and I both said a few words and a QR tag was later fixed to the plaque, meaning that future generations will be able to not only download the FA history directly from the plaque, but also watch a recording of the blue plaque ceremony. I was delighted that my friends Sir William and Lady McAlpine were able to attend, as the McAlpine family had built the original Wembley Stadium in 1923. This delightful couple live with herds of deer, a tribe of meercats, a full size railway line complete with engines and rolling stock, a family of capybaras, a railway museum, a fleet of dogs, a flock of alpacas and anything and anyone else that turns up.

Our next plaque commemorated Denmark Street, London, Britain's Tin Pan Alley, which was the centre for the UK's publishers and songwriters from the '20s and where the likes of the Rolling Stones, David Bowie, the Kinks, Donovan and hundreds of others began their careers. The heartbeat of the small street, just off the north end of the Charing Cross Road, was the Giaconda café, where the musicians and writers would hang out, in the hope of getting a gig or picking up a publishing deal. The café is still there, (re-opening this summer) with the blue plaque letting the world know that this is where many of the most successful songwriters began a journey that resulted in phenomenal sales around the planet. Donovan flew in to unveil the plaque, performing a song that he'd written specially for the occasion, appropriately called 'Tin Pan Alley'. I say unveiled, but the cord failed to pull the curtain away, so most of the unveiling shots were of my backside as I perched precariously on a ladder to remove the curtain by hand. Several of Tin Pan Alley's most successful songwriters attended, including Don Black, Tony Hiller, Barry Mason, Bill Martin, Mitch Murray, Guy Fletcher and John Carter. Thanks to the efforts of our PR guru, Dan Kirkby, with whom I worked at Radio One, the event made all the main news bulletins on ITV and BBC as well as getting into more than 100 newspapers. Guy is terrific company and we've spent many a happy evening or weekend together along with his lovely wife Cherry. A source of wisdom and knowledge in the music industry, he commands great respect as the Chairman of PRS for Music. When I was lucky enough to receive the British Academy of Composers, Songwriters and Authors Gold Badge of Merit in 2011 it was Guy from whom I received it during the annual lunch at the Savoy Hotel.

My interest in history also involves diving off on a whim to various Civil War battle sites such as Edgehill or Naseby. I have been known to wander over Wars of the Roses sites too, like Barnet and Bosworth Field, in fact anywhere that has some fascinating historical attachment. Many people get excited at seeing a celebrity. I get excited about famous buildings, rivers, monuments and the like.

Family history is also a passion, starting with my father's old football programmes and newspaper match reports, such as this write-up from an FA Amateur Cup match: 'A dominating share in Walton's performance was taken by their halves, of whom Read, a keen tackler and thoughtful distributor of the ball, was outstanding.' The old man's fair play was also reported in another match: 'There was a cry of "Hands, ref.," when a shot from Bunce hit Read's wrist on its way through the penalty area, but with Read making no attempt to play the ball with his hand, the incident was not deliberate or serious enough to warrant a penalty.' Here, that fleeting moment in time, that cry from the crowd, that incident, is again committed to print, my father, the pre-war lad at centre-half, not knowing that he'd soon be playing in the chilling-sounding War League North. I have several cards from that period summoning him to Manchester United's ground for training. Another newspaper cutting sees the young Read sitting proudly in the middle of the front row of the Guildford City team.

Prior to joining the Army at the outbreak of war my father was accepted for service in Division A of the Metropolitan Police War Reserve, stationed at Hyde Park. The acceptance letter is dated 26 April 1939, so they clearly knew that something was in the wind.

I've enjoyed poring through family history from a very young age and that interest has never waned. I have my great-grandmother's vehicle registration card from 1928, which declares: 'This council has been informed that a registered motor vehicle NC 2606 has been transferred to you.' The car was a Calthorpe, made by a Birmingham manufacturer that produced some 5,000 high-quality cars after World War One but by the end of the '20s had ceased production altogether. I read somewhere that fewer than ten have survived. I wonder if NC 2606 is one of them. Nestling next to the registration card is one of many speeches given by my grandmother, this one being dated October 1954:

Mr President, Madam Chairman, Mr Mayor, Mayoress, Ladies and Gentlemen, It is my very great privilege to propose the final toast of today's proceedings and that is to our guests. Looking back on the rallies we have had here in the Winter Gardens, Blackpool, must, I am sure, give all of us who've been associated with them a warm and homely feeling and to me they are becoming more like family re-unions. We have present our near relatives from Lancashire, Cheshire and north Wales and our more distant but nevertheless welcome relations from Yorkshire and the Midland counties...

Look, here's a menu from a dinner-dance at the Grand Hotel in Manchester in November 1946, the evening being rounded off with the seasonal Pouding de Noel with Sauce Rhum. No etymological wrestling needed that night, even for the uneducated. I note that post-pud, my godfather proposed a toast to the King and the Royal family, followed by a few well-chosen words from my grandmother. Public speaking was a baton taken up by my mother, who declaimed at dozens and dozens of dinners, sometimes in rhyme, usually with wit, often with an edge and certainly with a full glass. She was definitely a character. She was much loved by my friends for her *joie de vivre*, sense of humour, intellect and eccentricity, and she had the ability to see through the vainglorious and denounce the charlatan, sometimes to the point of embarrassing bluntness. She could also be belligerent, dogmatic and dismissive. She was one of the 'Oh get on with it, stop feeling sorry for yourself' school, the 'We don't talk about things like that in public' brigade and the 'I'll keep your feet firmly on the ground' tribe.

My mother was also highly capable and unflappable in an emergency. There was a ghastly accident across the road from us when a lorry knocked down and killed a young girl who was cycling with her mother and sister. Taking charge, Mater was first on the scene, coping with a distraught mother, a panicking truck driver and an almost delirious sister. The lorry had virtually run over the girl's head, but my mother was at the front, organising, keeping everyone calm and on a firm rein and dealing with the trauma, before the emergency services arrived. Exceptional. On the other hand she could be downright offensive. I was probably about fifteen and girls were beginning to filter into our crowd. One of them, not a girlfriend, came to call for me one day, and clearly didn't meet with my mother's approval, for as we were leaving, and within earshot, she flared her nostrils, raised her eyebrows and hissed, 'I don't think so, do you?' Reminiscent of Lady Chetwode's supposed comment about John Betjeman, her future son-in-law, 'We invite people like that to tea, but we don't marry them.'

Latterly she imagined scenarios. Here's a typical example. The telephone rings. I run down the corridor to answer it. Pretty normal stuff. I'm possibly breathing slightly more heavily than usual. 'Hello.'

It's Mater. 'We don't say "Hello", we give our number.'

I've had that one since I was four years old. I still haven't learned. 'OK.' I'm still breathing deeply.

'Oh, I've clearly interrupted something of a personal nature.'

I have to disappoint her. 'If you really want to know, I'm playing table-tennis.'

'Oh, it's none of my business.'

'Maybe not, but I'm still playing table-tennis.'

'Hmph! And how do play table-tennis by yourself?'

'It may come as a cataclysmic shock that I'm not proficient enough to play by myself.'

'There's no need to be rude, just because I've caught you out.'

'Caught me out doing what?'

'Whatever you were doing.'

'I was playing table-tennis!'

'Hmph, that's what you call it, is it?'

'Would you prefer ping-pong?'

'There's no need to be funny.'

'I'm not. I'm playing table-tennis.'

'What, with one hand, while you're talking on the phone along the corridor?'

'Well, clearly I'm not playing now because I'm talking to you.'

'So who's the girl you said you're playing with?'

'I'm not playing with a girl.'

'Oh well, it's clearly none of my business.'

'If you really want to know I'm playing with some friends.'

'You don't get out of breath playing table-tennis.'

'You do if you play properly. Anyway what did you call for?'

'Oh, it doesn't matter if you're … "busy".' Click.

Mingling with the Calthorpe motor, the speeches, the football write-ups et al. is my great-grandfather's *Gospel According to St John, Active Service 1914–1915*. This small book of some seventy pages also carries the words 'Please carry this in your pocket and read it every day'. It has a personal message from Lord Roberts dated August 1914 urging my great-grandfather, and others, to 'put your trust in God'. There are eight hymns at the back, including 'When I Survey the Wondrous Cross', 'Rock of Ages' and 'Abide with Me'. The final page is a 'Decision Form', a declaration to be signed with both name and address, the confession beginning, 'Being convinced that I am a sinner…'

I could fill a book with historical accumulations from the family. As for photographs, our lot were queuing up as soon as Fox-Talbot exclaimed, 'I've just had a negative thought.' Shots of my great-great-grandparents and some of their peers, looking fairly sombre, in keeping with the period, various cars that would now be worth a fortune, unidentifiable folk, my grandfather dressed in whatever daft garb he thought would look hilarious for the camera. In his finest comedic moment in a ballroom somewhere, he takes Elvis literally, as you may recall from Chapter 2, and is the only one on the dance-floor waltzing with a wooden chair. My grandmother's fox fur can be seen draped round his neck in this rather splendid snap. Also caught on camera are a procession of family dogs resignedly adorned with hats, necklaces and sunglasses, my mother and my grandmother in full flow at some of the aforementioned speeches, my great-grandparents standing upright and proud for the camera, my great-grandfather sporting his waxed moustache, my father the boy chorister looking cherubic outside a church, youthful cricket teams now almost a century old, for whom the Great Umpire's finger was raised long ago, snaps of pipes, firmly clenched in white teeth, boating parties on the Thames, ancestors taking off across heathland with a pack of upright-tailed beagles, Army boys in khaki shorts, a headless relative on a carousel, another playing a banjo in camp, friends lifting the casing of Bluebird, which held the Land Speed Record, back onto its wheels. Why? I have no idea. I wish I'd discovered a lot of these photographs when there were folk around to answer questions. There are photos of weddings, dinner parties and a thousand other events captured and frozen in time, that pose more questions than they give answers.

I have fairly complete histories of the two main houses I've owned. The Aldermoor at Holmbury St Mary had been built in the early 1860s for Henry Tanworth Wells RA, whose best-known paintings include *Victoria Regina*, depicting Victoria being informed that she was now the monarch and *Volunteers at the Firing Point*. Wells's circle included Dante Gabriel Rossetti, Ford Madox Brown, John Ruskin and William Frederick Yeames. He also hosted the fifth Earl Spencer, and William Gladstone was a not infrequent guest while Prime Minister. Wells's closest confidant was the Gothic revivalist architect George Edmund Street, who designed the law courts and who almost certainly had a major hand in designing the house. The Wells and Steet families also intermarried. In the '20s and '30s, the famous Harrison sisters, Beatrice, May and Margaret, performed regularly in the drawing room, around the time Beatrice was enticing some poor unsuspecting nightingale to sing along to her cello in her garden at Oxted, for a clutch of patient BBC sound engineers. It was a privilege to walk in the footsteps of these people who'd contributed much to our country. In 'Elizabethan Dragonflies' I wrote, 'The Jekyll-haunted gardens now are mine, I walk at will down long, untrodden tracks.'

The house's 23 acres and twenty-two rooms were full of history, with the oldest tree, a yew, being dated at something like 600 years old. Makes one wonder what was on the spot at the time. The property was 850 feet above sea level and, despite being some 25 miles from the coast, from the top windows, when the conditions were right, one could see the Channel glistening through the Shoreham Gap. There were a few cracking parties at the house that may well have rivalled those of Victorian and Edwardian incumbents. How often do you see Rick Parfitt from Status Quo and David Cassidy wiping the spinach and gruyère quiche from their mouths to join Beatles tribute band, Cavern to knock out a few favourites? Or David Grant and his girl-friend Carrie disappearing for an hour or two into the azaleas only to re-emerge as an engaged couple, eventually marry and live happily ever after. Or the guy who did the catering spending fifteen minutes warning his staff of the dangers of walking into the plate glass doors in the conservatory only to do it himself five minutes later and break his nose? Or the Marquess of Worcester and Lord Johnson Somer-set with a mouth full of vol-au-vents singing along to the Tremeloes' playing live by the rhododendrons? Those were fun days and I wish I'd kept the house and not listened to my 'advisers'. Years after I sold it for £550,000 it went for something like £4.5 million. Any 'sight' would have been good; foresight, hindsight, second sight, insight.

Then there was Little Brinsbury Farm, dating back to 1195 when the stronghold belonged to Brynis. Thomas de Brunnesbury and his delightfully named wife Celestrial lived on the site from 1327 until 1377, but the first mention of the building that I bought is in 1618. I have a list of the incumbents from then right through to World War One, a fascinating swathe of history.

In the spring of 2014, I persuaded BBC Berkshire at Caversham, which is where I broadcast from Monday to Friday, to let me bring in three archaeologists with their top-of-the-range metal detectors onto their vast acreage as there had been people living on the site since Saxon times and the area had never been explored. I was allowed to head this up and wield my own metal detector. During the dig we discovered that man had been there even before that, as I found knapped flints and tools from, I would guess, the Upper Palaeolithic – over 10,000 years ago. We also unearthed some medieval tokens and a beaten silver penny from the Commonwealth period, when Cromwell's troops briefly held Charles I captive in a house on the site. The grounds yielded Elizabethan buckles, a variety of buttons worn by young Georgian dandies and ammunition from the Civil War through to World War Two. There have been plenty of coins to go with that penny from the mid-1600s, including several from the reigns of George II, George III, Victoria, Edward VIII and George V. No hint of the Romans yet, but one of our goals is to try and locate the site of the Elizabethan manor. It almost certainly wasn't on the site of the current house, which was rebuilt on a site for which we have the 1720s design and layout of gardens. Capability Brown added his expertise to the gardens, but his work is now largely undetectable. I hope we can bring in geophysics at some point. The 'Big Dig', as the BBC have named it, continues.

CHAPTER 12

WHEN AN OLD CRICKETER LEAVES THE CREASE

MY FIRST INDUCTION into the world of leather on willow was in next door's orchard against the older and stronger neighbour Christopher Olsen. He could fling one down that whizzed past the imaginary wicket keeper and sent shock waves through the henhouse at long stop. It was, as you can imagine, a rather one-sided affair, but I took my punishment as was expected. My bowling was knocked elegantly past trees bearing the young fruits of Cox and Russet positioned at third man and long leg, and the designated tree that served as our wicket suffered many a dent as the lanky, blond bowler beat the bat time and again.

Playing cricket was one thing, but as a little boy, watching it was another. I would later reach the age where I'd sit in front of the TV with my scorecard, but in those early days the young Olsen, down for Eton and thus already brushing up on his cricket skills, would want to watch the Test Match and I voted for *Andy Pandy* or something equally feeble. It once led to an all-out fight. I had no chance of winning, but I did tear his shirt in the scuffle and went home in disgrace.

Once some of the England cricketers came to our house, of whom I only remember Denis Compton and Godfrey Evans. Why they came I have no idea. I didn't ask then and it didn't seem to matter. Kids just appear to accept things. They did rather generously give me a small cricket bat and a red rubber ball, the latter being eaten at one point by a thick hedge, never to be seen again. On another occasion, nothing to do with cricket, some members of what was then referred to as a Red Indian tribe, but would now be an American Indian tribe, were also guests at one point and brought me some beautifully tooled cowboy boots and a wooden tomahawk with a silver blade and green binding. Now it's too late I want to ask questions. Why did these people beat a path to our door bearing gifts of sporting equipment and weapons of war?

The war between the Test Match and *Andy Pandy* was healed by our respective parents and forgotten completely when a Fortnum and Mason van appeared in the drive bearing a wigwam that would not have disgraced a senior member of the Cheyenne. A perfect excuse to put on the hand-sewn boots and wield the tomahawk. Mostly, though, I wore my cowboy outfit, but never for cricket. I always had to have the correct attire for the occasion. I did get a pair of Christopher's old cricket boots that he'd grown out of, which served me well until I too grew out of them.

I once took 6-6 for Drake House in a school match. That was the peak of my career with the crimson rambler; from there on it was downhill all the way.

In 1973 Tim Rice formed his own cricket team, Heartaches. I occasionally opened the bowling and was sometimes first change, and I snatched a trophy or two as Bowler of the Year. It has to be recorded that the trophies were rather ugly, bizarre monstrosities that belonged on no self-respecting shelf or mantelpiece. They varied according to the availability of bizarre figurines on plinths being sold somewhere in bulk. Our early wicket keeper was Sinbad Coleridge, who bellowed like a rather stern sixth-former about to deliver a severe beating to some unsuspecting new boy. I was the new boy. He was related to the poet of course, but the wrath that fell from his position behind the timbers as I dropped yet another catch was anything but poetic. He scared the life out of me. I didn't dare tell him then. Recently I felt confident enough to confide my early fear to him.

Burly Johnny Chuter and Tim's brother Jo often swung into action with the new ball. Jo spoke Japanese, but it was of little benefit in pavilions of the Home Counties when asking for more cucumber sandwiches. In the fielding positions you might find the aspiring, and ultimately eminent, architect Piers Gough, who would make his name re-developing London's Docklands and receive a CBE for his services to architecture. His younger brother Orlando Gough could also be seen lurking near the boundary, ready to turn his arm. Orlando would later become a celebrated composer, writing for ballet, theatre and the contemporary arts scene. Malcolm Edwards, a very handy chap with the willow, became a major book publisher, and Mike d'Abo was and remains a superb songwriter and singer with assorted versions of Manfred Mann. His younger brother, Noel, also a bastion of the music business, I'd already known for years and he wasn't slow in donning the colours, such as they were. Noel is a most delightful fellow who greets everyone as though he's related to them. He probably is. In the slips and occasionally behind the wicket could be found A. W. Heath, horse-racing aficionado and my one-time band-mate in Just Plain Smith. Alongside him was the already successful lyricist, our golden-haired, slightly balding leader, T. M. B. Rice, unaware of the slew of awards and the knighthood ahead. Other lads in the slightly impertinent colours of red, pink and green were saxophone-playing Chris Brooker and my sometime room-mate Chris Pryke.

In the field Pryke kept his teeth. Behind the stumps he lost a few to a particularly lively ball. It was like a mass extraction without gas. I vividly remember the ivory shower spraying majestically from his gums to whistle their last at the feet of a surprised batsman. When we breakfasted in our room and I had the *Beano* delivered as my morning paper, he was simply 'Pryke'. He has since been elevated to Sir Christopher Dudley Pryke, fourth Baronet. It doesn't mean he got his teeth back, though. Another room-mate was Mark Nicholas, Hampshire skipper turned commentator and interviewer, and one of the professionals that were winched in when the going got tough. He once confessed that he wished he'd kept up his interest in the guitar, but he's doing wonderfully without it.

Among the finest with the willow during my main period as a Heart were big hitter 'Handy' Andy Rossdale, Tim Graveney, who had cricket in his genes, of course, his father Tom having captained England, and Torquil Riley-Smith, who had betting money in his jeans. Torkers lived near Borley Rectory, reputedly the most haunted house in Britain, and his own house wasn't without its spookiness with its cambered passages and odd noises.

I was occasionally able to get away for the Heartaches' annual Cornish tour, an excuse for a lads' week away in September. Housed chez Rice or at fellow Heartache Anthony Deal's house (there were simply a brace of Deals then; more have appeared since) the week consisted of testosterone-fuelled contests against swarthy Cornishmen from local teams such as Mannacan, Mullion and Cornish Choughs. Revered Heartaches names such as Harold Caplan, John 'Fingers' Fingleton, the late Dave Glenn, Jonty Horne, Peter Robinson, Richard Slowe and Nigel Cobb would appear on many a batting order, some with better stats than others, but who cared? That wasn't the point. Actually I'm not too sure what the point was, but that didn't matter either. Did there have to be a point? Only on the field of play, where point is situated between cover and gully.

On one night of the annual tour Tim and I would brandish guitars. Another night would be dedicated to table-tennis, then there'd be a tennis day, then a night in a restaurant. A tough and gruelling regime, I think you'll agree. One of the most intriguing evenings was stew night at the Deals'. The meal would be peppered with Hearts getting to their feet (where possible) and declaring that they'd like to take wine with anyone who … and there would follow a preposterous or embarrassing tagline. Was one man enough to stand and take wine, thus tacitly admitting whatever the charge was?

Of course we had awards ceremonies, stag evenings and Christmas parties. It would have been rude not to. In an amazing run of good fortune, our leader, the aforementioned golden-haired etc., has won the Personality of the Year award every year since 1973. By the most extraordinary coincidence he is also the sole judge of that award. What are the chances of that?

We recently celebrated the team's fortieth anniversary, with several of our former presidents attending the dinner. These lads, Alan Lamb, David Gower, Mike Gatting and Mark Nicholas, can play a bit as well as swanning around for a year as president. I looked around the tent – sorry, the expensive marquee – that Tim had erected in his garden and realised that if all 100 of us had been a team, I would have been put in to bat at about ninety-seven. A sobering thought. I mentioned this to Vanessa but she had no idea what I was talking about, nor who the cricketers were, as she was engrossed in assessing the decor.

As mentioned in Chapter 1, the door into radio was opened mainly by my alleged bowling prowess. Moderately fast. Moderately accurate. Nothing special. Those were the days of plenty, when Neil ffrench Blake could talk record companies into supplying cricket equipment and football kit for entire teams. Some of my fellow broadcasters appeared alongside me in that rather makeshift squad, including Steve Wright and Paul Hollingdale, neither of whom could play cricket. They'd agree with that assessment. For a while I was playing for both 210 and Heartaches. For a nomadic, coarse cricket outfit, the Hearts featured in many magazine photo shoots in our unflattering red, pink and green caps, pullovers, ties and blazers. Our 1987 spread was a riot of colour … more like *Gardener's World* than *You* magazine. There were shots of star batsmen with top crimper John Frieda and his then wife Lulu, the tea ladies with the Rices, a quality control panel comprising

Frieda, Tim Graveney and myself discussing the moistness of the sand-wiches, Tim Rice leading his squad in a round of laughter at a local tavern, and a candid shot of me at the centre of something sinister in the changing rooms. The caption says I'm modelling a straw hat, but judging by the expressions, the various stages of undress and the angle of the bodies, that was clearly a palliative for the easily shocked readers of the *Mail on Sunday*. We also held our tummies in and climbed into our clashing colours for a *Tatler* magazine shoot. Had we no shame? As Shakespeare might have said,

> *Once more into the breeches, dear Hearts, once more.*
> *Or close the batting down with our English Green, Pink*
> *and Red!*

Having presented my programme live at Windsor Castle for his seven-tieth birthday, my longest batting session was thanks to the Duke of Edinburgh. In July 1987 I was invited to Buckingham Palace to help start the TSB Million Mile Walk in aid of the Playing Fields Associa-tion. The charity had been founded in 1926 to protect playing fields and open spaces and provide the opportunity for people of any age to undertake any recreational activity close to their home. The Duke of Edinburgh, who had been its patron since 1947, was there to greet us and start the walk, of which a few of us were doing the first mile inside the Palace yard. As we lined up, Philip and his equerry came over for a chat. I assumed it would be about the charity, but the duke eagerly asked which roadshow week I was doing and what pranks I had lined up that year. I fleetingly thought how wonderful it would be for him to make a surprise appearance at Newquay and have Smiley Miley carted off to the Tower on some slight pretext, but the moment passed. Knowing I was a keen walker and sports enthusiast, Philip's equerry pointed out that I was the strong man of the team. The duke jokily raised his hands in the air as if he were a weightlifter pushing the weights above his head, but a photographer caught him midway and it looks as though he's about to punch my lights out. I still have the photograph in case it all kicks off, to prove that he started it.

Well through this escapade at Buckingham Palace, I was seconded for another bash for the charity later that year. It wasn't unknown for me to reach double figures when batting at number seven or eight, but this was something different. Some fiendish plan had been concocted that meant me batting non-stop for four hours for the Playing Fields Association. All I was told was that it would be 'on the lawn'. Not a bad gig, you might think – hitting a few balls on a beautifully mown strip on a balmy summer's day. Try it at a freezing cold Paddington Station in December, with a string of guys hurling deliveries at you non-stop. As for 'the lawn', that turned out to be the name traditionally given to the area between the Great Western Hotel and the station concourse.

A cricket net was set up, I put on the whites and then I was told about the prizes. Now we all know that if there's a freebie somewhere along the line (no railway pun intended) we try harder. The reward for bowling me out was a not insubstantial voucher which would have got you a return to most places on the network. I faced one railway worker who looked suspiciously like the Antiguan quickie Curtly Ambrose and another who had a look of Malcolm Marshall, the Barbadian fast bowler who was capable of slinging one down in excess of 90 mph. There was the odd furtive-looking moustachioed Antipodean – Dennis Lillee? And that Yorkshire chap. He might have been a little thicker round the middle, but I'm sure I heard someone call him 'Fiery Fred'. I'm not sure what record we were aiming at, I just did the hitting, but it had to be done in accordance with the rules of *The Guinness Book of Records*, so I was officially observed throughout by the area manager for British Rail's Western Region and the National Cricket Academy's youth development officer for Surrey County Cricket Club.

The scorers were the headmaster and teachers of Parkhill School in Croydon, as some of their pupils helped to field and got to throw a few balls down. After four hours of forward drives, sweeps to square leg and snicking it through the covers, I emerged with the jolly credible figure of 1,210-10. I'd faced 1,210 balls in 240 minutes and only been bowled on ten occasions. British Rail were delighted at having to hand out so few free tickets. It was billed as a 'World Record Cricket Attempt' and sponsored by TSB, with commuters chucking some money in the bucket to bowl a seamer or two. Well we did it, but I've never looked to see whether it made *The Guinness Book of Records*. If not, I still have the statistics and the verification. It may not be too late, even though the Playing Fields Association was re-branded in 2007 as Fields in Trust.

Elsewhere, I turned out a few times for Screaming Lord Sutch's Savages. To be a Savage was a noble thing; there had been many of us over the years. The self-styled Third Ear of Harrow and founder of the Monster Raving Loony Party was without doubt a character. He still holds the record for losing the largest number of election campaigns – forty in all. Musicians such as Jeff Beck, John Bonham, Paul Nicholas, Ritchie Blackmore, Jon Lord, Jimmy Page and dozens of other have performed as Savages over the years. At a book launch at Nomis Studios not long before Sutch was found dead, we discussed him hosting a party for everyone who'd ever been a Savage, which would culminate with a group photograph. He was very excited about the prospect, but of course circumstances prevented it from happening.

There were also assorted games for the Bunburys, a team of show-biz and sporting reprobates organised, drilled and skippered by the inimitable David English. I'd first encountered this extraordinary character in 1976, when he became a part of Neil ffrench Blake's on-air team. I was never quite sure of his role, but neither, I suspect, was he. My most vivid memory was of his newsreading. The news, as even small reptiles in the Vietnamese jungle know, is sacrosanct. If you're the newsreader, commenting on news items is strictly *verboten*. Unless, that is, you're David English. On one of those 'and finally' stories, a woman's handbag had been stolen in Reading. That says it all. The listener can draw their own conclusions. English had other ideas. 'What a bloody awful thing to happen. People like that make me really mad. It's absolutely despicable.' And so say all of us, but you'd never catch Trevor MacDonald interjecting personal feelings into a bulletin. I rather liked his matey style, but he wasn't there for long. Despite appearing wonderfully untogether, as former head of RSO Records, he looked after folk like Eric Clapton and the Bee Gees, who loved him to bits.

I was sitting in my old MG at traffic lights in the Fulham Road one afternoon when David pulled up behind me. Always affable, he leapt out for a chat as a queue formed. With one ear on the conversation and one eye on the red light, he chatted in his usual animated fashion. The lights changed.

'David, the lights are green.' I slid the car into gear. He remained unmoved both verbally and physically. 'There are cars hooting at us.'

'That's showbiz,' he laughed, his head firmly inside the car.

'I'm certain it's not because they recognise you from that old Head and Shoulders commercial you did.'

'It might be.' He turned, smiled and waved to a long and increasingly intolerant line of drivers. I wasn't quite sure where to hide. 'It's OK,' he said, 'nobody's business is that important.' He was probably right, but it didn't ease the situation. The lights, which had gone back to red, turned green again. Chaps were getting out of their cars. 'All right, all right,' he beamed, 'just having a chat.' Again he waved regally to one and all. By the third change to green we were off the grid. I was thankful for my pole position and made sure I'd outrun him by the next set of lights.

David had a wonderful knack of pulling the Bunburys together. I'm sure he kept a secret book of likes, dislikes, whims and favourite fielding positions. He knew how to bait the stream for the fish he wanted to catch, in the most genial and charming manner. Who could refuse? I have to admit that he is also a class batsman. Anyone who can hold his own in the company of such eminent cricketers as

Ian Botham, Michael Holding, Dennis Lillee, Chris Cowdrey, Geoff Howarth and Chris Broad has to be good. Apart from the professionals, the Bunburys often looked more like a festival line-up than a cricket team, with Eric Clapton, David Essex, Bill Wyman and Spandau Ballet's John Keeble taking to the field. Used to bigger balls, but equally handy with a smaller one, were Gary Lineker, Graham Taylor, Andy Sinton, Simon Barker and Dean Saunders. Graham Dene and I represented the broadcasters, with Andy Peebles supplying many a fine commentary.

An offshoot match in 1989 was probably the most festival-like, when Bill Wyman's XI played Eric Clapton's XI at Stocks Country Club in Hertfordshire. Eric fielded David English, David Essex, boxer Gary Mason, Frazer Hines, John Keeble, Chris Tarrant, Graham Dene and Johnnie Walker, while Bill's side featured Peter Scudamore, Deep Purple's Ian Paice, Errol Brown, Michael Holding, Mike Rutherford, Andy Fairweather Low and me. A good squad to assemble if there's a lot of singing, twanging, punching, riding and talking, but cricket? We failed to reach their total of 234, the last wicket falling at 180, but money, glasses and spirits were raised at the Dorchester Hotel and, like the tagline that Jimmy Kennedy wrote for 'The Hokey-Cokey', that's what it's all about.

In May 2014 the Heartaches lads and the next generation gathered at the Oxo Tower to show off fading red, pink and green blazers and ties. The effect was that of squinting through a kaleidoscope at a herbaceous border having had a few snifters. I attempted to explain some of the team's characters to Vanessa again, but in most cases they were unexplainable. I solemnly swore to many a fellow Heart that this year I would return for the annual tour of the Lizard, even if I'm not selected. If twenty first-class cricketers have played for the team during its colourful innings of forty years, surely I can return to lend them my camaraderie, wit and bonhomie, if not my dwindling skill at the bowling crease.

CHAPTER 13

ANYONE FOR TENNIS

A LTHOUGH I WAS too young to hold a full-sized tennis racquet properly, I'd bash around on the grass court we had at home. No coaching, no lessons. It was still the era of 'Right, kids off, the adults are coming on'. The tennis court was also the high jump section of my Olympics course. Not the net, as you may be thinking, but two fold-up chairs, standing all of 2 ft 6 in. in old money, with a bamboo cane stretched between them. We had a lot of bamboo, so no outsourcing needed. There was no raising of the bar, nor breaking of records. You either jumped 2 ft 6 in. or you didn't. No judges or umpires needed. That isn't to say there wasn't the odd difference of opinion.

Running a mini-Olympics from the age of five onwards took more than a little organising. I could usually round up half a dozen willing, or unwilling, participants and persuade them to have numbers pinned to their shirts, T-shirts or whatever. Again, this was no haphazard oper-ation. I meticulously drew numbers on sheets of A4 paper with AAA on it for Amateur Athletics Association and made the competitors wear them both front and back. The chief pinner-onner of numbers, my mother, would officiate at a distance. There was no professional-ism or lack of dress code in *my* Games.

Apart from the high jump, there was the relay (if there weren't enough competitors you had to run twice or even swap teams), the sprint, the long jump, putting and running. The running didn't have a particular distance as I recall.

Despite our garden having a hidden stream that ran behind some giant cedar trees there were no water sports. Water is like a magnet to kids and although I often went there looking for adventures (as you do), the stream was too narrow for even a makeshift vessel and too shallow to swim in. So it never made it into the Games.

And then there was the tennis. This was the most difficult to organise as not only did the scoring confuse the other kids, and me to an extent, but the word 'deuce' always made everyone shriek because it sounded the same as 'juice.' Ah, the simplicity of youthful humour. In all these endeavours I was assisted by Old Charlie, our gardener who, unbeknown to him, doubled as my groundsman for the Olympics. I doubt that he was a great age, he just stooped a little, wore a cheesecutter cap and didn't kick up too much when I jumped in his symmetrical piles of dead leaves, but he was 'Old Charlie' simply because our next gardener was also called Charlie and I suspect that he was marginally younger.

I'd trail round after Young Charlie; for kids, anyone that looks as if they're doing something interesting and anyone in the dead leaf, wriggly worm, odd frog and bonfire trade was a natural magnet. Once some chums along the avenue were due to have a brace of Scottish cousins delivered to them for a period. There was much discussion between myself and Charlie as to whether they would look disarmingly different to us and indeed, if they spoke a similar language. This childlike train of conversation spilled over into an earnest conversation about the distance from Scotland to Walton-on-Thames. At such a tender, unworldly age, my estimate when asked to make one was 20 miles. I did believe for a while that everywhere was 20 miles from Walton, which would have been convenient for holidays, but would have made the world a much smaller and more densely populated place. My guess made Charlie roar with derisive laughter. Now as all us kids know, we don't like being laughed at, we like to be taken seriously, so I took the only course open to me and burst into tears. Normally I would have wandered off, licked my wounds and possibly come back for a second guess having consulted my globe atlas, but somewhere behind one of the windows the scenario had been observed.

My father later demanded to know the facts. 'Why were you crying earlier?'

It was easiest to tell the truth. 'Charlie asked me how many miles it was from Scotland and I guessed incorrectly.'

'Now tell me the truth.'

'That is the truth.' I couldn't have made up a story that was any truer.

'Tell me the truth.'

I began to wonder if I was lying without realising it. No, it was what happened. I was sent to my bedroom to think about what I'd said and to revise my answer. Life is damned unfair when you're a kid. Or at least it was then. I thought about making up some other story, but wasn't sure that anything I could create could beat the truth.

The episode passed into history and only took on a new meaning many years later when Charlie appeared in the local paper for making what we'd now refer to as 'inappropriate advances' to children at a local park. All became clear. Had my father possibly heard a vague rumour that our gardener may be 'slightly strange' as he would have termed it and was keeping a weather eye out for anything untoward? These days, with young people being exposed to virtually everything via all aspects of the media, parents would sit down to explain gently and sensibly. But years ago, the social interaction between adults and children was nowhere near as close. Since then I have been incensed if I've been subjected to any kind of injustice.

I played tennis regularly at school, but although the Old Wokingians continued to trot out in their dotage to play soccer, there was no post-school tennis for those who were decanted year in, year out into the world beyond. Nevertheless I wielded diverse styles and makes of racquets over the years against many an opponent on a variety of surfaces, entered the odd tournament and thought I was more proficient than I was.

When I lived in St George's Hill, Cliff Richard was in the next road. We started hitting a few balls at the tennis club from around 1980. In 1983 Cliff's first pro-celebrity tennis tournament kicked off what was to become twenty-five years of volleys, smashes and drop-shots in the name of improving the lives and sporting opportunities of hundreds and hundreds of young players. The amateurs for the initial outing were Cliff, Hank Marvin, Trevor Eve and me. Trevor distinguished himself on court as he did on the stage, winning the debut event with Ann Hobbs. Of course, he was never asked back.

My serving style needed a bit of fine honing at the time, but there was no call for the gales of laughter. I thought they were laughing at Hank's humour, but it was my serve. Cheek. I could hear Cliff's mother remonstrating with a section of the crowd on my behalf. It seems I lifted my right leg up as I served and it looked … well … let's just say it didn't look butch.

Terry Wogan, Mike Yarwood and Hank wielded the racquets at the second tournament, held like the first one at the Brighton Conference Centre, and in 1985 Shakin' Stevens and Annabel Croft, Cliff and Sarah Gomer, Hank Marvin and Virginia Wade, and Ann Hobbs and I showed the audience a thing or two. Cliff and I sang a song or two, during which I didn't lift my leg once. What were the audience laughing at, then?

The following year saw the return of Hank B. Marvin, clearly desperate for a trophy, battling it out against such tennis giants as Ronnie Corbett and Peter Cook and an athlete who could give Hank a run for his money over 1,500 metres, Sebastian Coe. In non-playing capacity I trundled off to the 1987 Tennis Ball in aid of Young Tennis Players of Great Britain. At least I qualified in one of those departments: I was British. Later in the same week Cliff's office flew me up to Manchester to front his 'Search for a Star' day with Sue Barker. We had great fun among 200 enthusiastic kids with fearless forehands and sizzling serves. The result of this day was to lead to the lad setting up his own tennis foundation. The annual tournament raised some £40,000 for the LTA, although fear of my increasing prowess on court led to me doing the commentary instead of posing in my shorts and giving verbal abuse to that year's celebrity players, Elton John, Emlyn Hughes and Mike Yarwood.

On several occasions I presented the Radio One breakfast show from Wimbledon, catching the early morning atmosphere with players knocking up, tons of strawberries making their presence felt and the resident hawk circling Centre Court to put the wind up any disruptive pigeons. One year, following a barbecue at Cliff's with Sue Barker, I persuaded her to come and present the show with me as she had the knowledge and was still Britain's number one at that time. I sidestepped her self-effacing moment, knowing she'd be fine. She's become not only a fixture at Wimbledon, but a great TV presenter, and to many the face and voice of tennis. Maybe I should have been an agent.

The 1988 line-up at Brighton for Cliff's tournament comprised Cliff and Ann Hobbs, me and Virginia Wade, Aled Jones and Julie Mullins, and Jimmy Tarbuck and Annabel Croft. We were all wired up with microphones to catch any pithy or witty epigrams that might fall from our perspiration-flecked lips, but Cliff's kept crackling, breaking up and producing some ghastly feedback. The crowd found it amusing. So did Jimmy Tarbuck, coming out with the lightning line, 'I don't what you lot are laughing about, that's his new single.' At the end of our match with Aled Jones, I jumped the net. Aled followed suit. Then Virginia. I wonder if we'd all leap it so convincingly now? As you may have guessed I carried my partner, with her lack of experience, to an astounding victory. Silverware was ours.

How does it feel to be a winner, eh, Virginia? Stick with me,
kid. What? Seven grand slam titles, number two in the world
at singles and number one at doubles? Ah, well, yes. And

Wimbledon champion ... well, quite ... and the only British
woman in history to have won all four grand slams? Yes, but
I must have played some part in this victory. Not really? Ah.

At the end of the evening there was Cliff's usual festive serenading, one musically astute reviewer later commenting, 'Cliff asked Mike to join him in singing "Silent Night". This sounded really good. Much better than the same version sung by Bros.' I hope they got seats where they could hear properly the following year.

Clearly spurred on by my victory with my short-term doubles partner in 1988, I took another trophy two years later. I say 'short-term' but must emphasise that that was purely Virginia's decision. 'Forget Jeremy Bates,' I pleaded, 'we could make a go of this tennis thing. We make a good team. I distract the opposition with some lamentable shots and you put the winners away.' It made sense to me. Anyway, this second triumph occurred in the summer of 1990 at Marlborough College. It was the illustriously named Joan Hunter Dunn Tennis Tournament, organised by the Betjeman Society and its founder, Philippa Davies. The venue had been chosen as JB had been a schoolboy there, while Joan Hunter Dunn had been his muse for the poem 'A Subaltern's Love-Song'. It was a jolly day, with the chaps clad in blazers and boaters and the ladies in '20s dresses and the like. I turned up in my MG TF and proceeded, quoting Betjeman, to start 'whizzing them over the net with the strength of five'. In the afterglow of another fleeting moment on the podium of my mind, we lounged in the old cricket pavilion, drank tea and listened to some '30s Wimbledon tennis commentaries. No silverware this time, the prize being a rather decent racquet and a certificate signed by Miss J. Hunter Dunn herself.

I had a good-quality court when I lived at The Aldermoor, which usually had somebody playing on it. Errol Brown came to play one day, taking to the court in fashionable long trousers, a beautifully tailored shirt and a rather exotic-looking fedora. I wasn't sure how this would work in actual play, but Errol seemed to cope and effortlessly straddled the gap between tramline and catwalk. Jona Lewie was also on court, stopping balls rather than cavalry and giving a reasonable impression of a solid player. Who knows who won? Who cared? We had a jolly time and a feed at the local pub, the Royal Oak, was the post-match carrot. Now many's the time I'd been in that pub and heard the stentorian Gallic tones of Jacques the landlord, exclaiming, 'Oh, you 'ave meessed 'im again, your namesake, 'e was in yesterday.' The ''im' in question was Oliver Reed, who lived in the next village. Not exactly my namesake of course, with our Christian names being entirely different and our surnames being spelled differently, but that didn't deter Jacques. This evening, however, was different. Oliver and his wife and a couple of friends were also booked in for dinner. With only one table separating us (a golden wedding anniversary) we must surely fall into conversation and become the best of friends. Over a modest starter, Errol, Jona and I fell to talking about the media attention Oliver received and that most of it was probably exaggerated and unjust. Within two minutes of arriving he proved it wasn't. Returning from a quick trip to the gents, an old boy in blazer and tie on the next table turned to him and said, 'You're Oliver Reed, aren't you?'

The actor pushed his sleeve up and shoved his fist into the chap's face. 'What if I am? Want to make something of it?'

If I were a betting man I'd say that the chap didn't want to make anything of it. Nevertheless he'd probably done his bit during the war and didn't want to lose face. 'Think you're clever, do you?'

'Yes,' said Oliver, removing the flower from the guy's buttonhole and eating it.

'Oh, think you're a big man, do you?'

In retrospect I'm sure it was more of a statement than a question, but it was a gift to Oliver Reed. He unzipped his trousers and slapped his manhood on the table, declaring, 'Yes I do.'

As they say of bank robberies, it all happened so quickly. That being so, we felt that we should intervene at this point, so Errol and I rather cautiously got to our feet, without actually having discussed a plan of action. Before I could wrestle Oliver to the floor and force him to apologise (yeah, right) he'd zipped himself up again, just as Jacques came round the corner and grabbed him playfully. I'm never sure whether anyone ever grabbed Oliver Reed 'playfully', but at least he sat down ... and so did we. I wisely decided against going over and attempting to become bosom buddies with my 'namesake', for many reasons. Mostly because he might have punched my lights out.

The Federation Cup, the premier international women's tennis event, hadn't been to Britain since 1977, so it was quite a big deal when it was staged at Nottingham in 1991. I headed up there for a few days, as tennis and the Radio One Roadshow came together for the tournament, initially attending the official reception with British players Sam Smith, Monique Javer and Clare Wood. One of my duties was hosting the fantastic children's day, with tennis kids of all nationalities integrating through tennis. *Tennis World* revealed that Cliff and I would be on court to 'capture the excitement' of the first day. Not 'provide the excitement' you'll have noted, just capture it. They did us proud in the alliteration stakes with the headline 'Royalty, Read and the Radio One Roadshow'.

All the great female players, such as Monica Seles, Steffi Graf and Jennifer Capriati, were there, and security was high due to the presence of the Princess of Wales, but that didn't stop Smiley Miley. Following a hit on court, I returned in time for the radio show to see my MG some 80 feet in the air on the platform of a crane. I have no idea how he got it up there or how much it cost. I reasoned that at least I wouldn't get a parking ticket, but I have to admit that it was a trifle embarrassing to keep glancing up and seeing my car in the clouds. Even so, Diana thought it was a scream. I've often wondered why Smiley didn't latch on to this royal approval and use 'By Appointment'. An opportunity missed.

The Princess of Wales was also the guest of honour at a charity tournament in aid of the British Deaf Association, staged at the David Lloyd club at Raynes Park. Another opportunity to play with some of the greats. I partnered the delightful Peter Fleming, today a TV commentator but underused and underrated in that role. He'd won countless doubles championships with John McEnroe and now he was saddled with me. I knew the plan: 'Yours, Peter ... Yours again ... Yours, Peter ... You, partner.' A familiar but successful pattern. On this was a formidable partnership built, to face the might of Michael Chang, Stefan Edberg et al.

If the opposition was tough, the umpires, in the shape of Jeffery Archer and Bruce Forsyth, were even tougher. Frustrated by their inexplicable decisions, I proffered my racquet to Diana at one point, but obviously not being dressed for the occasion, she declined. Not scared of former Wimbledon Champions, surely, Ma'am?

There was also an art auction in aid of the charity and I'd fallen in love with one of the paintings. During the interval I was studying the art when an intrigued Diana came over. 'Have you bought anything?'

I nodded. 'Guess which one.'

She went through most of the works before pointing at a picture of two ladies in Edwardian dress playing tennis at twilight by an old country house. 'Not that one?'

'That's the one. Don't you like it?'

'Not particularly.'

'Good, then you won't be fighting me for it.'

'Absolutely not.' She looked at the ground and laughed. I wasn't certain whether she was scoffing at my taste or the painting. Probably both. One scoff fits all.

On another occasion my friend Charles Haswell and I had been playing with some former professionals at the Chelsea Harbour Club when Diana appeared from the pool, greeting us with a beaming smile and possibly a little envy that we'd been playing tennis with a handful of veteran champions. Her exuberance was such that we hugged and I gave her a kiss. It seemed the natural thing to do. I didn't notice, but Charles pointed out that she blushed rather deeply. An hour later I had a phone call from Ken Wharfe, Diana's protection officer.

'What have you been up to, Read?'

'What?'

'Don't give me that. The Princess came in here looking rather flushed a while ago and was full of it. Apparently you kissed her.'

'Ah, yes … not a good thing to do?'

'On the contrary, she seemed very happy.'

There seemed to be so many tennis tournaments played for good causes in the '90s. One such, in 1992, was at the old Vanderbilt Club, now buried under the Westfield shopping centre at Shepherd's Bush. In the name of Help Hammer Cancer, with fellow DJs David Hamilton and Ed Stewart alongside equally short-shorted television presenters Martyn Lewis and Jonathan Dimbleby, we once again took to the court. Our old pal George Layton took the honours that day, holding the not insignificant trophy triumphantly over his head.

Also in 1992 Cliff's annual tennis tournament celebrated its tenth staging by moving to the bigger National Indoor Arena at Birmingham, where Frank Bruno and Roy Castle joined us on court. Roy, Cliff, Tim Rice and I forced some of our own unique brand of rock & roll on the 14,000 or so on whom we'd bolted the doors. What a sound: two guitars, one trumpet, one gyrating Mick Jagger tribute act (T. Rice) and three voices. A rare and intriguing combination. Michael Ball later showed us how it should be done. At Birmingham, the format began to change to accommodate more players, so I never had a clue who was winning or losing. The tournament was always held a week before Christmas so everyone was in the festive mood. We mixed around, played it for laughs and often worked in teams, popping on court for a game or two and then off again. Slightly more Davis Cup. No, more like the Bette Davis Cup. As usual the Salvation Army band would play, march and get everyone into the spiritual side of the season and Cliff would follow with a hit or two and a carol or three. Following 'Mistletoe and Wine', I joined him for 'All I Have to Do Is Dream' and Brian Conley made it a trio as we launched into 'Whole Lotta Shakin''.

Maybe it was the way we harmonised on 'Dream', maybe it was our ferocious cross-court backhands, or more realistically maybe nobody else was available, but Cliff and I were invited to play at Eastbourne. No, not on the beach, but, as Alf Garnett might have said, 'Yer actual Eastbourne.' For the top women players, this was and remains the tournament leading up to Wimbledon. With temperatures up in the high seventies, Cliff and I joined former England footballer Colin 'Nijinsky' Bell, John Inverdale and Jeff Wayne, of *War of the Worlds* fame, to play on the main court with some of the planet's greatest. I'd played against Jeff in a tournament before and he was good. A one-time captain of Hertfordshire who used to play on the circuit in the States, he was virtually a professional, but all the while there's a racquet in one's hand, there's hope. Under the eye of the Duchess of Gloucester, seen studiously taking notes of my unorthodox but cavalier style, we strode into the arena. I eyed the opposition, which included Arantxa Sánchez Vicario and Nathalie Tauziat. I partnered the talented South African number one, Amanda Coetzer, but fell foul of Jana Novotná, who was umpiring. I climbed the chair to remonstrate with her over some seriously questionable line calls, but she was having none of it and put me firmly in my place, wherever that was. Clearly not on court. That worthy and austere organ the *Eastbourne Gazette* deemed this curtain raiser to the serious tennis worthy of the whole front page. 'The first game, between Sir Cliff and Arantxa against Mike and Amanda, was tremendous entertainment and was enhanced by reigning champion Jana Novotná's umpiring.' It says much for the match when the highlight appears to be the umpiring.

By the late '90s Cliff's festive tennis season had extended to a fundraising evening for his foundation at Hampton Court. What a setting, especially at Christmas. In 1990 I performed my regular 'Twelve Days of Christmas', a rabble-rousing, ice-breaking vocal start to the evening, with everyone, including the Duchess of York, taking part. In 2002 the Russian girls for whom I was producing and writing (see Chapter 10) performed at Hampton Court, singing 'Silent Night' in their own language to an enthusiastic audience that once again included the Duchess of York, alongside William Hague and Cherie Blair. The Hampton Court bash was always atmospheric, with the lighted torches, the lone piper, the Tudor kitchens and of course, the history. One year I performed in the Great Hall with Gordon Giltrap. He played 'Greensleeves', over which I recited 'Winter' from *Love's Labour's Lost*, as both Henry VIII and Shakespeare performed in the Great Hall. At different times of course – Henry was the warm-up man, with the Bard getting the gig a few years later.

The previous year I collected the largest piece of tennis silverware I'd ever seen. Partnering Guillermo Vilas, one of the greatest-ever South American players, we won the Mulberry Classic at Hurlingham. 'Guillermo,' I said, 'play your natural game. Don't tighten up.'

'What, you mean like I did when I won seven titles in a row, or when I was world number one alongside Björn Borg?'

'Yes, you've got it. Let me call the shots.'

'OK. Much like the time you were on court with me when I won the Australian, French and US Open titles.'

The boy was a quick learner. Rather decently he let me keep the trophy. 'I've got cabinets full of them. You have it. You probably don't have many.' He was right. I staggered out to the car park looking like I'd won the biggest trophy in the world, only to find it wouldn't fit in the boot. I kept it for a year and would have kept it forever but Mulberry insisted that I give it back. It was a *Lord of the Rings* situation, I didn't want to let go.

In 2002 I brokered an unusual union at Cliff's annual tournament. A year or two earlier, when we had been shooting the video for 'November Night', Cliff bemoaned the fact that he'd never met Roy Bennett and Sid Tepper, who had written 'The Young Ones', assuming (erroneously) that they'd passed on. An idea began to take shape. Again a few years earlier, I'd interviewed Roy for a book and knew that one of his ambitions had been to meet Cliff. He assumed that now it was too late and wouldn't happen. As well as 'The Young

Ones', these guys had written many songs that Cliff covered, including 'When the Girl in Your Arms' and 'Travellin' Light'. They'd also written for Frank Sinatra and penned over fifty songs for Elvis. So it was that in 2002 I flew Roy and his wife Ruth to London. On the day of the tennis tournament we travelled to Birmingham. The tennis over, Cliff took to the stage with his band, but before they could start playing, I walked on, unannounced.

'What are you doing?' Cliff mouthed. He might even have hissed a little, I can't be sure.

'Who loves "The Young Ones"?' I asked the crowd, to a rousing cheer. '"Travellin' Light"?' Rousing cheer. I listed many Tepper and Bennett songs that Cliff had success with and then many Elvis classics they'd written. I told the respective tales of admiration and how both parties assumed that it was a moment that would never happen. To tumultuous applause from 12,000-plus fans, I brought Roy on stage. Cliff was truly shocked. They hugged like two old friends. A moment to take it all in, and then they launched straight into 'The Young Ones'. Epic.

There have been countless pro-celebrity tournaments over the years. I've already mentioned many of the great women players I've been delighted to be on court with and I'm also so lucky to have played alongside the likes of Rod Laver, Roscoe Tanner, Ken Rosewall, John and David Lloyd, Frew McMillan, Roger Taylor, Jeremy Bates, Mansour Bahrami, Henri Leconte and Ilie Nastase. It was genuinely a privilege to be on court with such world-class players.

While living at Amberley, in the shadow of the glorious South Downs, I played extensively for Storrington, even spending a few years as club captain. Not, I suspect, through being an outstanding player, but more for standing still in the line of those press-ganged, while the wiser old owls took that regulation step backwards.

If I thought that my task was to swagger around the court with the word 'captain' emblazoned on my blazer, while fair maidens' hearts skipped a beat, I was wrong. There were the obligatory meetings, usually about carpets, curtains and paper clips, awkward members to be counselled, arguments over court bookings to be sorted and teams to be selected. Selecting four players for my particular squad was tricky enough, but there were five men's teams alone, who all had their regular share of problems: players crying off at the last minute, replacements to be found, opponents who were lost en route to a match and the unfathomable County League rules. These were enough to baffle the love-child of Euclid and Alan Turing (unlikely, I know, but it gets the point over). Many a time we've fallen foul of the County statute book. The opposition would scrutinise your team with more zeal than the cast of the Book of Judges from the Old Testament. 'Didn't we play against you in the second team a few weeks ago? Play for both, do you?' 'Not sure you're allowed to play down a league on the second Sunday after Epiphany.' 'Are you new to the club? Not seen you before.' The implication being that we might be fielding a ringer.

Let me slice open the cake for an example. Oh, on the subject of cake, the home team was duty bound to provide tea. That hopeless, haphazard, disorganised member of the human race known as a 'bloke' is never shown up in a more marked manner than in the area of tennis teas. Here's the scenario. It's a home game, ergo we provide the tea. With exceptional and uncanny male organisation we each turn up with mini chocolate rolls and a lump of cheddar.

'I thought you were getting the bread.'

'I thought *you* were.'

'Who's brought butter?'

Silence while we all look accusingly at each other.

'Milk?'

We all stare out of the window.

'Ham?'

Something has caught our eye through the window. It's the first team ladies approaching the pavilion laden with enough home-made food to satisfy Billy Bunter and the whole of the Remove at Greyfriars School.

Possibly, just possibly, food envy is pushed to the back of our minds during the battle for league points with the opposition, but as soon as the day is won (or lost) we begin to rue the fact all over again that we are Men. We may be able to smash a ball over the net in quasi-macho manner (or should that be Quasimodo manner?) but as hunter-gatherers and providers we are bottom of the league. As the ladies unveil quiches, cakes, delicate sandwiches, salads and pasta our opponents make their excuses and leave. They probably have plans to stop en route somewhere. Anywhere that serves anything other than cheddar and mini-rolls. If we look pathetic enough, the ladies may lend us a drop of their semi-skimmed to make our tea a marginally more acceptable colour.

I got diverted by cake. I was about to regale you with an actual case of scrutiny and how it can lead one into deep water.

We are playing a team further east than us. Not as far as Rye and not as close as Worthing. That day we are playing as the second four. With a player dropping out at the last minute, I call on a first-team player, who obliges. On arrival, he is immediately subjected to the gimlet-eyed appraisal of one of the opposition.

'I've played against you before.'

'I don't think so.'

'Yes I have. Aren't you in the first team?

'Me?'

'Yes, you. You've played down once before, I remember. You can't do that twice in a season or we can claim the match by default.'

Ben has been rumbled. This could be a wasted journey.

'What's your name?'

'Ben.'

'Ben what?'

Here another of our team rushes to Ben's aid. 'Ben Maddison.'

'Maddison? But you're a Maddison, you're Dave Maddison, I've played against you many times.'

'That's right.'

'Is he a relation?'

'Not really.'

'Not really? He either is or he isn't.'

It's getting tricky for Dave. He was only trying to help and now he's in the dock. 'He isn't.'

'That's a coincidence, two Maddisons.'

Dave clutches at a straw that is blocked at both ends. 'He's Madison, with one D.'

The unlikely farrago hangs in the air.

'Come on,' says their skipper, 'we're already fifteen minutes late starting.' I make a mental note to remember when we sign the score sheet at the end of the match to write Ben's name as Madison, with one D. It's not easy being the captain.

Mention must be made of our fourth team member that day, Tony James. A former Commonwealth athlete, when he was ten stones lighter of course, an exceptionally gifted artist and a collector of vintage cars. The trick with the cars, he says, is to have so many that your wife never knows when you've bought another. He was my on-court partner and a decent player, despite never knowing the score. His random idea of what the score might be baffled many an opponent as well as me, but he was my pal and if he thought we'd won the game he must be right. I'm sure we got quite a few points that way. I called him Rhino. When he charged the net, even the Saracens First XV would have taken cover, and the steam from his nostrils brought to mind an A4 4-6-2 locomotive bound for Glasgow on a frosty November morning.

It was in a delightful shop in Moreton-in-Marsh that I spotted it: a realistic model rhino. The sort you'd buy for a farm set if you were breeding rhinos. I bought five, the final destination of the odd-toed ungulates already firmly in my mind. They nestled in my tennis bag until teatime. We were playing a Sussex County match away: slap-up feed guaranteed. The timing was perfect. As Rhino popped to the loo the sandwiches and cakes emerged. The opposition gazed in wonder as I secreted five rhinoceroses among the cakes and sandwiches. I explained the gag. We could hardly contain ourselves. Rhino returned. This man is ultimately laid back, but he must notice them. He ate a sandwich, then another. He even moved one of the model rhinos to get to a cake. This was baffling. Another cake. More tea. Eventually he leaned over very, very casually, stretched out a laconic arm, picked up one of the rhinos, examined it, replaced it, turned to the opposing players and said at length, 'That's a really strange coincidence, because they call me Rhino.'

Before the groundsman takes the net down and I head off to the changing rooms, I must make a confession that may see me banned from any future matches. From 2005 until 2009, as I've mentioned elsewhere, I was presenting programmes at Frinton-on-Sea for the re-launched Radio London. Unsurprisingly, I played a lot of tennis at Frinton, one of the most delightful clubs in the country. Beautiful grass courts, fantastic location, lovely people and an incredible history. My biggest thrill on court at Frinton was playing in a doubles match with Mark Cox, former world number one, against former British number one Andrew Castle and Buster Mottram, once ranked fifteenth in the world. That array of talent makes you step up to the mark.

Well, that was nearly my biggest thrill. One wet evening after a strenuous indoor tennis session we were sitting in the bar discussing how exciting it must have been when it was only the second tournament to Wimbledon. Tales were told of the days when the Prince of Wales, later Edward VIII, took the courts, when Winston Churchill smoked cigars at the bar and when King Zog of Albania and Emperor Haile Selassie of Abyssinia visited the club. While we were talking about these great characters I felt words form unbidden on my lips. 'They'll also be talking about tonight for years to come.'

The gang looked at me as though I was mad. 'What on earth will they say?' someone ventured.

'They'll say, "Have you heard about the night they played naked tennis on the hallowed lawns of Frinton-on-Sea?"'

Accompanied by much shrieking, four of us disrobed and headed out on the moonless night with the rain driving in from the sea. We could hardly see to play so the assembled company couldn't have seen much either. If indeed there was much to see … It was hilarious … and wet. I'd say we were soaked to the skin by the time we'd finished, but we were only in our skin. Very exhilarating and who could even guess at the score, but we did it. Word spread very quickly, especially as this was Frinton, the last bastion of gentility. The last place in Britain to get a pub, the last to get a fish and chip shop, and the first to get naked tennis. The papers carried the story, which even made the nationals and some magazines. I was asked to deny it. I couldn't. The club got a local journalist (a good friend of mine) to write a piece for the local papers specifically saying that we'd made it up, that it was an urban myth. It wasn't. People still ask me about it years later.

CHAPTER 14

SKIING IN THE SNOW

MY FIRST SKIING jaunt was early in the early '90s, taking to the slopes with Cliff Richard, another new boy on the piste, and our friend Charles Haswell. As I was still less than enamoured of flying at the time, I took the train and met them at the picturesque Austrian resort of Lech am Arlberg. Through the window of the train, I spotted small dots on the mountainsides at about 10,000 feet. People? Impossible! Well, even if they were, at least I'd never have to ski down from there. The lower, gentler slopes would be fine for me. Wrong. After one day on the nursery slope our guide had me in a chair lift heading up to the Kriegerhorn, the nearest mountain, in a pretty fierce blizzard. At the top there was a biting wind. Cliff was concerned. Not for his safety, but for his showbiz persona. His face was going numb with the intense cold. 'I can't smile properly,' he shouted above the storm.

'I'm not sure anyone's going to notice in this weather,' I shouted back.

'Even so, it's a bit worrying.'

To my surprise, I made it down the mountain without serious mishap. Well, until the last 50 yards or so, when I overegged it a tad in the confidence department and virtually fell into the hotel, a flurry of arms, legs and one ski. I found the other ski about 100 feet away buried in snow.

The following day I spotted a guy in the hotel foyer who looked familiar. He obviously felt the same about us. 'Hi guys, we knew you were here.'

Who was he? A spy? Superintendent of the skiing police? Press? No, he was royal protection officer Ken Wharfe. He explained that our presence was known as they had to check the other guests before the Princess of Wales and Princes William and Harry were booked in. It was all very relaxed and great fun, Diana being happy to join in our regular sessions when we got the guitars out after dinner. Don't think me lazy or plagiaristic but let me lift one Lech session from Cliff's book, where Diana asked if William and Harry could join the singing session one night.

> We agreed that it shouldn't be too late because they had to go to bed, so Diana suggested we do it at about eight o'clock, after the boys had had their meal and before we had ours. So Mike and I joined them in the empty bar and I sang all my hits ... after one of the songs I stopped for a moment and Harry said, 'Do you know "Great Balls of Fire"?' I said, 'Of course, but how on earth do you know it?' ... He said, 'Because Mummy likes it...' So I sang it and Harry was beside himself with excitement. He grabbed a Toblerone packet that was lying on the table and, using it as a microphone, gyrated like Michael Jackson while Mike and I did the number.

There have been some extraordinary groups in the history of music, but a five-piece featuring the future King of England, the Princess of Wales, Prince Henry of Wales and the most successful British singer of all time must cap the lot. I recently had a note from William, who remembered the Lech days with great fondness.

I did make it down from 10,000 feet by the second year, but there were a few hairy moments, like a 100-yard-long ice path about two feet wide, with a mountain on the left and a sheer drop on the right. I made God all sorts of outrageous promises during those 100 yards if I came through it safely. I hope he doesn't remember them. OK, it wasn't the most graceful descent, but that was never part of the plan. Actually there was no plan, unless it was 'Come down as upright as possible and if upright isn't possible, try to slither down without being spotted'. Harry was fearless, although the royal security team kept an eye on the two princes from a discreet distance. I seem to remember the boys carrying some sort of tracking device with an alarm, so if they got into difficulty of any kind, Ken and his team would lock onto their co-ordinates and locate them within minutes.

In March 1992, Prince Charles came out to join the royal party, and he and Diana invited Cliff, Charles Haswell and me to have supper with them on the Sunday. Unfortunately, circumstances dictated otherwise. On that day, Diana's father, Earl Spencer, died. There were already dozens of photographers outside the hotel, but that now intensified. What a ghastly situation for her and the boys. A father and grandfather passes away and you're in a goldfish bowl until a suitable flight can be organised. It was difficult to know how to commiserate without being intrusive. I wrote a note with a small poem and slipped it under her door. Two weeks later I received the most gracious and charming letter from her, at a time when she must have had many more pressing matters to attend to. I was very touched.

Amazingly, neither did she forget the dinner. We re-convened at Charles H.'s house in Barnes some while later. Of course we sang a few songs as she'd insisted we take the guitars along. We even had a rehearsal in Cliff's kitchen. Heaven knows why we bothered rehearsing, as we rattled through some old favourites with Ken joining us on a third harmony here and there. Someone commented that he sang like a bird, so I called him 'Canary Wharfe', which Diana thought was a terrific name for him. We'd all adopted daft names when skiing, like the Count of the Mount, the Artiste of the Piste, the Lush of the Slush and the Wizard of the Blizzard.

One year, a TV crew came out to film Cliff's antics on the slopes, so we all tried to look as professional as possible. We were instructed to 'stand in a line and all hold one ski in the air'. Of course I slipped, and the rest went down like ninepins. Uncool.

A bonus of skiing in Lech was the indoor tennis centre, despite the higher altitude causing the ball to whizz through the air that much faster. The most magical aspect of Lech was the horse-drawn sleighs, their festive bells jangling as they pulled us up the mountain through the sharp evening air to a wooden restaurant another thousand feet up.

On one occasion, Ken Wharfe talked me into staying an extra day. He was planning to go up into uncharted territory and promised it would be rather special. Our guide knew the mountain like the back of his ski glove. Something told me to go home. I stayed. That night in the bar, the locals looked aghast. 'You're going up tomorrow with Gurt?'

'That's the plan.'

'Gurt, the Madman of the Mountain?' The plan wasn't looking so hot. The place shook with laughter. 'He is a crazy man. Sleeps all night on the mountain. Drinks lots of schnapps.'

'Hmm.' Thanks, Ken.

The day dawned. What could go wrong? I'd been skiing all week. It was just another day, I tried to convince myself. We went high and came down through the trees. Very pretty but very scary. Suddenly there seemed to be more trees than space in between them. Without warning, I rounded some pines, ploughed through some deep snow and collided with a stationary Wharfe. He was taking a breather. My skis slid under his, I went over backwards and one of his skis smacked me a massive crack on the head. I was poleaxed and expected our concerned guide to have me airlifted off the mountain at once.

'Come on let's go,' he said.

'Go where?' I wasn't sure where I was, let alone where I was going.

Ken was giving me a strange look. 'Crikey, you've got a bit of a bump.'

I felt my head and there was a lump the size of a rugby ball. Well, a sizeable hen's egg at least. Common sense, not that I'm overendowed with it, told me to discontinue the exercise and get off the mountain. I spent most of the afternoon attempting to translate stories in the local paper while I waited for the doctor and felt my lump expanding by the minute. I survived, but only just.

A move from Lech one year saw us skiing at Megève in the Rhône-Alpes region of south-eastern France. It was a superb place, turned into an alternative to St Moritz by the Rothschilds in the '20s, but getting to the slopes from our hotel meant a trip across town. The place where we lunched, a few thousand feet up, afforded us the most fantastic view of neighbouring Mont Blanc, but the snow was beginning to melt some way down. Time and time again I skied into pools of water. Very tiring, very wet. I decided to head off earlier each day to play tennis at a local centre with their coach. Less tiring, less wet. I missed out on a trip to Aspen, but each year there's loose talk about reviving the crack skiing team and taking to the slopes again in earnest. Now where's my 'Wizard of the Blizzard' T-shirt?

CHAPTER 15

BALL OF CONFUSION

I SUPPOSE I'VE HAD three stages of sport, football as a kid, then cricket and then tennis, although I've always played all three. I also enjoy croquet, a demonic game that I think is a cross between chess and snooker. An early girlfriend, Gillie Palmer, had regular croquet in her family's garden and I also played on the island of Herm in the '80s and '90s, when it was owned by my friends the Woods. Rules varied of course. During one particularly tight match on the island with Rupert Wood and his sister Rosie, my ball rolled onto the pie-crust shoe of the Dean of Guernsey and lodged there. I wasn't in the market for forfeiting a shot at that decisive stage of the game and looked hopefully at the surprised clergyman. I had to make an important decision in a nanosecond.

Step One, as Eddie Cochran once sang: I knew that Guernsey came under the episcopal jurisdiction of the Bishop of Winchester. Step Two: I supposed therefore that he wasn't a suffragan bishop and therefore 'Your eminence' would be incorrect. I couldn't afford to get this wrong. Did that make the correct address 'Your Grace'? Step Three: An innocent upturned face and a polite 'Your Grace?' Nothing needed adding. Being a man of the world, or at least of the Channel Islands, he got my drift. He nodded. I clicked the ball neatly off his shoe with my mallet and away it rolled. He smiled and spoke at last: 'Divine intervention.'

In 1987 I was invited, with Rupert Wood, to the British Open Croquet Championship Final at Hurlingham. Worth it for the champagne breakfast, lunch and afternoon tea alone, but enhanced by many an awe-inspiring roquet, croquet, hoops run and even the odd attempt at a triple peel. After having watched the game for some while, I went in to buy a lemonade, or maybe something less appropriate. Coming away from the bar, pint in hand and with a copy of *The Times* under his arm was one of the finalists. Impossible.

'Aren't you actually playing in the final…?' I began, incredulously, pointing to the great outdoors.

'Oh yes,' he smiled dismissively. 'I know his game very well, he'll be about another fifteen minutes on his turn.'

Casual, assured, British. A Francis Drake moment.

When I moved to Little Brinsbury Farm and bought a few acres of extra land I created a full-size croquet lawn with the expert help of my girlfriend Alison's father, Stanley Jenkins. He'd been Our Man in Singapore when Wimbledon champions Lew Hoad and Ken Rosewall broke their journey from Australia there, en route to defend their title in 1954, and the Foreign Office had insisted he create a court for them. His own tennis lawn had always been the benchmark of excellence. So who better for my croquet lawn? I came to look upon Stanley as a second father. He is a man equipped with humility, humour and a sense of fair play, and he makes good chips. He'd been one of the World Youth leaders with Olof Palme and Che Guevara, had worked with Mountbatten and was referred to by the head of the KGB as an 'arch-imperialist fascist beast'. Maybe Khrushchev hadn't experienced the canny Welshman's expertise on the tennis court, or the croquet lawn. We cut, we rolled we trimmed, we marked, we encouraged the moles to colonise someone else's land and we turned out a pretty respectable patch measuring the required 35 yards by 28 yards, virtually twice the size of a tennis court.

As well as social games, I organised a well-attended croquet tournament twice a year, when the marker flags went up, a gazebo was erected and the silverware was displayed on a table alongside all the trappings that heralded an old-fashioned afternoon tea. The names engraved on the shield, which still sits gleaming atop shelves of books, reveals that the 1997 winner was singing supremo Colin Blunstone. Many a rock star was humbled on that lawn, but not the man from St Albans with the velvet voice. Could there be a revamped Zombies album in the pipeline? 'She's Not There (She's Playing Croquet)', 'Tell Her No (I Can't Play Croquet)' and 'Time of the Season (For Croquet)'? Probably not. There seemed to be a plethora of croquet tournaments in the '90s and while my diary might not be dominated by them, they certainly rank among the multiple entries. One classic, at Wiston House, Steyning in the shadow of the South Downs was an all MP affair … well apart from me, with Howard Flight, Tim Loughton, Peter Bottomley and Nick Gibb throwing caution to the wind and running those hoops as if they were on the campaign trail with one week to go to the elections.

Encouraged by my father, I kicked leather footballs from an early age, until getting hooked on Frido balls. These were dimpled plastic, or maybe PVC, affairs, the first cheap alternative to a leather football, and were less inclined to smash windows. The ideal way to carry them was in a plastic string bag, then you could kick them, as you walked to whichever patch of green you were going to grace, without them actually departing into the traffic or over a wall. Apart from the puncture kit, I was quite passionate about them. They were fairly susceptible to thorns and other sharp objects and while they were still serviceable when flat, the shape wasn't ideal. The puncture kit, simple to most, was complex to me.

As mentioned earlier, my father played centre-half for one of the top amateur teams, Walton & Hersham, meaning there were always full-size leather balls around. Even at the age of five I did nothing by halves. Even if I was having a kickabout with friends in the garden

I had to dress accordingly. I had to put on the whole kit, including proper boots, or I didn't feel properly dressed. Weird kid. As Walton played in red and white, I felt that these were the only acceptable colours and was aghast when a lad a year or two older than me turned up to play in the garden one day in a green top with green and white socks. I remember trying to send him home to change.

My father was a good player and, like all sportsmen of his era, humble. After he died I found a stack of old football programmes from some of the teams he'd played in. As well as Walton & Hersham, there were many local sides as well as The Army XI, the Combined Services XI and Guildford, who were semi-professional. He'd never mentioned it to me, but one programme mentioned that he'd been asked to turn professional on several occasions. Another declared him to be one of the most popular players in the amateur game and one of the strongest centre-halves.

My mother would embarrass him with the odd soccer story. He was standing in a doorway in Manchester, where he was stationed with the Army, sheltering from the rain, when a police car pulled up. 'Les Read?'

'Yes.'

'You're wanted, sir.'

'What am I supposed to have done?'

'I believe it's what you're going to do.'

He was passed a call-up card to train with the war-torn Manchester United squad.

My father was selected for a post-war game at Gigg Lane, home of the mighty Bury FC, for which my mother was in the stand. That shows that it was early days in their relationship! Concerned at his non-appearance on the pitch, she was equally surprised when he slid into the seat next to her fifteen minutes into the match.

'Why aren't you on the pitch?'

'I was held up.'

'Tell them you're here.'

'No, it's too late now, anyway someone else is already playing.'

'You didn't want to face their right-winger, did you?'

'Don't be silly.'

'Are you sure?'

'Don't be ridiculous.'

He never did go on the pitch, even for the second half. In later life he still got annoyed when my mother told the story of how he was afraid of facing Stanley Matthews. I'll guarantee he's looking down as I write. 'Don't be ridiculous.'

Not many mess with a tall, strapping centre-half, but in the first thirty minutes of one game he took a hard knock on the head. The game proceeded, as games do, until a brief respite midway through the second-half, when one of the team was getting dousing from the trainer's 'magic sponge'. During the break in proceedings, another player asked generally, 'Does Les keep asking you the score?'

'Actually, yes.'

'Me too.'

'And me.'

He hadn't a clue where he was, or what was going on. He'd played most of the match with concussion.

I used to laugh at the story when I was a kid. Until it happened to me. I was playing in a match on Desborough Island on the Thames at Weybridge. It was a foggy, footbally type of Sunday morning. Our side were awarded a corner. And as the ball came over, we all went up for it. I connected and it went in the goal, but of that I had not an inkling. Somewhere in the melee a boot connected with my temple. I do recall someone asking me what I was doing. What did they think I was doing? I was running around in small circles behind the goal. I later discovered that some thought it might be my individual way of celebrating. It wasn't.

I was driven to St Peter's Hospital in Chertsey and thrown into A&E. I was lying quite happily on a bed, when a doctor came in and asked me my name. I hadn't got a clue.

'Do you know what you've been doing?'

I looked down at my muddy football kit. 'No, not really.'

I had amnesia. Nobody mentioned the word of course.

'Can you remember anything?'

'No.' I have to say I wasn't perturbed. I felt as though I'd had a couple of bottles of cheap wine. All was well. But it wasn't. The doctor asked again. 'What's your name?'

'Give me a clue.'

No clues. This game went on for a few hours. I was still unconcerned. I didn't know who I was, where I lived, what I'd been doing or the names of any of my friends.

After what was apparently some four hours, a chink appeared. 'Wait a minute. Call Walton-on-Thames 23806.' I'd remembered the number of my girlfriend, Gillie. 'Call that number. They'll tell you who I am.' The doctor didn't move. I began to get agitated. 'Go on, call that number, they'll tell you my name.'

Of course, they already knew my name, as someone had driven me in and supplied all the necessary details. How was I to know that? I was on my own planet.

This was getting frustrating. I was trying to help and the doctor was ignoring me. Then came another doctor's voice from the next cubicle. 'You say you slipped on an ice cube coming out of a party at four in the morning and broke your arm.'

'That's right,' which was presumably the voice of the patient.

I laughed out loud. 'Ha … that's really funny.'

The voice belonging to the broken arm said, 'That sounds like young Read.'

I knew that voice. 'Gabriel!'

'The very same.'

Piece by piece my life started to return, although I felt as though I had a head full of jelly for a week or two. I thought I was on the mend, but there was an unexpected side-effect.

I was at the front of the queue at Tesco one day with the usual pile of tinned baked beans and sausages and tinned soup when I threw them all down and ran out. By the time I got back to the house I was sharing, I was perspiring heavily. What the hell was wrong? I didn't go to the doctor although my head still felt fragile and I didn't confide in anyone. I tried to walk the 100 yards to the local record shop. Impossible. I turned back in a panic time and time again. I assumed that it was some form of agoraphobia brought on by the thump in the head from the unknown assailant on the pitch. Whenever someone asked if I was coming out to play football I made ridiculous and implausible excuses. This was crazy. Would I never go anywhere or do anything ever again? I really wished I'd never been kicked in the head.

I reasoned that although you can go to someone for help, all they can do is listen. The first and subsequent steps have to come from within. Right, that was the reasoning sorted. What was the worst that could happen? I fall over. I faint. So what? I probably wasn't going to die from it. So I borrowed a bike, the premise being that if I panicked at least I could get home more quickly. It also gave me something to focus on in the act of cycling. That was a start, focusing on something. I imagined that the brain was a circle, and an irrational fear suddenly and completely fills all 360 degrees of it. OK, so if I was in the street and panicking and let's say, the Queen wound down the window of her car and wished me a very good morning (which would actually happen years later), I would be so surprised that for a moment that 360 degrees would be filled with something other than irrational fear. I worked at that notion, like going to the gym.

I was asked to play in a cricket match on the green at Claygate, the home of Leverets CC, but of course playing would be impossible. What if I was fielding at slip and panicked? There would be no sympathy. But I wanted to play and decided that I'd make it a real test. I wrote my own set of rules. I'd insist on fielding on the boundary (easy escape if needed), I'd allow myself four loo breaks (sorry, skipper, too much beer, back in a second) and if things got really bad I'd feign an injury (slight if I felt I could return to the pitch, more painful if I felt I couldn't).

I concentrated on filling the 360 degrees with as much as I could. One or two TV stars were playing, including Mick Robertson from *Magpie*. They might not have been HM but it worked to a degree. Very slowly, but very surely, I cured myself. Today the only legacy from that Sunday morning match on Desborough Island is a dislike of tall buildings. I'd wandered around the top of St Pauls taking panoramic shots of London quite happily, but I couldn't now. Funny old game.

As a boy I'd practise keepy-uppy for hours or kick a ball against a wall if there was no one around to play with. With a tennis ball or a Frido ball, I got quite tricky. Too tricky for one of our schoolmasters, Mr Scammel, who took sport when needed. He was refereeing in the match that got me my nickname at school. When the ball arrived on the left wing (my father had taught me to play with both feet) I dribbled, I tapped it up and down on my foot and knee and was having enormous fun until a bison-like bellow echoed across the pitch. Yes, Mr Scammel, florid of face and incandescent with sporting rage. In his book the ball was to be punted upfield, not to be held up, as we'd say now. 'Get rid of it, Twinkletoes!' Twenty-two young players quaked in their boots. I duly got rid of it. I didn't, however, get rid of the nickname. 'Twinkletoes' morphed into 'Twinkle', which by the schoolboy law of shortening everything became 'Twink'.

I'd played for the School XI up until the age of eleven, but at Woking the competition was stiffer and I found myself playing in the school third XI when I achieved that exalted age. My first mention in print was as goal scorer against King Edward's, Witley, I think it was. We were soundly beaten and I netted the only goal, but I didn't look at the result, only the 'Read' after our single goal. I also played for my House, Drake, but goals there weren't of such great importance in the great scheme of things.

One of the guys I was occasionally in the team with was Alan Hamlyn. A big, solid lad, whose house in Cobham we sometimes went to for coffee when we were of an age to consider ourselves 'young gentlemen' with great affectation. Some of us took to carrying brollies and calling each other by our Christian names, which was weird after years of surnames. As I recall Hamlyn was a fair if not outstanding footballer, so it came as a surprise to find him not only playing for the USA, but also captaining them. I haven't seen him since school, but I felt a surge of pride. It's always great to see an Old Wokingian doing well.

If the school selectors hadn't seen the raw talent in me, the powerful calves ready to find the net, the delicate body-swerve and the pinpoint accuracy of my inswingers, then I was unlikely to grace any First Division grounds. That's *old* First Division, younger readers, in other words the Premiership. But I was always up for a match and when I started in the wireless game, played many times for Radio 210. There and at Radio One, as with tennis, I was so lucky to play for and against guys at the top of their profession and run out onto many famous pitches. The stuff of dreams.

I joined Radio One just too late to play in a charity match at Roker Park, to raise money for a Variety Club Sunshine Coach, but was asked to head up to the north-east to present the keys. The fiasco that ensued is covered in no small detail in Chapter 2, and I'm not sure I can bring myself to re-live it again.

Actually to go off piste for a moment, that did happen a few years later. I'd just collected my Mercedes from the garage, as it had been in to have the brakes fixed and tested. With the certificate verifying that my brakes were in tip-top order sitting snugly on the passenger seat I drove off. Within half a mile a car pulled out in front of me. I slammed on, with enormous confidence, my fabulous, stop-on-a-sixpence brakes. Nothing. The car sailed on. I yanked on the handbrake and went down the gears as fast as a Tom and Jerry cartoon. I stopped within inches of the driver's door.

A pale and shaking individual got out of the passenger door and came round to my window. 'I'm going to report you.'

'What for?'

'Nearly hitting me.'

I tried to explain about the brakes, waved my piece of paper with all the confidence of Neville Chamberlain at Heston Aerodrome, and flapped my arm in the direction of the garage.

He was having none of it. 'Don't think I don't know who you are.'

Whoops.

'I know exactly who you are.'

Crikey.

'You're that Gary Davies!'

'Game's up.'

And off he went. Bloody Gary Davies. I wish he'd check his brakes.

However, playing at the grounds of teams like Manchester United, Norwich City, Cardiff City, Leeds United and Tranmere Rovers more than compensated for it. We also played at Meadowbank in Edinburgh, the stadium built for the 1970 Commonwealth Games.

Our opposition for one match in the '80s, comprising celebrities and sportsmen, at Ninian Park, Cardiff featured one J. P. R. Williams in their XI. The Welsh international and triple grand slam winner made his mark on the world of sport as a rugby player and his opposite number that day (me) may have been slightly foolish to underestimate him. In retrospect, it would have made more sense to have tried to run round him, or even let him have the ball. 'All yours, JPR. No problem. Away you go, son.'

Did I really try to run through him? Surely not. What a crass decision. He was on me before I had time to think. It was like running into a concrete wall reinforced with steel girders. I lay on the ground without any breath in my body. Not only had it been completely knocked out of me, I swear there was a vacuum there. I sucked hard, but it was still tricky. I concentrated on survival. I could check for broken bones afterwards.

'Are you OK?'

The answer was 'No, not really', but I think it came out us 'Uuu-urghh', although I'm not 100 per cent sure about the spelling. But if you're going to break something, at least let an orthopaedic surgeon such as JPR do it for you, then he can tell you in gleeful detail about the musculoskeletal trauma you might suffer to your left acetabulum in later life, which would be reassuring.

There were no mishaps at Old Trafford, except that we were one man short. Teddy Warwick, Radio One producer and team manager, seemed to have got his maths wrong.

'Teddy, there are eleven in a team.' 'Get your boots on, Teddy.' 'Being reduced to ten men happens, but starting with ten men?'

He rode the stick and the banter with a knowing smile. Seconds before kick-off he came back into the dressing room. 'I've got you a sub.'

'Brilliant. Who is it, Teddy, you?'

'No, it's a guy who reckons he can play a bit.'

Enter Bobby Charlton, kitted up and ready to go. I think the term 'Wow' went for all of us. I played alongside Bobby in the forward line. Hey, it feels great just writing that.

Do I remember every word? Come on. 'Good ball, Mike … back to me, son … that's it.' There he was, waiting for the return ball, Munich survivor, World Cup winner, selected for four World Cups, European Cup winner, 106 international caps and forty-nine international goals.

'Come on, Mike, give it that extra yard … keep the pressure on.'

I gave it that extra yard. 'Sure, Bob.' I was on first-name terms now.

Twinkletoes makes it to Old Trafford. I still have the team photograph, with Peter Powell, Steve Wright, David Hamilton and the rest of our team-mates, including the music industry's finest like Dave Most and Alan James, looking like real players in our United strip, thanks to the presence of one of the all-time greats.

'Who won the match?' I hear you ask. I was going to tell you anyway. We did. The second photograph is of triumph and jubilation, with Bobby and me holding the all-important trophy aloft in the centre of a packed stadium at Old Trafford. As one might hashtag on Twitter, #RadioOne #Theatre #Dreams #BobbyCharlton #Result.

I later took Bobby on one to one, man on man and drew 1-1 after fifteen minutes. I can tell you're impressed, but there is little cause to be, because we were playing Subbuteo at a toy fair. To be fair I often tell the story and leave out the table football part. Well, you would, wouldn't you?

A few photographs linger of a lithe, long-haired specimen playing alongside such eminent sportsmen as Emlyn Hughes, Kevin Keegan and Mick Channon for England footballers in the annual six-a-side match against the England cricketers. For the life of me I have no idea why I kept being selected. Possibly for my fashionable '80s shorts? Maybe for my dressing room bonhomie and camaraderie? Certainly not for my playing skills. My Radio One pal Kid Jensen was also lucky enough to run out on those occasions. The lovely Emlyn ruined my once modest talent as a bowler. At this annual tournament we played both football and cricket and knowing I was fairly handy with the old crimson rambler, Emlyn chucked me the ball. 'There you go, Readie. Sort them out.'

For indoor cricket the ball was smaller and lighter than a normal ball. I should let it go earlier, then. No, later. No, earlier. No, later. Blimey, I'd psyched myself out. Earlier, definitely. The ball flew up into the rafters and the crowd howled with laughter. Later, then. The next ball smashed into the ground at my feet and the crowd howled again. Great entertainment, but it was doing nothing for my mental approach. The next four balls were a nightmare that lasted several weeks in my mind. I have never been able to bowl properly since.

As a kid I'd run for hours without stopping. It was just something I enjoyed doing. I was never a sprinter but I was a stayer. It started when staying with my grandparents, when I'd watch future Bury footballer George Jones running around the park and the golf course. I bumped into George a year or two back at a Bury match and discussed his influence on my daily long-distance jaunts.

Our family have supported Bury FC since the late 1890s and I attended my first match at the age of eight, standing in the old blue and white boys stand, and still try to get to as many games as possible during the season. Home games can take a good three hours at least and, while I do get up to Gigg Lane (or the JD Stadium as it's become), I'm more likely to make the closest away games. After I met Vanessa, my broadcasting pal Greg Upwards said, 'you'll know she likes you if she's sitting next to you at a far-flung away match watching Bury losing 3–0 on a cold November day'. Fast forward a year and it actually happened. Having said that it wasn't without its problems.

'Don't stand up and cheer.'

'Everybody else is.'

'That's because they're Colchester fans.'

'Who are we fans of?'

'Bury. We only stand up when *they* score.'

'That was very sporting of the home fans to applaud our player's shot.'

'They were applauding their goalie's save.'

'Oh.'

It couldn't have been without some rustic and physical charm as she also made it to Brentford. Mind you most of the time was spent checking the emails.

'What's she doing,' someone asked, 'It's not a great game but it's not that bad,'

'Oh … just checking the goal alerts for the other games I expect.'

Anyway back on track, from running I later transferred to long distance walking because you see more, have more time to take in the history, can stop if you want to and aren't moving against the clock. In the late '90s I walked the South Downs Way from Winchester to Eastbourne in four days, the rough equivalent of a marathon a day. On one of the days I ate my lunch with a long-dead German pilot who had been commemorated with a small obelisk. He was 25-year-old Hauptmann Joseph Oestermann, who'd been flying a Ju 88 bomber on the first day of the Battle of Britain on 13 August 1940. The other two members of the crew had bailed out and survived. A young man, thrust into the fray like many of our young pilots. I sat with him for half an hour and then said my goodbyes.

I'd taken a week off from the Classic FM breakfast show to do the walk and of course my colleagues were mentioning it at intervals. To my delight I found notes on gates and posts along the way: 'We are the farmhouse in the dip, do call in for a cup of tea', 'Cakes await you if you deviate from your path and follow the signs to the half-timbered cottage' and so on. Well worth the deviation. I encountered Betjeman's grandchildren out with their nanny, walked one whole day with two teachers and met the man who pulled Virginia Woolf from the river Ouse at Rodmell in April 1941 at the behest of two small boys.

It was on that walk that I discovered the difference between wanting a cup of tea and needing a cup of tea. The rain was driving off the sea and I knew that I had at least another three hours to go before I would be anywhere remotely near finding a steaming cup of Earl Grey. OK, there are people with more serious things to pray for but nevertheless I had a word or two with the Man Upstairs about the situation. Within two minutes a shape loomed out of the mist and squalls. Unbelievably, it was a BBC mobile unit. I knocked on the door. An engineer opened it. 'Hello Mike, what the heck are you doing up here?' After another two minutes I had not only the tea but also biscuits. What a bonus. The unit was relaying a race meeting from 'Glorious Goodwood' back to London. Either God works in mysterious ways, He had a winner in the three-thirty or spiritual traffic was light that day.

I took an even longer walk in the spring of 2007. Well, a walk and ride. Two hundred and 50 miles on foot and 250 by bike. Peter Kay and Matt Lucas had re-visited the Proclaimers' '(I'm Gonna Be) 500 Miles' for Comic Relief and were sitting at number one. Out of a conversation came the idea of actually walking 500 miles for the charity. Poring over maps to see which points were around 500 miles away from Frinton (for this was during my Radio London days), I alighted on Edinburgh. If that was the start point, maybe I could persuade

Charlie and Craig Reid to walk the first mile with me. I also called the editor of *The Beano*, based not too far away in Dundee, to see if Dennis the Menace would start us off. Boxes ticked all round, Dennis, the Proclaimers and I were snapped by *The Beano* and subsequently appeared in the comic's Summer Special. The lads duly wished me goodbye and good luck after the first mile. Only another 499 to go. I pushed east past Leith, Musselburgh and Prestonpans. I'd been warned about the 'burn' I'd experience as I cycled up the Scottish hills. Now I felt it. Avoiding the A-roads I cruised into Dunbar some 28 miles east of Edinburgh. Then it was south-east past Reed Point and Eyemouth and so to Berwick-upon-Tweed. At Berwick, instead of relaxing and preparing for the next day, I went to Duns Castle, at the invitation of Alexander and Aline Hay. The Laird of Duns and Drumelzier and his good lady are always terrific hosts. The following morning we walked the grounds as part of the 500 miles, around the two lakes and the past the keep, dating from 1320, before getting back on course. Further south the great trek also took in Alnwick Castle, which was used extensively in the Harry Potter movies, St James's Park in Newcastle and Sunderland's ground, the Stadium of Light. The 35-mile stretch of Jurassic coastline from Staithes to Flamborough is quite breathtaking but not easy on the sections where bikes are banned. Walking is fine. Cycling is fine. But pushing a bike over rough terrain is no fun. It prohibits you from breaking into a jog if you need to make up some time. There were also so many occasions when people wanted to have a chat. I'm fine with that, but that meant covering the next section at a faster speed.

I was used to seeing places like Bridlington and Skegness from the Radio One Roadshow stage with 20,000 people out there and a car to whizz you in and out, but here I was walking into town at a steady 4 to 5 miles an hour with no reception committee except for the Big L support vehicle. No decking rooms out as gardens now, no rounders on the beach, no Captain Sensible to challenge at crazy golf, no jingle being sung by a mighty crowd and no luxury hotel.

Where A-roads made cycling or walking impractical, I put the miles in doing circuitous routes. Around the Wash I must have cycled hundreds of desolate lanes to make up for the trunk roads. I had the support vehicle, but we could only reconnoitre at accessible points and it was tough to know when to leave the bike and when to take it. East Anglia? 'No problem,' I'd said, 'it's flat.' It may feel it in a car and walking's not too bad, but cycling you could feel the slightest incline that often went on for miles. Now some regular cyclists may sneer at this as much as they would at a pair of plastic-coated cycle clips, but I'd hardly cycled since I was a kid. There were times when I wondered what had possessed me to raise my hand for this lunatic scheme, but as I gobbled up the miles I could sniff the sea air at Frinton. I made it in exactly two weeks. What an adventure. Will you have me certified if I tell you that I played tennis that night? Clothed.

CHAPTER 16

I COULD WRITE A BOOK

IN THE WEEK that I joined Radio Luxembourg and was offered my first TV series, the first *The Guinness Book of British Hit Singles* was published, co-written with Tim Rice, his brother Jo and my future Radio One colleague Paul Gambaccini. We just thought that it'd be quite useful for us to have all the hit records listed in one book. The project had been given the thumbs-up by the 'Guinness Twins', Norris and Ross McWhirter, a short while before Ross was tragically gunned down on his own doorstep. We assumed that Norris wouldn't want to continue with the book, but he must have had amazing fortitude, as things carried on and he remained firmly in the saddle. For my part, I spent weeks and weeks at Colindale, where the British Library's magazines and newspapers were stored until 2013, requisitioning the old music papers, logging every chart entry and its weekly movement on huge sheets of graph paper. Having ordered my periodicals for that day, an expressionless porter would eventually glide towards me with my 'kill' on a trolley fitted with specially muffled wheels. I would then toil away for hours at a time. Looking back, it seems such a cumbersome and lengthy process now that everyone is so laptop friendly and computer literate. There was a strict 'no food' rule at Colindale and as I became a notorious grub smuggler and as such a marked man, I was frisked on a regular basis. I did manage to sneak the odd snack past the Colditz-style guards, but trying to consume stuff without being spotted was like trying to eat in class; you never really enjoy the pork pie or sausage roll as much as when you can savour it with a cup of tea and reading a book. Shovelling in the odd mouthful when you think no one's looking doesn't hold as much appeal for me. The moment is to be savoured. Nevertheless avarice won the day.

We had no idea that the books would take off in the way they did, with the second edition even topping the bestsellers. We assembled an intriguing mix of chart artists from different eras to grace its cover. Cliff Richard, Joe Brown and Craig Douglas posed alongside Elton John and Kate Bush as Errol Brown and Danny Williams lined up with the Drifters, Hank Marvin and Paul Jones. The four most senior representatives were Vera Lynn, Russ Conway, Johnny Ray and David Whitfield. The new breed were represented by Bob Geldof, Billy Idol and Tom Robinson.

It was fascinating watching the interaction between the artists, one of the most memorable moments being Elton sidling up to Johnny Ray asking for an autograph for his mother Sheila, who was apparently a huge fan. Tim, Jo, Paul and I were photographed with Kate Bush with the happy snap being captioned 'Three men with Kate Bush in their eyes', a bastardisation of one of her song titles. Another edition had a front cover that featured the artists who had been the most successful each year. Then we started issuing albums books and other spin-offs. One of these was *Hits of the '70s*, when again we assembled a rather decent crowd of hit makers, this time at the House of Commons, with Norman St John-Stevas, Minister for the Arts, as our host. The criterion for inclusion was a number one hit from that decade. The Village People in full stage gear seemed delightfully outrageous in those surroundings and Freddie Mercury was his usual charming and erudite self. Lieutenant Pigeon and Bryan & Michael mingled with members of Mud and Slade and dozens of others, and we ate, drank and made merry. It was Elton, though, who grabbed the next day's headlines. He perched himself on the Speaker's Chair and shouted 'Order! Order!'

We also published *The Guinness Hits Challenge* and *The Guinness Book of 500 Number Ones*. The launch for our number ones book, which came out in 1982, was held at Abbey Road Studios, where more UK chart toppers had been recorded than any other studio. It is famous for recording the Beatles, Cliff Richard and the Shadows and Pink Floyd among hundreds of major acts including, outside rock and pop, Glenn Miller, Sir Edward Elgar, Sir Malcolm Sargent and Yehudi Menuhin. We invited everyone who'd topped the chart, with Billy Fury as a special guest representing all those great acts who almost made it to the coveted number one spot. Among his string of success running from 1959 to 1983, Billy had seven top five hits. It was an emotional re-union for Billy and Cliff, who hadn't met up since the early days of rock & roll. It wasn't long before Sting appropriated a patrolling policeman's helmet, which he sported for some of the evening. I think there must have been a timeshare on the helmet as Cliff also wore it for a while before it appeared on the head of former Shadows drummer Tony Meehan. The brothers McCartney were there, Mike representing the Scaffold and Paul representing the Beatles, for whom this studio had been the crucible for most of their global success. Linda McCartney was there too, representing Wings with Paul. Unit Four Plus Two swapped stories with Bucks Fizz; The Hollies, who topped the chart in 1965, chatted with one of the Johnston Brothers, who'd been at the number one with 'Hernando's Hideaway' in 1955. Of course George Martin was there, and how could he not be? He practically kept the place going single handed and produced a heck of a lot of number ones. In fact I'm not sure that we didn't interrupt one of his sessions to start the party. The other great Abbey Road producer of the era was Norrie Paramor, responsible for hits from Cliff and the Shadows, Helen Shapiro and more. We invited

his widow in his stead. Even St Winifred's School Choir made it …
well, not all of them, obviously. Brian Poole and the Tremeloes were
photographed with Alvin Stardust, Bob Geldof with Ray Dorset of
Mungo Jerry and Des O'Connor with Ricky Valance. Roger Waters
of Pink Floyd shared a drink with Aneka of 'Japanese Boy' fame, the
first UK number one to be recorded in Scotland. And for the big
finale, a happy snap of the most number one artists ever assembled.
Among them was Micky Dolenz, who'd written the lyric 'The four
kings of EMI are sitting stately on the floor', referring to the Beatles,
for the Monkees' hit 'Alternate Title', and here he was, sitting stately on
the floor, next to one of the four kings, Paul McCartney.

We soon sailed through the half-million sales mark and on, with
Guinness presenting us with 'Half Million Club' awards in front of
another crowd of major artists, including Lonnie Donegan and Adam
Faith. From 1978 to 1986 our Guinness books were phenomenally successful, and they continued to be after that, but I bowed out after a
delightfully long run.

There were books off the back of the TV series *Saturday Superstore*
and *Pop Quiz*, as well as *The Cliff Richard Chronicle*, which was re-
packaged and re-written a few times, and a biography of the Shadows.
The Story of the Shadows was enormous fun to write, with Hank Marvin, Bruce Welch and Brian Bennett giving me a colossal amount of
time, some of which was spent on Hank's or Brian's tennis court. If
we ran late they'd give me a bed for the night, even though I had to
get up at the crack of dawn for the Radio One breakfast show. Hank
had been my inspiration for learning the guitar, but I could never
have imagined back then that he'd be bringing me a cup of tea at five
o'clock in the morning. The book has now acquired some sort of rarity value, one guy even telling me how he'd heard of one in a shop in
Haverfordwest on the west coast of Wales and had driven the round
trip from London just to secure a copy. Many Shadows fans have asked
me to bring it up to date, so who knows … one day?

As I've mentioned here and there, I'd always written poetry from a very young age and had a few bits and pieces that I added to for my first collection of poems. I ended up buying as many copies as I could, not through vanity, but the juvenilia soon made me squirm a little, so I reasoned that the more I snapped up the less other people could buy them. I guess there are still a few copies of *The Aldermoor Poems* out there somewhere that I missed. The next collection, *Elizabethan Dragonflies*, was better, with poems on places such as Rutland, Invergowrie, Badminton, Hurlingham, Land's End, Loch Lomond and St Enedoc. There were also poems on diverse characters including the painter Georges Braque and 'William Hickey'. I was asked to write some lines for the last-ever Hickey column in the *Daily Express*, so I had the final word in the diary that had been going since 1928, when Tom Driberg, later a Labour MP, became the first journalist to use the pseudonym of the infamous eighteenth-century diarist. In the '60s Nigel Dempster took the helm, perhaps the most famous name to do so, and the last of some fifty journalists to fill the role was Richard Compton Miller.

My poem 'William Hickey – 1933–1987', had the final word:

> *From '30s to '40s,*
> *From Driberg to Miller,*
> *Collecting the crumbs*
> *From society tables,*
> *Steering the blue-blooded*
> *Beaverbrook tiller,*
> *Through the sea of reality,*
> *Fiction and fables.*

It has been pointed out that the column started in 1928, but the date the Daily Express gave me at the time was 1933. So we re-write history?

A 'funeral' was held in which the theatrical procession marched across Fleet Street to the journalists' and printers' spiritual home, St Bride's Church, complete with New Orleans-style jazz band and a coffin filled with champagne bottles, topped by a rusty typewriter. The contents of the coffin were consumed, naturally, in a nearby pub. It was a privilege to be a part of the send-off.

I was delighted to have many of my poems featured in the *Poet's England* series, each book representing poetry about each county down the ages. Several poems were spread around the volumes with Surrey, rather wonderfully, featuring four of them; *Effingham Station, High Surrey (Coldharbour,) Along the Banks of Mole and Wey*, and *The Great Fire of 1951. Effingham Station* was also featured in a volume of railway verse, *Marigolds Grow Wild on Platforms*.

During my time at Classic FM, one of the programmes had a feature where they asked various folk to talk about the favourite room in their house. I decided, unquestionably, that mine would be the library. On reflection I thought that the word 'library' might come over as being a little stuffy so I called it 'a room with books', and wrote a poem to go with it. Not surprisingly, it would end up being the title of my next book of poems, published in 1996. After reading 'A Room with Books' for the programme, I found myself inundated with favourite poems from listeners. This led, rather inevitably, to my producer, Tim Lihoreau, and myself compiling the listeners' top 100 poems. Thousands and thousands of votes poured in, giving us a logistical, but ultimately rewarding, nightmare. Wordsworth's 'Daffodils' and Kipling's 'If' came out as the top two, with de la Mare, Browning, Tennyson, Masefield, Keats, Brooke and Rossetti all featuring in the top ten. I edited the volume of poems, and wrote a one-page biography of each poet in the top 100 and a foreword that included the poem that had started it all off, 'A Room with Books'.

There's feeling in a room with books, the love,
The depth, the warmth of something that's alive.
The ranks and rows of old campaigners stand,
Passed from hand to hand, friend to friend, to me.
The flames in shadow dance upon them all,

Who themselves once danced upon this earth;
Burns, Belloc, Blunden, Bridges, Beardsley, Brooke;
Inscribed with care from lover, mother, friend:
In faded hand 'December 1910.'
Books from the libraries of laureates,
Volumes revered as bibles at the front;
Diaries of dear, dead days, letters of love,
Classics, passions, open wounds; injustice.
As full-bodied wine, verse, chapter, stanza,
Spill and flow out across the floodlit lawns,
From leathered desk to some dark, secret place.
And here I sit, surrounded by my friends,
Their words remain though they themselves are gone,
Their lives re-lived within my favourite room.

In 1998, we followed *One Hundred Favourite Poems* with *One Hundred Favourite Humorous Poems*, again with a single-page biography of each poet. While pondering on how to write a more novel introduction, I began to amuse myself by thinking of links between the various poets featured in the top 100. I ended up with something called 'Stanley Holloway in Thirty Moves', starting with Holloway and seeing if I could get back to him in thirty moves using poets featured in the book. I was allowed to use a poet more than once if applicable. It's a wedge of literary fun, so let's include it here.

Stanley Holloway made his London debut in Kissing Time *in 1919, which was co-written by P. G. Wodehouse. Wodehouse wrote with Ira and George Gershwin, whose song 'I Don't Think I'll Fall in Love Again' was influenced by G. K. Chesterton. Chesterton was such good friends with Hilaire Belloc that people referred to them as 'ChesterBelloc.' Belloc's farrago 'The Four Men' heavily influenced 'The Soldier', Rupert Brooke's most famous poem. Brooke's early poems were*

published in the Granta *magazine, once edited by A. A. Milne.
Milne successfully adapted Kenneth Grahame's* The Wind
in the Willows *for the stage, as did Alan Bennett. Bennett contributed to the book* Larkin at Sixty, *a celebration
of Philip Larkin's life and work. Larkin was the librarian
at Hull University, where he met and influenced a young
student called Roger McGough. McGough wrote hit records,
as did Cole Porter. Cole Porter wrote the music and lyrics
for* Kiss Me Kate, *based on* The Taming of the Shrew *by
Shakespeare. The Shakespearian characters Othello, Richard III, Hamlet and Macbeth were all portrayed on stage by
William McGonagall. McGonagall's American counterpart
was Julia Moore (known as the American McGonagall), who
was a major influence on Ogden Nash. Nash wrote the musical* One Touch of Venus *with Kurt Weill, who collaborated
on* Lady in the Dark *with Ira Gershwin, who wrote with P. G.
Wodehouse. Wodehouse was knighted, as was John Betjeman.
Betjeman was a pupil at Marlborough with Louis MacNeice.
MacNeice described John Cornford as 'the first inspiring com-
munist I have met'. Cornford had actually been christened
Rupert in memory of Rupert Brooke. Brooke was remembered
in the poem 'At Grantchester' by Charles Causley. Causley
wrote the poem 'Betjeman 1984'. Betjeman bought a new book
of poems in 1976 and praised it as being full of 'good, honest
country poems'. It was a collection of poetry by Pam Ayres.
Pam Ayres presented a radio documentary about Jane Austen,
who read and was influenced by William Cowper. Cowper's
father was a rector, as was the father of Lewis Carroll. Carroll's* Hunting of the Snark *was influenced by* Bab Ballads
*by W. S. Gilbert. Gilbert almost became the artist for the Alice
books by Lewis Carroll. Carroll was educated at Rugby, as
was Walter Savage Landor. Landor was the model for Lawrence Boythorn in Dickens's* Bleak House, *while the Dickens*

musical Oliver! *once starred Barry Humphries. Humphries was a regular contributor to* Private Eye *magazine, home of their fictitious poet-in-residence, E. J. Thribb. Thribb was created by Richard Ingrams, one of the* Private Eye *founders, while the founder of the Eton College magazine,* The Etonian, *was W. M. Praed. Praed's work was often compared to that of Thomas Hood. Hood was the joint editor of the London Magazine, while the editor of the* Classical Review *was A. D. Godley. Godley's translations of Horace were published in 1898, while another poet to translate and write poems in the style of Horace was Rupert Brooke. Brooke's cousin Erica was infatuated with George Bernard Shaw, whose play* Pygmalion *became* My Fair Lady *and starred … Stanley Holloway!*

Thankfully the two volumes have been selling consistently since 1997 and 1998.

I've always had Rupert Brooke's poems around for as long as I can remember. He looked too modern for his era and I always thought that he and his circle were the forerunners of the Swinging Sixties set, but were curtailed by two world wars and two periods of austerity. They went barefoot, had unchaperoned weekend camps, played guitars, read poetry and planned to change the world; the girls were emancipated and Brooke grew his hair long. Brooke was feted with eulogies and effigies after his death at the age of twenty-seven. Much has been made of our stars who died at this age, such as Jimi Hendrix, Jim Morrison, Amy Winehouse, Brian Jones, Janis Joplin, Kurt Cobain and Robert Johnson, but Brooke was the first icon of the twentieth century to do so and create a stir in the hearts of those he left behind. He was referred to as a 'Young Apollo', whence the name of my Rupert Brooke musical, and Winston Churchill wrote a glowing obituary in *The Times*, commenting, 'We shall not see his like again.'

Brooke's Commander-in-Chief, General Sir Ian Hamilton, reflected on why so many people thought him charismatic and rather special:

Is it because he was a hero? There were thousands.
Is it because he looked like a hero? There were few.
Is it because he had genius? There were others.
But Rupert Brooke held all three gifts of the gods in his hand.

After a couple of decades the inevitable iconoclasts appeared in an attempt to swing the pendulum the other way, so in the '90s I decided to write a balanced account of his life, neither being eulogistic nor iconoclastic. In working on *Forever England* I travelled the length and breadth of the country, taking in places that he'd been drawn to for one reason or another. I motored from Becky Falls to Llanbedr, East Knoyle to Dymock, Lulworth Cove to the Lizard and Rye to Moffat. All were able to add something to a fuller and more rounded story that uncovered some unknown facts and facets of Brooke's character and 27-year journey. On my travels I met with the son of Brooke's great friend Dudley Ward. Peter Ward was one of only two people I encountered that had been alive during Brooke's time, albeit as very young children. Peter was mentioned in Rupert's correspondence twice, once in 1914 and again early in 1915 following a long-lost letter being delivered to him from his Tahitian girlfriend Taatamata. There were hints in that letter that she may have been pregnant with his child. As Dudley Ward had been Rupert's main confidant, I asked Peter if he could throw any light on the possibility of a child. Boxes came down from the loft that had never seen the light of day, containing hundreds of snapshots sent back to England from Tahiti with the intention that some would be enlarged when Brooke returned. The outbreak of World War One consigned them to sit in an attic for decades and decades. In the bottom of one of the boxes were a few letters that told an extraordinary tale. Late in 1935, twenty years after Brooke's death and a respectful time after the death of his mother, Dudley Ward, a man not given to flights of fancy, began to make serious enquiries about the possibility of Brooke having had a son or daughter. It appeared that Rupert had asked him to put these wheels in motion. With little to go on, he wrote to Viscount Hastings, who owned a property on Moorea, an island north-west of Tahiti. Hastings thought that Norman Hall, who had recently directed *Mutiny on the Bounty*, might be able to help as he had a wide circle of friends there. Word came back from Hall that Taatamata was still alive, but he was leaving Polynesia for San Francisco and wouldn't be able to contact her. Hall died in 1951, but I tracked down his daughter Nancy, who confirmed that her mother had told her in confidence that Arlice Rapoto, a great friend of theirs, was the daughter of Rupert Brooke and Taatamata. A photograph she sent me of Arlice, taken around 1950, shows an uncanny resemblance to Brooke. And so I was able to add to the Brooke legend and publish a photograph of his daughter, who sadly died a few years before I wrote the book.

The other person I met who had known Brooke was his second cousin, Winifred Kinsman, whose grandmother, Lucy Hoare, had been Rupert's mother's sister. Winifred was a charming lady and it turned out that she also used to ski at Lech, but back in the '30s. She kindly opened our Rupert Brooke Museum at the Orchard, Grantchester in 1999. There were three of us who founded the Rupert Brooke Society: the late Robin Callan, the owner of the Orchard, where Rupert had lived; Dr Peter Miller, former chairman of the Brooke Centenary Committee; and me. Peter, no inconsiderable age himself, took on the mantle of president, Robin enabled the re-construction of the museum building and staffed it, while I chaired the society and edited the magazine as well as ensuring that the museum contained the story of Brooke, books, artefacts and some of his belongings. Between us we had his steeplechase cup from Rugby School, the binoculars he wore en route to a Gallipoli that he never reached, buckles from his uniform, signed books, a lock of his hair and a growing amount of things that people offered or brought in.

I was lucky to beat an American university to one of several poems that Brooke lost somewhere in Canada, en route to San Francisco in the summer of 1913. The poem, 'For Mildred's Urn', was in Brooke's handwriting but experts had no idea what the subject matter was. I adore literary sleuthing, and was soon able to come up with a rational explanation by bringing together the literary, genealogical, historical and geographical. When Brooke sailed to the USA on the SS *Cedric* from Liverpool in May 1913, he discovered that the poet Richard Le Gallienne and his wife Julie were also on the ship. Rupert was disparaging (probably a pose) about the man, 'who mooches about with grizzled hair and a bleary eye', in a letter to Eddie Marsh. Le Gallienne would also have been carrying the ashes of his former wife in an urn. Case solved; the poem is on sometime loan to the museum. Fifteen years on the society is still going strong, spurred on by *Forever England*, which will be re-published in 2015, the centenary of Brooke's death. Sadly Robin Callan won't be here for the anniversary and the erection of a blue plaque, having passed away in April 2014. I read 'The Old Vicarage, Grantchester' at his memorial service.

For twenty years I've been in and out of the Orchard, letting many an hour slip away with Robin, discussing Brooke, Virginia Woolf, Lytton Strachey, Henry James and many others who passed through these gardens and stayed at the house. We also talked of England, its past, present and future, and the future of the Orchard, which he put into a charitable trust to preserve this piece of history. In the Orchard an hour turns into a morning turns into a day; as Brooke himself wrote, 'I only know that you may lie, day-long and watch the Cambridge sky…' Robin was a quietly spoken but brilliant man, who invented a method of learning English at four times the normal speed, the Callan Method. At his memorial service the vicar mentioned that he'd lived life as an eighteenth-century aristocrat.

Sometime in 2000, I was at a small gathering on the south coast that included several musicians. Tales were swapped and old photographs from the '60s were dragged out, and I knew this could provide the foundation for another book. The photographs could be dated almost to the month, by the hairstyles, clothes, stances, and the makes of guitars and amplifiers. Putting the book together was a labour of love. I didn't realise it would take me a year with my nose firmly to the grindstone, or in this case the Fender Stratocaster. I interviewed hundreds of singers, guitarists, drummers, bass players, pianists, organists, managers and other folk of all kinds, many still playing, who were on the scene during the decade of musical excellence. Long-disbanded groups got together round kitchen tables to reminisce, recall, sometimes argue over historical points and laugh about old disputes or the musical differences that had brought about the outfit's demise. For some, their roots went back to the days of skiffle or jazz; others had bought instruments and learned as they went, and there were those who'd tried to run before they could walk and had fallen by the wayside. There were some tragedies, some success stories, but mainly tales of almost making it. All of them were delighted that *The South Coast Beat Scene of the 1960s* brought their own stories to life and gave them their own personal place in musical history. Tim Rice's school group at Lancing College had cunningly called themselves the Aardvarks, so that when fame arrived they would always be top of the bill alphabetically, even when touring with the Rolling Stones and the Beatles. I was glad to be able to fulfil his distant schoolboy dream when the Aardvarks opened the batting for the groups, listed alphabetically, in the book. The Urchins, the Vikings and the Web clearly hadn't thought it through. There were potted histories too of south coast clubs, including the Shoreline at Bognor Regis, the Top Hat at Littlehampton and the Mexican Hat at Worthing. A good year's work.

About the same time another book, *Major to Minor*, was published. I'd been working on and off on this book for a year or two, looking at the reasons behind the rise of the professional songwriter from the mid-1800s to the present day. Classical composers aside, for one could make a great case for someone like Schubert being a writer of popular songs, Stephen Foster was the man that led the way. Songs became so powerful that they almost became weapons in the American Civil War, with the Confederates singing 'The Yellow Rose of Texas', 'God Save the South' and 'Dixie's Land', while the Unionists gave out with

'The Minstrel Boy', 'Battle Hymn of the Republic' and 'John Brown's Body'. Both sides used 'When Johnny Comes Marching Home', a hit exactly 100 years later for Adam Faith. While those songs were firing up the South and the North in the US, we were cheerily chirping the smash of 1862, 'Blaydon Races'.

Stephen Foster died prematurely and in poverty. Like Elvis he earned more after his death than he did during his lifetime. Despite the racial divide, especially in the South, there were successful black writers too. James A. Bland wrote over 700 songs, thirty-seven of which are in the US Library of Congress. The music halls opened the door for songwriters in Britain, although they also encouraged charlatans who claimed they owned the publishing rights. Performers would often cough up a relatively small amount rather than go through the extensive and complex system of checking credibility or getting entangled in litigation.

By the end of the nineteenth century, sheet music had become phenomenally popular, with upwards of twenty million copies being sold annually from 40,000 song titles. Eminent UK songwriter Leslie Stuart came to blows with someone on a street corner illegally selling sheet music for one of his songs, while in the US the songwriters fought to get royalties from the newly formed gramophone companies. New York restaurants were brought into question: should they be paying for playing music on their premises? Did the diners come because of the music or was it incidental?

My next book of poetry, *New Poems for Old Paintings*, which came out in 2003, was inspired by a birthday present. When Julie Dene, the wife of my pal and radio colleague Graham Dene, sent out the invitations to her celebrations, I hit upon a wheeze for a unique present. She is a direct descendent of the painter J. M. W. Turner so I got Tony James (you remember, Rhino) to copy Turner's *Rain, Steam and Speed*, which famously depicts a railway engine going over Maidenhead Bridge. He did such a stunning job that I had it framed and was moved to write a poem to go with it, as part of the gift. I have to say, it went down rather splendidly. The night of the party Tony Blackburn and I had a slow waltz to encourage other people to get on the dance-floor. A tender moment, but we remain just good friends.

The poem, and Julie's enthusiasm, spurred me to write some more. Music has inspired art, art has inspired music, words have inspired music and music has inspired words. In this book, art was the inspiration for poetry. Sometimes the poems took the title of the painting and sometimes not. The paintings appeared on one page and the poem, unless longer, on the facing page. I wrote poems based around paintings by the likes of Pissarro, Monet, John Singer Sargent, Cézanne, Constable, Holman Hunt, Lowry, Toulouse-Lautrec and, of course, Turner. I also had to include a couple of my favourite paintings by John Atkinson Grimshaw, *Golden Light* and *October*.

The following year I collaborated with Richard Havers on *Read's Musical Reciter*, intriguingly subtitled 'Lids lifted, stones turned, tales told, stars stripped, rock mined, pop plundered and pseuds cornered'. Bursting with tales of all kinds from the world of music, it sits on the shelf of many a downstairs loo. Neither friend, acquaintance nor the coolly cordial can deny the fact. I have visited some loos even when unnecessary, with the sole purpose of checking the location of their *Read's Reciter*. I've lost count of how many loos I've flushed without reason and how many taps I've washed my hands under for the sake of appearances. The book seems to have found its spiritual home.

Having inherited the spirit of enjoying comics from my maternal grandfather, as a boy I read them, re-read them, studied the characters, and even smelled the paper. I've already touched on the US comics that I obtained from our American neighbours, but *The Beano*, *The Dandy* and later *Wizard* and *Roy of the Rovers* were favourites. My mother also had old copies of *Film Fun* and *Radio Fun* kicking around, both of which ran until the early '60s. *Radio Fun* had strips featuring the likes of Benny Hill, Arthur Askey, Petula Clark and Norman Wisdom. I reflected, if indeed young boys do reflect, on how marvellous must be to actually feature in a comic. I would never have imagined then that I'd not only feature in Britain's most popular comic, *The Beano*, but on three occasions. As my grandmother pointed out, 'Your grandfather would have been tickled pink.'

The first time I was written into a Dennis the Menace strip where his dog Gnasher has gone missing and Dennis pops into my studio to ask if I can help. Top stuff. My second *Beano* appearance was in a Biffo the Bear story, with, rather bizarrely, a woodpecker carving my face in a tree in the final frame. The trio of appearances was rounded off by being the subject of a whole Billy Whizz page, with the speedy schoolboy hero desperate to hear the show and hoping that his uncle is going to buy him a mug that we were giving away on Radio One at the time, Mike Read's Tee Hee Mug. There were also appearances in lesser organs, such as *Oink!*, where I had my guitar stuffed down my throat, much to the consternation of a brace of perplexed doctors. I was featured in my *Saturday Superstore* persona in *Whizzer and Chips* and as one of Roy Race's mates in *Roy of the Rovers*. I popped up again in a 1981 issue after Roy had been shot (shades of JR in *Dallas*) and a few of his friends were asked to send 'get well' messages. Cripes, I was in esteemed company on that double-page spread, alongside More-cambe & Wise, Alf Ramsey, Kevin Keegan, Trevor Francis, Malcolm McLaren and Lawrie McMenemy.

As was alluded to in the Preface, even the cobbling together of this book was not without some excitement. By the end of 2012 I had writ-ten just short of 100,000 words. Whether any of it made any sense I can no longer judge, as some lazy bastard who couldn't be bothered to work broke in and, stole my car, my laptop and my cards. The car and the cards were sortable of course, but the laptop contained the second novel, the autobiography, the history of the FA Cup Final and hundreds more literary gems. I know, I know, I should have backed it up. You're right, of course, and I do now. Horse, stable, door, bolted. Got it. I'll never write the novel again, but with this weighty tome I had to start from scratch. If you don't like it, I can always claim the original to be superior.

CHAPTER 17

MORE LIKE THE MOVIES

FILMS? INDEED, SAY I, films. Not blockbusters, I grant you, but certainly the silver screen. No Baftas or Golden Globes, but every iceberg with its glittering peak has nine-tenths submerged. My film career so far is the submerged part.

Where to begin? Well, to be frank, the distance between the start and the finish is not all that great. In the late '80s, I was asked to be in a film about rock & roll. I have no recollection of the title, so for all you know I could be lying through my teeth and to be honest it's of little consequence as it was never made. I did attend a couple of meetings, was given a script and, I confess, got mildly anticipatory.

A few years later I actually made it to the shooting stages of a film. My scenes were to be on the Isle of Man in a two-hander with Simon Callow. One of my waggish pals bade me farewell saying, 'Norman Wisdom lives on the island, say hello from me.' Right. As if I was bound to bump into him. It's similar to 'Oh, you're going to San Francisco; if you see a bloke called Simon who has a dry-cleaning company give him my best'. Life's not like that. And yet … as I parked my car on the ferry, the motor that pulled in behind me decanted none other than N. Wisdom. I fought hard against launching into a 'Mr Grimsdale' voice and just managed to restrain myself as he came up and said hello.

'Hello, Norman,' I replied, as you do, and without a trace of a comic trip.

'Going to the Isle of Man then?'

With anyone else I might have responded with 'No, Newfoundland actually', but this man was a legend, so I nodded eagerly.

We ascended from the car deck together. I say *we* as if it were simply a brace of bonding males, but there were three of us in this temporary relationship. The lady looking after him said nothing, but her face and demeanour gave away her inner thoughts. 'Come away, Norman.' 'Don't talk to him, Norman.' 'Make him go away, Norman.' Norman, however, was happy to talk. In the end she carted him off physically. I was delighted and privileged a few years later to be at Norman's ninetieth birthday party, especially when he sang 'Don't Laugh at Me'.

Norm – you can tell how familiar we'd become – having been swiftly extricated from my presence, I was able to settle down to studying my script. I was to play a public schoolmaster, which sounds above board, but I seem to remember an element of skulduggery in the plot. I wish I could recall what the heck it was about, but I'd be making it up, much like I did with the script. I remember doing the scenes with the lovely Simon Callow and having supper with him on the two nights I was on the island, but beyond that is a veil of mist such as hangs over Ramsey on a November morning. Was I paid? Probably not. Was the film released? No, they ran out of dosh.

Somewhere around 2006 I was cast in the film *Inside Out*, which was being shot at Pinewood. Henry Hadaway, who'd had the idea and had co-written the script, had suggested me. Henry was the sagacious record company boss who'd once signed me to his label Satril. The suggestion came out of the blue, as I hadn't seen him for some while. After some post-production legal wrangles, I think I'm safe to say that it was an HHO/Palm Tree Productions film, with various credits being shared and meted out here and there. I'm told that it was released abroad. Probably just as well.

This time I do remember the story. It is a romantic thriller, filmed in London and Cannes, and centres on the tempestuous relationship between a student doctor, James Silverdale, played by Tony Streeter, and a girl from Prague called Christabel, played by Charlotte Radford. Christabel is ambitious; she wants her own nightclub and gets involved with a couple of wealthy guys including East End record producer Mickey Taylor, skilfully, powerfully and meaningfully acted if any directors are reading this. If they're not, then I guess I was passable. Mickey appeared to be rather partial to the 'F' word, so I spread it around with large helpings of vitriol and menace, in equal measure. The part called for me, in one scene, to push a musician into a swimming pool in Cannes. I pushed, accompanied by a liberal sprinkling of 'F' words and a modicum of venom. Robbie Moffat, the director, exploded. Really? I thought I'd pushed and sworn jolly well. It transpired that he hadn't shouted 'Action' so the cameras hadn't been rolling. We had to wait half an hour for the actor and his clothes to be dried sufficiently for me to push him in again. 'Who cares?' you're thinking. 'You were in Cannes and you were getting well paid.' Don't be silly, the scene was shot in Hertfordshire and I got paid something.

My role must have been fairly substantial as the publicity proclaimed, 'The cast includes Tony Streeter, Charlotte Radford, Saeed Jaffrey and Mike Read!' Charlotte and I ran around a lot together during the filming, were mischievous and a more than a little irreverent, but it was fun. We had one torrid scene which we played more to shock the crew and director than as serious drama. If you can't be bothered to watch the whole 95-minute saga to check out my East End accent and my Anglo-Saxon language, you can enjoy two small clips of my contribution on YouTube. If you can't even be fagged to click the YouTube button, you'll just have to take my word for it that I was perplexed, nay mortified, that I wasn't nominated for Best Supporting Actor. The question continues to baffle critics south of Bognor Regis.

All I can say is thank goodness I'm not an actor, for the call didn't come again until the tail end of 2013. Even the most rejected thespian can't rest for that long and live with themselves. It was my one-time co-star, albeit my role was as nothing compared to hers, Charlotte Radford, who called me while I was on my way back from attending some shindig in London with Vanessa to ask if I could film the following day. Despite the aeon between engagements and the desire to leap at another triumph on the silver screen, I kept my powder dry. Clearly this was either a hastily written part or somebody had let the film makers down. After several discussions with La Radford I was given to understand that an actor of major importance had been unable to fly in for the occasion. The part was so small that, whoever it was, he could have got it in the can as the wheels touched the runway and taken off again without actually troubling customs.

The American Banker was directed by the ebullient Jeff Espanol, complete with giant unlit cigar and headgear purloined from an unwary and vodka-soaked Cossack. We filmed my scene in London at Brown's Hotel. I was a Liverpudlian banker. Jeff, his millinery appendage shaking like a great furry Yorkshire pudding, put me through my paces. He got me to slow my delivery right down. 'Slower … Slower still … Even more, Mike … You can still take it down a notch.' The more observant among you will have noticed that in this exchange of creative ideas, I failed to exchange. I felt it more prudent to listen. I slowed. I menaced. I whispered. I had lunch and off I went, creatively if not exactly financially richer.

Looking at the powerful cast list has provided me with a few silver screen aces to play when needed. They'll be handy when interviewed by the critics.

'When was your last film?'

'This year, actually.' It's always good to throw in the odd 'actually'.

'And who else was in it, anyone we've heard of?'

'Oh, you know … the usual crowd, Faye Dunaway, David Carradine…'

Best to leave it at that point, although I did have an email from Jeff 'The Hat' Espanol in Hollywood, which said, 'See your face each day for the editing and I want to tell you thanks for being so humble on the set of my film. You are great in the film.' Listen, I don't care if it is showbiz director-speak, I can live with it. He ended, 'See you in Cannes.' Now I have no idea whether that means he flies me down in a Lear Jet or I fork out myself for the Eurostar. In May 2014 he called again to ask if I could do another scene. I checked my filming commitments. I appeared to be surprisingly free. We shot the scene in Dover Street, in Mayfair, with Japanese tourists banging off rapid-fire snaps imagining they had captured a British film star or two. Again. I had to be menacing, only more of the smiling assassin this time, who, rather bizarrely, ends up playing blues guitar. I'm forbidden to say more as Jeff has promised me a river scene with concrete shoes if I say too much. I realised how long this film has taken to make when someone pointed out that one of its star names, David Carradine, died in 2009.

In 1991 I wrote the music for the film *How's Business*, starring Ron Moody and Brett Fancy and with Ben Brazier in the lead role, who later went on to star in *Layer Cake* with Daniel Craig. I recorded the score at the University of Surrey in the John Lennon Studio, which I'd opened with Nigel Kennedy a year or two earlier. Bizarrely the film hasn't yet emerged on DVD and I was unable to go to the premiere, so I still haven't seen the finished version.

On the film script front, the colossal amount of writing time has been rewarded with not one jot. Several have been acclaimed, but acclaiming doesn't buy the cheese and chutney on granary. They sit on my laptop straining to get out and do their stuff, but money seems to be the main stumbling block. We once did a read-through of my Rupert Brooke film, *Forever England*, based on my book of the same name, and even started some auditions when we thought the backing looked good. Hundreds of hours writing, re-writing, sitting in meetings, getting money, losing money, getting director, losing director have resulted in no film having been made as yet, but as weary souls of the celluloid will tell you at length, it is a tedious process that can take years. I did have a long chat with actor Paul Bettany about possibly playing the lead role, but I fear we weren't ready financially at the time.

The director that was attached for a good while was the highly experienced Bryan Forbes, a formidable screenwriter, actor, and director for both film and TV who became MD of Associated British, which became EMI Films. When we had lunch at Pinewood to discuss the project, the whole place was buzzing. The word had gone round that 'Bryan was back!' Many an afternoon we went through my script, cutting this section, expanding that scene, examining the characters and often touching on the *raison d'être*. As well as working with one of the greats of the film industry, there was a culinary bonus in that Bryan's wife, Nanette Newman, would prepare a banquet for our lunch where lesser mortals would have had us make do with a ham sandwich. Brian and I grafted during the mornings, but the afternoons became more convivial as we'd flick through some of Bryan's amazing memorabilia, especially a plethora of royal correspondence in tandem with the relevant stories. We went different routes in the afternoons, Bryan down the scotch and cigarette road and me down the tea and biscuits avenue.

The producers at some length announced, 'Now let Bryan write his director's script.' He did, but it was a totally different take to the actual story and took place on a film set, from the actor's perspective. An interesting idea, but not for me. We still haven't made the film, so maybe he was right and I was wrong, but we agreed that one had to be firm in the pursuance of perfection. With the 100th anniversary of Rupert Brooke's death looming in 2015, and all the World War One commemorations, I'm having yet another crack at breathing life into it.

With the millennium looming, I began to work on a major project that would hopefully see a combination of history, the arts and more performed at a dozen castles around the UK, with a cast of thousands and some great effects. The basic idea was a thousand years of history, with a character from each century telling the story of their 100 years through the music, dance, conflicts, inventions, art, sculpture, fashion and more. I had a couple of very positive meetings with Prince Edward and his company, Ardent, but the year 2000 arrived faster than we could fund or organise it.

The battle of good and evil in *Wenceslas: King of Bohemia*, set in Prague in the early 900s, also languishes expectantly on SkyDrive awaiting its moment, alongside *The Greatest Game*. I was initially slated to be a consultant on the latter film which was to be written by Julian Fellowes, a capital chap with whom I chatted about the project on several occasions, but he was busy with a new series of *Downton Abbey* so, not surprisingly, he had no time to attend to the likes of Old Etonians v. Blackburn Olympic. I was commissioned to write the script and was delighted with the result. I got an extremely good response to the story, which was essentially one of the old school versus the new school and the struggle of professional football to be born. The trouble is, the longer you pass a good idea round the more chance there is of it being filched by some knave keen to get on the red carpet for their hour of glory.

Two versions of *Great Expectations* are juxtaposed with these other scripts-in-waiting. Both musical films, one is traditional and the other an early '50s US version with a black Magwitch and a Pip whose expectation is to be a singer in New York. The latter works so well I'm convinced that I'll get it away. Well, you have to remain positive and upbeat. If you don't have the passion yourself, the piece will never take root. There are others, but there seems no point in dwelling more on greyhounds that are still in the traps.

I did make it to the Cannes Film Festival on three occasions, with three or four of us taking a house for a fortnight. This worked out cheaper, so I was told, than booking hotels. It was also more fun. Diaries note meetings with such glorious names as Matador Films, Azure Films, a meeting on the *African Queen* and a party at Villa Estella, of which I remember little.

I was informed that it would be useful to get a meeting in with Steven Paul, Jon Voight's partner in the film production company

Crystal Sky. If I was lucky enough to get a one-to-one, the covert voice told me, I would have to pitch my script in double-quick time. The tip came with an attention span warning: 'If you don't get him in two minutes he'll be off.' I wasn't sure I could sell an entire film in the time it takes to announce and play the Beatles' 'And Your Bird Can Sing', but at least I was given an appointment. This, said my inform-ant, was a good start.

Ten minutes before the scheduled meet at the Majestic came the call. 'Steven can't make today, can we re-arrange for tomorrow?' We re-arranged. The re-arranging went on for three days. Miraculously, and against all filmic odds, it happened on the fifth day. Seated opposite him with a glass of something unmemorable, I launched into my two-minute pitch at roughly the pace of Plastic Bertrand attacking a live version of his 1978 classic 'Ça plane pour moi'. I must have impressed him as I ran well over the two-minute mark. He showed no signs of being distracted by passing actresses or nodding off in the eighty-degree heat that surrounded us. We spent an hour chatting about this and that before retreating to his business suite to meet the rest of the team. I was in. No question. I got a call on my return home and we subse-quently had several dinners in London, including one with the Crystal Sky lawyer. All terrific. Camaraderie, bonhomie, fine wines, part of the gang, being talked up, I was the 'golden boy', or so it seemed, but hey, that's the US film industry. They love you and they keep on lov-ing you, but not much happens.

Another cove was so enamoured of my creative writing that he asked me to look at doing a script based on a book he had the rights to. What I should have said was, 'Show me the contract and the advance and we can talk.' What I actually said was, 'Great, OK,' and got on with it. The gentlemanly way. Several months later, having put in more 'Hard Work' than American jazz saxophonist John Handy, I accidently dis-covered that he'd asked somebody else to do it. Now I try not to sally forth without putting on a stout pair of shoes.

My old friend Lisa Voice (great dinner parties and a good heart) was in Cannes with a film script so we hooked up and had supper. She insisted that I went with her to a hotel, where she was looking to buy something. Security seemed unnecessarily tight around the suite where she was doing the deal. Having been scrutinised, checked and frisked I was allowed in. It was the only time that I've even seen a £7 million diamond, let alone held one. Was it possible to scrape some off under the fingernails? I doubted it.

Small screen appearances might not carry the kudos of a cinema release, but blimey guv'nor, do they get repeated. My fleeting, but crucial, role in *Only Fools and Horses* still comes around with incredible regularity, for which, I presume, a small postal order wings its way to someone, if not with equal regularity, at least occasionally. For a rather grand third billing in that august journal *Radio Times*, I did very little. The episode 'It's Only Rock 'n' Roll' centred on Rodney's group A Bunch of Wallies. Initially Del mocks them but he soon changes his tune when he smells money and becomes their manager, taking them to ever greater depths. It wasn't a demanding role for me as I simply had to introduce them on *Top of the Pops*. However, being in formidable company, I didn't hold back. I gave it my all … whatever that was. I read recently that David Jason would consider re-visiting *Only Fools and Horses* if the right scriptwriter could be found. Ahem…

I was let loose on the set of *Midsomer Murders* for the episode 'The Axeman Cometh'. I played myself, which is always a tricky call. Getting into a role is far more rewarding (fill in your own cheese and ham gags here). The gist of the story was that Badgers Drift was playing host to the Midsomer Rock Festival, with an old local rock group, Hired Gun, re-forming for the occasion. The episode featured great actors including James Cosmo, Philip Davis and Rupert Vansittart, so clearly I had to step up to the mark. Wandering past John Nettles's Winnebago, I poked my head in (why not? I was part of the gang now) as I'd heard the sound of a guitar. Was it Suzi Quatro, who was also a member of Hired Gun? I peered in. No leather-clad lady, but in her stead, John Nettles coming on like Jimi Hendrix. On his invitation

I went in, hung out, strummed a bit and discussed a mutual love of John Betjeman's poetry. His sidekick Jason Hughes joined us and I now felt that I would be slated for every episode. We were a trio now, surely? I could berate sinister vicars, unmask wicker men, break up an ancient cult or spot the odd village psychopath with the best of them.

I fear, though, I'm getting ahead of myself. There I was backstage at the rock festival, the cameras were rolling. Allowed free rein on the script, I was issuing last-minute instructions punctuated by such deep and soul-searching comments to Hired Gun as 'have a good one', and then I bounded onto the stage to announce the group that the Midsomer area had been waiting years for. John Nettles and Jason Hughes were at the front by the crush barriers, with John, as Barnaby of course, about to re-live his youth. After my big moment, I was to join Laura Howard (Cully Barnaby) at the side of the stage to watch the band in action. No sooner had we passed a few pleasantries than Suzi Quatro was electrocuted. Well, her character, Mimi Clifton, was. I'm sure it's easier for an actor or actress to die than to react. Does one throw one's hands up as if in a Victorian am-dram melodrama, stagger a little, like someone at turning-out time at the Dog and Duck or underplay it? I underplayed. The episode also featured snatches of other acts on stage, to give it that sense of authenticity, including former Family frontman Roger Chapman and my old pal Geno Washington, with his Ram Jam Band.

That day's shoot was at Twinwood Arena in Bedfordshire, the airfield from which Glenn Miller had taken off back in December 1944, so naturally it was worth exploring. The control tower still stands, and there are three typewriters from the era, clothes from the period hanging up, a board marking planes that have or haven't returned and a wealth of photographs. Down the cold, stone steps you go to the side door where Miller's UC-64 Norseman would have been waiting, and imagine the decision being made that the fog wasn't too bad and they would make it to Paris. A pity Chief Inspector Barnaby wasn't around then; he'd have solved the mystery.

CHAPTER 18

POLITICAL MAN

THIS ISN'T THE RIGHT TOME in which to expound one's theories and beliefs in detail, but here's an overview. Despite the snappy chapter headline, I am not actually a political man; I am just one of some sixty-three million people with a view. It goes without saying that not all sixty-three million will agree with each other. That doesn't mean one can't be civilised and allow other people their points of view. I thank God we are a democracy and enjoy freedom of speech, which also means that everyone is entitled to an opinion, be it right or wrong. If we didn't have different views, the world would be a rather bland place.

I've spoken at four Conservative Party conferences in support of William Hague, sometimes adding a song with political lyrics to the event. Satire, if indeed it is perceived as such, is not always construed in the way it was intended. One such ditty, in 2007, brought forth two entirely different results. The lyric, not exactly biting, but with enough thrust to make it work, included the line 'turning the country Brown', which was erroneously bandied about in the following day's nationals as a blatant piece of racism that caused many angry folk to storm out of the room in disgust. Confronted by one dogged and determine journalist on the phone, I explained that is was 'Brown' with a capital 'B', in other words Gordon Brown, who was poised to become Tony Blair's successor. If any humble pie was eaten by the press, it was an exceedingly small slice.

The other side of the coin was being almost set upon by various key figures muttering something that sounded extraordinarily like 'London mayor'. They couldn't be serious? It seemed they were. It was something that had never crossed my mind. Within a couple of weeks I was summoned, in a polite way of course, to meet with the then Conservative Party chairman, Francis Maude. There was no coercion. No press gang offering me the King's shilling. The gist of the meeting went something along these lines. I telescope them to make it more digestible.

'Why me?'

'You're intelligent.'

'But surely I don't know enough about politics.'

'But you're interested enough to speak at the conferences.'

'Well…' I was losing ground.

'And you're known. We have a lot of up-and-coming politicians who are interested in standing for London mayor.'

'Probably better qualified than me.'

'Not at all. You're smart, you can absorb facts very easily, and as I said you're known.'

'Does that have a bearing on it?'

'Very much so. We'd have to spend millions on trying to give someone else a profile as high as yours, and in a very short space of time. It just wouldn't work.'

'Isn't there anyone with a high profile?'

'No one has thrown their hat in the ring.'

I reasoned that I wasn't using my brain at that time at anywhere near its maximum capacity. That's like not exercising and putting on weight. I didn't want a fat brain.

Francis Maude could see me wavering. 'Look, you're used to the media. However much we train someone, they'll have to get used to being in the limelight, appearing live on television and radio and knowing how to deal with the press. That's what you've done for years.'

'Hmm.'

'Anyone else will have a standing start. You'd have a flying start. You're up to speed.'

Francis dispatched me to have tea with Gillian Shephard, once billed as Margaret Thatcher's successor. It was a delightful occasion and Gillian a most gracious hostess. On the business end of things, she sent me along to the corridors of power at City Hall, that odd glass thing plonked near Tower Bridge by Norman Foster in the name of architecture. It has the appearance of a pile of those streamlined modern cycling helmets just about to keel over. Inside it feels like a combination of the Tower of Pisa and one of those caterpillar rides at the fair. I had more meetings, was given literature to absorb and was informed that although the party were enthusiastic about me pushing forward, they couldn't be seen to only be supporting one person. Fair enough.

As soon as the news leaked, as news does, I found myself having to give interviews on the possibility of standing for London mayor, TV crews turned up at Radio London (Big L) the radio station where I was working and the press called for quotes. They were much fairer than I imagined. Iain Dale suggested I appear on his political internet station, 18 Doughty Street, which ran from 2006 to 2007, to discuss my candidature and generally answer questions from both him and viewers. I believe I was the last of the ten people in the running who appeared on there and apparently gave such a good showing that I was pointed up as being the most likely to succeed. I had a massive vote of confidence from the London taxi drivers and the Jewish community, neither camp being major supporters of the then mayoral incumbent, Ken Livingstone.

Global PR guru Chris Lewis, who had his finger very much on the political pulse, started to build a team for me. We had many meetings and suppers at Westminster, with the likes of Liam Fox and other powerful MPs. I guess they were sounding me out. We had meetings with Steven Norris, who had been the official Conservative candidate for the mayoral office in 2000 and 2004 and had lost both times to Ken Livingstone. He imparted his knowledge of, and passionate interest in, public transport, saying that if I landed the position, he would love to be responsible for Transport for London and if he became mayor I could head up Culture, Media and Sport. From that I assumed that he intended to stand for a third time. Our spies in the Commons chamber and the Strangers' Bar informed us that Steven Norris was indeed not only intending to stand for a third time, but had a strong team and the money for his campaign in place. I wavered. If that were true, I wasn't off the starting blocks. I was told not to believe all I heard and also to sharpen up. I'd assumed that I was smartly dressed for these occasions at Westminster. Clearly not. For one very important meeting I turned up in suit, tie and polished shoes only to be informed by Chris Lewis that I wasn't smart enough.

'You're joking?'

'No I'm not, this is a seriously important meeting. You have to look 100 per cent.'

'Not much I can do about it now, the shops are closed and there's only half an hour until we convene.'

'You'll find a suit of clothes, another tie and a pair of brand new shoes in the bedroom … just through that door.'

'Are you serious?'

'Absolutely.'

It was at that moment that I realised that this was business.

Chris also put me through my paces on the media front. 'This would be a doddle,' I reasoned, 'my strong point.' I had to think again. With the cameras rolling he fired questions at me from all angles. I thought I'd acquitted myself reasonably well. Until we watched the playback, that is.

'Look at you, you're lolling back in the chair as if you're not interested.'

'I was being laid back. I was relaxed.'

'Not good enough. You sit up straight and look like you mean business.'

'OK.' If it was only my posture, I could deal with that. It wasn't only my posture.

'You're looking around the room. You must look the interviewer right in the face. If you don't want to look in their eyes, look at the bridge of the nose and keep your gaze right there.' It was a good lesson. I still try to adopt a 'hold the bridge of their nose' policy.

Like a rebellious tube train announcer, Chris told me 'not to mind the gap'. 'Although a one- or two-second silence will feel as if you could drive a bus through it, don't worry, it's fine. It looks as though you're thinking about a point that has been raised or considering the question that's been put to you. Don't trot your answer out so fast, even if your brain works that quickly, that it sounds glib.'

Another ploy he used 'to sharpen the brain' was to answer a question with a question.

'Did you come here by car?'

'Is it important?'

'Are you refusing to answer my question?'

'What do you think?'

'Why are you being so evasive?'

'Do you seriously think I'd be evasive?'

And so on … you have to be up to speed, that's for sure.

With one week to go before the declarations, Ian Sanderson at party HQ called to ask if I had my papers ready to send in. I did. There was still talk of Steven Norris making a strong bid and rumours abounded. Just when it seemed that the declared runners were heading for the final furlong a backmarker appeared to be making headway with the odds shortening all the time. I was at a tennis party at Tony Samuels's house in Burhill, near Weybridge, when I chanced to be paired in the doubles at one point with the backmarker's father. 'I hear you may be standing for London mayor,' he beamed, admiring my backhand.

I gave a self-effacing laugh. In hindsight, as a response that was probably a tad weak. A real leader would have boomed in stentorian tones, 'Yes I am.'

How much Stanley Johnson knew of his son's intentions to stand for London mayor I didn't know. In between volleys and half-volleys I asked him the question, but either he was keeping his cards close to his chest or genuinely had no idea.

A week later the final phone call came from HQ. 'Could you ensure your declaration papers are faxed in by eleven o'clock, to be on the safe side?'

'Has Steven Norris declared yet?'

'Not yet.'

Boris Johnson?

'Not yet.'

Maybe the field was clear.

Half an hour later Boris declared. Steven Norris didn't declare. I didn't declare either, reasoning that Boris must have had talks with David Cameron so there would be heavy support at the top. One or two doubting Thomases asked what I would have done had I been chosen. The answer is I'd have stepped up to the mark without any qualms, given it my very best, learned where necessary and delegated when I needed to.

A year or two later it was mooted that the government were after ambassadors in various areas to act as a bridge between them and the people. Crikey, I thought, in true schoolboy annual style, if they feel they're that out of touch with the public, there's a problem. Following a lengthy phone call with Nigel Farage in the summer of 2012, we agreed to meet and have a chat. I found him charming and intelligent with a pretty good take on where the country was going and where the country should be going. I liked his policies and I delivered my first speech alongside Nigel at the UKIP south-east conference in 2012 and spoke at the National Conference a few months later. I became their spokesman for Culture, Media and Sport, three areas I love and in which I work. I have since spoken all around the country, in Birmingham, Wiltshire, Gloucestershire, Hampshire, Tyne and Wear, Oxfordshire, Sussex, Humberside and Kent. The extraordinary thing is that despite not yet having a single seat in the Commons, the daily YouGov polls consistently show UKIP in third place. The party also created the 'earthquake' that Nigel predicted by securing the most MEPs at the 2014 European elections, UKIP becoming the first party for 100 years to beat the two main parties in a national election.

What has slightly soured the world of politics for me is the smear campaigns and the deliberately misleading information and propaganda that's put about. I'm a great believer in being positive about yourself rather than being negative about someone else. When parties openly admit that they're trying to knock back any potential opponents it all becomes pointless. If you are selected to serve, either as Prime Minister, governing party or MP, your primary duty is to serve the country in the best way you think possible. Executing U-turns and appropriating other parties' policies to maintain popularity, when they have never been part of your manifesto, is shallow and weak. The racist nonsense which had been levelled at UKIP was suddenly and deliberately brought back with a vengeance as the party's popularity rose. In every field I work in I'm friends with people of all creeds and colours. Just diving off-piste for a moment, I was recently at a gallery where my very talented friend Ros Lloyd had an exhibition of her sculptures, and met a triple amputee called Dan. Having had a good chat with him, I reflected on the drive home how difficult life must be for him now. He was upbeat and trying to be positive, but facing an uncertain future. Not surprisingly the phrase 'there but for the grace of God' came into my head and by the following morning the emotion had become a song, the chorus of which was:

There but for the Grace of God
Go you or I or anyone,
Culture, creed or colour,
They're all somebody's son.

During 2014 the BBC made me aware of a possible conflict of interest with regard to being a spokesman for Culture, Media and Sport, especially as part of my brief included broadcasting. This meant having to turn down various programmes on which I was scheduled to appear. I still do talks every few weeks but without wearing an official hat. Several papers reported that I was going to stand as an MEP, but that was never discussed. I have been approached to stand in the 2015 general election, which is flattering and of course I have to give that serious consideration. How extraordinary that a party with, at the time of writing, no MPs could have such an effect on British politics, create so much media interest and shake the foundations of a structure that has possibly outlived its usefulness. Nigel Farage is a leader who communicates. We talk on the phone, or text. Even the morning after the EU elections, when the media circus was pursuing him after UKIP's historic victory, we remembered a conversation from two years ago. I told Nigel then of a day when I went to a local pub in Weybridge. I'd just started the Radio One breakfast show and was forever being given pieces of paper to say hello to someone the following morning. I was always pretty good about remembering, so stuffed some thirty scraps of paper in my pocket and took them in with me the following day. Even though they were from different groups of people and both sexes, virtually all of them asked me to play Duran Duran's 'Planet Earth', which had just been released. I looked at my producer and said, 'This group is going to be huge.' I told Nigel that he would know when that moment came for UKIP, which is why he texted after the EU earthquake to say, 'This is the Duran Duran moment.'

It's healthy to have different ideas and opposition, but I can't believe that we are really so diametrically opposed on so many aspects of life in the UK. And what makes the country work. Politics has become rather a dirty word, so as I say, I'm not a politician just a bloke with a view. I chatted with Tony Blair over dinner one evening at a friend's birthday and found him quite delightful, extremely charming and good company. I have never been a Labour voter but he was a statesman and a gentleman whatever you think of his politics. At one point he enquired about Robin Gibb's state of heatlth, after which he and Cherie sent a long and heart-warming email to Robin and Dwina at what must have been something like two in the morning. Very caring.

CHAPTER 19

TOMORROW
NEVER KNOWS

So HERE I sit by the timeless waters of the River Thames, which has been flowing to the sea, via one route or another, for fifty-eight million years and shows little sign of letting up. I've 'seized the day': made decisions, some right, some wrong, some beneficial and some downright catastrophic. Time passes quickly. I didn't believe that when I was a teenager. I assumed it would stand still ... for me at least. I believed the maxim expounded by Pete Brown and Piblokto, 'The Art School Dance Goes on Forever'. My relationships have been fun and I've stayed on excellent terms with my long-term girlfriends, but clearly, for one reason or another, they weren't meant to be life-time partners. As the Beatles opined, Tomorrow Never Knows ... or maybe they were wrong.

On the radio front, I have worked with so many incredible people, but Neil ffrench Blake and Doreen Davies cannot be credited enough for their inspiration, common sense, passion and belief in me, for which I thank them with copious amounts of gratitude and love.

On the songwriting side, my earliest publisher and promoter of my first hit, Dave Most deserves a special mention, as does Barry Mason for listening to my early songs and being encouraging and supportive. Bless you both.

As a galvanising force and inspiration to young people, Eric St John Foti, inventor and mentor, gave many the belief in themselves they needed to face the world.

I salute three great writers with whom I've worked extensively, Rupert Brooke, Oscar Wilde and Sir John Betjeman.

I was genuinely delighted for Vanessa when she was awarded the OBE. A just reward for a lot of hard work, determination and fortitude. Well done Vanessa Brady OBE.

I still try to uphold the school motto, taken from Milton's tractate *On Education*: 'Justly, Skilfully, Magnanimously'. Having visited his blue plaque at Berkyn Manor near Colnbrook, where he lived from 1632 to 1638, I like to imagine the seeds of Milton's statement on comprehensive reform were sown there before being published a few years later. Ergo, I can feel I have re-tuned to the original roots of the Wokingians' motto.

We're told that it's not a good thing to have regrets. What rubbish. If I wish to wallow in the odd regret or two, why shouldn't I? They're *my* regrets. Everybody tells me what a good father I'd have made. I wish that I'd had children, but either the circumstances, timing, or nature of the relationship dictated otherwise. I could certainly have been more judicious with some of the business advice I took. I love radio and TV but I also wish I'd concentrated even more on the songwriting. It's always been a deep and abiding passion. There have been copious amounts of fun, however, so no complaints there and it's a great bonus to leap out of bed on a daily basis eagerly looking forward to the day. The crazy years of the rock & roll business flashed by before I noticed, and carried the past away, but the future, as always, holds allure, mystery and promise. As J. B. Priestley said, 'I've always been delighted at the prospect of a new day, a fresh try, one more start, with perhaps a bit of magic waiting somewhere behind the morning.'

I've believed in the magic of the morning since being a child. The knowledge that the day could bring anything; that one could achieve anything … that there may just be some magic lurking somewhere, or if not it might be possible to create some.

As Horace scribbled in a wise moment after a particularly good breakfast, *carpe diem quam minimum credula postero* – 'seize the day, but put little trust in tomorrow'. I do both.

INDEX

100 Years of Prime Ministers and Prime Music 266
210 Thames Valley 11, 22, 28, 31
  Read and Wright Show 13
24 Hours 200
7-UP 42

A Christmas Carol 227
A Hard Day's Night 48
'A Room with Books' 343–4
Aardvarks, The 350
Abba 85, 259
d'Abo, Mike 291
Action, The 166
Adam and the Ants 85
Addis, David 25
Adventures of Ozzie and Harriet, The 234
Adventures of Robin Hood, The 158, 185
Adverts, The 27
Aerosmith 20
Ainsworth, Peter 232
Air London 202
Alan Bown!, The 262
Alarm, The 191
Aldermoor Poems, The 213, 342
Alexander, Arthur 165
Alexander, Danny 266
Alexandra, Princess 206
Alexandra, Queen 59
Allwood, Ralph 203
Ali, Muhammad 142
Alison 197, 323
Alison, Jenny 25
Alldis, Barry 38–9
Allwood, Raplh 236

Almond, Marc 84, 240
Altman, John 247
Amateur Athletics Association 299
Amber 170
Ambrose, Curtly 295
America 254
American Patrol 247
Anderson, Jon 242–3
Anderson, Ray 79, 253–4
Andre, Peter 1, 5, 8–9, 245, 263–4
Andrews, Dawn 197
Andrews, Eamonn 148
Andrews Barbara 153–4, 172–3
Andrews, Julie 153
Aneka
  'Japanese Boy' 341
Angel Air 212, 257
Angie 170
Anglesey, Henry 210
Animals, The 85
Annie 118
Apollo Leisure 226
Archer, Jeffrey 146, 307
Ardent 360
'Are You Ready' 26
Arista Records 205–6
Artwoods, The 165
'Ash Grove, The' 157
Ashcroft, Lord 278
Askey, Arthur 249, 352
Aspel, Michael 143
Astley, Rick 84, 112, 191
Atkins, Billy 51
Atomic Kitten 1
Atomic Rooster 262
Austen, Jane 212

Australia 2–3, 9, 30, 207, 224, 245, 262–3, 323
  Gold Coast 1, 133
Australian Open 4–5
Avon
  A World of Colour 196
  On the Move 196
Ayres, Pam 195

Bahrami, Mansour 311
Baish, John 81
Baker, Colin 228
Baker, Richard 135
Baldry, Long John 165
Ball, Bobby 91
Ball, Michael 308
Ballantyne, Celia 162
Ballantyne, David 162, 181–2
  'I Can't Express It' 162
  'Love Around the World' 162
Bamigboye, Baz 220–1
Bananarama 137
Barbados 253, 255
Barker, Simon 298
Barker, Sue 303
Barlow, Gary 197
Barrett, Syd 172
Barry 91
Barry, Michael (Michael Bukht) 74–5
Bates, Jeremy 311
Bates, Simon 84, 100–1
'Battle Hymn of the Republic' 351
Bay City Rollers 14, 20, 84, 149
Beach Boys, The 84, 188, 254

Beadle, Jeremy 259
Beano 156, 248, 292, 346, 352–3
Beatles, The 48–50, 61, 64, 85, 120, 148, 204, 249, 340–1, 350, 373
  'And Your Bird Can Sing' 361
  'Being for the Benefit of Mr Kite!' 51
  'Lucy in the Sky with Diamonds' 51
  Sgt. Pepper's Lonely Hearts Club Band 91
  'She Loves You' 188
'Beatles Lullaby' 183
Beautiful Game, The 233
Beck, Jeff 296
Bee Gees, 22, 64, 66, 130, 263, 265, 297
Belgium 184
Bell, Colin 'Nijinsky' 309
Bellinger, Chris 67, 134, 136
Belolo, Henri 258–9
Bennett, Brian 341
Bennett, Mike
  White Wedding 247
Bennett, Roy 310–11
Bennett, Ruth 311
Bermuda 122–3
Berry, Chuck 137
  'Promised Land' 189
Berry, Mike 17, 199
Berry, Vivien 273
Bertrand, Plastic 361
  'Ça plane pour moi' 35
Best, Alex 1
Best, George 1
Best of British 266
Beston, Ted 108
Betjeman, John 195, 202, 205, 209–12, 215–16, 239, 244–5, 257, 284, 363
  'A Subaltern's Love Song' ('Joan Hunter Dunn') 201, 203, 304
  'Archibald' 204
  'Fete Champetre, The' 201
  'Harrow-on-the-Hill' 201–2
  'Hunter Trials' 202

'Newest Bath Guide' 201
'Parliament Hill Fields' 202, 216
'Tregardock' 202, 205, 216
Betjeman, Lady 209–10
Betjeman Society 335
Joan Hunter Dunn Tennis Tournament 304
Bewes, Rodney 112
Bi Maybelle
  'Whole Lotta Shakin' Goin' On' 309
Big Norm 31
Black, Don 235, 281
Blackburn, Tony 45, 70, 73, 81, 181, 352
Blackmore, Ritchie 296
Blair, Cherie 310, 372
Blair, Lionel 143–4
Blair, Tony 365, 372
Blake, Neil ffrench (NffB) 10–13, 15, 17–19, 21–4, 26–7, 30, 118, 267, 293, 373
'Blaydon Races' 351
Blondie 82
Bloodaxe, Erik 275
Blue Beat Records 167
Bluesology 165
Blunstone, Colin 217, 240
Bo Street Runners 169
Boat That Rocked, The 3
Bolan, Mark 14
Bolt, Ian 27, 141
Bolt, Usain 57
Bond, Jennie 1, 10
Bond, John 39
Bonham, John 46, 296
Bonnie Prince Charlie 92
Bonzo Dog Doo-Dah Band 46
Borough, Steven 128
Bottomley, Peter 324
Bowie, David 49, 165
  'Dancing in the Street' 150
Brady, Vanessa 279–80, 298, 374
Braque, Georges 342
Breeze, Alan 125
Breeze, Olivia 125
Breeze, Renee 125
Brice, Ann 270

Brice, Roger 220
Briley, Martin 185
Bristol University 46
British Broadcasting Corporation (BBC) 17, 42, 44, 63, 67–9, 135, 180, 187, 255, 268, 286, 335, 371
  Andy Pandy 289
  Antiques Roadshow 218
  BBC Four 85
  Benny Hill Show, The 12
  Berkshire 287–8
  Beyond Our Ken 75
  Billy Cotton Band Show 125
  Blue Peter 19
  Call My Bluff 8
  Chart Quiz 54
  Crackerjack 188
  EastEnders 173, 192
  Easy Beat 158
  Give Us A Clue 143
  Juke Box Jury 158
  Mastermind 77
  Multi-Coloured Swap Shop 134
  One Man and His Dog 100
  Only Fools and Horses 362
  Paul Temple 153
  Pop of the Farm 54
  Pop Quiz 42, 54, 141, 180, 341
  Radio Berkshire 81
  Radio One 12, 27, 34, 41–3, 45–6, 49, 52, 55, 57–8, 60, 64, 66–7, 70, 72, 75, 77–9, 87–8, 92, 95, 97, 105, 111, 114, 117, 135, 146, 184–8, 191, 198, 203, 205, 208, 226, 248, 274–5, 281, 303, 306, 330, 332–3, 338, 341, 371
  Roadshow 336
  Radio Six Music 64, 198
  Radio Two 12, 15, 33, 64, 69, 118, 330
  Round the Horne 75
  Saturday Club 158
  Saturday Superstore 54, 61–2, 67, 75, 136, 150, 188–9, 203, 275, 341, 353
  Seaside Special 83

INDEX

Singled Out (Round Table) 54
Teady Bears' Picnic 114
This Is Your Life 12, 147
Three Men in a Boat 60, 113
Through the Keyhole 141–2, 173
Tomorrow's World America 60
Top of the Pops (TOTP) 44, 54, 62, 67, 82–5, 182, 192, 206, 246, 256, 362
Two Ronnies, The 83
World Service 236
British Deaf Association 307
British Empire 129
British Library 338
British Open Croquet Championship Final 323
British Rail 295–6
Broadcast 12
Brocket, Charlie 1, 5–6, 8–9, 246
Brooke, Rupert 213–14, 220, 235–6, 241, 245, 267, 343, 346–9, 358
'For Mildred's Urn' 348–9
'Old Vicarage, Grantchester, The' 146, 349
Brooke Centenary Committee 348
Brooker, Chris 291
Brooking, Sir Trevor 280
Brooklands College 48, 271, 273
Brown, Errol 84, 191, 298, 339
Brown, Ford Madox 286
Brown, Gordon 365
Brown, Joe 150, 198
Brown, Pete 373
Browning, Elizabeth Barrett 126, 343
de Brunnesbury, Celestrial 287
de Brunnesbury, Thomas 287
Bruno, Frank 308
Bryce, David 183
Bucks Fizz 340
Buddy Holly Story, The 234
Burgess, Guy 241

Burma 273
Burnett, Paul 70, 190
Bury, Martin 169
Bury Football Club 325, 333–4
Bush, Kate 191, 339
Buster, Prince 167
Byrds, The
'Mr Spaceman' 72
Byron, Lord George 8, 212

Calcut, John 99
Callan, Robin 241, 348–9
Callow, Simon 354–5
Cambridge University King's College 236
Cameron, David 204, 369
Campbell, Nicky 108
Canada 348
Cannes Film Festival 68, 356, 358, 360, 362
Cantabile 216
Capes, Geoff 94
Capital Gold 70, 72–4, 79, 198
Work Experience Scheme 71
Capital Radio 70, 194
Caplan, Harold 293
Capriati, Jennifer 306
'Captain Noah's Floating Zoo' 183
Captain Sensible 107, 190, 202, 205, 216, 337
Cardiff City Football Club 331
Carlin Music 164
Carradine, David 357–8
Carroll, Clive 257
Carter, John 281
Carter, June 126
Cash, Dave 70
Cash, Johnny 126, 181
'Ballad of Annie Palmer, The' 126
Cassidy, David 13, 287
Castle, Andrew 315
Castle, Roy 59, 308
Caudwell, John 278
Caught in the Act 236
Cavendish, Lady Elizabeth 210–12
CBS Broadcasting, Inc. 205
Cézanne, Paul 352
Challenge Anneka 195

Chamberlain, Neville 184, 331
Channel Four 150
Channel TV 60
Channon, Mick 333
Chaplin, Charlie 124
Chapman, Roger 363
Charles I, King 288
Charisma Records 202
Charlemagne 119
Charles, Prince of Wales 47, 60, 250, 319
'Charley Brewster's DJ Show' 163
Charlton, Sir Bobby 332–3
Chatsworth House 116
Chegwin, Keith 136, 150
Cherry, Celine 254
Chetwode, Lady 284
Chinnery, Derek 41, 43–4, 96, 100
Christie, Agatha 205
Christos, Jon 256
Churchill, Sir Winston 124, 172, 346
Chuter, Johnny 291
Ciani, Paul 83
'Cinema Saint' 49
'City to City' 245
City Sounds 163
Clapton, Eric 40, 255, 297–8
'Tears in Heaven' 255
Clark, David 143
Clark, Petula 352
Clarkson, Roger 255
Clash, The 27
'White Riot' 27
Classic FM 25, 76–7, 81, 230, 242, 248, 335, 343
'Morning March, The' 230–1
Cleobury, Stephen 236
Cliff Richard Chronicle, The 341
Cliff the Musical 249
Coates, Eric
By the Sleepy Lagoon 153
Dam Busters March, The 153
Knightsbridge March, The 153
Cobain, Kurt 346

Cobb, Nigel 292
Cochran, Eddie 14, 322
Cocker, Joe 149
Coe, Lord Sebastian 302
Coetzer, Amanda 309
Cohen, Michael 42–3, 135
Cole, Tony 183
Coleridge, Sinbad 290–1
Collins, Pete 187
Collins, Phil 62
    'Groovy Kind of Love' 84
Colman, Stuart 55, 188–9
'Colours, The' 112
Comic Relief 190, 335
Commonwealth Games 331
Compton, Denis 290
Conley, Brian 309
Conservative Party 364, 367
Constable, John 352
Conway, Russ 339
Cook, Peter 277, 302
Corbett, Ronnie 302
Corcoran, Chris 227
Covenanter Wars
    Battle of Rullion Green
      (1666) 139–40
Coventry City Football Club
  136
Coward, Noël 124–6
Cox, Mark 315
Cox and Kings 118
Craig, Daniel 358
Crane, Andy 84
Craven, John 136–7
Crazy World of Arthur
  Brown, The 262
Cream 164
Crickets, The 24–5
    'My Little Girl' 187
    'Teardrops Fall like Rain' 187
Croft, Annabel 198, 302
Cromwell, Oliver 72
Crosby, Bing 205
Crowder, Alan 204
Crowe, Sarah 237
Crystal Sky 360–1
Cumbria Tourist Board
    'Baarmy Sheep' 260
Curtis, Sonny 25
Czech Republic
    Prague 356, 360

Daily Express 98, 221, 234–5,
  251, 278, 342
Daily Mail 260
Daily Mirror 98, 251
Daily Star 110
Daily Telegraph 278
Dale, Ian 366
Dalyell, Tam 139
Dando, Jill 106
Dandy, The 156, 352
Darwin, Charles 212
Dave and the Diamonds 167
Dave Clark Five, The 84
    'Everybody Knows' 180
David, Soundarie 254
David Cup 10
Davies, Doreen 42, 55, 60,
  78, 373
Davies, Gary 101, 331
Davies, Philippa 304
Davis, Miles 62
Davis Jr, Sammy 149
Davis, Sandy 182
'Davy Crockett' 152, 154
Day, Darren 228
Dead Poets Society, The 259,
  262
    'In Flanders Fields' 267
Deal, Anthony 292
Decker, Carol 112
Dee, Dave 205
Dee, Simon 23–4
Deep Purple 162, 298
Dempster, Nigel 342
Dene, Graham 298, 351
Dene, Julie 351–2
Dennis 194–5
Denver, John 72
Desmond, Richard 278
Dickens, Charles 163, 227
    A Christmas Carol 226–7
    Great Expectations 226, 360
    Oliver Twist 8
Dietrich, Marlene 125
Dimbleby, Jonathan 308
Disasters Emergency
    Committee 253, 256
'Distant View' 244
Distel, Sacha 59
'Dixie's Land' 350
'Do You Remember Me' 199

Dolenz, Micky 341
Don Wimble and the Aces 199
'Game, Set and Match' 198
Donaldson, Walter
    'On the Gin Gin Ginny
      Shore' 152
Donegan, Lonnie 198, 341
Donovan 163, 166, 216, 281
    'Newest Bath Guide' 217
Dooley, Jim 278
Dore, Michael 213
Dorset, Ray 341
Douglas, Craig 339
Downton Abbey 360
Doyle, Sir Arthur Conan 212
Dr Hook 137
Drake, Milton
    'Mairzy Doats' 151
Drake, Nick 184
Drake, Sir Francis 92
Dribrg, Tom 342
Drifters, The 191, 339
Droudge, PC Keith 98
Dunaway, Faye 357
Dundas, David 246
Dunn, Joan Hunter 304
Duran Duran 55, 67, 85, 189
    'Planet Earth' 371
Durrell, Gerald 75–6
Durell, Lee 75–6
Durr, Cookie 270
Dvořák, Antonín 231
Dylan, Bob 163, 166

Eater 27
Eaton, Chris 235
Echolettes, The 161–2
    'Our Love Feels Now' 162
Ed Sullivan Show, The 267
Eden, Lady 126
Eden, Sir Anthony 126
Edge, Molly 173
Edge, Valerie 192
Edmonds, Noel 45, 57–8, 101
Edward, Prince 360
Edward VII, King 59, 163, 205
Edward VIII, King 90, 288, 315
Edwards, Malcolm 291
Edwards, Rod 196, 202, 204,
  216
Egypt

Suez Crisis (1956) 126
Eileen 4, 252, 257–8
Eilers, Mike 220
Elderton, Nigel 200
Electric Light Orchestra (ELO) 85
Elgar, Sir Edward 231–2, 245, 258–9, 340
   Pomp and Circumstance No. 4 258
Ellis, Janet 234
Ellis, Sir Vivien 65
Elizabeth II, Queen 19, 47–8, 62, 124, 135, 144, 228, 279, 328
Elizabeth, Queen Mother 124, 228
Elizabethan Dragonflies 213, 342
Elsbury, Gordon 206
Emburey, John 46
EMI Films 359
EMI Music 11, 162, 183, 192, 194, 341
'England My England' 260
English, David 22, 296, 298
English Speaking Union 252
Equals, The 165–6
Eric the Eel 31, 33
Errol 305
'Esmerelda Fufluns' 175
Espanol, Jeff 358
   American Banker, The 357
Essex, David 84, 108, 204–6, 215, 298
   Christmas EP, The 216
   His Greatest Hits 198, 216
Estefan, Gloria 84
Etherington, Steve 248, 259
Eton College 203, 236, 289
European Union (EU) 371
Eurovision 248, 250
Evans, Godfrey 290
Eve, Trevor 302
'Evening Paper' 163–4
Evening Standard 221, 251
'Ever Decreasing Circles' 160
Everett, Kenny 70–2, 84
   'Knees' 72
Everett, Rupert 101
Everly, Phil 54–5
Everly Brothers 207

Facebook 159
Fairweather Low, Andy 298
Faith, Adam 95, 341, 351
Faithfull, Marianne 15, 212–13
Falklands War (1982) 113
Fall, The 207, 247
Fancy, Brett 358
Farage, Nigel 369–71
Fat Mattress 262
Featherstone, Roy 183
'February's Child' 172–3, 175–6, 178, 192
Federation Cup 306
Fédération Internationale de Football Association (FIFA)
   World Cup (1966) 2
   World Cup (2006) 259
Feld, Malcolm 243
Fellowes, Julian 360
Ferguson, Sarah (Duchess of York) 310
Ferry Cross the Mersey 12
Fingleton, John 292
First World War (1914–18) 87, 175, 238, 267–8, 282, 287, 347, 359
   Western Front 269
Flack, Roberta 148
Fleming, David 307
Fleming, Ian 124–6
Fletcher, Guy 281
'Flight 19' 16, 199
Flight, Howard 324
Flintlock 19–20
Flower, John 22
Floyd, Eddie
   'Things Get Better' 46
Flying Burrito Brothers 13
Flynn, Errol 124
Flynn, Patrice 124
Football Association Challenge Cup (FA Cup) 266, 276, 353
Forbes, Bryan 359
Forbes, Emma 195
Foreigner 149
Forever England 347, 349, 358
Formby, George 101, 249
Forsyth, Bruce 307
Foss, Paul 187
Foster, Norman 366
Foster, Stephen

'Oh! Susannah!' 152
'Old Folks at Home, The' 152
'Some Folks' 152
Foti, Erich St John 166, 374
Four Lads
   'Standing on the Corner' 188
Four Tops, The 84
Fox, Sam 101
Fox, Tony 22
France 9
   Aigues-Mortes 119–20, 122
   Calais 111
   Canal du Midi 118
   Megève 321
   Paris 101, 258, 363
   Seine, River 119
Sète 119
Francis, Stu 91
Francis, Trevor 353
Franco, Francisco 62
Frankie Goes to Hollywood 85, 191
   'Relax' 66–9
Freddie 121–2
Freeman, Alan 14, 84, 265
Freeman, Ian 280
French, Samuel 221
Freud, Emma 146
Frieda, John 293–4
Frisby, Elliott 259–62, 264–5, 267
From There to Uncertainty 170
Frost, David
   'Cricket Bag, The' 142
Fudge, Kenneth 159
Furnace, Zoot 21
Fury, Billy 340

Gabrielle 217
Gaius Marius Ltd 119
Gallagher, Don 219
Galvin, Joshua 28
Gambaccini, Paul 26, 84, 113, 338
Game, The 169
Garafalo, Robert 255
Garland, Judy 249
Garnett, Alf 309
Gates, Gareth 59

Gatting, Mike 293
Gauge, Alexander 158
Gay, John 163
Geldof, Bob 147–8, 339, 341
   'Great Song of
     Indifference, The' 111
George, Boy 191, 253–4
George II, King 288
George III, King 288
George V, King 210, 288
Germany 187, 260
Gibb, Dave 169–70
Gibb, Dwina 263–5, 279, 372
Gibb, Ian 158
Gibb, Maurice 84, 263
Gibb, Nick 324
Gibb, Robin 84, 129, 253, 256,
   262–4, 277–80, 372
   'I've Gotta Get a Message
     to You' 263
Gibson, Barry 187
Giffin, Colin 186
Gilbert and Sullivan
   Iolanthe 163
Gilbert of Sempringham 275
'Ginger You're Barmy' 155
'Girls Were Made to Be
   Loved' 183
Girouard, Mark 210
'Glad That I Live Am I'
   (hymn) 154
Gladstone, William 286
Glaister, Gerry 193
Glenn, Dave 292
Glover, Brian 228
Go West 84, 191, 207
'God Save the South' 350
Goddard, Geoff 16–18
   'Johnny Remember Me'
     199
   'Just Like Eddie' 199
   'Son This Is She' 199
   'Tribute to Buddy Holly'
     199
   'Wild Wind' 199
Gomelsky, Giorgio 161
Gomer, Sarah 302
Good, Jack
   Oh Boy! 42
   Six-Five Special 42
'Good King Wenceslas' 267

Goodier, Mark 84, 115
Goons, The 162
Gorbachev, Mikhail 190
Gormley, Peter 183
Gospel According to St John,
   Active Service 1914–1915 285
Gough, Orlando 291
Gough, Piers 291
Gower, David 293
Grace, Bob 231
Gracious 182
Graf, Steffi 306
Gramm, Lou 149
Grant, David 216
   'Conversion' 216
Grant, Eddie 166
Graveney, Tim 292–3
Great Expectations 227–9
Green, Al 148
Green, Candida Lycett 208
Green, Mick 159
Green, Peter 41
Greene, Richard 158, 185
Greene, Sarah 136
Greenslade 185
Greenstreet, Mark 193
Grenside, Dorothy 271
   Open Eyes 272
'Grief Never Grows Old' 256–
   7, 267
Grimshaw, John Atkinson
   Golden Light 352
   October 352
Grossman, Loyd 141–2
Guardian, The 221
'Guernica' 62
Guernsey 59, 322
Guest, Christopher 246
Guevara, Ernesto 'Che' 323
Guinness Book of 500 Number
   Ones, The 340
Guinness Book of British Hit
   Singles, The (1977) 26, 29, 87,
   213, 338
Guinness Book of Records, The
   26, 101–2, 295–6
Guinness Hits Challenge, The 340

Hadaway, Henry 355
Hadley, Tony 217
Hague, William 310, 364

Hale, Tony 44
Hall, Norman
   Mutiny on the Bounty 348
Hamilton, David 69–70, 79,
   84, 261, 332
Hamilton, General Sir Ian
   346–7
Hamish 161
Hammond, Albert 232–4
   '99 Miles from LA' 231
   'Free Electric Band' 231
   'It Never Rains in
     Southern California' 231
Hampstead & Highgate 217
Hampton Court 309–10
Hancock, Herbie 148
Handy, John 361–2
Hanson, Alex 220
Hardy, Bert 11
Harley, Steve 202, 205
Harriet 9
Harris, Chris 118–19
Harris, Jet 15
Harrison, George 55, 180, 198
Harry, Debbie 82
Harry, Prince 204, 318
Harum, Procol 84
Haslam, Annie 202, 205
Haslam, Dorothy 271
Haslam, Jack 270–1
Haswell, Charles 317
Hatt, Chris 175
'Have You Seen Your Daughter
   Mrs Jones' 26, 183–4
Hay, Alexander 336
Hay, Aline 336
Hayward, Justin 89, 205, 216
Heartaches, The 17, 40–1,
   290–3
Heath, A. W. 291
Heath, Bill 175, 177
Hello! 228
Help Hammer Cancer 308
Hendrix, Jimi 162, 202, 346, 363
Henley, W. E. 259
Henman, Tim 199
Henry, Stuart 34–5, 104
Henry VIII, King 274, 310
Hepburn, Audrey 125
Herbert, A. P.
   'Liberty Song, The' 258

Herd, The 165

Hereford United Football
Club 136

Heritage Foundation 276–8

Herman's Hermits 162, 164

HHO/Palm Tree Productions
355–6

Hickey, William 342

Hill, Benny 352

Hill, Dave 46, 226

Hillier, Bevis 210

Hillier, Tony 281

'Hills of the North, Rejoice'
(hymn) 154

Hines, Frazer 298

Hines, Justin 167

Hirley, Justin 202
'Tregardock' 202

Hitler, Adolf 117, 184

Hits of the '70s 339

Hoad, Lew 323

Hoare, Lucy 348

Hoban, Michael 149

Hobbs, Ann 302–3

Holden, Tony 'Jogger' 22–3

Holder, Noddy 46

Holding, Michael 298

Holland, Merlin 218–19, 223

Holley, Ella 25

Holley, Lawrence 25

Hollies, The 85, 340

Hollingdale, Paul 12, 23, 293

Holly, Buddy 14, 24–5, 120,
187

Holman Hunt, William 352

Holoway, Mike 19

'Home, Home on the Range'
154

Honeyz, The 254

Hooper, Dave 167

Hopkin, Mary 14

Hopkins, Gerard Manley 163

Horne, Jonty 292

Hot Chocolate 84

'Hot, Hot, Hot' 197

Hothouse, Greenfingers 21

'House of Usher, The' 245

Housemartins, The 207

How's Buisness 358

Howard, Frankie 194

Hugenouts 119

Hughes, Emlyn 303, 333

Humperdinck, Engelbert 58,
84, 174
'Last Waltz, The' 180

Hunniford, Caron 5

Hunniford, Gloria 5

Hunt, Jeremy 266

Hurll, Michael 83

Hussey, Marmaduke 194

Hustlers, The 159

Hymns Ancient & Modern
(book) 154

'I Vow to Thee, My Country'
(hymn) 154

'I Wouldn't Leave My Little
Wooden Hut for You' 152

Icke, David 136

Idle Race, The 178

Idol, Billy 339

'If She's a Day' 163

'If You Were the Only Girl in
the World' 152

'In Memory' 240

Independent Singles Chart
256

India 210
British Raj 120

Inside Out 355–6

Institute of Contemporary
Arts 62

Inverdale, John 309

Irons, Jeremy 216

Italy 239
Milan 239
Venice 257–8

iTunes 196

ITV 255
Army Game, The 75
Blind Date 248
Bootise and Snudge 75
*I'm a Celebrity . . . Get
Me Out of Here!* 2, 5–8,
245, 296
Man about the House 12
Oh Boy! 248
Ready, Steady, Go! 162
*Sunday Night at the
London Palladium* 248
Thank Your Lucky Stars 158
This Morning 246

*Who Wants to Be a
Millionaire?* 265–6
X-Factor 149

Jackson, Linda 213

Jackson, Michael 84, 189

Jackson, Philip 278

Jackson, Richard 213

Jacobs, David 84

Jagger, Mick 163, 174
'Dancing in the Street' 150

Jake 175

Jam, The 187

Jamaica 126–7, 266, 275
Oracabessa 124

James, Alan 332

James, Edward 163

James, Henry 241, 349

James, Tony 351

James VI of Scotland 92

Jameson, Peter 205

Jamieson, Peter 205

Janey 58

Japan
Taipei 101 6

Javer, Monique 306

Jay, Margaret 266

Jazz FM 79, 81

Jensen, Kid 70, 333

Jersey Islands 59, 75
Alderney 59

'Jerusalem' (hymn) 154

Jet Bronx and the Forbidden
142
'Ain't Doin' Nothin'' 142

Jibson, Tim 276

Jimmy Brown Sound and
Horse 175

Jock Swon & the Meters
'New Wave Band' 185

John, Adrian 67, 79–80

John, Elton 149, 165, 255, 303,
339–40

'John Brown's Body' 351

John Mayall & the
Bluesbreakers 164

John's Children 262
'Arthur Green' 176

Johnny Hates Jazz 202–3

Johnson, Boris 204

Johnson, Holly 68

Johnson, Robert 76, 346
Johnston Brothers
 'Hernando's Hideaway' 340
Jones, Brian 346
Jones, Davy 61
 *They Made a Monkee Out
 of Me* 61
Jones, George 333–4
Jones, Paul 257, 339
Jones, Rob 30
Jones, Tom 58, 101
 'Delilah' 180
Joplin, Janis 346
Journey through Music 237–8
Joyce, William 39
'Just a Little Bit Crazy' 260
Just Plain Smith 170, 175–6,
 181, 291
 'Crazy, Crazy' 181
 'If (Would It Turn Out
 Wrong)' 181
Juste, Adrian 109

Kaiser Chiefs 260
Kay, Peter 335
Keats, John 8, 343
 'When I Have Fears that I
 May Cease to Be' 125
Keeble, John 298
Keegan, Kevin 28, 333, 353
Keen, Alan 30
'Kelly from the Isle of Man'
 152
Kennedy, Jimmy 298
Kennedy, John F. 116–17
Kennedy, Kathleen 'Kick' 116
Kennedy, Nigel 358
Keith 91
Kern, Jerome 277–8
 'I've Told Every Little
 Star' 278
 'Old Man River' 278
 'Smoke Gets in Your
 Eyes' 278
 'Way You Look Tonight,
 The' 278
Kershaw, Nik 191
Khrushchev, Nikolai 323
King, Ben E. 206
King, Graham 11
King Jr, Martin Luther 193

Kinks, The 84, 166, 176, 281
Kinnock, Neil 136–7
Kinsman, Winifred 348
Kipling, Rudyard 343
Kirkby, Dan 281
Kitchingham, Gerry 193–4
Kitchener, Lord Horatio 269
KLM Airlines 239
Knopfler, Mark 191
Knox, Buddy
 'Party Doll' 157
'Kiss Me Goodnight Sgt
 Major' 155
Knights Templar 119
Korean War (1950–3) 60
Kosta, Peter 224
Kretzmer, Herbert 277

Labour Party 342, 372
'Lady of the Lamp, I Won't
 Look Back' 175
Laguna Festival 237
Lamb, Alan 293
Lambrettas, The 46
Lancaster, Osbert 210
Land, David 179
Langtry, Lillie 205
Lauper, Cyndie 149
Laurel & Hardy 249
Laver, Rod 311
Layer Cake 358
Layton, George 308
Le Bars, Tessa 194
Le Gallienne, Richard 349
Lea, Jim 226
Leale, Eva 278
Leconte, Henri 311
Led Zeppelin 46
 'Communications
 Breakdown' 173
Lee Rose, Randall 79
Leeds United Football Club 331
Leicester City Football Club
 'Swinging for England' 260
Leigh, Vivien 124
Lemarque, Francis 200
Lennon, Cynthia 49, 51
Lennon, John 48–51, 63, 142,
 148, 184, 263
 'Imagine' 51
Lennon, Julia 51

Leonard, John 109, 116–17
Lettermen, The
 'Way You Look Tonight,
 The' 71
Level 42 149
Levine, Steve 254
Levy, Michael 204–5
Lewis, Brian 271
Lewis, Chris 366–7
Lewis, Jeremy 271
Lewis, Ken 271
Lewis, Martyn 308
Leyton, John 17, 199
Leyton, Lawrence 137–40
Liberace 149
Licorish, Vicky 136
Lieutenant Pigeon 339
Lihoreau, Tim 343
Likes of Us, The 244
Lillee, Dennis 295
Linda, Solomon
 'Lion Sleeps Tonight,
 The' 246
Lineker, Gary 298
Lipman, Maureen 195
Liverpool Football Club 1
Liverpool Philharmonic
 Orchestra 149
Living in a Box 84
Livingstone, Ken 366
Lloyd, David 311
Lloyd, John 311
Lloyd, Ros 370
Lloyd Webber, Andrew 18, 65,
 179, 212, 215, 234, 244
 Jesus Christ Superstar 18,
 176, 179
 *Joseph and the Amazing
 Superstar* 18, 179, 248–9
 Richard the Lionheart
 18, 179
Lloyd Webber, Julia 162
Lloyd Wright, Frank 228
Lloyd's List 247–8
Loch, Gare 104
'London Town' 49
London Weekend Television
 (LWT)
 Pillow Talk 146
Lord, Jon 296
Loren, Sophia 124

Loudermilk, John D.
  'Angela Jones' 190
  'Ebony Eye' 190
  'Indian Reservation' 190
  'Language of Love' 190
  'Sittin' in the Balcony' 190
Loughton, Tim 324
Louis IX of France 119
Love
  'Alone Again Or' 77
Love, Mike 84
Love, Poetry & Revolution 262
Lowry, L. S. 352
Lucas, Matt 335
Lukas, Jon 182–3
Lumley, Joanna 195
Luxembourg 28–31, 35, 41–2
Lyall, Billy 149
Lydon, John (Johnny Rotten)
  1, 5, 68
Lynam, Des 198
Lynn, Vera 339
Lynne, Jeff 178
Lynton, Jackie 173
Lyttelton, Humphrey 276

McAlpine, Lady 280
McAlpine, Sir William 280
McCallum, David 193
McCartney, Linda 340
McCartney, Paul 24–5, 62–4,
  137, 204
  'Let It Be' 191
McCrae, John 267
MacDermott, Mike 230
McDevitt, Chas 198
MacDonald, Trevor 297
McEnroe, John 307
McFadden, Kerry (née
  Katona) 1, 6–7
McFly 256
McKay, Staff Sergeant
  Thomas 92
McKenna, Paul 3
McKeown, Les 84
McLaren, Malcolm 353
Maclean, Donald Duart 241,
  243–4
McMenemy, Lawrie 353
McMillan, Frew 311
McPherson, George 138, 140

McWhirter, Norris 338
McWhirter, Ross 338
Mad Bongo Player of Powis
  Terrace 171
Maddison, Ben 314
Maddison, Dave 314
Madness 259
Magic Roundabout, The 34
Magnet Records 204–5
Magpie 329
Mail on Sunday 209–10, 229,
  294
Major to Minor 350
Maitland, Lady Olga 212
Mallett, Timmy 197
  'Itsy Bitsy Teeny Weeny
    Yellow Polka Dot
    Bikini' 197
Malta 129–30
  Valletta 129
Mamma Mia 226
Manchester Evening News 168
Manchester United Football
  Club 282, 331–2
Mandrake Paddle Steamer 185
Mann, Manfred 291
Marconi, Guglielmo 112–13
Marconi, Maria 112–13
de la Mare, Walter 343
Margaret, Princess 126, 150
Marillion 101
Marlborough College 304
Marriott, Steve 104
Marsh, Eddie 349
Marshall, Malcolm 295
Martin, Billy 51, 281
Martin, George 195–6, 202, 235
Marvin, Hank 302, 339, 341
Mary, Queen of Scots 92
Masefield, John 343
Mason, Barry 180, 281, 374
Mason, Gary 298
Matchbox 200
  Flying Colours 187
Mathis, Johnny 14
Matt Bianco
  'Get Out of Your Lazy
    Bed' 136
Matthews, Mike 23
Matthews, Stanley 326
Mattison, Major Ian 280

Maude, Francis 365–6
Mauldin, Joe B. 25
Maxwell, Robert 146
May, Brian 42, 84, 198
May, Simon 236–7
'May Day Song for North
  Oxford' 203
Mayall, John 165
Mayo, Simon 115
Mazelle, Kym 194
  'Woman of the World' 193
'Me and Jane in a Plane' 151
Meehan, Tony 340
Meek, Joe 16, 277
Melody Maker 177
Memba 58
Men They Couldn't Hang,
  The 112
Menuhin, Yehudi 340
Mercury, Freddie 63, 149, 339
Mexico
  Acapulco 132
Mike and the Mechanics 240
*Mike Read & Sir John
  Betjeman: The Sound of
  Poetry* 257
Mike Stuart Span 169
Miley, Smiley 57, 79–80,
  88–9, 91–2, 104–6, 109–10,
  112, 114, 294
Miller, Dr Peter 348
Miller, Glenn 340, 363
Miller, Judith 218
Miller, Martin 218
Miller, Richard Compton 342
Mills, Gordon 58
Mills, Sir John 277
Millwall Football Club 1
Milton, John
  On Education 374
Mindel, Dave 181–2
'Minstrel Boy, The' 157, 351
Miss Saigon 228
Mitchell, Granddad 43
Mizell, Hank
  'Jungle Rock!' 246
Monet, Claude 352
Monkees, The 61
  'Alternate Title' 341
  'Cuddly Toy' 61
Monster Raving Looney Party

296
Montague-Drake, Blair 165
Montand, Yves
 A Paris 200
Montez, Chris
 'Let's Dance' 188
Monty Python 75
Moody, Ron 358
Moody Blues, The 148
Moon, Keith 58, 277
Moore, Gary 191, 254
Moorea 348
Morecambe & Wise 249, 353
Morgan, Sir Henry 124
Morley, Paul 68
Morris, Joan 153–4
'Moscow Nights' 245
Moss, Stirling 59
Most, David 164, 206, 279,
 374
Most, Dot 279
Most, Mickie 147, 164, 202–3
Mothers of Invention, The 167
Mottram, Buster 315
Moulin Rouge 155
MS *Herald of Free Enterprise* 191
Mud 84, 339
Mungo Jerry 341
Murdoch, Rupert 11
Murphy, Alan 149
Murray, Andy 199
Murray, John 205, 212
Murray, Mitch 281
Murray, Pete 84
'Music, Music, Music' 152
Mussolini, Benito 113
'Mutual Admiration Society' 152
My Fair Lady 228
'My Old Man's A Dustman' 196
Myers, Judie (Judie Tzuke) 179
Myers, Sefton 178–9
'Myfanwy' 204–9, 215–16,
 240, 267

'Narcissus' 240
Nash, Robin 83
Nastase, Ilie 311
National Children's Orchestra
 of Great Britain 254
National Cricket Academy 295
National Singles Chart 256

Needletime 12
Nelson, Charlie 192
Nelson of Corsock 140
Nelson, Ricky 234
 'Believe What You Say' 25
Nemeth, Joe 172
Netherlands
 Holland 140
Nettlefold Studios 158
New Musical Express (*NME*)
 65, 158
New Poems for Old Paintings
 351
New Seekers, The 183
New Ventures 179
New Zealand 280
Newman, Nanette 195, 359
News International 11
Newton-John, Olivia 183
Nicaragua 131
Nicholas, Mark 292–3
Nicholas, Paul 296
'Nicola' 163
Nine Below Zero 46
Nixon, Richard 142
'No Smoke without Fire'
 232–4
Nocito, Mike 202–3
Norris, Stephen 367–9
Northern Ireland 128, 144–5
 Belfast 129
 Derry-Londonderry 129
 Troubles, The (1963–98)
  129
Norway 191
 Bergen 118
 Kristansand 118
 North Cape 128
 Stavanger 118
Norwich City 331
Novotná, Jana 309
Nowell, Percy 165

Ocean, Billy 19
O'Connor, Des 341
O'Connor, Liam 278
Odo, Bishop 273
Odysseus 119
Oestermann, Hauptmann
 Joseph 335
Old Charlie 300–1

Olivier, Laurence 125
Olsen, Christopher 289
*One Hundred Favourite
 Humorous Poems* 344
 'Stanley Holloway in
  Thirty Moves' 344–6
One Hundred Favourite Poems
 344
One World Project 256
Oscar 220–2, 225
O'Sullivan, Gilbert 58
Ottoway, Scott 261
Oxford University 220
 Christ Church 241
 Magdalen College 205

Page, Ian 186
Page, Jimmy 296
Page, Mark 66
Pahlavi, Mohammad Reza
 (Shah of Iran) 142
Palme, Olof 323
Palmer, Annie 126
Palmer, Carl 58
Palmer, Gillie 106, 322, 327
Palmer, John 126
Panasonic Rock School 149
'Papa Piccolino' 151
Paramor, Norrie 176, 340
Parfitt, Rick 287
Park, Andy 261
Park, Richard 70–2, 194
Parker, Major Sir Michael 47
Parkhill School 295–6
Parkinson, Michael 56, 143
Parnell, Ric 173–4, 188, 262
Paul, Steven 360–1
Payne, Trevor 248
Pebble Mill 217
Peebles, Andy 298
Peel, John 44
Peer-Southern Music 200
Peers, Donald 69
'Peggy' 240
Pentland Rising (1666) 139
Pepsi and Shirlie 101
Pet Shop Boys 84
 'Go West' 258
Pete Waterman Limited
 (PWL) 191
Peter Pan 270

Petty, Norman 24–5
Petty, Vi 25
Phantom of the Opera 228
Philby, Kim 241
Philip, Prince (Duke of
 Edinburgh) 117, 135, 294
Philip the Bold 119
Philip the Fair 119
Phillips, Lesley 237
Photos, The 46
Piblokto 373
Picasso, Pablo 62
'Pictures on My Wall' 163, 175
Pillar, Admiral Sir William 60
Pillar, Lady Ursula 60
Pinewood Studios 355, 359
Pink Floyd 165, 340–1
Pinky and Perky 154
Pissarro, Camille 352
Pitney, Gene 14, 240–1
 'Something's Gotten Hold
  of My Heart' 241
 'Twenty-Four Hours from
  Tulsa' 241
Pitt, Bill 182
Pitt, Ken 166–7
Playing Fields Association
 295–6
Poet's England 343
Poetry in Motion 216–17
Police, The 85
Polynesia 348
Pomus, Doc 249
Poole, Brian 341
Pop One Up 94–6
Porter, Nyree Dawn 228
Powell, Dave 226
Powell, Don 46, 226
Powell, Peter 27, 60, 84, 92–3,
 115, 332
Presley, Elvis 132, 149, 207,
 249, 256, 285, 311, 351
 'Big as Memphis' 187
 'Jailhouse Rock' 43
Preston, Billy 167
Price, Harvey 9
Price, Katie (Jordan) 1, 5–6,
 8–9
Priestley, J. B. 374
Prince, Tony 188
Proclaimers, The 84, 103

'(I'm Gonna Be) 500 Miles'
 335
Project X 149
Prokofiev, Sergei 231
Pryke, Chris 291–2
Pryke, Sir Christopher
 Dudley 292
Public Image Ltd 8
Punch 206
Purnell, Keith 173
Pursey, Jimmy 185–6
Pyrotechny, The Musical 234

Q-Tips 46
Quadrophenia
 'We Are the Mods' 123
Quatro, Suzi 191, 363
Queen 217, 259
Queen for an Hour (TV
 programme) 62–3
Quirke, Pauline 19

Radford, Charlotte 356
Radio City 30
Radio Fun 352–3
Radio Guide 12
Radio London 79, 315, 336, 366
Radio Luxembourg 27, 37,
 148, 184, 188, 338
Radio One Club 177–8
Radio Times 115, 362
RAK Studios 204
Ram Jam Band 363
Ramones, The 27
 'Blitzkrieg Bop' 27
Ramsey, Alf 353
Ray, Johnny 339
Rea, Chris
 'Myfanwy' 204–5
Read, Beryl 173
Reading Festival 19–20, 161
Reading Football Club 10
Reading University 16–17, 199
Reagan, Ronald 137, 190
Real Thing, The 91
Record Collector 176, 196
Red Arrows 76
Redding, Otis 167
Reed, Lou 148
Reed, Oliver 305–6
Reed, Sir Bartholomew 273–4

Reed, Michael 228, 238–9
Reeve, Christopher 148
Regent Sound 166
Reid, Charlie 103, 336
Reid, Craig 103, 336
Reid, John 192
Republic of Transkei 74
RG Jones 169, 183, 185–6,
 188–9, 193
Rice, Anneka 195
Rice, Eva 217
Rice, Jo 26, 291, 293, 338–9
Rice, Tim 26, 41, 64, 175–6,
 206, 215–17, 220, 222, 225,
 233, 244, 264, 290–3, 308,
 338–9, 350
 Evita 26, 41
Rice-Davis, Mandy 68
Richard, Cliff 4, 15, 48, 65,
 70, 130, 183, 189, 192–3,
 198–9, 217, 220, 245, 248–9,
 253–4, 302–4, 306, 308–11,
 317, 320, 339–40
 I'm Nearly Famous (album) 15
 'Livin' Doll' 189
 'Mistletoe and Wine' 309
 'November Night' 240,
  310
 'Ocean Deep' 240
 'Saviour's Day' 193
 Small Corners 193
 'Travellin' Light' 311
 'What Car' 79
 'When the Girl in Your
  Arms' 311
 'Young Ones, The' 311
Ricky Nelson – Teenage Idol
 235, 240
'Riders in the Sky' 15
'Riders of the Range' 154
Ridgeley, Andrew 89
Right Said Fred 195–6
 'I'm Too Sexy' 194
Riley-Smith, Torquil 292
Rivers, Tony 188–9, 216, 235
Roach, Rod 161–2, 174, 182
Roberts, Rachel 205–6, 215
Robertson, Mick 329
Robinson, Peter 292
Robinson, Smokey 206
Robinson, Tom 339

Robson, Bobby 136
Robson, Linda 19
Rockolas, The 89–91, 116,
    187–8
    Born to Roll 116
Rodgers, Anton 227
Roe, Tommy
    'Dizzy' 188
Rogers, Kenny 202
Rogers, Roy 249
'Roll the Cotton Down' 153
Rolling Stones, The 149, 207,
    281, 350
Rose, Bernard 67
Rosewall, Ken 311
Rosie May 192
Ross, Diana 149
Rossdale, Andy 292
Rossetti, Dante Gabriel 286,
    343
Roswell, Ken 323
Rothermere, Lady 126
Roussos, Demis 13–14
Rowles, John 183
Royal Albert Hall 204
Royal Variety Performance 150
RSO Records 297
Ruddock, Neil 'Razor' 1, 4–5,
    245–6
Runcie, Robert 135
Rusedski, Greg 199
Ruskin, John 286
Russell, Bertrand 241
Rutherford, Mike 298
Rwanda
    Virunga Mountains 58

Sad Café 240
Sandford, Christopher G.
    216, 227
Sargent, John Singer 352
Sargent, Sir Malcolm 340
Sarstedt, Peter 216
Sarstedt, Robin 19
Sassoon, Siegfried 267
Savile, Jimmy 84
Sawalha, Nadia 237
Sayer, Leo 28, 217, 240
Schofield, Philip 115, 195
Scholl, Andreas 242
School for Scoundrels (film) 78

Screaming Lord Sutch's
    Savages 296
Screen Gems 162
Scudamore, Peter 298
Seaman, L. C. B. 159
Searchers, The 261
Second World War (1939–45)
    39, 59, 67, 129, 258, 263,
    268, 288
    Battle of Britain (1940)
    335
    Munich Summit (1938)
    184
    Normandy Landings
    (D-Day)(1944) 81
Secret Affair 186
Sedaka, Neil 262
Seeger, Alan 267–8
Seeger, Pete 268
Seles, Monica 306
Setzer, Brian 54
Sex Pistols, The 1, 85
Shadows, The 14–15, 27, 183,
    340–1
Shaffer, Peter
    Amadeus 211
Shaggy 217
Shakespeare, William 224, 294
    *A Midsummer Night's
    Dream* 157
    Love's Labour Lost 310
Shakin' Stevens 55, 112, 189,
    276, 302
Sham 69 185
    'Hersham Boys' 83–4
Shapiro, Helen 340
Sheen, Charlie 235
Sheen, Martin 235
Shelley, Percy 8, 213
Shepherd, David 150
Shepherd, Gillian 366
Sherman, Alan
    'Hello Muddah, Hello
    Faddah' 190
Sherrin, Ned
    Loose Ends 41
'Shirley' 169
Shooting Star Chase Hospices
    217, 260–1, 265
Shoreline, The 165–7, 350
'Shoreline Surfin'' 167

Showaddywaddy 14, 185
Shuman, Mort 249
Sibelius, Jean 231
Siddle, Dave 162
'Silent Night' 304, 310
Silhouette 197
Simon 192, 194
Simpson, Wallace 90
Sinatra, Frank 132, 198, 249
Sinton, Andy 298
Skatalites, The 167
Sky TV 260
    Sky News 253
Slade 70, 85, 226, 339
    'All Join Hands' 226
    'Merry Xmas Everybody'
    46
    'Radio Wall of Sound'
    225–6
    Walls of Hits 198
Slattery, Tony 75
Sledge, Percy 206
Slowe, Richard 292
Small Faces 104
Smith, Alan 169
Smith, Delia 136
Smith, Dodie
    Dear Octopus 157
    I Capture the Castle 157
Smith, Sam 306
Somerset, Lord Johnson 287
Sondheim, Stephen 225
Songs from the Shows 238
Soul Sounds 254
South Africa 224
    Cape Town 133
*South Coast Beat Scene of the
    1960s, The* 165, 350
Southampton Football Club 1
Soviet Union (USSR)
    Committee for State
    Security (KGB) 323
Spagna 84
Spain 224
Spaim 62
Spandau Ballet 298
'Spanish Harlem' 15
Spencer, Earl 319
Spencer, Lady Diana (Princess
    of Wales) 47, 306–8, 318–19
Spencer Davis Group 262

INDEX

Spinal Tap 174, 246, 262
St John-Stevas, Norman 339
St Lucia 121
Stadium Dogs, The 186
Stage, The 220
Standfast, Alison 137
Standring, Colin (Big Stan) 182
Stardust, Alvin 14, 24, 147, 189, 216, 219, 341
    'Christmas' 216
    'Executive' 216
Starr, Edwin 191
Starr, Ringo 55
Status Quo 84, 189, 287
Stax Records 167
Steel, David 136
Stephenson, Pamela 54
Stewart, 'Baby' Bob 32
Stewart, Ed 308
Stigwood, Robert 65–6
Stilltoe, Alan
    Saturday Night and Sunday Morning 235
Story of the Shadows, The 341
Strachey, Lytton 241, 349
Stratton-Smith, Tony 202
Stray Cats 54
Street, George Edmund 286
Streeter, Tony 356
Striker, Micky 21
Stuart, Leslie 351
Stubbs, Una 143
Studholme, Penny 25
Sue Records 167
Sugarman, Karen 217, 266
Sullivan, Dean 217
Summer Holiday 248
Sun, The 11, 30, 96, 98, 191, 218
Sun Studios 15
Sunday Night at the London Palladium 207
Sunday People 146–7
Sweet, Jon 240, 242
'Sweet Polly Oliver' 157
Swinging Blue Jeans, The 84
Swinton, Ellen Schroeder 269
Swinton, John Liulf 269
Swinton, Maj. Gen. Sir Ernest Dunlop 269–70
Swinton, Tilda 270

Switzerland 191
Sydmonton Festival 212, 232–5
Symons, Alan 22

Taatamata 347
Tahiti 348
Tallack, Roger 177–8
Talmy, Shel 166
Tamla Motown 167
Tanner, Roscoe 311
Tarbuck, Jimmy 303
Tarrant, Chris 298
Tate, Dave 114
Tatler 203, 294
Tauziat, Nathalie 309
Taylor, Elizabeth 124
Taylor, Graham 298
Taylor, Lady Helen 212
Taylor, R. Dean 120
Taylor, Roger 84, 311
Teenage Idol 234
'Tell Me I'm Wrong' 189
Temptations, The 167
    'Since I Lost My Baby' 168
Tennyson, Lord Alfred 343
Tenth Planet 170
Tepper, Sid 311
Terence Higgins Trust 149
Test Match 289–90
Thames Television 11, 147
    You Must Be Joking!/ Pauline's Quirkes 19
Thames Water Authority (TWA) 114
Thatcher, Margaret 136–7, 366
'They Were Only Playing Leapfrog' 155
Third Reich (1933–45) 39, 59, 67
'This Is Not Goodbye' 264–5
Thrashing Doves 137
Three Fivers, The 75
Thyrds, The 169
Till the Clouds Roll By 277
Tillotson, Johnny
    'Poetry in Motion' 72
Time 220
'Time and Tide' 169
Times, The 87, 213, 221, 323, 346
Tomes, Barney 181–2

Tonight (newspaper) 72
Took, Barry 75
Tottenham Hotspur Football Club 1
de Toulouse-Lautrec, Henri 352
Tourists, The 46
T. Rex 85
Trainer 193–4
Trainspotters, The 186
    'High Rise' 185–7
    'Hiring the Hall' 187
    'My Town' 187
Tranmere Rovers Football Club 331
Travis, Dave Lee (DLT) 52, 86, 188
Treherne, Nicola 235
Tremeloes, The 84, 341
Trent d'Arby, Terence 148
Trigger 249
Trinidad and Tobago 122
Troggs, The 84
TSB Rockschool 148
Turner, General 139
Turner, J. M. W. 352
    Rain, Steam and Speed 351
Turner, Tina 149, 206
Turner Prize 71
'Twelve Days of Christmas' 310
Twin Towers Rock & Rolls Tour (1987) 101–2
Twitter 68, 85, 333
Twitty, Conway 119
Tyson, Mike 121

UB40 207, 217
UK Independence Party (UKIP) 369–71
Unit 39
Unit Four Plus Two 340
United Kingdom (UK) 30, 33, 40–1, 133, 148, 174, 182, 184, 191, 225, 234, 259, 267, 306, 341, 351, 359, 371–2
    Arbroath 103
    Badminton 342
    Berkshire
        Compton 193
        Newbury 193
    Berwick-upon-Tweed 102, 336

Birmingham 52, 308, 311, 370
Blackpool 87, 101
Bognor Regis 124, 164, 167, 169, 189, 350, 356
Bournemouth 90–1
Bridlington 86, 90, 107, 336
Brighton 247, 303
Bristol 57, 92, 100
Bromley 56
Cambridge 188
Carolyn Bay 90
Channel Islands
  Herm 59
  Sark 59
Civil War (1642–51) 281–2, 288
Clacton-on-Sea 79, 110
Cleethorpes 86, 90
Colwyn Bay 87
Devon 91
Dover 101
Dumfries 139
Dunbar 336
East Anglia 109, 337
East Grinstead 189
East Sussex 63
Eastbourne 334
Eastbourne 111
Edinburgh 92, 102, 336
Exeter 90
Exmouth 90
Eyemouth 336
Falmouth 87, 89
Foreign and Commonwealth Office 323
Frinton-on-Sea 10, 79, 315–16, 336
Glasgow 314
Gloucestershire 15, 370
Great Yarmouth 90, 106, 110
Guildford 325
Hampshire 370
  Basingstoke 24, 189
  Winchester 334
Hastings 90
Haverfordwest 341
Helensburgh 103

Hertfordshire 298
Hounslow 189
Hull 260
Humberside 370
Hurlingham 342
Isle of Man 355
Isle of Wight 60
Kent 111, 370
Lancashire 271
  Colne 167
Land's End 189, 342
Leeds 27, 92, 186
Leicestershire 76
  Leicester 177
Littlehampton 350
Liverpool 149, 243, 349
Loch Lomond 104, 342
London 13–14, 18, 27–8, 37, 43, 47, 49–50, 52, 66, 71–2, 83, 98–9, 121, 149–50, 171, 179, 181–2, 189, 193–5, 206, 213, 215, 217, 225, 229, 231, 247, 250, 254, 262, 273–4, 281, 291, 311, 329, 338–9, 356–7, 366
Manchester 43–4, 84, 168, 283, 303
Margate 111
Ministry of Defence 279
Moffat 347
Morecambe 87
Moreton-on-Marsh 314
Newbury 24
Newcastle-upon-Tyne 59, 336
Newquay 90, 294
Norfolk 166
Nottingham 227, 229
Oxfordshire 370
  Oxford 113, 146, 188, 206, 240
Parliament
  House of Commons 266, 339, 367
  House of Lords 266–7
Perth 145
Plymouth 87, 90, 92
Portsmouth 90, 230
Reading 23–4, 296
Reed Point 336

Rhyl 87
Rutland 76, 342
  Oakham 76
Rye 313
St Austell 87–8, 90
St Enedoc 342
St Albans 324
St Ives 87, 89
Scarborough 86
Scotland Yard 99
Skegness 86, 90, 106, 336
Slough 13, 203
South Shields 86
Southampton 90
Southend-on-Sea 12
Southport 87
Southsea 91, 112
Staines 189
Sunderland 336
Surrey 48, 152, 169–70, 190
  Chertsey 326
  Claygate 173
  Dorking 51
  Hersham 83
  Walton-on-Thames 48, 99, 158, 162, 272, 278, 300–1, 327
  Weybridge 48, 58, 99, 162, 172, 231, 272, 274, 326, 368, 371
Sussex 111, 150, 229, 252, 315, 370
Swanage 91
Torquay 87, 90, 96
Wear 370
Westminster 367
Weston-Super-Mare 105
Whitehall 99
Wiltshire 208, 370
Woking 274
Wolverhampton 46
Worthing 313, 350
Yeovil 240
Yorkshire 56
  York 275
United Nations (UN) 47
  International Year of the Child (1979) 47
United States of America (USA) 32, 58, 60, 93, 148,

INDEX

162, 174, 176, 182, 224, 237, 253, 280, 309, 330, 349, 351
  Aspen, CO 321
  Chicago, IL 189
  Civil War (1861–5) 263, 350
  Dallas, TX 116
  Honolulu, HI 133
  Houston, TX 131, 189
  Memphis, TN 76
  Nashville, TN 190
  New Orleans, LA 189, 342
  New York, NY 189, 194, 225, 351, 360
  San Francisco, CA 130–1, 189, 348, 354
Universal Music 255
University of Surrey
  John Lennon Studio 358
Untamed, The 166
Ure, Midge 90, 147

Valance, Ricky 341
Van Zandt, Steve 101
Vaughan, Sarah 148–9
Vee, Bobby 178, 234
Verdi, Giuseppe 231
Vicaro, Arantxa Sánchez 309
Vickers Armstrong 274
Vietnam 10, 296
Vilas, Guillermo 310
Village People 85, 258, 339
  'In the Navy' 258
  'YMCA' 258
Vincent, Gene 137
Virgin Sleep 173
Voice, Lisa 361–2
Voight, Jon 360–1

Wade, Virginia 302–3
Wakeman, Rick 254
Walker, Johnnie 69, 298
Walker, Trisha 190
Wallace, James 139
Wallis, Barnes 274
Ward, Dudley 347
Ward, Peter 347
Warrell, Andy 206
Warwick, Teddy 332
Washington, Geno 162, 165, 257, 363
Waterer, Lt. Col. Richard 230–1

Waterman, Pete 187–8, 191
Waters, Roger 341
Watson, Russell 253
Waugh, Evelyn 120
Wayne, Carl 216–17
Wayne, Jeff
  War of the Worlds 309
We Will Rock You 226
Webb, Sir Aston 47, 278
Weedon, Bert 62, 120, 190, 197–8
  Play in a Day 61
Welch, Bruce 198, 341
Wells, John 216
Wells RA, Henry Tanworth 286
Wenceslas: King of Bohemia 360
Wesley, Mark 36
West, Keith
  'Excerpt from a Teenage Opera' 185
  'Tomorrow' 185
West, Paul 187
West Ham United 280
West Side Story 228
'Westering Home' 157
Wet Wet Wet 148
Wham!
  'Club Tropicana' 89
Wharfe, Ken 318, 320
'What the Dickens' 173, 262
'When Johnny Comes Marching Home' 351
'Where Have All the Flowers Gone' 168
Whistle Down The Wind 233
Whitfield, David 339
Who, The 165–6
Whole Scene Going 167–8
Wiedlin, Jane 84
Wignall, WPC Marilyn 98
Wilde, Kim 101–2, 149–50
  'You Keep Me Hangin' On' 102
Wilde, Marty 25
Wilde, Oscar 70, 218–22, 224
Wilde, Paul 25
William, Prince (Duke of Cambridge) 204, 318
'William Hickey – 1933–1987' 342
William of Orange 113

William the Conqueror 273
Williams, Danny 339
Williams, Kenneth 143, 277
Williams, Nigel 221
Williams, Paul 63, 67, 87–8, 93–4, 102, 106, 117
Wilson, Hugh 165
Wilson, Nick 189–90
Wimbledon 198, 232, 237, 248, 303, 307, 309, 315, 323
Wongs 340
Winehouse, Amy 346
Winsor, Kathleen
  Forever Amber 169
Winston 58
Winters, Bernie 143–4
Wisdom, Sir Norman 277, 352, 354–5
Wittgenstein, Ludwig 241
Wizard 261
Wogan, Terry 302
Woking Grammar School 185
Wood, Clare 306
Wood, Ken 48
Wood, Rosie 322
Wood, Roy 261
Wood, Rupert 322–3
Woolf, Virginia 241, 335, 349
Woolworth 246
Wordsworth, William
  'Daffodils' 343
Wren, Sir Christopher 135
Wren Orchestra 216
Wright, Steve 11–13, 19–21, 31, 293, 332
Wyman, Bill 254, 298

Yardbirds, The 161
Yarwood, Mike 302–3
Yeames, William Frederick 286
Year of the Child, The 46–7
Yello 84
'Yellow and Red' 169, 172
'Yellow Rose of Texas, The' 350
Yes
  'Survival' 243
'Yesterday's Heroes' 16, 199
York, Susannah 193
York Archaeological Trust 275

Yorke, Dwight 9
Yorkshire TV
  Pop Quest 28, 42
YouGove 370
Young, Paul 46, 240
Young Apollo 214–15, 230
Young Ones, The 189
Young Tennis Players of Great
  Britain 302–3
'Youth and Age' 241–2
YouTube 16, 58, 69, 85, 174,
  187, 206–7, 257, 262, 265,
  356

Zappa, Frank
  'It Can't Happen Here' 167
Zavaroni, Lena 14
Zodiac Mindwarp 207
Zombies, The
  'She's Not There' 324
  'Tell Her No' 324
  'Time of the Season' 324